The Mahdi and Africa

The Mahdi and Africa

Muhammad Ahmad and Sudan's Mahdist Revolution in Context

John D. Grainger

Pen & Sword
MILITARY

First published in Great Britain in 2025 by
Pen & Sword Military
An imprint of Pen & Sword Books Limited
Yorkshire – Philadelphia

Copyright © John D. Grainger 2025

ISBN 978 1 03613 744 1

The right of John D. Grainger to be identified as
Author of this Work has been asserted by him in accordance
with the Copyright, Designs and Patents Act 1988.

A CIP catalogue record for this book is
available from the British Library.

All rights reserved. No part of this book may be reproduced, transmitted, downloaded, decompiled or reverse engineered in any form or by any means, electronic or mechanical including photocopying, recording or by any information storage and retrieval system, without permission from the Publisher in writing. NO AI TRAINING: Without in any way limiting the Author's and Publisher's exclusive rights under copyright, any use of this publication to 'train' generative artificial intelligence (AI) technologies to generate text is expressly prohibited. The Author and Publisher reserve all rights to license uses of this work for generative AI training and development of machine learning language models.

Typeset by Mac Style
Printed in the UK by CPI Group (UK) Ltd, Croydon, CR0 4YY.

The Publisher's authorised representative in the EU for product safety is Authorised Rep Compliance Ltd., Ground Floor, 71 Lower Baggot Street, Dublin D02 P593, Ireland.
www.arccompliance.com

For a complete list of Pen & Sword titles please contact

PEN & SWORD BOOKS LIMITED
47 Church Street, Barnsley, South Yorkshire, S70 2AS, England
E-mail: enquiries@pen-and-sword.co.uk
Website: www.pen-and-sword.co.uk
or
PEN AND SWORD BOOKS
1950 Lawrence Road, Havertown, PA 19083, USA
E-mail: uspen-and-sword@casematepublishers.com
Website: www.penandswordbooks.com

Contents

List of Illustrations		vi
Maps		viii
Foreword		xi
Introduction		xii
Chapter 1	The African Muslim Context	1
Chapter 2	The New Islamic Expansion	10
Chapter 3	Egypt Rising	25
Chapter 4	Egyptian Rule in the Sudan, 1824–1880	43
Chapter 5	An Empire of the Red Sea	60
Chapter 6	Ethiopian Revival	72
Chapter 7	Egypt: The Limits of Empire	86
Chapter 8	Revolutions and Invasions	100
Chapter 9	The Destruction of the Egyptian Empire: I – Egypt	116
Chapter 10	The Destruction of the Egyptian Empire: II – Sudan	131
Chapter 11	The Destruction of the Egyptian Empire: III – The 'Debris'	146
Chapter 12	The Wars of the Mahdists	159
Chapter 13	The Upper Nile Problem	177
Chapter 14	The Contenders: Italians and Ethiopians	194
Chapter 15	Advances to Contact	207
Chapter 16	The Invasion of Sudan	218
Chapter 17	Fashoda and Other Places	238
Notes		252
Bibliography		269
Index		274

List of Illustrations

Muhammad Ahmad el Mahdi; the only portrait of him.

The Suez Canal; a sight to see for Egyptians, who, after all, built it. The ships are depicted as sailing rather too closely together. Much of the canal looks the same today.

Ferdinand de Lesseps, the inspirer of the canal, a true entrepreneur, wheeling and dealing, ignoring debts, and ultimately successful, against heavy odds. He tried the same magic with the Panama Canal, and was defeated.

Sir Evelyn Baring, effective ruler of Egypt for two decades. Later, as Lord Cromer, a high potentate in British politics, especially during the Great War, but always essentially a bureaucrat.

Urabi Pasha, pictured in 1906; the first native Egyptian to have effective rule of Egypt since the pharaohs, but unable to hold on to the power he captured. (*Wikimedia Commons/CC BY-SA 2.5*)

Alexandria under fire from a British fleet in 1882 – unplanned and unintended, but Admiral Beauchamp Seymour was undeterred by possible criticism.

Brigadier General Sir Garnet Wolseley, conqueror of Egypt (and Ashanti and central Canada earlier). A modern general, as Gilbert and Sullivan pointed out, but a planner rather than an inspiring leader. He failed in Sudan, where he had to improvise. But he got a peerage.

General Charles Gordon, an exciting commander and boss, but generally unable to complete any task he began. He was also disobedient, and over-confident, which brought his death at Khartoum.

Brigadier General Herbert Kitchener, adorned with his medals as *sirdar* of the Egyptian army in Egypt. He was an organiser rather than a fighter, and later organised himself into power in India and as a recruiter for the British Army against Germany. The victor of Omdurman, and Captain Marchand's nemesis.

The Mahdi's tomb, before British shells damaged it, and before General Kitchener rifled it and removed the Mahdi's skull as a souvenir. Queen Victoria was horrified and compelled him to replace it. The tomb is now rebuilt and a Sudanese shrine.

Captain Marchand lands to meet Kitchener at Fashoda. Kitchener was being unusually diplomatic – as per his instructions, of course – and was dressed in his Egyptian uniform and flew the Egyptian flag; no doubt unwilling to play this game, he nevertheless did so, successfully, and may have avoided a war. Marchand's face was thus saved, but he still ended up at the meeting with nothing.

Captain Marchand became, for a time, a French hero, but he had still been humiliated, and France learned a lesson in not challenging a stronger power – until 1914, of course.

Menelik, *negusa nagast* of Ethiopia, was the real winner in the imperial struggle for north-eastern Africa, winning battles, founding cities and unifying his country. Politically, he was head and shoulders above all others involved in the area.

Al-Zubayr Rahma Mansur, slaver and dupe. He was successful as a slaver, and as a founder of a principality in the Bahr el-Ghazal area, from which he seized control of Darfur. But he was asked to go to Cairo and there he was held in gilded captivity for the rest of his life – the clever politician outmanoeuvred so easily.

Henry Morton Stanley, reporter and self-proclaimed explorer, but also a brutal killer of Africans. He excelled at newspaper stunts on a large scale, seeking out men – Livingstone, and Emin Pasha, who did not wish to be found. He also excelled in developing distractions to hide his brutality.

The Ripon Falls in Uganda. The river Nile, so long, so essential to life, is also thoroughly awkward for travellers, with six cataracts in its lower course, and a series of ten waterfalls and cataracts in its upper course – not to mention the great swamp of the Sudd. (*Andyessex via Wikimedia Commons/CC BY 3.0*)

Maps

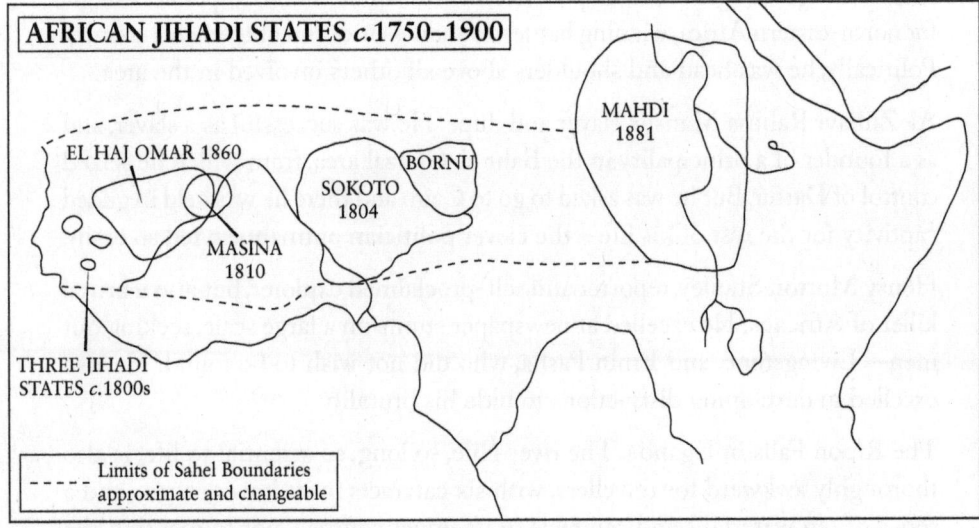

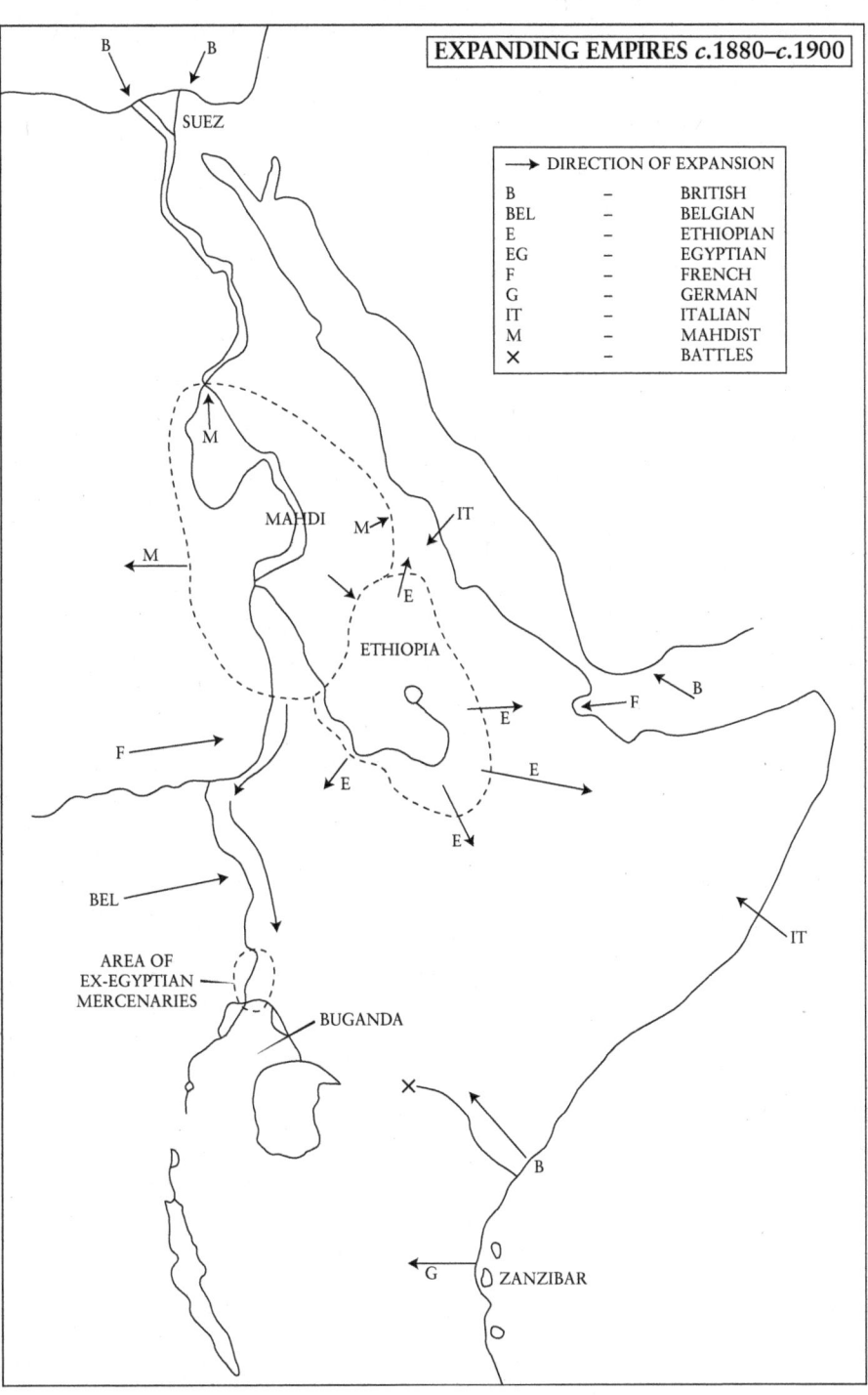

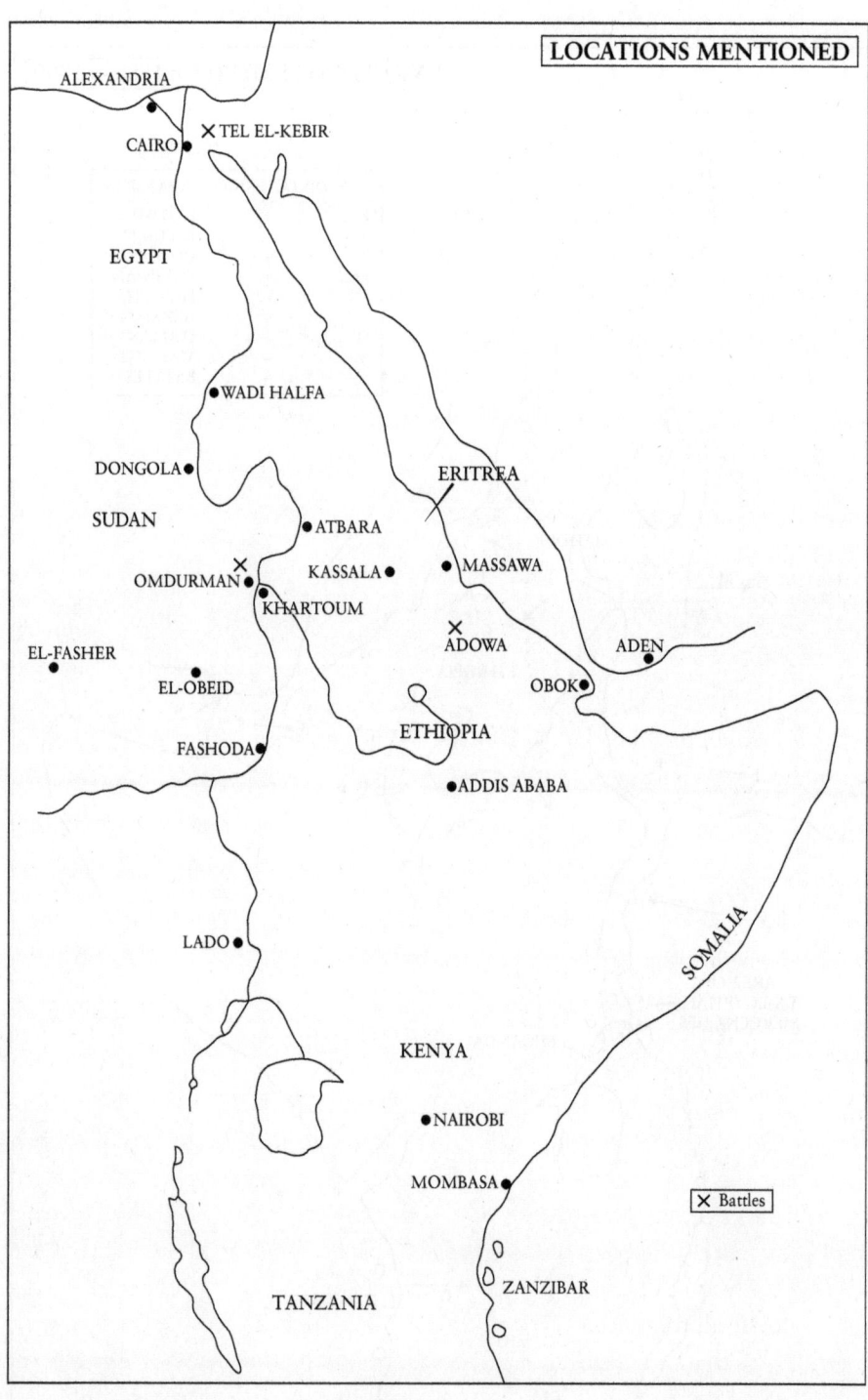

Foreword

Many years ago, I travelled to East Africa, where friends of mine had taken up posts as teachers at a school in Ethiopia. In a perhaps misguided moment, they asked me to visit. I accepted and spent several months travelling around that country and its neighbours. The visit included a month spent as a temporary teacher in the school until a teacher on leave returned – a factor whose pay allowed me to stay considerably longer than I originally intended. I had a return plane ticket, but after a little research I found that the fares from London to Addis Ababa and from London to Nairobi were the same and I persuaded the Goanese clerk in the Ethiopian Airlines office (his name was 'da Gama'!) to issue me an extra return ticket (that is, free) between Addis and Nairobi. So, with the pay of my month's teaching and free tickets I could travel about Kenya, Tanganyika (as it then was), and Uganda, all three countries which had recently become independent. I returned briefly to Addis at the end of this and then flew home, stopping for a week in Egypt on the way.

One of the results of this fascinating trip has been this book, somewhat belated perhaps (half a century late), but the time since then has been occupied by earning a living. I had hoped to be able to return by way of Sudan, sailing down the river Nile, but this proved impossible to arrange (or afford). Getting to Sudan from Ethiopia or Kenya seemed almost impossible, except by air, but at least I saw six of the countries involved in this book – Ethiopia, Eritrea (these two then united as one country), Kenya, Tanganyika (now Tanzania), Uganda and Egypt). Of the places that appear in this study, I visited Addis Ababa, Adowa, Axum, Gondar, Massawa, Asmara, Harar, Nairobi, Mombasa, Mount Kilimanjaro, Ngorongoro Crater National Park, Serengeti National Park, Lake Victoria, Kampala, Cairo, and Luxor; since then I have visited Egypt again, seeing Aswan, and sailed the length of the Red Sea, and through the Suez Canal. I travelled by car and train in Ethiopia, by boat, bus and train (the Uganda Railway) in East Africa, train in Egypt – and plane between all these.

I catalogue all this because it is one of the necessary matters in writing about distant lands that one needs to have some idea of what they all look like. I trust some of this experience of travel appears in this book. For one thing, it brought home to me the sheer size of all these countries – a revelation to one from cramped and small Britain, who had studied the area beforehand only from maps.

Introduction

The most dramatic events in north-east Africa in the nineteenth century were the revolution of Muhammad Ahmad, called al-Mahdi, the conquest of the Nile Valley by him and his followers, from the Egyptian border at Aswan to the southern swamps, and the contemporary British conquest of Egypt, and then the Anglo-Egyptian conquest of the Mahdist regime in the Sudan. The defeated Mahdist state, apparently eliminated, has however been the origin of its modern successor, which has continued under the name of Sudan. This relationship is all the more clear since the southern part of Sudan has now escaped, and has succeeded in constituting itself as the Republic of South Sudan. The Mahdi was the creator of both of those states, just as he was the originator of the curious 'Anglo-Egyptian Sudan', which succeeded his regime.

It is on these events that attention is generally concentrated, in Britain in part because it involved British forces, and a couple of unusually interesting and charismatic commanding generals, Charles Gordon and Herbert Kitchener. It also involved a major political crisis in London, and another in Paris. It is thus normally seen as an episode in British imperial history, or as one item on its own – the 'Mahdist War', the 'Conquest of the Sudan', and so on – or as an episode in British foreign policy. It is rarely seen as part of the history of its historico-religious-geographical region, which is in fact all North Africa, from the Red Sea to the Atlantic Ocean.

There were other equally astonishing events in that much wider region at the time. In the north, Egypt went through the sequence of an internal revolution, and a British invasion which suppressed that revolution; this was part of the same process as the Mahdist Revolution, which was also eventually suppressed by a British military expedition, but it happened in Egypt in the much shorter time frame of two years, whereas in the Sudan, the process of revolution lasted two decades. In Ethiopia, a European invasion by an Italian army at the same time as Kitchener's conquest of the Sudan resulted in the decisive defeat of the invaders by the Ethiopians. The condition of Ethiopia before and after that attack, however, which includes a British armed raid, Egyptian invasions and Mahdist attacks, cannot be ignored, for the Ethiopians became a much more serious enemy of the Mahdist state than the British and Egyptians for most of its existence. One of the major consequences of the Mahdist War was that the British moved into Kenya and Uganda, one of their excuses being that they had to defend those lands against the Mahdists (or others). One of the origins of the Italian move into Ethiopia was their earlier move into the neighbouring lands of Eritrea and Somalia, in part encouraged by Britain. And the Kitchener conquering expedition encountered a French expedition at Fashoda, coming across country from the Congo, aiming for Ethiopia, and this almost sparked off a European war. As if that was not enough, the greatest battles in the region in that time were not conducted by any of the European armies but were between the Mahdists and the Ethiopians, each fielding armies of up to 100,000 men.

This is a series of events, conducted during a couple of decades, which is quite enough for several books, and indeed the Mahdist adventure has produced a library-full, though all too many simply discuss one or other of the British campaigns – 1882, 1885, 1896–9, in heroic and/or personal terms. To understand what was happening it is not enough to follow the British actions, or even those of the Egyptians or the Sudanese. The Sudan was instead the epicentre of a whole series of events, so that to begin with the Mahdi is to start, like Homer, *in medias res*, at a point where a long series of preliminary events had already taken place, some already noted in the previous paragraph, and which have to be followed to understand what was happening in Africa – Europe's actual interest was minimal. These were not only the events that were contemporary in time with the Mahdist adventure but many had taken place long before it – centuries before – and were spread over a much wider geographical area. (The working out of the religious history of the whole region is still continuing.) Without taking these widespread events into account, it is impossible to understand what happened in and around the Sudan and its neighbours in the late nineteenth century. And, of course, the explosion in the Sudan has had consequences reaching through to our own days. One of the consequences has been grievous misgovernment in both Sudan and South Sudan, resulting in rebellions and civil wars. The Mahdist trouncing of the European and Egyptian forces in their rebellion, and then their seeing off an invading British expeditionary army, may be counted as one of the inspirations for anti-colonialist risings throughout North Africa and the Middle East ever since.

Perhaps this political, temporal and geographic connection is not explicitly acknowledged, but it is surely a subconscious assumption and inspiration. If a group of African Muslims, ill-armed by the standards of any contemporary European or Asian army of the late nineteenth century, could defeat an Egyptian army and then a British army, and then resist the subsequent British expedition of reconquest for three years, fighting to the last, by which time the British were armed with machine guns, steamships, and quick-firing artillery, then the

Taliban in Afghanistan, the FLN in Algeria, the Boko Haram in Nigeria, and others, could well aspire to the same level of victory – and two of these clearly have succeeded.

These considerations suggest that the crisis in north-east Africa between 1881 and 1898 is not just one of the British against the Mahdi, as British accounts of these events tend to imply. By ignoring any other factors, and thereby suggesting that it was a peculiar, particular and singular affair without wider relevance, much is removed from the story. It was actually part of a much wider business of empire-building in Africa by every participant – the Europeans (British, French, Belgians, Germans and Italians), and the Africans (Egyptians, Mahdists, Ethiopians, Sudanese and others). And it is too seldom noted that the larger majority of the fighters on the 'British' side were Egyptian and Sudanese, plus Indians; the British soldiers were rarely as much as a quarter of any imperial 'British' army; it may be claimed without serious dispute that the Mahdist Wars were wars between Africans.

In the longer perspective that results from the passage of seventy years since the abandonment of empire-building in the region by the Europeans, it can be seen that the whole matter was not only one of Europeans invading the African countries, but also of Africans building their own empires. For the Mahdi and his successors were doing exactly that, and were still invading new lands when they were stopped; the Ethiopian emperors were building an empire at the same time and indeed had started earlier and continued later than the Mahdists and the British; the Egyptians had built an empire in Syria, Arabia, and the Sudan, and had maintained much of it for two generations; they had conquered the Sudan, an event which was the main cause of the Mahdist Revolution. Only after these events had taken place did the Europeans intrude. Empire-building in north-east Africa was originally an African enterprise, in Egypt, the Sudan, and Ethiopia, and it can be argued that the Europeans simply took over what the Africans had constructed earlier, and their empires – Italian, British, French and Belgian – lasted about the same length of time as the earlier Egyptian Empire in the Sudan.

The events in the nineteenth century in north-east Africa must therefore be set into two much wider contexts. One, the more familiar in Europe, is the extension of European control over virtually all Africa, a process that, in its decisive phase, began a century before Kitchener's attack on the Mahdist state – in South Africa or Algeria, or West Africa – but did not achieve much land acquisition until the 1880s. The first invasions came at the end of the eighteenth century with the British invasion of the Dutch colony at the Cape of Good Hope, and the French invasion of Egypt two years later. (The preliminary coastal acquisitions by various European countries from the fifteenth century onwards, all the way round from Morocco to Zanzibar, had been small, limited, and in the context of empire-building, unimportant, though they did provide bases for later expeditions of conquest.) This is the imperial context, which is mainly what is noted in European history, as though Africa was a blank sheet waiting for Europeans to write history upon it.

The second context is that of internal African history, and in the context of this book, particularly of African Islam. In 1804, a Muslim holy man in what is now Northern Nigeria declared a *jihad*, and in a few years he expanded his control over a substantial area, creating an African empire, the Sokoto Caliphate, as quickly and as large as that of the Mahdi. He was not the only one of his type at this time, nor even the first; there had been similar movements in West Africa in the eighteenth century and they continued to erupt throughout the nineteenth, in Libya, and, of course, in the Sudan, and his success produced emulating *jihads* next door. (Indeed, it is possible to trace these Muslim movements back to eleventh-century Morocco, and forward to the present.) These men were operating in a long tradition of similar activity, going back to the original Arab Muslim conquests in North Africa in the seventh century, and this was one of the inspirations for the Mahdi of the Sudan. It is also exactly in the area of the jihadist states of the early nineteenth century that renewed jihadist activities have been taking place in the last few decades. The European conquests suppressed this activity for a few decades; it has now revived, and appears to be succeeding.

This book, then, is an attempt to set the events of European conquest in north-east Africa – by the Egyptians, the British, the Italians and the French – into a wider context, specifically an African and a Muslim context. And the central event was in all this the jihadist ('Mahdist') rising in the Sudan. The British conquest of the Sudan in 1896–8 in effect closed down the imperial contest in the wider region for the next two generations, until the British withdrawal from the region in the 1950s – notwithstanding the Italian invasion of Ethiopia in 1935, and gradual French advances until about 1912. Yet the Sudanese experience of Kitchener was not the endgame in a long process stretching back to the beginning of the nineteenth century, and encompassing much more than north-east Africa, but geographically much of North Africa from the Atlantic to the Red Sea was affected, and the Mahdist explosion in the Sudan is only properly understandable if that wider context is taken into account, and that the political evolution of both the Sudan and South Sudan is still ongoing.

The purpose of this book, therefore, is to set the episode of the Mahdist rising in the Sudan in a much wider context, in particular in a wider African context. It will therefore be seen that the episode of British conquest in the 1890s is no more than that – a brief episode that produced a brief British empire in succession to the Mahdist state, which itself was a successor to the previous states that had occupied the Sudan, back to the pharaonic period in Egypt. It was the British reaction to the Mahdist state's foundation and victories that brought them into Kenya and Uganda, the Belgians into the eastern Congo, and the French into competition with both.

This wider context is the subject of this account.

Chapter 1

The African Muslim Context

The central event in the nineteenth-century contest for control of the river Nile was the uprising led by Muhammad Ahmad, the Mahdi, in the Sudan in 1881 and after. He established a viable state, usually called the Mahdist Sudan. His early death prevented him from establishing a working and unifying administration, and from expanding his rule as he would have wished. He and his successor (the Khalifa) became involved in a contest in which all his neighbours – Egypt, Britain, Ethiopia, Italy, France, and the small states to his west, Darfur and Wadai, and others to the south – were concerned; its existence also affected the Congo, and the East African states in what became Uganda and Kenya.

It was the conquest of the Mahdist state by the combined British and Egyptian army in 1896–9 that settled the wider contest in Britain's favour, if only for a couple of generations: France was shut out from the Nile Valley by being blocked at the conference between Kitchener and Captain J.B. Marchand at Fashoda after the British/Egyptian conquest; Italy had failed in its own invasion attempts against Ethiopia in 1896 and before, but retained Eritrea and Somalia under a distant British protection. This was the case simply because Britain was the most powerful element in the area and, after the Sudanese conquest, did not want further changes. But the origin of the whole contest lay not with any of these states and peoples, nor with the Mahdi's ambition, but in the West African cities of the Hausa and the nomadic Fulani in what is now Northern Nigeria, and even before that in the Muslim conquests in the far west of Africa, and still earlier in the Muslim conquest of Morocco, the Maghreb, and Egypt. In his day, the Mahdi was the latest manifestation of jihadism in this wide region, a factor that had always to be taken into account since the days of the Prophet Muhammad. The Mahdi's adventure was far from an issue to be settled by Egypt and Britain alone; it was the latest stage in the Islamisation of the Sahel belt in Africa. The range of concerned countries and regions involved makes the Mahdi's state and his revolution a world crisis.

The Muslim conquerors first moved into Africa when their armies reached Egypt in 640, soon after the death of the Prophet.[1] They took that country from the Byzantine Empire without difficulty, but at first they went no further west than Cyrenaica, nor south beyond the first cataract at Aswan (the traditional western and southern boundaries of Egypt under the pharaohs, the Macedonian Ptolemies, and Rome). This was their limit for the next half-century; then in the 690s, in a new surge of conquest they reached into the west, the Maghreb,[2] and in 711, a further expedition invaded Spain, where the Visigothic kingdom forthwith collapsed.[3] Expansion southwards from Morocco did not take place for several more centuries, but travel across the Sahara was age-old by then, and Muslim merchants and caravaneers travelled these old routes, and many of the people of West Africa became familiar, in a superficial way, with Islam.

The early Muslim conquerors everywhere were not notably interested in converting their conquered populations to Islam; for one thing, as infidels, their non-Muslim subjects paid a special tax, which they would cease to pay if they converted. Nevertheless, conversions did begin, partly because of Islam's attraction, partly to escape the taxation regime, and partly to have easy access to the power and the governing set. It took time for many to accept the new religion, conversion being a slow process at first, but after a century or so, the movement speeded up. In West Africa, however, many converts retained many of their 'pagan' beliefs and practices even after adopting Islam.[4]

One of the results of the vagueness of the Koran, Islam's original simplicity, and the rapidity of the first conquests, was a dispute over the interpretation of the new religion and its application to ordinary life. These rifts tended either to follow pre-Islamic ethnic lines, with neighbours already at enmity adopting different Koranic interpretations (a process also visible with Christianity), or it might be a dispute between those of the desert and those of the cities; theological disagreements also played their part, once the religion came under scholarly and theological scrutiny and hence subject to nitpicking disputations.

These disputes included the major schism of Sunnah and Shi'ah, and there were various other separations and divisions. The desert tended to produce lean and bitter versions of Islam, cities were more tolerant and luxurious, which the desert Muslims saw with both contempt and jealousy, and which produced the characteristic conquest of the cities by the desert men, followed by the latter's adoption of the city's luxury – followed by another cleansing by the next desert uprising.[5]

In addition, a series of holy men emerged who set themselves to meditate, mediate and interpret, and were often used as judges and arbitrators. Such men set up their bases, called *ribats*, in isolated spots; in Africa they notably chose places on the edge of the desert, and there they gathered followers around them, teaching and preaching – in effect, attempting to convert their audiences to their particular belief and version of Islam. They gained reputations as teachers and interpreters of the word and the world; their fame gathered further followers to them. They frequently saw faults in the surrounding societies, and some at least set out to reach out to reform those societies, which is one form of *jihad*.

The earliest of these *ribats* in West Africa seem to have been situated on the desert edge, to the south of Morocco, in what is now the republic of Mauritania, inhabiting fortified buildings in the desert. They and their followers became fixed on the need to cleanse the surrounding neighbouring Islamic communities of contamination and deviation – which often meant surviving Christian and pagan beliefs and attitudes that had been incorporated into Islamic practice. This, it was understood, had to be done before any further progress could take place in converting non-Muslims. Only pure Muslims could then succeed in expanding and expounding the faith.

This, of course, was a political decision and process. Many people did not wish to be subjected to this cleansing; as a result, it was eventually seen to be necessary to use force to ensure it, though persuasion was usually attempted, sometimes over several decades, before a reformer decided that only force would work. In the Maghreb, this resulted in the emergence of a succession of reforming dynasties, the Murabitin and the Muwayhidin (Almoravids and Almohads in Spanish), intent on cleansing first Muslim Morocco and then Muslim Spain. These were, therefore, *jihad*-states, *jihad* being the term used to describe the internal cleansing process. It was then relatively easy to extend the concept of *jihad* to wars against non-believers, infidels, though this final stage was rarely reached, since the preliminary cleansing process was never completed – and could never be completed – to the teachers' satisfaction.[6]

The effects of the reforming and cleansing process were therefore limited, in both time and space. Typically, the warfare resulted in the conquest of a particular country, but the task of ruling, as opposed to conquering and killing, absorbed those energies of the conquerors that were originally devoted to war. And the reformers may have campaigned against luxurious living, but soon tended to succumb to it themselves, as they acquired the wealth taken from their victims. Ibn Khaldun in the fourteenth century, who travelled throughout most of the Muslim countries, from the Maghreb to India, Indonesia and China, remarked that a *jihad* state usually lasted only three or four generations, by which time it was ripe for an attack by a new reformer.[7]

In Morocco, the Almoravids campaigned from their original *ribat* on the Atlantic coast of Mauritania (just north of the Senegambia area) into Morocco and then into Spain in the second half of the eleventh century AD. A simultaneous expedition went south into West Africa (after a dispute between two of the original leaders, who then literally went their different ways). The northern movement was halted by the Christian states in the northern half of Spain, and the southern by the pagan African states in the Sahel and the tropical forests in West Africa, notably by the kingdom of Ghana, the first securely known organised state in the region. Knowledge of Ghana, however, is largely due to the fact that the sources are Islamic writers and historians, who knew of Ghana only from its enmity to Muslims. No other African states of the time excited their interest; it is clear from archaeological investigations, for example, that several well-established and comparatively ancient trading cities existed eastwards of Ghana along the Niger River.[8]

The Almoravid dynasty lasted from c.1050 for about a century, and was then overthrown by the Almohads, who aimed to repeat the reforming process that the Almoravids had abandoned. Their regime in turn lasted for even less time, and ended in the 1230s. Succeeding rulers managed to prevent any further disruptive manifestations of reform, but even so, each dynasty tended to last only a little longer.

From the desert edge in Mauritania and Morocco, therefore, the *jihad* could go north into Morocco, the Maghreb, and Spain, or it could go south into pagan Africa. It was, of course, far easier to campaign to cleanse existing Islamic societies than to conquer and convert those who were not Muslim in the first place and were more naturally hostile. Usually, some support could be expected for reform from the existing and settled Muslim population; it was hard work to take on the generally difficult and unrewarding task of converting people from pagan (or Christian) to Muslim. And so the expansive Almoravids were succeeded by the Almohads, who confined their actions to North Africa and Spain, while the southward movement had little overt success, at least in the short term. The jihadists concentrated above all on existing Muslim societies, which they felt should be cleansed before setting out to convert the rest of the world, and so none of these *jihads* seriously expanded the realm of Islam.

For Africa, therefore, the Muslim presence was for centuries less a violent attempt at conquest and more a slow penetration of the pagan countries by individuals. Africa produced trading goods that were valued in the societies of the north, notably gold and slaves. Muslim merchants travelled through the Sahara Desert to buy these goods and transport them for sale in Egypt and the Maghreb, which they would expect to be sold further on; some merchants paused in the desert to collect salt from the mines, a product that was much needed in the south, and at times they could exchange salt for gold, weight for weight.[9] The mining of the salt was, of course, done by slaves; other slaves were trafficked to North Africa, Egypt and Arabia.

Some of the Muslim merchants settled among the pagans of the Sahel, the long strip of land that stretched right across Africa between the desert to the north and the tropical forest to the south, from the Atlantic coast to Ethiopia. This was territory that was cultivable where there was water; otherwise it was generally good for pastoral farming. In that long narrow land a series of agricultural and/or urban societies had developed before Islam arrived, and in particular, this included a number of cities along the Niger River and in Hausaland, which were, of course, particularly attractive to the merchants. That is, the Muslim immigrants successfully inserted themselves into the existing African societies, either as temporary visitors and travellers, or itinerant merchants, or as true migrants, and they were generally tolerated. The numbers of Muslims in the societies increased, but only slowly: some pagans converted, Muslim immigrants came in from North Africa, slaves were purchased and employed by those immigrants and were converted by them, and family members joined the original migrants. The merchants built mosques for their worship and, besides making money and actively trading, they tended to proselytise in a quiet way.

For seven centuries, the peoples of West Africa, and in particular those living in the Sahel region, were subjected to these increasing religious pressures. This was a country where a complex interplay of states had developed: forest kingdoms, such as Benin, Oyo, Dahomey and Ashanti, close to the Atlantic coast; mercantile cities along the Niger River, such as Gao, Jenne and Timbuktu; a group of seven cities in Hausaland; there were also less organised, non-urbanised tribes, such as the Fulani pastoralists and Berber and Tuareg communities from the desert, leading a nomadic life. All these jostled and fought and traded with each other from at least the tenth century onwards, and probably before. States condensed out of tribal societies that came under pressure; the cities tended to be fortified, and the states were kingdoms.

The arrival of Islam had therefore added a further element of complexity to an already complex society.[10] This complexity was increased still further by the coastal intrusions of European merchants beginning with the Portuguese coastal explorers in the fifteenth century. The Portuguese were originally in search of gold, but they also found other goods that were equally profitable – above all, slaves – especially once the routes across the Atlantic to America had been worked out.[11] In some regions, particularly the Congo, the Portuguese promoted their own religion of Catholic Christianity, but in other regions they seem not to have bothered; other European merchants made little attempt for a long time to convert the Africans.

Slaves, particularly those captured in the forest areas, were exported in all directions, along established routes into the Islamic states of North Africa and the Middle East, after a gruelling journey across the Sahara, or carried on the new routes across the Atlantic in even more unpleasant voyages in European ships to, mainly, America; some were taken east into Arabia or India. The enslaved victims were sold by all the societies along the Atlantic coast, in a system in which they were sold in exchange for guns, which were then used to establish and expand the kingdoms and to raid for more captives to sell in exchange for more guns. And so on. The Sudanic kingdoms of the Sahel were as avid for the profits of the slave trade as any other societies, as well as to acquire slaves for their own internal use. In the eighteenth century, a plantation economy developed using slave labour in that region, which was perhaps as cruel as that in the Middle East or the West Indies or the southern states of the United States; probably as many were enslaved and employed by African societies as were exported to the north and the west.[12]

Islam had arrived, as noted, from North Africa, by way of Egypt, from Libya, from Algeria and from Morocco. The Muslims came along well-established desert routes, though each source produced slightly different versions of the religion.[13] The most potent religious source was Morocco, whose merchants had reached across the Sahara to the early kingdoms that had already developed in the western Sudan by the eleventh century. (The routes across the desert had been known since well before Roman times.)[14] But, whereas in the Middle East, in India and in Spain, Islam had expanded often enough by conquest, in West Africa the process was less bloody and less dangerous; it was also very much slower, though there were Muslim empires in the thirteenth and fourteenth centuries – that is, empires with Muslim rulers, though much of their populations remained pagan. Rooted in local customs and beliefs, part of their societies, paganism was obstinate.

Muslim influence, mediated through merchants and travellers, was slow but increasingly pervasive, and was focused especially on the African rulers, for it was obvious that the quickest way to convert a society was to convert the kings and then to rely on them to compel or encourage the conversion of their subjects. (In Europe, this was *'cuius regio, eius religio'*, a political system developed in the Reformation, which helped to bring peace to societies torn by religious war at the cost of expelling the minority.) But these rulers were often less than convinced of the efficacy of the Islamic religion, and they were equally addicted to the African content of the pagan beliefs they had grown up with. As kings, they owed much of their power and influence and authority to their practice of, and participation in, the traditional African pagan religious ceremonies. These ceremonies were understood by their people to be essential to the well-being of their societies; the conduct of those ceremonies was regarded as an essential element in binding the societies together. In many kingdoms, a Muslim king might abandon Islam, or he might be succeeded by a non-Muslim, ending any royal proselytism; at the same time, the theoretically Muslim kings also believed in, and practised, many of the pagan African customs. Tolerance of both sets of beliefs was therefore necessarily widespread.

This was hence a complex society, a mixture of religions, pagan and Muslim, of lifestyles, rural and urban, agricultural, mercantile and pastoral, addicted to warfare of a predatory sort (the main loot, of course, was human beings, to be enslaved). It continued with city-states and expansive empires; it welcomed immigrants, both mercantile and pastoral. All of the states or cities or tribes might or might not be in conflict with neighbours. It was, in short, from the Muslim point of view, a most difficult society in which to proselytise. It was also a very tempting Muslim target for cleansing and reform, being a mixture of Islamic and pagan beliefs, the latter infecting the former (or vice versa), but one in which the only solution in the end could be violence.

This was where the ascetic Muslim holy man had his influence. These men were isolated, but only in the sense that they lived separately from the rest of African society, often at the edge of the desert and the sown land. Their fame soon attracted followers and so they became teachers, emphasising the correct Muslim way of life (or their version of it), and their criticism and example contrasted this with other societies, both pagan and Muslim. The teacher began by isolating himself from contamination by pagans and their beliefs, a dedication admired by both pagans and Muslims. The latter provided the holy man's followers, who gradually grew to a community. Together they formed a devout group, usually relatively small, but they were a steady example to other Muslims, and in effect to the rest of African society also.

The kings who formed the government of the area were usually pagan, but the people of their kingdoms were generally a religious mixture of pagans, Muslims and converted pagans; the last were often holding on to their pagan beliefs even when attending the mosque; the Muslims were also often of several varieties, strict and less so. Then there were also the indifferent, who were probably the majority. The middle group, the converted pagans, had typically retained a set of beliefs and practices from their pagan lifestyle. They worshipped in the mosques, and sometimes adopted some Muslim practices, such as the five-times-a-day prayer, but also took part in such pagan practices as the ritual celebrations their pagan society felt was necessary; they often worshipped the old gods alongside the practice of Islam, dancing and singing the old songs. They would also normally use the pagan language – this, of course, would carry with it all the old beliefs and practices – rather than using the immigrants' Koran and Arabic.

The eventual reaction by the growing Muslim community around the teacher, and the teacher's successors, was often a campaign of persuasion, which was liable to become forceful. The essential element was the cleaning out of the continuing pagan practices that contaminated Islam – at least in the reformer's view. This would bring the community to the true religion, and to its proper and true practices. The target was, at first, not the pagans who formed the greater part of the surrounding society, but the semi-Muslims, those still using pagan rites yet attending the mosque. (This is not, of course, a peculiarly Muslim practice, as many Christian communities can attest, for many Christian festivals are rooted in ancient religious practices – Christmas is a prime example.) It was difficult work, with supposedly fully converted pagans often sliding back into the old ways.

The kings had a particular difficulty, since they were expected by the pagans, the unconverted, and even some of the Muslims to conduct the proper pagan religious ceremonies in the traditional way; if they became Muslims their status as king was clearly in danger, since, in theory, they would have to abandon the old rites. This is the background to Muslim complaints about the kings' backsliding. It was necessary for the rulers to conciliate all their people, pagan or Muslim, if they were to hold on to their positions. They were also, because of their power and position, particular objects for the persuasiveness of the holy men. A king who became a devout Muslim was in a decisive position to work at converting his pagan subjects, as well as reforming the partially converted. For some time the kings had to balance themselves between the two persuasions, and they often fell off the balancing pole.

The overall effect of this conflict was to increase the numbers of Muslims, though slowly, but in a general atmosphere of toleration amid a continuing mixture of beliefs and traditions. However, this mixture, and the repeated relapsing of Muslim kings into paganism, and with Muslim kings being followed by pagan successors, or vice versa, made for a particular but increasing religious instability. By the early nineteenth century, that instability resulted in a great Muslim revival, aimed primarily at believing Muslims. Most pagans were not affected, unless an excess of Muslim zeal produced a massacre. The eventual result was a series of *jihad* campaigns, which effectively constructed a set of new Muslim states and, in the end, a new empire, populated by the same mixture of Muslims and pagans as before the *jihad*, but with Muslim rulers firmly in control.

This Islamic 'revival' could easily move on to expansion, and so it was often more a Muslim conquest. The process began, as did the original Muslim communities in their *ribats*, in the western part of the Sahel, the area referred to Senegambia, where a number of minor local states adopted Islam in the period after the collapse of a series of large pagan-cum-Muslim empires of the medieval period. The last of these, the Songhai Empire, was destroyed by a Moroccan invasion in 1591. That collapse left pockets of Muslims in many areas, in the cities more than the countryside, and these were vulnerable to campaigns of reform and conversion. There was a group of small Muslim states in the far west in Senegambia in the eighteenth century, which were created by

Muslim teachers who had adopted *jihad* of the violent sort, such as Futa Jalon, Futa Toro, and Khasso.

The violence began in Futa Toro in about 1725, and became integral with the development of the social role of the state.[15] Fulani pastoralists were thus progressively accepting Islam, but they were well scattered across West Africa. These communities were in relatively small states, small, that is, in size and population; it took much of the eighteenth century for them to become firmly established as strongly Muslim states.[16] They did not indulge in much expansionist action, being too small in population to have a serious effect, but were the source of a good deal of Islamic influence. They and their pagan neighbours gathered wealth by participating in the slave trade with the seagoing Europeans, and in the more traditional trade with Muslim merchants who crossed the Sahara in search of, above all, the gold that was mined in the region.[17]

Then at the end of the eighteenth century there began a new phase of major Muslim expansion. Already, *jihad* in West Africa had been pursued by the teachers and holy men who founded and reformed the small Muslim states in the Senegambia region, and the founders of mosques and Islamic schools were also a part of this movement of reform and revival. The example was one of the roots of the movement that produced the new Muslim empires.

Chapter 2

The New Islamic Expansion

The social environment in the Sahel in West Africa, stretching from the Atlantic coast in Senegambia to Lake Chad – 2,000 miles – was, as the last chapter implied, in a condition in which many of its societies were receptive to a religious revolution. Most of the societies were mainly pagan in religion but were not unfamiliar with Islam, for Muslims lived amongst them, and these were in many areas increasingly assertive. It was this mixture that persuaded the Muslim preachers they had a particular task to perform.

Into this environment there arrived some notable leaders, such as Ahmad ibn Idris, whose follower, Muhammad ibn Ali as-Sanusi, founded the Sanusi movement in Cyrenaica, which had influence in the Nile Valley and Sudan, and throughout the central region of the Sahel. Ibn Idris's own influence was felt particularly along the Nile. His missionaries travelled along the trade routes south from Cyrenaica and into Darfur and Wadai, and on to Bornu by Lake Chad, the whole region between the Nile and the Niger. Once in the Sahel, they could use the east–west trade route, which was also used by West African *hajj* pilgrims, but they also remained in contact with the Mediterranean states along the several trans-Sahara routes – a new route, from Cyrenaica to Wadai, was pioneered and developed in the late eighteenth century.[1]

This development typified the new religious movements, which were usually dependent on one man's initiative, possibly continued by a follower. They did not, however, have any clear overall aims, other than to preach and teach; they were certainly not aiming to begin a *jihad*, and, in fact, as-Sanusi and his followers were vehemently anti-*jihad*. So the general reform movement was without any clear political direction, though a Muslim revival among the believers was regarded as necessary. As a result of this weakness and vagueness in direction, such a movement had a tendency to fade after a single lifetime, unless the movement was re-energised by a new teacher.[2] As-Sanusi's movement was more resilient than most, but these revivalists' activities were preliminary to a wider *jihad* of the violent sort, whether they intended that or not, and the explosion in the Niger region was one result; more distantly, so was the explosion in the Nile Valley later.

Usuman dan Fodio was one of those Muslim holy men. He operated for a long generation in the late eighteenth century among the Hausa states between the mid-Niger and Lake Chad, working to convince the population and the kings that a reform movement among the Muslims was needed. This was the region where the kings existed on that difficult Muslim-pagan balance, and so were vulnerable to his persuasive teaching. In some cases, they were hostile to Usuman, perhaps because he made them feel guilty, but certainly uncomfortable. He had been taught by al-Hajj Jibril ibn Umar, who had been expelled by the king of the Hausa kingdom of Gobir because of his troublesome preaching and teaching.[3] He had emphasised and criticised the mixture of pagan and Muslim beliefs that were held by too many of the local Muslim clerics, and by the kings such as Bawa Jan Gworzo of Gobir (1777–85), the man who had expelled him from the kingdom.

Usuman (also known as Uthman) adopted ibn Umar's attitudes but delivered his campaign from a new base in the north of the region. He moved about between the Hausa kingdoms, spreading his influence slowly but more widely. He was able to speak to, and upbraid, the kings with relative freedom, since he was of an aristocratic family, and he always addressed them as an equal. Above all, he acquired a reputation for intelligence, persuasiveness and bravery, all of which protected him.

For thirty years, Usuman pursued this regime of talk, persuasion and discussion as a typical holy man, of whom there were several active in the region at the time.[4] He preached throughout Hausaland, targeting in particular the kings of the Hausa cities, with the usual mixed results. He had more success with the Fulani, a nomad, cattle-herding people who had spread throughout the Sudan lands and grazed their flocks and herds in the lands between the cities, with which they also traded. The Fulani were already familiar with the reform movements that had developed in the *jihad* states in the far west; indeed, some of the Fulani in the west had taken part in those *jihads*. As nomads, however, they were often regarded as uncomfortable neighbours by the settled populations of farmers, merchants and city populations. Conflict between desert and sown was as endemic in West Africa as it was in Arabia and Central Asia and elsewhere. Islam appealed more strongly to the Fulani nomads than to the settled city populations, and this intensified that conflict.

The Hausa, among whom Usuman primarily worked, were a distinct people who inhabited the fertile lands between Lake Chad and the middle section of the Niger River. The land was mixed grassland and forest, and so the country's economy was a mixture of cattle raising, farming and commerce. They had developed from communities of villages and small towns into a group of city-states, which by the eighteenth century were articulated politically into seven independent city-kingdoms with a continuous history of several hundred years, and ruled by dynasties of *sarkins* (kings), whose long history gave them considerable dynastic pride and authority. As with such political organisations wherever they existed – in Greece, ancient Mesopotamia, India, early China, Mexico and so on – they fought each other, with successive cities enjoying a period as the most powerful for a time, and then replaced by another.[5]

Islam was present in all the cities, but with limited effect so long as the *sarkins* remained pagan. It was a country whose mixed economy, mixed allegiances, mixed religions, and mixed politics made it a fertile source of wealth and culture, but also an obvious target for Muslim reformers.

Usuman dan Fodio was born in 1754 in Gobir kingdom, and was given a classical Arabic education. His father was a well-known Islamic scholar and both father and son were authors and poets in both Arabic and Hausa; all this served to protect him personally and to enhance his reputation among the local Muslim population. He and his teacher had grown up in Gobir, one of the more important of the cities in their lifetime; as a Hausa from a noble family, and as a well-known Muslim teacher, Usuman was in a particularly strong position to exercise influence.

There was another source of conflict in the region. The pastoral Fulani had gradually spread from the west, herding their cattle and occupying the dry grassland areas that the merchants and farmers of the cities had ignored, or could not exploit. The pastoralists' animals grazed the grasslands between and around the cities. This produced a relationship between the nomads and the cities' populations, but also prompted the usual intermittent conflict between desert dwellers and farmers, between Hausa and Fulani.

In 1774, Usuman began a career of itinerant preaching in the several kingdoms of Hausaland, appealing to both Hausa and Fulani, and preaching a need for the purification of Islamic practices, to remove the infusions of African pagan practices that had survived and accreted on to the practice of Islam in the region. He was also an intellectual, producing large numbers of books and poems in both Arabic and Hausa, but also others in the language of the Fulani, so widening his reputation and the reach of his influence. He made some progress in his purification campaign, but only to any real extent amongst the poor and the Fulani, to whom his ascetic preaching particularly appealed. It was often directed in criticism of the cities, but the kings and elite remained resistant.

So this was Usuman dan Fodio's field of action, building on the basis of local Muslims, and because of his origins and status he was able to criticise the part-pagan, part-Muslim kings and the supposedly Muslim clerics he encountered. He preached and persuaded for almost thirty years. Although he made converts, the kings proved elusive, as he had probably expected. One king of Gobir became a devout Muslim, but his successor was resolutely pagan. By 1804, Usuman was getting old, and perhaps he was afraid that his work would end before Hausaland became fully and properly Muslim, as so many one-man campaigns ended. His influence was, after all, still largely personal and so only temporary; he saw too many brief reforms end in a relapse to the old ways. Two years earlier, he had survived an assassination attempt, apparently initiated by King Nafata of Gobir, who had succeeded two brothers who were both Muslims, but was himself a determined pagan.

Usuman withdrew north to the town of Gudu, on the edge of the desert. The incident emphasised that he had not achieved all that much, and if he died, anything he could claim as an achievement would probably fade away. At the same time, a king would not have attacked him if he did not feel threatened, so Usuman could take comfort from that. It certainly appears to have pushed him to reconsider his purposes and methods. In the two years following the failed assassination attempt he decided that he must change his tactics. Persuasion had not succeeded; after thirty years, he clearly felt that he had failed. So his decision was to turn to violence. He would mount a *jihad* directed at the cities in Hausaland, using the Fulani as his warriors, men who were already antagonistic towards the cities.

Usuman knew of the successes of the small *jihad* lands in the west, and he had made contact with emissaries from there, who no doubt encouraged him. In 1804, he declared a *jihad* in Hausaland. He was driven to it when he demanded the freeing of some prisoners, who were being taken off into slavery, because some of them were Muslim. It was, of course, against Islamic law to enslave Muslims. The king of Gobir, the pagan Yunfa, Nafata's son and successor, and Usuman's declared enemy, probably in this incident finally found his excuse to suppress the troublesome cleric. He launched an attack on dan Fodio's base at Gudu; Usuman fled, and thereby survived, and this became the date of his *hijra* – 21 February 1804.

This first defeat, and the preceding assassination attempt, aroused dan Fodio. He called on his followers to help and they gathered to defend him. He was proclaimed *Amir al-Mu'minin*, commander of the faithful, or in Hausa, *Sarkin Musulmi*. King Yunfa, obviously the first likely target for this new army, launched a new attack with his army of mercenaries and the Gobir militia. His attack was defeated. His reaction was to warn his fellow Hausa kings that a 'fire' had been lit that was likely to consume them all – an accurate prediction, though he may have neglected to mention that he himself had been the incendiary.

All the Hausa kings knew of, or knew, Usuman dan Fodio, who had been a familiar visitor to their kingdoms and their courts for a generation; they had all been subjected to his criticism at one time or another. They plainly understood the danger they faced, and may well have understood that Usuman's career actually seemed to be leading to this development. So some of them will not have been surprised at the new turn of events. They all turned on dan Fodio's followers in their own kingdoms, and the whole of Hausaland rapidly dissolved into a confused sequence of local warfare. It cannot have escaped Usuman's knowledge of the extent of his influence and the existence of his followers throughout Hausaland; by declaring his *jihad* he must have known that the 'fire' King Yunfa predicted would spread quickly, though no doubt there was an element of gambling in his decision. This element of preparation on his part gave him a distinct edge in the wider conflict.

The explosion in Hausaland attracted some Muslim interference and encouragement from the *jihad* states of the west, but it still left considerable numbers of the Fulani indifferent, though it was the Fulani in Hausaland who were most enthused by the uprisings, with the prospect of looting the cities. It was a highly confused situation, which involved not only civil wars in each Hausa kingdom, and a large element of social conflict, as well; in addition, there were also attacks launched against and by neighbouring lands.

The almost instantaneous reaction throughout Hausaland to what was only a minor battle in Gobir suggests strongly that social, religious and political tensions in that land had by 1804 brought the whole social system to breaking point. A healthy society does not collapse into internecine conflict on this scale so quickly, and on so relatively minor a pretext, unless it was fully prepared for it. King Yunfa's fire was laid and ready for the spark. Usuman dan Fodio may well have been aware of the possible results of his actions, but even if not, he was certainly able to profit by the collapse when it occurred.

To the east of Hausaland was the kingdom of Bornu, an even more ancient state than the Hausa cities, and normally a Hausa enemy, but also normally fairly passive. Now it was invaded by jihadists from Hausaland. A successful battle by the invaders, however, had the result that the victors then grabbed any loot that was available and went home. Evidently, it would seem that one of the elements in the *jihad* forces was the presence of numerous opportunists who were using the wars to their own pecuniary advantage – not a surprise, of course, but also a sign that the fighting was not always on behalf of Islam. Furthermore, the attack on Bornu was countered by the emergence of Muhammad al-Amin al-Kanemi, who inspired his followers in the Bornuan army to resist the jihadists successfully in the name of Islam, and established himself as the new ruler; his dynasty replaced the ancient royal family over the next generation. In a sense, this was a success for Usuman's *jihad* in that he had provoked another *jihad* campaign in imitation; but it was also yet another civil war.

The war of Usuman's *jihad* in Hausaland lasted for five years. It was conducted by the Shehu Usuman in command (Shehu was one of the titles he was given) and was hard-fought on both sides. He had only infantry forces at the start, and faced a heterogeneous army that included Hausa levies, armoured knights on horseback and various other groups, usually mercenaries. The advantage he had in the beginning was command of a united and well-motivated army, which was fighting against mixed and apparently less than united enemy forces – the cities fully retained their traditional rivalries, even though the royal families felt equally threatened. The various civil wars within the several kingdoms were a distraction away from forming a united opposition to the jihadists, and, on the other side, the enthusiastic invasions of Hausaland's neighbours such as Bornu were less than helpful to the Hausas who were fighting at home. The Shehu's cause was also helped by the revolt of various peasant groups who had been ground under by the oppression of the ruling elite and now seized the chance to rise in rebellion – further evidence of the social tensions of the country; the slaves working on the plantations that had been developed in Hausaland in the previous half-century could be another source of support for the uprisings.

In the circumstances, the progress of the *jihad* was only gradual. The northwestern kingdom of Kebbi was largely conquered during 1805, but fighting still continued there for several more years. In the south-west of Hausaland was the Zaria (also Zazzau) kingdom; it was attacked by an army of just seventy-four men, who were assisted as they campaigned by the villagers, who supplied them with both food and intelligence. The invaders, with these rebels helping, were able as a result to avoid the formidable royal cavalry, and at Zaria city, they drove the *sarkin* and his followers out.[6] These, however, moved as a group away from the city and settled in the neighbouring area centred on Abuja, which remained a staunchly pagan area all through the *jihad*. (This city was selected by the independent Nigerian Republic as the site for its new federal capital, its continuing paganism placing it as a neutral amongst the conflicts of Muslims and Christians.)

The other cities fell in similar fashion to a mixture of social revolt and religious enthusiasm – Katsina in 1807, Dawra and Gobir in 1808, and Kano in 1809. These at least are the dates of the capture of the capital cities, but, as with Zazzau and Kebbi, it proved impossible for Usuman's forces and supporters to establish full control or even domination of the countryside, much of which remained pagan. The cities became largely Muslim as a result, but large sections of the old kingdom retained their pagan beliefs. Abuja was not the only region of the country holding on to the old ways.[7]

The *jihad* might have been largely successful in seizing power in each of the city-states, but it was at that point that Usuman dan Fodio's political imagination went no further. The old kingdoms were assigned to individual followers to rule as emirs, or to be conquered by them, if that had not yet been done. The old kingdoms thus continued in existence and became semi-independent emirates, owing an allegiance to the *Sarkin Musulmi*, which became increasingly nominal. Sokoto was founded as Usuman's capital. As a result, Hausaland as a divided political community effectively survived, enlarged somewhat by conquests of neighbouring lands, but still divided into the old city-states, now called emirates; the incomplete nature of the conquest left pagan areas continuing within and between the jihadist emirates. There was an overall monarch, the *Sarkin Musulmi* – the local term for caliph – but it proved increasingly difficult for these caliphs to enforce obedience over the more distant sections. Usuman's new headquarters at Sokoto grew into the imperial capital,[8] but he also divided the empire by putting his brother Abdullahi in command at Gwandu to the west. (Sokoto was within the boundaries of the former kingdom of Gobir; it and the former Kebbi had been the first of the old kingdoms to be conquered.) When Usuman died in 1817, his son, Muhammad Belo, seized power at Sokoto, while Abdullahi continued to rule at Gwandu. These two founded separate ruling dynasties. Thus, the empire was divided into two monarchies within a few years of the success of the *jihad*, each of which was also divided into a group of hereditary emirates, which they theoretically oversaw. As one would expect, however, the emirates developed into effective independence while always swearing theoretical allegiance to the *Sarkin Musulmi*. The pre-existing Hausa system of city-state monarchies revived and continued.

The division of the caliphate was partly aimed at encouraging expansion, on the principle that each would have a section of the frontier to operate on, and in this, the scheme was only somewhat successful. Gwandu expanded towards the south, taking over the kingdom of Nupe, and establishing a vague suzerainty over the Yoruba state of Ilorin, but expansion further south was blocked by the difficulties of campaigning in the tropical forest, which the men of the north found inimical for their warfare, not to mention their health. Sokoto expanded to the south-east – Bornu to the east being as strongly resistant to Sokoto's forces as the forest states – into Adamawa and adjacent areas. The division of the monarchy, however, also inhibited concerted action so that continuing expansion had ceased by the time of Usuman's death in 1817. This expansion had been left to the individual emirs, with the result that by operating individually, their expansion was limited; their independence of activity was confirmed, so that the Sokoto Caliphate as a political unit remained only very loosely constructed and was always liable to internal disputation and disruptions.

It would seem that Usuman and his followers were quite content with this loose political structure, probably because they habitually concentrated on the religious aspect of reforming local Islamic practices. This is quite reasonable since this was their original purpose, but once having achieved their conquests, it was evidently their responsibility to organise and rule them in such a way as to maintain the caliphate's continued existence and well-being. The actual lifetime of the caliphate was about the same as that which Ibn Khaldun had postulated four centuries earlier – three or four generations – which translated for this caliphate into about ninety years. Here was a basic weakness in the construction of a *jihad* state: if it was small, such as those in the far west of West Africa – Futa Jalon and the others – it could survive more or less indefinitely, particularly since, after its initial eruption, it was no threat to its neighbours; if it was large, it was liable to disintegrate, lapse from its original ideals, and was therefore vulnerable to its enemies, pagan and reforming Muslims. The Sokoto Caliphate did not succumb as many others of its type did to further reformers, but instead to British and French imperialists. (This whole western Sahel region is now under attack by the Boko Haram jihadists and other similar groups – a development hardly surprising, but perhaps a century later than might have been expected; the Muslim states subject to the jihadist attacks show all the evidence of complacency and corruption in the usual manner.)

The new caliphate was followed by internal divisions and quarrels. The conquest was largely superficial, and the conversion of the population was less than complete; the main result was the removal of the old Hausa dynasties in the conquered area, which all disappeared, though some survived in unconquered pagan regions.[9] The political links of the new emirates back to Sokoto and Gwandu, however, continued, and one of the crucial succession events in each of them was for the new emir to send a present to the *Sarkin Musulmi* in Sokoto, or to the emir in Gwandu. This ceremony – acceptance implied recognition – was still being performed while the whole set of the caliphate's polities was being attacked by the British at the end of the nineteenth century. It was perhaps only an association of states by this time, rather than the empire it started as, and they did not always support each other.

The paroxysm of violence in Hausaland between 1804 and 1810 did not therefore force a very great change on the geopolitical condition of the region, as the old kings were mainly replaced by the emirs. It did, however, hoist a new Muslim elite to power in the wide region between Lake Chad and the Niger bend and somewhat extended the region under Muslim rule, even though the conquest of Hausaland itself remained incomplete. The failure to follow through from the religious change to a more thoroughgoing political revolution limited its effects. There were large areas of paganism still within Hausaland after the *jihad* commotion had declined, though conversion to Islam had clearly been facilitated.[10]

On the other hand, it is clear that the *jihad* in the Hausa cities had originated in two basic causes – first, the internal social condition of the Hausa polities, in which a fraught society, particularly amongst the peasantry, was looking for rescue from its oppressors; this became the field in which the Muslim reformers, culminating in Usuman dan Fodio, came to be working; the *jihad* wars were in part social revolutions. Second, the fact that the *jihad* risings in the far west had already taken place and had succeeded, thus providing a useful indication of probable success.

The Hausa *jihad* was thus working and growing in prepared soil, and had examples of success that it could use, and which provided it with a pattern of action. There were men from the older *jihad* states in the far west – Futa Jalon, Futa Toro, and others – who were active in Hausaland in promoting the *jihad* there alongside Usuman dan Fodio and his followers.[11] Similarly, it is evident that the uprisings in the Hausa cities quickly affected the situation in Bornu to the east, and that there Muhammad al-Amin al-Kanemi was able to lead the Bornuans in a defensive war against the invading Hausa jihadists, ironically in part by inspiring his people with Islam in much the same way as Usuman did the Hausa and Fulani. He followed up his victory against the resisters by taking the title of Shehu, and effectively became king of Bornu. The success of the jihadists was also an example to be followed by ambitious warriors in the territory to the west of the new caliphate, where men like al-Hajj Umar and Samori could adapt Usuman's methods to their own campaigns.

To the west of Hausaland, without a Fulani-Hausa invasion, the kingdom of Masina suffered the same process of uprising and religious revolution. Ahmadu ibn Mahmud Lobo Cissé of the Cissé dynasty, which had ruled in neighbouring Segu, was in contact with Usuman, and had served as one of his commanders in his *jihad* wars. Ahmadu used his skills and experience to develop his own *jihad* war in Masina. The old dynasty was overthrown, and Ahmadu Lobo emerged victorious. He took control with the title of Shehu Ahmadu. He always acknowledged his debt to the events in Hausaland, but as inspiration rather than in material or military help. He also expanded his rule along the Niger as far as Timbuktu; Masina was regularly at war with Kaarta further west (a pagan kingdom) and with Segu (from which the Cissé rulers came) to the south. His aim in both areas was conquest, and he failed.

That is, one result of the Hausa-Fulani revolution in Hausaland was that the whole region from the Atlantic coast to beyond Lake Chad was disturbed, above all by Muslim religious activities. There is, however, no reason to assume that this was the only imported disturbing influence, for one of the origins lay in the communications across the Sahel. There were, for example, strong links with North Africa due to the long-lasting trading connections, and these links were extended and strengthened in the eighteenth and nineteenth centuries. In the nineteenth century, the new route from Cyrenaica to Wadai, the kingdom east of Lake Chad and Bornu, was developed; it was along this route especially that the Sanusi brotherhood extended its influence.[12]

Some of this influence penetrated into the Nile Valley. The Sanusi headquarters in Cyrenaica made them neighbours of Egypt, and to some extent the Sanusi were enemies of the Egyptian government. Some of the advocates of *jihad* certainly looked to the Nile Valley as promising territory; the activities of the slavers there created a thoroughly fertile soil for Muslim jihadist exploitation, just as did the oppression of the Hausa peasantry by the Hausa elite. But not long after the success of Usuman's *jihad*, and while its victorious elites were consolidating their hold on their conquests and extending them in the Central Sudan region, the Nile Valley was seemingly removed from the possibility of a successful *jihad* by the arrival of Muslim forces from a different direction. This conquest was Muslim, but was more political, commercial and exploitative in intent than the jihadists elsewhere in Africa. It came from Egypt, a straightforward traditional conquest, rather than the Muslim 'revival'. The Egyptians were as Muslim as Usuman dan Fodio and others of his ilk, so their intrusion into the Nile Valley south of Egypt may be said to have delayed the Mahdi's revolution there for a couple of generations.

The Egyptian conquest took place from 1822 onwards, while at the same time, Muslim conquests in West Africa were taking place. In 1825 or thereabouts, a Muslim from West Africa called Umar had made the pilgrimage to Mecca, and had stayed there for some time. He was a native of Futa Toro, one of those minor jihadist states that had emerged during the eighteenth century in far western Africa. Even before going on the *hajj*, he was well known as an Islamic scholar and local aristocrat; his participation in the *hajj* only enhanced his reputation; it also provided him with important connections and familiarised him with the Muslim revolutions in other lands along his route.[13]

His journey east to Mecca started from his homeland close to the Atlantic Ocean, and took him through the long sequence of states along the Sahel – Kaarta, Masina, into the new Sokoto Caliphate and the Bornu Sultanate. In the latter two, he would be in states that had only recently gone through the Islamic reform, and Masina was in the process of doing so under Ahmadu when he visited it. He stayed for several months in Sokoto, recently revolutionised. Beyond Bornu was an area of small states that had survived the nearby religious revolution without too much damage, then Wadai, a state that resisted any reform or attack from any direction longer than any other states in the area (it was the last to be taken by the French), then Darfur and the Egyptian-ruled Sudan, when the Egyptian conquest was still in progress. He could cross the Red Sea through Suakin and Jeddah, the traditional route for *hajj* pilgrims from West Africa. He was a wealthy, alert and intelligent man, and the conditions in all these states would be noted as he passed through. He made the acquaintance of the leading men in each city and state he visited; his aristocratic status and his participation in the *hajj* would guarantee that.

He was in Arabia at a period when the Wahhabi sect, extreme Islamic puritans, was prominent in the area. He spent several years studying and deepening his understanding of Islam in Mecca and elsewhere, no doubt absorbing at least some Wahhabi influence. He also took due note of the Wahhabis' violent methods, which were more intensive and brutal than those of Usuman dan Fodio in his Hausaland *jihad*. He began his return in about 1830. On his way home, he passed through the Egyptian-ruled Sudan, and then on westwards, reversing his earlier journey, through Wadai and Bornu. In Bornu, he acquired a wife, Mariatu. He then stayed in Sokoto for several years. The successor in Sokoto to Usuman dan Fodio, the founder of the *jihad* state, Muhammad Belo, presented him with one of his daughters, Aissa or Mariam, as another wife, and he also acquired a third, a slave girl called Fatma. His return to Futa Toro was equally leisurely, briefly interrupted by his detention by the king of Kaarta because he had arrived by way of Masina, which was at war with Kaarta. (Masina had now gone through its own Muslim revolution.) Even in detention, he was hardly uncomfortable, since his wealth enabled him to live well there, and his aristocratic status prevented any mistreatment.

After his release, he returned to his home country, and then moved to Futa Jalon, another state that had had its jihadist revolution in the past. There he set up as a merchant, dealing in slaves and local agricultural produce, and buying, among others things, guns from the British and French merchants on the coast. The guns were used to arm the men he employed as guards for his caravans.

Again, he spent a period of several years in this activity. He became rich, gaining an entourage of soldiers and religious followers, and acquiring an even wider knowledge of the region and its inhabitants. His reputation increased, both because he was a wealthy man, and as a scholar, assisted, of course, by his description as 'al-Hajj' Umar. It would seem that this was not sufficient, and his attention shifted more decisively towards his religious beliefs. He was by this time over 50 years of age.

While in Mecca, and under a degree of Wahhabi influence, he is said to have received secret instructions from Sheikh Sidi Ahmed al-Tijani, the leader of a puritan group, to leave Medina and 'go and sweep the countries of the West'. Interpreted, this was understood to be an instruction to organise a *jihad*.

But Umar – now al-Hajj Umar – was clearly in no hurry to commit himself to a *jihad* campaign. He spent the next twenty years in what later would be thought of as a time of preparation, building his wealth, recruiting soldiers – employed as guards for his caravans at first, but useful in any fighting – acquiring weaponry, preaching – a career reminiscent of that of Muhammad the Prophet. This has all the hallmarks of deliberation, a well thought-out process.

His religious beliefs were tainted by the inclusion of a strong infusion of violence, in part from the example of the Wahhabis he had met in Arabia, and partly by the example of the success of the Fulani *jihad* of Usuman in Hausaland; the Sokoto Caliphate was a Fulani state, overthrowing the Hausa governments that had ruled before the revolution of dan Fodio. And the small jihadist states in the west – Futa Toro, Futa Jalon and others – were also Fulani. A whole series of pressures, including his religious experience, his tribal origin, and his own experience, his home background, and his wives, who came from *jihad* states, and that curious instruction to 'sweep the West' acted on Umar to produce his reaction to the new events in his homeland in the 1840s.

He was becoming a nuisance to the government of Futa Jalon. His wealth and aristocratic status gave him an audience, his success as a merchant increased his renown, and now his outspoken views on religion increased his influence and his nuisance threat to the governing elite still further. (Futa Jalon was a formerly jihadist state, but its rulers had evidently relaxed into less rigorous religious observance.) He thus lived in a land that had already gone through a *jihad* period, and the original fervour had faded, to be contrasted with the more recent *jihad* successes in neighbouring Sokoto and Bornu. It was not surprising that the Futa Jalon rulers were uneasy at his increasing influence.

He was compelled to leave Futa Jalon and moved eastwards, across the mountains that marked its eastern boundary, to settle in the town of Dinguiraye. There he finally began his own *jihad* war. He could interpret his life as a replica of the career of Muhammad, and claimed an understanding of the need to cleanse the Islamic lands of their errors, their slack and infidel ways, and to convert the heathen; his expulsion from his homeland was his *hijra*. And he had an armed following, loyal to him – his armed caravan escort men – and a party of capable men and women to organise affairs. (Usuman dan Fodio's life and career had also copied that of the Prophet; in both cases, this was no doubt wholly deliberate.)

He prepared quite deliberately to foment a politico-religious revolution, aimed at the overthrow and dethronement of the existing rulers of the local states. This, of course, was what dan Fodio had done in the Hausa kingdoms and Mahmadu al-Amini al-Kanemi in Bornu. The old ruling elites had, inevitably, opposed his demands for reform – just as the elite of Futa Jalon, and probably Futa Toro as well, had opposed his presence and his work. In Sokoto, they had then been replaced by dan Fodio's own elite rulers of the old states in the persons of the new emirs.

The *jihad* that Umar launched lasted for a decade and a half. His *jihad* was less a cleansing of Islam, which had been dan Fodio's aim, and more an intention to convert the pagans, both those who did not know Islam and those who had rejected it. The basis of his campaign was the Tukulor people, related to the Fulani and speaking a similar language. He also from the start used guns in his campaigns, presumably because his own caravan men had them, but also because some were already in the hands of his target states.

This first target was the kingdom of Kaarta, which he had visited during his *hajj*. It was the obvious beginning, for it was a pagan kingdom amidst several Muslim states. But from the start, he came up against a whole series of sources of resistance. His troops overran Kaarta and pillaged it, as Usuman's men did in Bornu, but failed to convert many of the people, who resisted his rule and his attempts to convert them, and resented the thorough sack the kingdom had suffered. (This latter activity was clearly the aim of a large part of Umar's forces, rather than religious reform or extension.) Next door was Masina, which he must have hoped would join him. It had been subjected to a small *jihad* campaign at the same time as that in Hausaland, and it had, as he knew from his own experience, been at war against Kaarta. But the king of Masina, Ahmadu Lobo, and his people were unimpressed by Umar's successes, and disliked his methods. At least he did not attack Masina yet, but turned against several small pagan states to the west of Kaarta, notably Khasso and Galam. But this time he came up against an even more formidable enemy, French soldiers, armed and disciplined, and more formidable fighters man to man than his own less disciplined forces. The French were also well established in several forts within the pagan countries, over which they had established their protection. In clashes with the fairly small French forces Umar's troops were repeatedly defeated.

Umar recoiled. He turned east again, and attacked the kingdom of Segu, which fell to him, but only after a fairly lengthy two-year campaign. Masina, probably acquainted with the methods of its attacker, since it was a *jihad* state itself, was next attacked and overrun. Umar thus more or less controlled a large area of the western Sudan, along the line of the upper Niger River, a territory about 500 miles in length.

Yet his control was unsteady. Not only was there still resistance to his rule in Kaarta, his first conquest, but continued opposition existed in both Segu and Masina, where the opposition was inspired in the name of local independence, not religion. He was able to mount a raid further east, and captured and sacked Timbuktu, ironically the most noted centre of Muslim scholarship in the whole region. He then had to turn back to put down risings against him in his recent conquests. In the process of this internal campaigning, he was killed (1864).

There followed a larger series of rebellions, against his successors, not to mention disputes among those successors for the position of leader. He had placed some of his sons as provincial governors – reputedly, he had twenty-five sons and twenty-five daughters – and they each wanted the full control that Umar had exercised, or, alternatively, independence. It took nearly a decade before one of the sons, Ahmadu Seko, governor of Segu, emerged as the victor.[14]

The condition of the whole region, from Futa Jalon to Timbuktu, had been seriously damaged in all this fighting, first by the brutal and violent methods of Umar's soldiers, then by the scorched-earth tactics employed in the succession war. Ahmadu faced continual opposition to his rule, and eventually left his main centre, in Segu, for Kaarta, but he was driven out by the French and ended his life in exile in the Sokoto Caliphate, just before it was conquered by the British.

To the south of the Tukulor Empire, which Umar constructed and which began to disintegrate under Ahmadu, an alternative process of revival and resistance – or empire-building – developed under the leadership of a local man, Samori. He operated in the upper Niger regions and along the streams feeding that river from the south. His origins were somewhat similar to that of Umar in that he had first specialised in trade, and only later did he turn to military matters. He was not a Muslim and at first laid emphasis on his pagan credentials. His particular genius was to develop and build an effective army, based on possession of guns and the enforcement of proper discipline. With this, he conquered a kingdom as large as that of Umar and Ahmadu.

At a fairly late stage in his career he co-opted Islam into his scheme, but then abandoned it once he had suffered a bad defeat. There is no sign that he believed in Islam, only that he was prepared to use it for his own purposes if he felt it was worthwhile. His career lasted about twenty years, contemporary with that of Ahmadu in the Segu Tukulor *jihad* state, roughly 1870 to 1890. It seems clear that although he was indifferent to Islam, and tended to emphasise the efficacy of the pagan religions, he took lessons from the experience of the Tukulor empire-builders to the north. But like Ahmahu Seko, he eventually collided with the French – an even better military group than his own army.[15]

A third major military-cum-political leader in the region was Mahmadu Lamine. He operated in the land to the west of the Tukulor Empire, but he was far too close to the French territories to be allowed to construct a major state; he was fairly quickly brought down by French attacks. He had learnt his revolutionary trade while a prisoner of Ahmadu Seko, and applied the lessons of Umar's military developments to his own followers. He operated mainly in the 1880s.[16]

There is in all these nineteenth-century West African revolutionary developments a clear connection. We may begin with the small *jihad* states of the far west, which had emerged in the eighteenth century, though they came from older roots reaching back to the original Muslim conquests in the north. Usuman dan Fodio had connections with some of those *jihad* states – Futa Jalon, Futa Toro and so on – and took his inspiration from their work, and from personal contacts with emissaries from them.

The revolution in the Hausa states, which replaced them by the Sokoto Caliphate within a few years, was the most important development in whole region; it was copied in Masina and in Bornu to either side of the new caliphate, where the revolutions were led by local imitators of dan Fodio's success – Ahmadu Lobo, the conqueror of Masina, had been one of dan Fodio's commanders in the Hausa wars. Umar passed through Masina, Sokoto and Bornu on his *hajj* journey, and on his return journey in Bornu and Sokoto he married women of those lands, whose knowledge of events and processes in their homelands was useful to him; in Sokoto, the daughter of the successor of dan Fodio, Muhammad Belo. It is reasonable to conclude that this experience was part of the inspiration for his own declaration of *jihad* twenty years later, and that his potential for *jihad* was noted by his new relatives. Mahmadu Lamine learned of military affairs while in detention under Ahmadu Seko, Umar's most successful successor; Samori was apparently influenced by the success of the Tukulor *jihad* to his north. The Muslim revolutionaries were frequently inspired by the Prophet Muhammad's life, spending much of their early lives in preparation for their later work.

These religious and national revolutions were thus all conducted independently, but with a common inspiration. They also overlapped in time. Umar's journeys in Sokoto and its neighbours happened not long after the Sokoto Caliphate was organised, and while it was still expanding. Samori and Mahmadu Lamine were actively building their empires while Ahmadu was still fighting to maintain his hold on Umar's inheritance. And at the start, Usuman dan Fodio owed some of his inspiration to his contacts with men from Futa Toro and Futa Jalon.

Umar's *hajj* journey was only one of numerous such journeys by West African Muslims in the eighteenth and nineteenth centuries, so much so that Suakin was one of the major ports they used, having walked across the Sudan; special arrangements were made in Darfur to safeguard them and speed them on their ways.[17] The turmoil in West Africa, from dan Fodio's *jihad* from 1804 to the activities of Samori and Mahmadu Lamine in the 1880s, were undoubtedly well known in Sudan, where the condition of the people during that time under Egyptian rule could hardly have been worse. The ability of the Fulani and Tukulor and others to throw off the rule of their oppressors, inspired in many cases by Islam, was an obvious inspiration, and this eventually came to fruit in the success of Muhammad Ahmad the Mahdi.

Chapter 3

Egypt Rising

The Hausa *jihad* in West Africa in 1804–9 occurred just after the first European intervention in Egypt in 1798 to 1803. This began first with the French, then the British, and resulted in the emergence of a semi-independent regime after 1803, though it was technically returned to Ottoman rule in that year by the withdrawal of the British forces. It is not easy to detect any direct connection between these events in the two areas, other than contemporaneity. The most obvious connections are Islam and the slave trade, since both Egypt and the West African Sudan were avid consumers and exporters of slaves, as were Britain and France. The African kingdoms were the suppliers of the human trade goods to Europe, America, and the Muslim countries, and the hunting of the Black slaves went ever deeper into the interior of Africa as the sources of supply near the coasts were exhausted. This was clearly a major source of warfare throughout the continent.

Neither the French nor the British stayed long in Egypt on this occasion – the British removed the French in 1801, and finally left themselves in 1803 – and neither of them was in Egypt for the benefit of the Egyptians. The effect of their relatively brief presence, however, was to stir up the government of the country, which remained technically an Ottoman province all through the several invasions, but which had actually been under Mameluke rule. These were a selected and highly trained group of warriors, originally enslaved Christian children imported from the Ottoman provinces, most particularly from the Caucasus region; there were selected Blacks from Africa amongst them as well. They were trained as expert horsemen, swordsmen and cavalry, then freed and made into a warrior elite from among whom the head of the Egyptian government and the army was selected by his fellow warriors. The pattern was a common one throughout Islam, in the Ottoman Empire – where they were called janissaries – and in Mughal India. In Egypt, the Mamelukes, however, had established themselves as an autonomous governing system.[1]

The British and the French and later the Turks between them physically destroyed most of the Mamelukes, which was the only means of removing them from control in Egypt. Only when the Mamelukes had been physically removed – that is, in most cases, killed, though some escaped – was it possible to begin any reform of the Egyptian government. The removal took twenty years to accomplish, with only a relative few of the Mamelukes surviving the violence; those who did survive and adapt, however, often rose to high positions in the new government.

The French were the first invaders, in 1798, under the command of General Napoleon Bonaparte. It was essentially his expedition, originated, planned and conducted by him, and consequently designed primarily for his personal glory. He conquered the country, had it surveyed and explored, but found that expanding out of it was impossible. He was up against constant opposition within Egypt, at least once the Mamelukes had been defeated and the Egyptians saw through his pretensions of liberation and Islamic conversion. He was up against the Turks and the Palestinians in his vain attempt to invade Syria, where his forces were defeated. He was also up against the British, with whom revolutionary France had been at war for several years already; the Royal Navy dominated both the Red Sea and the Mediterranean, and on his voyage from France to Egypt, he had been very fortunate not to be found by the searching British fleet. Between them, these Napoleonic enemies boxed in the French within Egypt as soon as the French landed, and this continued until they were ready to surrender and be removed. Napoleon's expedition was a political and imperial cul-de-sac.[2]

The results of the European intervention in Egypt were profound for the country, but were also of a wider effect than in Egypt itself. The victory of the British Mediterranean Fleet at Abukir (the 'Battle of the Nile') finally established the Royal Navy's superiority in the Mediterranean after a brief eviction a few years before. The victory of the British Army – the new, better trained and professionally commanded British Army – over the previously all-victorious French marked the beginning of the destruction of the Napoleonic system even before it had spread from a reform of the army to an autocratic government of France. It took a lot of hard fighting still, but the Egyptian expedition had given a clear sign that revolutionary France could be defeated.[3]

The French expedition to Egypt was a substantial one, perhaps 40,000 men, but once in Egypt they were cut off from easy contact with France by the destruction of the fleet that had brought them. At the Battle of the Nile, the British Mediterranean Fleet, commanded by Vice Admiral Nelson, destroyed or captured almost every French ship.[4] The French fleet was thus defeated, but so also, partly as a result, and rather more surprisingly, was the French invading army. A Turkish force and the local Palestinian militias prevented the French from campaigning in Palestine,[5] and the British landed two armies in Egypt to fight the French, alongside a Turkish army. The main force from Britain under General Abercrombie was landed at Abukir, and a secondary force, mainly from India under General Sir David Baird, but with a contingent from Britain, landed at Quseir on the Red Sea coast.

This British intervention was an impressively coordinated campaign, with armies and fleets sent from Britain and India and a Turkish force joining together in Egypt to fight the French. Abercrombie's army from Britain met and defeated the French army close to Alexandria,[6] then marched to Cairo, where it was joined by the Turkish invading army; they jointly laid siege to the city. The French in the end surrendered *in toto*, and only then did the British discover that the French forces had outnumbered them decisively all along. A victory like this was something to boast about. The French were not disarmed on surrender, and were consequently watched by the British forces as, cheerfully, and loaded with loot, they marched to the ships that would take them home – British ships, of course. Baird's British army from India had meanwhile marched across the desert from the Red Sea to the Nile, then hired boats and travelled north along the river. This was an impressive logistical achievement, though the force never got into action against the French, arriving in the north after the French surrender. The war in Egypt was over before they reached Cairo.[7]

The British forces – mainly those from India – stayed in Egypt for two more years, a gradually diminishing presence, until the Treaty of Amiens brought a temporary end to the wider war with France. These events had had a usefully disturbing effect on the Mameluke system in Egypt. Confusion gradually took over that government as the Mamelukes were destroyed, so that for several years it was not clear who was in control in the country. Eventually, after the appointment of an Albanian military adventurer, Muhammad Ali, as commander-in-chief by the Turkish imperial government, matters were sorted out with some ruthlessness. The massacre of most of the surviving Mamelukes, who were attempting to revive their former regime, occurred at Muhammad Ali's command. (The French and the British had already accounted for a large proportion of them.)

The result was that Muhammad Ali emerged as the *wali*, the official Ottoman governor, in 1805, though it took him several more years to secure full control. Surviving Mamelukes escaped southwards, and maintained their hostility to the new regime for another decade – a perfect excuse for Muhammad Ali to remain in power, of course. Muhammad Ali was in fact a military dictator, effectively independent of the Turkish government (as the Mamelukes had been), though he paid lip service to the Ottoman sultan's authority, more as a political protection against further interference from outside than in any loyalty to the sultan in Constantinople. His model may well have been Napoleon as emperor in Paris (and he was the more successful of the two *parvenus*).

It had taken several years for Muhammad Ali to emerge – fighting his way – from the crowd of Ottoman officials and soldiers who entered Egypt when the French were evacuated in 1801. At first, the Ottomans were welcomed, but they very rapidly wore out that welcome by their incompetent and greedy behaviour. They treated Cairo as an occupied enemy city, and set about looting and murdering.[8] There was conflict between the Ottomans and the surviving Mamelukes, between the Ottomans and the people, and within the Ottoman personnel, all of which groups gradually wore each other down. Muhammad Ali emerged as the commander of the Albanian contingent in the Ottoman forces; this was eventually the last effective and more or less disciplined Ottoman force in the country.[9]

Muhammad Ali used his position as the Albanians' commander to muscle his way to become the *wali*; he used his position to remove rival governors and authorities, to strike alliances with the clerical establishment, and at times used his Albanian troops to riot when such a method was useful to him. Eventually, he used them to massacre the last of the Mamelukes who were still in Egypt.[10] This process of emergence took ten years, beginning from the return of Ottoman authority in 1801, but it was the elimination of the Mamelukes that was a lesson to others, and a relief to the ordinary population. By then (1811), Muhammad Ali was invulnerable, even though he was repeatedly threatened by internal conspiracies during the rest of his rule, which lasted until 1848 (and his dynasty until 1953). He developed an effective police force and a secret police system with which he successfully countered these plots.[11]

The brief French and British military presences in Egypt had been further lessons for him. It was evident to Muhammad Ali that the Western Europeans had developed a set of skills and procedures, military, economic and governmental, which he and Egypt needed if the country was to emerge from the depression, economic and psychological, into which the long centuries of Mameluke/Ottoman rule had pushed it. (The Mamelukes had actually ruled since 1250, and the Ottoman conquest in 1517 had left them in power as rulers on behalf of the sultan.) The civil conflicts in that period of ten years, often provoked by Muhammad Ali himself in order to secure an extension of his power, or to destroy rivals, had caused widespread damage, on top of that caused by the French and British and Ottoman invaders. Muhammad Ali had cleverly played off each power centre in the country against the others, let them destroy each other, and had emerged as the dictatorial authority, the single power centre left. At that point, he could put into effect the lessons he had been learning from these turbulent years. He began to hire Europeans, to import new techniques, new skills, new machines, and to reform the administration. Building an army and a fleet were priorities.

Once clearly in power and in control, Muhammad Ali set about his reforms and innovations.[12] During his reign, he adjusted the provincial system three times, seeking ever more efficient methods of rule, and more effective officials and administrators – he found that the surviving Mamelukes were usefully efficient as administrators. He reformed the army, stimulated to do so by a riot by his own Albanians in Cairo, which demonstrated that they had become a nuisance even to him, and he recruited Turks, Maghrabis and others to replace them; in particular, he recruited European officers, at first experienced men who had served under Napoleon – French, Piedmontese, Neapolitan and Spanish – to officer his new army. In 1825, there were at least thirty-eight of them in senior commands.[13]

He established factories, particularly textile factories, this being the recognised essential beginning of any industrial development, producing early profits and creating immediate unskilled employment.[14] The development of factory manufacturing had the effect of squeezing out the cottage industry of weaving, which had long been a secondary occupation of the peasantry. This was replaced by the cheaper machine-made variety of cloth, and this in turn brought the peasantry into full-time employment. Similarly, the introduction of cash crops such as sugar and cotton, rice and indigo, and numerous fruits, required a considerably greater, and more skilled, workforce than the traditional Egyptian agricultural peasantry had displayed.[15] As a result, many of the men who had spent time at home weaving now had to work with the new crops; for this they earned a rather higher pay than they had earned as peasant proprietors, though it was much harder and more continuous work. (This was, of course, replicating the contemporary experience of the spinners and handloom weavers of the north of England as the Industrial Revolution there took hold.)

Muhammad Ali established state monopolies in the export of many of these goods, notably in the export of grain during the Napoleonic Wars, when much of the British Army's needs in the Peninsular War were supplied from Egypt – at a very high price, of course.[16] Whenever he noticed a product likely to turn a profit, especially as an export, he made it a state monopoly. Some regard this as commercial acumen; others as excessive taxation. It may be identified as one of the reasons that the incipient industrialisation of Egypt did not develop – too much state interference, and probably a too-heavy state extraction of taxation revenue. (Think neo-Communist autocratic China, or contemporary army-dominated Egypt.)

All this was not achieved without considerable internal Egyptian trouble and disturbance. Establishing internal control – 'law and order' – had been Muhammad Ali's initial and overriding intention once he had gained complete control of the government system, and after destroying or recruiting the last of the Mamelukes in the country. But change begets opposition and he had to face repeated insurrections, none very threatening, but all of them awkward and distracting. One solution was to recruit troublemakers into paid employment – which, of course, they usually preferred. Bedouin tribes had to be tamed, in some cases by paying them very well for guarding the desert caravans which they would originally have looted – the British expedition from India adopted this system to ensure an easy and trouble-free crossing of the desert; it seems that the Bedouin were amazed at British generosity. Piracy on the river Nile had to be suppressed since this tended to interrupt the supply of food for Cairo and Alexandria (and export); the number of boats on the Nile was increased by a deliberate programme of construction, and the erstwhile pirates were recruited as boatmen. All this development was repeatedly interrupted by outbreaks of plague and cholera, and by the erratic Nile, where a low water level always brought drought and death.[17] Here were major reasons for Muhammad Ali's deliberate expansion of state authority, and for the heavy tax regime.

Despite all these problems, and the difficulties caused by the changes, the population of Egypt rose steadily during Muhammad Ali's control – a clear result of his measures. The population had been declining slowly but steadily for centuries under the erratic misrule of the Mamelukes, who had been in control of Egypt since Saladin's time in the twelfth century. The population when Muhammad Ali seized control in the 1810s was about 3.5 million; it rose to about 5 million during his reign, i.e., between 1811 and 1848.

Muhammad Ali was rumoured to be aiming to achieve complete independence from the Ottoman Empire. Since the Ottoman government was unable to involve itself with any success in Egyptian affairs, this ambition probably had a low priority for him as being hardly necessary. He did, however, exercise his new army as an imperial instrument – in the name of the Ottoman sultan, of course, and at times by the sultan's request. Another rumour had it that he aimed to construct an empire that stretched from Damascus to Yemen, though this was a considerable underestimate of his ambition, and even of his achievement.[18] As early as 1812, only the year after establishing his full control in Egypt, his army was campaigning in the Hejaz region in Arabia, and he gained control of Mecca and Medina. This, of course, was Ottoman territory, though it was under threat from the Wahhabi sect in central Arabia. He was able to carry through a series of contra-Wahhabi expeditions into Arabia because the Ottoman government had failed to defend its territory; he was thus able to claim to be restoring that authority.[19]

The authority of the Ottoman sultan was not always acknowledged by the *wali*, though when it chimed with Muhammad Ali's own inclinations and ambitions, the sultan would be obeyed. An instance was in 1818, when the

British East India Company sent a naval force against Yemen. The excuse was to investigate a dispute over the ill-treatment of a British merchant (who was in the wrong) at Mocha. The expedition was really aimed at extracting commercial concessions from the defeated imam of the region. As a precaution, the sultan then ordered Muhammad Ali to occupy the ports along the African coast of the Red Sea, and Suakin and Massawa were seized; neither the sultan nor the *wali* wished to see the British Empire expanding into the Red Sea or Arabia if they could prevent it.[20]

He later used his newly built fleet to intervene in the Greek insurrection – the 'Greek War of Independence' – in the 1820s, this time at the sultan's request. Commanded by his able son Ibrahim, his forces acquired an unpleasant reputation for cruelty and for the practice of enslaving Greeks (a continuation of the enslavement of Blacks in Sudan, or of Causasians – but to enslave white men and women in Europe was seen as illegitimate; illogical but true). Then, in 1830, he sent his forces to conquer Syria. Neither of these enterprises was particularly successful, though he did hold Syria for ten years. His fleet was badly damaged in the Battle of Navarino when it came up against the joint European fleets of intervention, dominated, of course, by British ships, and he had to remove his forces from Greece.[21] He also had to withdraw his forces from Syria in 1840, again as a result of European, particularly British, diplomatic and armed opposition.[22]

These attempts to expand in the Near East were generally unsuccessful because they quickly came up against the European states that entertained ambitions and interests contrary to Muhammad Ali's, and, more important, greater power. But his expansion into Africa did not evoke such opposition, at least not in his lifetime. His most successful long-term imperial adventure was in the Sudan. (For this, see later in this chapter.)

This was the time when Europe was becoming increasingly conscious of the existence, not only of the modern Egypt being developed by Muhammad Ali, but primarily of the fascination of the remains of ancient Egypt. There had been premonitory notices in the eighteenth century, but it was Bonaparte's expedition, and in particular, his inclusion in that expedition of a group of scientists – *savants* – which had begun to reveal the rich and fascinating remains of the distant past of that country. It affected everyone who spent even a short time there – the British forces stayed only until 1803, but the officers made plans, and developed a subscription scheme, aiming to take home an obelisk when they withdrew, though their plan did not work out.[23]

It became the custom for visitors to take items away, often hacking off sections of statue, and many who were in the country for any length of time had the opportunity to gather considerable collections. The French consul general, posted to Cairo by Napoleon, was Bernardino Drovetti. He was a Piedmontese and spent twenty years in Egypt. He carried off enough materials to found a museum in Turin; the British consul general, Henry Salt, acted in the same way.[24] Numerous visitors travelled up the Nile and described their experiences in print when they got home, thus, of course, widening the number of potential visitors. Some even went beyond the southern boundary of the country at Aswan and penetrated into the lands that were being conquered by Muhammad Ali's army in the 1820s.[25] As early as 1815, William Banks at Aswan could feel that he was under Muhammad Ali's protection.[26]

The number of these travellers, archaeologists, antiquarians and adventurers – and looters – increased considerably once the wars in Europe ended in 1815, and one result is that we have a library full of descriptions of the country. Above all, the visitors were interested in the ancient remains; so we have accounts of travel and of ancient remains, but rather fewer of the Egyptians themselves, or of Muhammad Ali's development activities. And relatively few went much further south than Aswan, the northernmost cataract on the Nile.[27] Despite their rather narrow viewpoint, however, many of these accounts do provide incidental information about contemporary Egypt.

Until 1820, the extent of control exercised from Cairo along the Nile Valley ended at the first cataract, where Aswan was the last Egyptian town going southwards; a garrison had been pushed forward to Wadi Halfa at the second cataract, but beyond that was a desolate area, with only the minimal human occupation along the river for 1,000 miles, and desert dwellers, probably hostile, spread over the adjacent lands. This land, from Aswan southwards, was Nubia, though the European travellers tended to include the Aswan area in that description. Travel south of Aswan was difficult, not only because of the cataracts (at Aswan, Wadi Halfa, Firket and then three more) but because the river flowed through desert and savanna for all that distance, land that was just capable of supporting scattered nomadic groups and their animals, with settlements close beside the river, but not much else. It was also dangerous: travellers could be regarded as fair game by the desert dwellers.

At Dongola, where there was an area of fertility, an oasis alongside the river, a small surviving group of refugee Mamelukes eked out a miserable existence, planting pearl millet for their food 'with their own hands', as al-Jabarti remarks, almost disbelievingly. Probably most of the little community had died off by 1816, when their existence became known in Egypt. Al-Jabarti lists the most prominent of these survivors in 1816.[28] After the death of Ibrahim Bey al-Kabir, their chieftain, who was in command, they sent an envoy to Cairo to petition Muhammad Ali to allow them to return to Egypt. He did not refuse, but stated forbiddingly difficult and restrictive conditions, including that they must live where he decided. He was clearly intending that they should be scattered about the country and supervised by his police. So far as is known, most of them found the conditions unacceptable, and did not take up his 'offer'. In 1819, a group of European travellers encountered three of the Mameluke officials who had joined their caravan and had decided to seek to submit to the *wali* Muhammad Ali. That is, the Mameluke state in Dongola was still leaking deserters. (The caravan consisted of over 200 laden camels, and carried gum arabic, ostrich feathers, elephant tusks, tamarind, and other goods; also, there were '200 young female slaves, who look very sorrowful for their fate'. It was a good summary of the economic value to Muhammad Ali of the conquest that in that year he was deciding to aim for.)[29]

The Mamelukes had exaggerated their distress, and concealed their present circumstances in their petition for clemency, but it is likely that Muhammad Ali knew plenty about them. Certainly, al-Jabarti, whose writing was contemporary with the *wali*'s time, knew which Mamelukes had died and which had survived their exile from Egypt in the past five years. They had campaigned in northern Sudan and had finally settled at Dongola, where they had formed a violent and predatory 'bandit state',[30] attacking and looting all their neighbours; it is no wonder Muhammad Ali imposed impossible conditions on their return to Egypt.

On the other hand, he was a cunning enough politician not to waste the opportunity they presented. He would use the threat they posed to their neighbours, and more distantly to Egypt, as a perfect excuse to intervene in the south. He prepared a military expedition to campaign along the Nile. This had several aims in view: first, the suppression of the surviving Mamelukes, but then the conquest of the lands to the south, and the location of the source of gold, which was one of the region's exports – and, of course, the capture and export of Black slaves. What he knew of the refugee Mamelukes, however, was little, though it was dwarfed by his ignorance of the lands further south.[31]

The river Nile is almost as dominating to life in the Sudan as it is to Egypt. In the region to which the last Mamelukes had retreated it twisted and turned, with Dongola, an isolated area of fairly well-watered good land, in the midst of all this. It flowed north from the junction of the Blue and White Niles, where Khartoum is now, past Berber and Abu Hamad, then turned to flow south-westwards past the old Nubian city of Napata, and then turned north again, past Old Dongola, another ruined city, and the recently founded New Dongola, close to the third cataract, and on to Egypt. Travel along the river was by no means easy; there were six cataracts, where resistant rocks created stormy rapids. The cataracts, however, could be navigated at a time of high Nile (July to November), though only with great care even then.

The last tributary of any size to join the Nile on its way north to the sea was the Atbara River, which joined close to Berber, at which point the Nile still had 1,500 miles to go to reach the sea. South of that junction the land became steadily less dry, and the river received tributaries in greater numbers, fed by monsoon rains in Ethiopia, and by the constant wet climate of tropical Central Africa. The Atbara and the Blue Nile came in, powerful reinforcements for the river, enough to see it through as far as the Mediterranean. Both of these rivers flowed from the Ethiopian Highlands.

The two rivers, the Blue and the White Niles, have complementary regimes. The White Nile, originating in the Great Lakes region of East Africa, has a fairly constant flow, regulated by a series of lakes – Edward, Albert, Victoria and Kyogo, reliable and capacious. It then feeds into the permanent swampland of the Sudd, south of Fashoda, where again the flow of water is controlled. In turn, this large area of swampland receives the flow of several tributaries – the Sobat, the Bahr el-Ghazal, and others. By contrast, the Blue Nile originates in Ethiopia, and it is the monsoon climate in that country that was the source of the floodwaters, until the Aswan Dam was built in order to regulate the flow. This river provided a regular annual flood every year, reaching Egypt in July and lasting until October or later – at least so long as the monsoon had arrived. It is this increase in the water in the river that facilitated boats attempting to pass the cataracts, and it was the failure of the monsoon in the Ethiopian Highlands that resulted in a low Nile and subsequent famine and disease in Egypt. But, even without the annual flood from the Blue Nile, the White Nile continued to send water from the Equator to the Mediterranean.

For Egypt, therefore, the desert between Aswan and Berber was a protective device, making travelling north from the steppes and well-watered lands difficult, especially for larger groups, such as armies. At the same time, this desert area protected the lands south of Berber from Egyptian attack. The six cataracts rendered river traffic difficult to impossible much of the time, and laborious at all seasons; traffic, therefore, tended to use the land routes. It was certainly possible for Egyptians to reach the Sudan, as Muhammad Ali's expeditions were to prove, and for Sudanese to reach Egypt, as the regular traffic in Black slaves to Egypt testified, but for both of these the passage was rare, and was mainly possible for small parties, such as the caravan including surrendering Mamelukes, which was seen by the travellers in 1819.[32] Invasions, obviously requiring much larger numbers, going in either direction were difficult and only took place very occasionally, and then by relatively small forces, who could be stopped when they reached fertile and populated land. Water existed, of course, in the river, but supplies of anything else were scant, and it is a mistake to assume that only water is required in crossing desert lands. Attempting to get through the desert region was not just a matter of needing water, it was also a matter of needing food, and the resources of food along the river were quickly exhausted by a large party. Muhammad Ali's invasion force was relatively small, partly for that reason, but its possession of guns made it effective.

Muhammad Ali had a variety of motives for invading his southern neighbour, which we call the Sudan.[33] It was not a single state at the time. The northern half of the land, from the Egyptian frontier (at the first cataract) along the great bend of the Nile, was divided among several mutually hostile Arab tribes, of which the most important were the Ababda, living north of Dongola, and the Shaiqiyah, south of that point. Both of these had suffered from the hostile attentions of the refugee Mamelukes; the Shaiqiyah had put up a good fight and had eventually driven the invaders back, and both of them tended to be friendly towards the Egyptian invaders for that reason.

These Arab and part-Arab tribes were descended in part from medieval invading Arab groups, who had intermarried with the existing inhabitants, some of whom were originally Christian and some pagan, though all were now more or less Muslim, if usually less than orthodox. As a result, the Arab blood had been diluted, and their spoken Arabic had acquired so many non-Arabic words that it was largely incomprehensible to most Egyptians.[34]

From the trading centre of Berber south, there were better-organised states, in particular the Sultanate of Sennar along the Blue Nile, and Kordofan and Darfur to the west of the main river. Beyond Sennar was Ethiopia, a Christian empire going through one of its bouts of disunion; it was very largely separated from the Nile Valley by its high mountain homeland, though it was the source of the Blue Nile, and of the annual flood.

Economically, the region had certain attractions for the Egyptian ruler. Beyond Sennar, in the foothills of the Ethiopian Highland at Fazoghlu, was an old source of gold that had been exporting that metal for so long that it was legendary. In northern Sudan, there was a partial slave economy of plantations, particularly along the river. To the south was Black Africa, a well-populated region that was the main source of slaves, who could be collected by armed kidnapping raids. The whole country, from Wadi Halfa to the Upper Nile (that part of the river from the Sudd swamplands to Lake Victoria), was therefore politically disorganised and weak. The main kingdom, Sennar, on the Blue Nile, was on its final route to disintegration; Kordofan to the west had broken away, but had slid into chaotic tribal independence. To the greedy and ambitious Albanian viceroy in Egypt this all looked very enticing. He had sent spies to investigate, and though he still had a relatively poor notion of its geography, and of the strengths of the various political units, he had no doubt that his own firearms-wielding forces would have no difficulty in conquering.

His first priority, however, was the violent Mameluke survivors at Dongola, since he knew their military capabilities. Having ruled in Egypt for six or seven centuries, they could be assumed to have little more than a residual appeal as rulers among parts of the Egyptian population, and revulsion among the great majority. Muhammad Ali also had an old-fashioned wish to possess quantities of gold, which was thought to be plentiful in the Sudan – a result of the old trade in the metal from Fazoghlu. He wanted to collect Black slaves, partly to work them in the plantations he was establishing in Egypt (the same were being organised at the same time in Usuman dan Fodio's Sokoto Caliphate), and partly for the captured men to become soldiers for his new army – a new, but more loyal, obedient and cheaper version of the Mamelukes. The Greek War was becoming more serious during the Sudan conflict and he intended to form the slaves that were physically suitable into new army units – he was, after all, a man who had grown up in the Ottoman Empire (and in Albania, the northern neighbour of Greece). It had been, for centuries, the Ottoman state's policy to collect male children and to train them and educate them as janissaries – an Ottoman version of the Mamelukes. He may have been a champion of modernisation in Egypt, but he started out as an Ottoman Muslim.

The Mamelukes at Dongola had been violent rulers, substituting violence for competence. They were ignorant of the river's regime, and twice they built their houses on low ground only to see them then destroyed by the flood. The chief of the group, Abd al-Rahman, intended to fight when the Egyptian army commanded by Muhammad Ali's son Ismail approached, but instead he set off to Darfur before it arrived, then went north to Cyrenaica, seeking refuge. Those left behind did surrender, and were able to go back to Egypt, where they were able to 'obtain positions according to their abilities'.[35] A group of twenty-five of them were noted at Giza, all dressed in white (the Muslim colour of mourning), waiting to be told what to do.[36]

Muhammad Ali used his sons, Ismail and Ibrahim, as his main commanders in his expeditions in Arabia, in Greece, and now in the Sudan, and his son-in-law, Muhammad Bey Khusraw, as well. Khusraw was the *daftardar*, technically a financial post (he is usually referred to by this official title rather than his name), and he conducted a secondary campaign against the Sultanate of Darfur, west of Kordofan. Ibrahim had already been his father's commander in Arabia, and now Ismail, his third son, was to command in the Sudan.

As to the campaign, the geography of the territory dictated the process and its progress. The Nile provided the route south, from Wadi Halfa, which was the assembly place for the army.[37] The invasion under Ismail began on 11 September 1820, at the time when the annual flood of the river made it easier to pass the cataracts. The tribe that lived around Dongola, the Ababda, received the invasion with equanimity, being victims and enemies of the Mameluke band. Ismail's initial target was the surviving Mamelukes in Dongola, who scattered before they could be attacked. The next target, in fact the main enemy – of both Ismail's army and the Abdaba – was the Shaiqiyah tribe, based further south around the bend of the river beyond Old Dongola. They were defeated in two battles, at Korti and Jebel Daiqa, a show of resistance more determined than anyone else achieved in this whole campaign. Then they accepted Egyptian rule, evidently impressed by the quality of the Egyptian army and the common sense and generosity shown by Ismail to the prisoners. They enlisted in considerable numbers in Ismail's army, proving to be a loyal and efficient force of irregular cavalry.[38] Crossing the steppeland of the Bayuda due east, so avoiding the next (northward) bend in the river, and two of the cataracts, the army arrived near Berber, which, again, surrendered at once.

The army that was accomplishing this easy conquest was a mixture of Turks, Arabs, Maghrabi mercenaries, Arabs from Egypt, Bedouin and Blacks – and now Shaiqiyah as well. There were about 4,000 men in all. Turks formed the cavalry, and Egyptian Arabs were the camelmen; there was an artillery group, with ten cannon as field artillery, a mortar, and two howitzers, all commanded by an American from Massachusetts, George B. English; the Bedouin were irregular cavalry, and were now reinforced by some of the Shaiqiyah, whose style of war was similar.[39] It was a useful mixture of infantry, cavalry and artillery, well suited to the needs of the campaign.

It took Ismail's army nine months to march from Wadi Halfa to the junction of the Blue and White Niles (where neither Khartoum nor Omdurman yet existed). In June 1821, after a march along the Blue Nile, the army reached and occupied Sennar, the capital of the sultanate. The Sennari Sultan Badis VI could not wait to surrender, and came out of the city to do so even before the army reached his capital. There was no resistance at any point after the defeat of the Shaiqiyah.

At about the time that Ismail's army occupied Sennar, the *daftardar*'s force started out from Aswan on the Nile. His army was smaller than Ismail's, about 3,000 men. His target was Darfur, a geographically large sultanate of which the nearest province, and the first target, was the Darfurian province of Kordofan, which had until recently been part of the Sennar Sultanate, but had seceded; it was only nominally Darfurian, having sunk into internecine tribal chaos. The *daftardar*'s army was mainly cavalry, regular and irregular. It followed a desert route developed relatively recently by trading caravans connecting Darfur with Aswan and Egypt, and when it reached Kordofan, it first defeated the army of the provincial governor at the Battle of Bara. At the provincial centre of al-Ubaiyid (el-Obeid), they found they were welcomed by the Egyptian merchant community that dominated the area economically and which hoped that the imposition of Egyptian government would reduce the oppression they claimed to have suffered at the hands of the nearby tribal chiefs. The non-Egyptian inhabitants were less welcoming than these merchants were, and in particular, the inhabitants of the Nuba Hills to the south of al-Ubaiyid were a source of opposition.

The *daftardar* succeeded in occupying the main town, al-Ubaiyid, and a couple of smaller towns nearby, but could get no further in the face of local hostility outside the city. As a result of the invasion of his province, the sultan of Darfur was as hostile as the people of the Nuba Hills. The intention had been to campaign further, and to take over Darfur completely, as well as Kordofan, but the hostility of Kordofan's inhabitants and neighbours, and the prevalence of the Darfur forces, plus the evident difficulty of the campaign – the route they would have to follow was mainly loose sand – persuaded Muhammad Ali to order the *daftardar* to abandon further operations.[40]

The *daftardar*'s campaign was thus cut short about a month after the Battle of Bara, but Ismail had done well in the main campaign, though he now had a very large territory to govern, large parts of which had yet to be visited and subdued. His father decided he needed reinforcements and a superior commander, and the experienced Ibrahim was given a small force, said to be only 150 men, and sent south with the title of commander-in-chief. Meanwhile in Greece, the Greek revolt against the Ottomans had developed into a war of independence, and Muhammad Ali thought, rightly, that the Ottoman sultan would soon be asking for his help, which he would readily give, but for reasons of his own, as in the Red Sea and Arabia. This was one of the reasons for the restriction of the activities of the Darfur expedition. New instructions went to Ibrahim to consolidate his brother's conquest, and then concentrate on securing slaves, which was now one of the main purposes of the expedition. It was suggested that they be sent to the Red Sea port of Suakin (recently seized from the Ottoman authorities) to be shipped across to Jeddah and sold in Arabia, the receipts being used to purchase supplies for the Egyptian army in the Sudan. He was clearly intent on making the conquest pay for itself.

The other main task for the brothers was to impose an administrative structure on the conquered lands with the object of collecting taxes from the new Egyptian subjects. The size of the conquered area dictated the division of the land into several provinces. Sennar was an obvious one. The stretch of the river from Wadi Halfa to Old Dongola became a province, and the next section of the river as far as Berber another. Sennar itself proved to be wet and unhealthy, so Ismail moved his headquarters down the river to the supposedly better site at Wad Madani, though this proved to be no improvement. The real problem was the psychological depression that settled on all the Egyptians because of the wet local climate. The Egyptians at home were only used to occasional rain, but from January to April the monsoon climate drenched southern Sudan. Disease spread throughout the army, particularly malaria and dysentery. Ibrahim himself suffered from dysentery and was doctored, successfully, by Alessandro Ricci. Ricci had arrived in Egypt as a visitor; he had collected antiquities, explored Sinai and Siwah, dabbled in archaeology, and was now practising his main skills as a doctor with the Egyptian army. He had followed the army's route along the river, sightseeing and recording ancient monuments and recording his experiences.[41]

Ibrahim remained for a few months in the south but his dysentery persuaded him very quickly to return to Egypt, leaving Ismail in charge once more. Dr Ricci arrived at his camp just as Ibrahim's own doctor died, and then succeeded in curing him. Ibrahim, nevertheless, returned to Egypt, risking the long and difficult desert route from Abu Hamad to Saras to save time, cutting out the long southward bend of the river through the Sharqiya country and Dongola, though starvation threatened the party along the way.[42]

The conquest had been too easy. The operations by the *daftardar* in Kordofan were not really challenged internally, presumably because the Egyptian rule there had the support of an influential part of the population. Even so, Egyptian garrisons were still established in forts within the towns, and the countryside was barely under control. Slave raiding began, but with too little success for the moment for Muhammad Ali's pleasure. Ismail went on a slave-raiding expedition into the south.

Things soon began to go wrong in the Sennar province. The general approach of the Egyptian conquerors was exploitative, both in acquiring slaves and despatching them to work in Egypt, and in extracting wealth from the conquered territory. A new system of taxation was imposed, which in Sennar replaced the much less onerous system used by the previous sultans. This was done without apparently considering the likely effects on the population – typical autocratic behaviour, of course – and was developed because the new rulers were impressed with an exaggerated notion of the wealth of the region. The initial ease of the conquest had evidently persuaded the Egyptians that the Sudanese population was docile enough to be squeezed unmercifully without complaining.[43]

That the treatment of the Sennar province was thoughtless is emphasised by the different treatment of the northern part of the conquest. In Dongola and Berber provinces, there was apparently little trouble. The changes, and the new taxation, were certainly unpopular and resented, but this did not lead to serious violence. The governor in Dongola, Abidin Bey al-Arnaut, one of Muhammad Ali's Albanians, imposed a tax system that was more or less just, even if it took more tax revenues than before – but then it had been the Mamelukes' rapacious and inequitable 'taxation' system they were comparing it with. Abidin began as the garrison commander at New Dongola and was promoted to governor of the province in April 1821.[44] He was probably helped by the Ababdas' memories of being rescued from the Mamelukes, while the Shaiqiyah further along the river had the alternative of enlistment into the Egyptian army, which then counted as their tax contribution; Shaiqiyah soldiers in fact were employed in a tax collection role elsewhere in Sudan.

The reaction against the new oppression and the more vigorous financial exploitation was much more severe in Sennar province than elsewhere, and became violent in February 1822. Ibrahim, ill, had left for Egypt, and was then sent to campaign in Greece; Ismail had gone south, upriver along the Blue Nile, to collect slaves and, if possible, find the source of the expected gold. The Egyptian forces had suffered badly from the local diseases since arriving, and February was the middle of the rainy season, rife with malaria and dysentery. The absence of the commanders and the sickness of many of the troops was evidently visible to the local malcontents. Two aspects of what soon became a full-scale revolt were evident at the start – ambushes of small or isolated groups of Egyptian soldiers, and the fleeing of large parts of the population out of reach of the Egyptian tax collectors and their violent escorts.

Brief expeditions were launched south beyond Sennar and south-west towards the Dinka tribe who lived along the White Nile in the Sudd region. (The course of the White Nile was little understood, and suggestions were made that an expedition should go to explore that river, but this did not take place.) Slaves were collected, by the hundred. The army also spent much energy chasing and killing recalcitrant local chiefs who continued to oppose the Egyptian conquest. The initial easy campaign of conquest had turned into a much more difficult campaign to gain and keep control in detail.

Ismail returned to Sennar from his slave raiding, and made conciliatory gestures – he did not have enough troops to do much else – and this calmed the atmosphere somewhat during the middle of the year. In Berber province, the governor Mahu Bey Urfali was similarly conciliatory. On the other hand, those who had fled did not return; one group had gone as far as Ethiopia, while others camped out in the wilderness, out of sight and reach of the Egyptians, and mounted a careful watch. Until October, this near-revolt seemed to be contained and Ismail was recalled to Cairo by his father.

It appears that Ismail wished to return to Egypt with a substantial monetary bonus. When he reached Shendi, he laid a demand on the Ja'aliyin tribe, who lived along the Nile south of Berber, of $30,000 and 6,000 slaves, to be paid in two days. Shendi was a major market centre in Berber province and no doubt had been a major source of tax revenue for the Sennar sultans. But there Ismail became involved in a dispute with the *mek* (king) Nimr of the Ja'aliyin. Nimr complained that his people could not possibly pay the new tax assessment. Ismail lost his temper and struck the *mek* in the face with his pipe. That night, members of the Ja'aliyin tribe came into Ismail's camp, which was apparently unguarded. They piled straw and forage around the building he was occupying with his staff, and set it all alight. All within, including Ismail, were burned to death.[45]

This was the signal for the discontent to develop into a full-scale rebellion. As the news of Ismail's death spread, so did the revolt. The small garrisons along the river south of Berber were killed or driven out, but most of Berber province was kept quiet under governor Mahu Bey Urfali, especially when he defeated a huge Ja'aliyin army that attempted to gain control of the region to the tribe's north.[46] The *daftardar* in Kordofan gathered his forces and marched to assist in suppressing the trouble. He made no conciliatory attempts, being especially enraged by being knifed by an annoyed slave during a supposed truce conference. He marched along the Nile as far as ad-Damar, just south of Berber, destroying many settlements, including Shendi, and killing anyone who resisted; then he turned south and did the same along the Blue Nile as far as Wad Madani, whose Egyptian garrison had held out under blockade.[47]

The Egyptian forces ceased operations at the beginning of 1823, but in the latter part of that year, they made several wide-ranging campaigns through the lands east of the Nile, and succeeded in destroying or suppressing those communities that were involved in the rebellion. Some of these were canny enough to submit after only a short resistance, and were rewarded. The loyal Shaiqiyah from the north were awarded lands close to the confluence of the White and Blue Niles, where they held allotments of land as soldiers; the Abdullab tribe, which had originally held these lands, had taken up arms, and had now been driven out; the Shukriya tribe, who lived in the Butana region between the Atbara and the Blue Nile, received the former lands of the Rufa'a tribe, which faded away after having lost those lands. Elsewhere, lands were left deserted, notably the fertile and productive Jazira, between the two Niles, and food production in the region declined drastically. The one notable survivor of all this was Mek Nimr of the Ja'aliyin, who moved his base several times under Egyptian pressure, and ended by moving over the Ethiopian border into the region called Wolkait. By the end of 1823, the Egyptian conquests were recovered, but the land was ruined, littered with dead, and silent in death. It was time for a new start.[48]

In many ways, the history of Egypt and the Sudan in the early nineteenth century suggests a comparison with the process of the French Revolution thirty years before, in that having secured control of Egypt after a very difficult civil conflict, Muhammad Ali was then able to use the social power it had generated to embark on a series of reforms, innovations and external conquests. These conquests naturally generated opposition, as did his internal policies, and his adventures in Greece and Syria and Arabia all failed. In the end, though, he managed to secure himself an empire to the south by the conquest of Sudan. His purpose, of course, was not to benefit Sudan – he was not that much of a revolutionary – but to secure certain resources, gold and slaves in particular, for his own use and enrichment. This scarcely interested the Sudanese, who were steadily opposed to the Egyptian enterprise. Nevertheless, for the moment he had been successful, and by pushing into neighbouring lands, which were less well armed and less well organised than the new Egypt, he and his successors were able to continue their expansion for the next several decades.

This was a new state on the world map, but one that was a curious mixture of the new – new weapons, an incipient industrial revolution in Egypt, increased government intervention in economic matters – and the old, in the form of an increase in slavery, the use of slave labour and slave soldiers, which was a well-established Muslim institution, and the establishment of slave-worked estates in both Egypt and Sudan on a similar pattern to those of the European colonies in America, though Muhammad Ali had found such estates in existence in the Sudan when he conquered it. And on top of this, Muhammad Ali had established a rigorous autocracy. While inheriting some practices from the past – Muslim, Pharaonic, Greek, Roman and mediaeval – in a sense his system also looked forward to the dictatorships of the twentieth century; it seems probable that his model was Napoleon Bonaparte, than whom he was rather more successful.

Chapter 4

Egyptian Rule in the Sudan, 1824–1880

The slaving raids in the Sudan netted a varying number of victims, but never enough to satisfy the demands of Muhammad Ali. If they were brought to Egypt by means of a long slow journey, often on foot, and if they survived that journey, many of the enslaved succumbed quickly to the local diseases in Egypt. If they were retained in the Sudan, the able-bodied men were put in the army, where, as slaves, they were treated badly, poorly trained, badly fed, and had little and poor equipment; as a result, they likely did not live for much longer than those who ended up in Egypt. Others were put to work in agriculture on plantations, or, for the women, in domestic service or as concubines; no doubt they were equally badly treated. And the slave trade and slave capture continued inexorably throughout the period of Egyptian rule. It was a most conspicuous waste of human life; profit can only have been minimal.

The military occupation of Sudan was concentrated along the White and Blue Niles, with a large force also in insurgent Kordofan. 'Large force' is perhaps a misnomer, since the entire Egyptian garrison consisted of 5 battalions, each of 800 men, before wastage, 3 of them along the rivers and 2 in Kordofan. Their purpose was, first, control, and second, slave raiding. This latter attracted merchants, so, just as Khartoum grew as a garrison-cum-mercantile town, so al-Ubaiyid, already a town in 1820, quadrupled in size of population by 1840. Of these inhabitants, a substantial fraction were slaves, used particularly in irrigation and agriculture. The death rate among the slaves ranged between a third and a half each year – the deficit was made up from captures taken on raids to the south.[1]

Ibrahim's experience during his brief visit in the south, during which he was ill much of the time, had convinced him that the climate and the diseases of the Sudan were too dangerous for an army of men habituated to the climate and diseases of the Mediterranean area. He convinced his father that an occupation army of Black slaves would be much better, for they would already be fully acclimatised to the climate and its diseases. A large training camp was established at Aswan to train the recruits. They still died off quickly – they were in a different disease environment at Aswan, just as Ibrahim had been in the Sudan – and had to be reinforced by still more kidnapping expeditions. The regime as a whole was enormously wasteful, but the slave raiders were in effect surrogate occupation forces, and so contributed to maintaining a precarious control. An example of the early regime is the *daftardar*'s raid into the Nuba Hills in 1822 (before he had to turn his forces on to the rebels in the Nile Valley). He is said to have captured 40,000 people in the first years of Egyptian rule, who were then enslaved, and dispatched north to Egypt. Then the usual problems of disease, despair, desert travel, desertion and escape, ill-treatment, and probably starvation at times, so reduced their numbers that only 5,000 managed to reach Egypt alive.[2]

But this was the process by which the manpower required by the Egyptian government was acquired, and some of those hapless people from the Nuba Hills will have been included in the 1st Regiment, which was stationed at Omdurman from 1824 onwards. This group therefore formed part of the earliest population of Khartoum. Their presence constituted a market around which the town could grow.

By one of those ironies in which history abounds, the Nuba Hills became the destination for the refuge for slaves escaping from bondage, some still shackled and pursued by the merchants, and for villagers from Kordofan escaping the tax regime imposed by the Egyptians. The tax collectors complained that 700 Kordofani villages had become deserted by the 1830s, and so were untaxable, without appreciating, or perhaps carefully not acknowledging, their own heavy responsibility for such a condition. The refugees were accommodated in the kingdom of Taqali, whose resistance to the slave raids ensured its continued independence throughout the period of Egyptian rule (which is locally known as 'the Turkiyya').[3] The early role of this kingdom in the 1820s was as protection for the refugees, but it became much less accessible as the Taqali resistance became effective. The slavers, finding the Nuba Hills difficult and hostile country, shifted their activities southwards from the late 1830s.

The Sudanese, apart from the slaves, who had their own grievances, kept green the memory of the massacres of the campaign of 1823, and this, amongst other causes, included the incessant slave raids that fuelled the continual resentment at Egyptian rule of both the enslaved and the conquered. There is no indication that the Sudanese ever became reconciled to foreign rule by anyone, Turk, Egyptian or British, and this is, of course, the fundamental fact that leads us eventually on to the great uprising led by the Mahdi and the general support his regime attracted. In this, it has distinct similarities with the experience of the peasantry and poor in the Hausa lands (a condition that eventually led them to support Usuman dan Fodio's *jihad*). It was, in consequence, necessary for the Egyptian rulers to keep relatively large garrisons in the country, which simply perpetuated the dislike, perhaps especially when it was slaves, captured and enslaved in the Sudan itself, who constituted the garrisons.

The rate of attrition amongst the captured slaves (as in the *daftardar*'s 5,000 survivors out of his 40,000 captures) did not continue, for measures were taken to take more care of the captives. Even the slave takers were apparently shocked at the losses, though from a financial point of view, no doubt, not because of its inhumanity.

The result of these ameliorative measures was the acquisition of enough fit male slaves to form 6 regiments of 4,000 men each, which were trained by French soldiers from the former Napoleonic forces. These large regiments were equipped with artillery, and were intended to be able to operate as independent units, and at a distance from Egypt. This again was reminiscent of the Napoleonic military system, if on a much smaller scale than the emperor's methods.[4]

The slaves who were transported to Egypt continued to suffer from Egyptian diseases, just as Egyptians tended to fall ill from Sudanese infections. The slave soldiers therefore had to be employed in the Sudan, though those who survived in Egypt could be used in such different climates as Mexico (a battalion was sent to help the French there in the 1860s) and the Crimean War. The difficulty experienced in building up a substantial slave force in Egypt meant that Muhammad Ali ceased to be interested in the issue of the slave army except as a garrison for the Sudan, and turned to recruiting Egyptian *fellahin*, who turned out to make very steady infantry. They had no tradition of military service, for the Mamelukes, rightly, saw that trusting them with weapons would be too dangerous. The *fellahin* soldiers proved later on to be conscious of their power as armed men; the slave soldiers were also liable to mutiny, and had no loyalty at all to their 'employers', though a competent commander could certainly lead them. (Sudanese battalions under British command, employed in the campaigns in the 1880s and 1890s, were excellent 'military material', as the language of the time had it – a variation, of course, on the attitude towards slavery.)

The general neglect of the slave forces – poor food, poor pay that was too often confiscated by their officers, and so on – made it necessary that constant slave raids be conducted to keep the units up to some sort of nominal strength. As well as the corruption in which the officers of the units were mired, and who all too often stole their men's pay, the physical mistreatment of the slave soldiers reduced the army to a condition in which it was easily defeated. Its soldiers were liable to desert, hardly surprisingly, and this eventually allowed easy conquest by the Mahdi's men. (Many of these slave soldiers joined his armies, and fought much more effectively in his cause than they ever did for the Egyptians – again a similar attitude to the peasants in Hausaland who joined Usuman dan Fodio's forces and provided them with useful intelligence.)

Individual units, despite all this, did tend to fight well in Mexico and Crimea or under such skilled commanders as General Charles Gordon. Their existence, however, is an indication that Muhammad Ali, despite his reputation as a moderniser and his successful resort to employing *fellahin* in the Egyptian army, was still to a degree a man of his Ottoman past; the use of slave soldiers was a Muslim practice from deep in the Middle Ages; he could never fully escape that heritage.

The main economic gains of the Egyptian conquest were expected to be slaves and gold. The first was a constantly wasting product, as noted; the captured people died so quickly, of new diseases, overwork, mistreatment or despair, or deserted to freedom when they could, so that the main purpose of slaving in the Sudan became simply to replace the losses among those who had been captured and recruited earlier. The other main hoped-for product, gold, was even more disappointing. The gold was washed from the streams in the area upstream from Fazoghlu, which was on the Blue Nile close to the Ethiopian border, but it was always retrieved in only small quantities. The two rivers involved, the Tumat and the Khawr al-Adi, small tributaries of the Blue Nile, were the sources of the metal dust, which was found in the streambeds. The production process was laborious, involving excavating mud from the stream, then washing the non-gold content away. Only small quantities were ever gained. Ismail had taken a mineralogist, Frédéric Cailliaud, with him on his initial conquest, and Cailliaud investigated the gold source. He produced a seven-volume treatise on the region, but little improvement in production resulted. A decade later, Muhammad Ali sent more European experts to investigate, and contradictory reports resulted. Soldiers were being used to wash for the gold, but they were ignorant of the task and were inefficient; a thousand other soldiers protected the investigators and workers as guards. Muhammad Ali came in person in 1838–9 to investigate, and appointed a controller to push on the work, again with little result. The product was so small that after another decade or so the works were closed down, but only after Muhammad Ali's death; he apparently never lost faith, or his lust for gold.[5]

The settlement that was established near the gold source was named Muhammad-Ali-Polis, but it failed along with the gold mining project. (It is a precursor of the ghost towns of the American West fifty years later – again, Muhammad Ali was leading the way; the mining methods used in the Sudan were those used in the West also.) He had a secondary purpose in this southern journey, as would be expected of the clever politician that he was. His Syrian and Anatolian war was heading for disaster, and he was looking for a bolthole to which he could retreat if his base in Egypt came under serious attack.[6] This new city was intended to be it, with a gold source from which to replenish his treasury. In the event, he was cunning enough to retain control of Egypt, even if he lost Syria. Muhammad-Ali-Polis failed as a city, therefore, because he no longer needed it; Sudan he retained, of course.

A more successful urban development had been Wad Madani, which Ismail had taken as his main camp in preference to Sennar because it was higher above the river and so drier and supposedly less unhealthy.[7] Its successful defence and survival in the rebellion in 1823 no doubt helped to increase its attraction. And yet, the new governor, sent in by Muhammad Ali in 1824 along with a newly recruited and more efficient army, was unimpressed by the place.

This new governor was Uthman Jarkas al-Birinji, an old Mameluke who had joined Muhammad Ali early on in his career. He was clearly intended to be a new broom after the suppression of the rebellion, the death of Ismail, and the savagery of the *daftardar*'s reconquest. One of his early decisions was that Wad Madani was not suitable as the administrative centre for the whole conquered territory. He selected a new site, at the confluence of the Blue and White Niles. There was a scatter of establishments already in and near the site he chose, a *kashif* (a tax collector and assessor) had been stationed there, the 1st Regiment of the new army was stationed on the west side of the White Nile – which became Omdurman – and a holy man had lived there until he was killed by the Egyptians during the suppression of the rebellion.[8] But only al-Birinji, perhaps with his trained military eye, seems to have appreciated its valuable strategic situation. He made it the replacement for both Sennar, the old royal capital, and Wad Madani, the army camp. It became the future city of Khartoum.

Why the advantages of the site for the new capital, or at least for an urban site, were not appreciated earlier is evidently due to the previous geopolitics of the region. The Egyptian conquest was the first time the whole of the country that became Sudan was under a single government, at least in modern times, and the earlier kingdoms were based elsewhere – at Berber and Sennar, for example, and further back at Meroë and Napata. And, of course, the Egyptians were very busy until 1824 with their conquest and the rebellion. Neither Ismail nor Ibrahim had time to consider the question of a new governmental centre, though the move from Sennar to Wad Madani indicated the need, Sennar being too far distant from the real centre of the Sudan, which was Khartoum. In fact, the Egyptian administration was quick enough to locate the essential centre at Khartoum – they had done so within only two years of the conquest. A year after the conquest and rebellion were over, the geographical usefulness and importance of the new site became obvious – and by then the political advantage of abandoning Sennar, the former royal capital, and starting anew would be clear. The place was named Khartoum, and its foundation marked a clear break from both the previous Sennar regime and from that of the conquerors.

Muhammad Ali welcomed the Europeans who arrived in Egypt, some of them as tourists, some as archaeologists – this was the great age of stealing monuments for European museums to display – and some as experts, or quasi-experts (or charlatans) of various sorts. His welcome was partly aimed at finding ways to increase the efficiency of his government and his army, and so to encourage the development of his empire. The drawback, of course, as in all European colonies (which Sudan came to resemble even under Egyptian rule), was that importing foreign experts was bound to retard the development of indigenous talent. A few senior posts went to well-connected Egyptians (or Turks), not necessarily the most appropriate or most experienced men, though they were thought to be loyal, if not wholly competent. Rarely were men promoted from below based on their abilities and experience. In this, of course, Sudan and Egypt were not really very different from other nineteenth-century states whose systems ran to cronyism and nepotism.

The economic development of Sudan was retarded even more by the use of slaves, which by definition was an inefficient labour force, and by the climate of the southern area, which was distinctly unhealthy for both Europeans and Egyptians. As an example, eight artisan miners were recruited from Britain to begin an excavation for iron ore, and to build an iron foundry; within two months of their arrival in the Sudan, six of them were dead from disease; even within that time they had also proved to be recalcitrant and independent-minded, complaining of the food and drink and the lack of pay, while failing also to follow instructions.[9]

The employment of Europeans and Americans is, of course, much better known than the experience of the Sudanese population, partly because Arabic sources are little studied and perhaps because few were produced,[10] but mainly because the European visitors tended to be literate, unlike many of the Sudanese. Many of the Europeans tended to write about their experiences in the exotic places they went to, largely because those were exotic, and because there was a European market for such books. In actual fact, most of the Europeans who went to Egypt and on into the Sudan did so for commercial reasons, seeking to profit from the trade in goods imported from abroad or exported from Sudan, though these were not the sort of men who wrote books about their experiences. The goods for export were largely those noted by Dr Ricci in the caravan at Aswan in 1819 – gum arabic, ostrich feathers, tamarind, sesame, and some other minor products, and slaves. A major export added during the Egyptian period was cotton, both raw and woven (of a very high quality), which received a major boost by the high prices paid for it during the American Civil War. Most items produced for trade were agricultural products, or items gathered from forests or in hunting. These tended to be high in volume and low in value, and so had to be moved in bulk.

Al-Ubaiyid in Kordofan, under the stimulus of the presence of the garrison and the profits of the slave trade, became a major entrepôt, receiving goods from the south, such as those noted by Ricci, and from Europe – 'metalware and swords, spices, sugar, coffee, rice, and soap'[11] – though most of these were actually tropical products imported in European ships. To this last may be added guns, at first military surplus weapons, bought from the large stores existing in Europe after the Napoleonic Wars. The steady improvements in the efficiency of firearms that characterised the nineteenth century then created its own trade, as demand for the latest guns grew. Khartoum and other Nile towns trafficked in the same goods.

A major difficulty was therefore transport within Sudan. The Nile was of limited use for moving goods for any distance, because the cataracts dictated that the goods must be unloaded at each one, carried past the rapids, and then loaded again on to different vessels. Exported goods were therefore usually carried in caravans, with only a small amount going by boat (small vessels could get past the cataracts when the river was in flood). A caravan might take up to six months to carry goods from central Sudan to Egypt, scarcely a profitable process, except in high-value goods, but these were not usually carried.

Several efforts were made in the 1850s to bring steamboats up the river, but they had even more difficulty in passing the cataracts than the sailing and oared vessels. By 1860, one steamboat was operating along the upper White Nile; it was owned by an Egyptian prince. This part of the river is free of cataracts for most of its course, but the steamer was small, and even if it could sail as far north as the sixth cataract (at Berber), the goods would normally have to go by caravan from there on.[12]

The answer to the transportation problem was railways. Muhammad Ali, during his visit to the gold mines south of Fazoghlu, had mooted the possibility of building a line from Dongola to the source of iron ore in Kordofan, more or less along the line of the trading route, which had earlier been used by the *daftardar*'s army of invasion. An alternative was a line from Shendi or Berber to Suakin on the Red Sea. Both of these routes were well used by caravans. The Berber–Suakin route would also be available to carry Muslim pilgrims travelling from West Africa to visit Mecca and Medina, thus generating some revenue. It was actually too early for all this, and the development of locomotives was hardly sufficient yet for extreme desert travel, but one must praise Muhammad Ali's insight, only a few years after the first British railway intended to carry both passengers and goods, from Stockton to Darlington, had been opened.[13]

There were further suggestions for transport improvement in the 1850s, at the same time that the experiments with steamboats were demonstrating the intractability of the cataract problem. None of the suggested schemes (which were stimulated by the success of the Cairo to Suez line, opened in 1857) succeeded in getting built, but in the 1860s, the Khedive Ismail (1863–79) finally tackled the basis of the problem for the Sudan. He pushed forward consideration of possible routes, and sent ten steamboats to ply the Upper Nile. The steamboats were a modest success, but the railway schemes looked too expensive. At last, in 1871, once the Suez Canal had been opened and was seen to be a success, a worthwhile plan for a railway to bypass the first cataract (at Aswan) was agreed. This was the essential first step, since it would then permit the transport of railway equipment past that prime obstacle. Boat slips would permit ships to be drawn up and transported by rail past the rapids. All was ready to begin in 1873, and the contracts were agreed, but the Egyptian government fell into a financial hole just at that time, and the project had to be stopped. The result was a line 33 miles long, which did bypass the first cataract, but went no further.[14]

One activity that was encouraged by the Egyptian conquest was the pilgrimage traffic. It was not really a commercial business, for the pilgrims were often poor and depended on alms and charities during their travels, but they had to be fed and sheltered, and locals could supply this and possibly turn a small profit. There was a major *hajj* route from West Africa through the kingdoms that lay along the Sahel south of the desert, the Sokoto Caliphate, Bornu, Wadai, Darfur and Kordofan and into the Nile Valley, usually crossing the river at Shendi (the pilgrims were one of the original sources of that town's prosperity). Their route then was directly east to Suakin, whence the pilgrims would sail across the Red Sea to land at Jeddah, relatively close to their Arabian destinations. The conquest of Kordofan, originally part of the Darfur Sultanate, had resulted in hostility between Darfur and the Egyptian rulers, and a frontier guard was then mounted by Darfur for defence; the pilgrimage traffic got through, as would be expected, but the cold war between Darfur and Muhammad Ali's Sudanese state prevented much other traffic.

One puzzle of perennial interest, to Europeans above all, was the source of the White Nile. The source of the Blue Nile had been more or less solved back in the 1780s by James Bruce, though access along the river beyond Fazoghlu was blocked by the impassable gorge the river had carved through the Ethiopian Mountains. Bruce had reached the main Ethiopian urban centre and imperial capital at Gondar, which is on Lake Tana, which he correctly identified as the source of the Blue Nile, but he could not explore the river fully since it was too difficult to get through along the gorge; also he was in great danger by the time he was travelling to leave the country, and so he took a more direct route to Sennar. He was correct in his claim to have found a source, but, as is the way with such pioneering men, he was not believed by the stay-at-homes in Britain, whose pet theories he claimed to disprove.[15] But at least it was agreed that Ethiopia was a source of the Blue Nile.

The White Nile question arose once the Egyptian conquest of Sennar and Kordofan allowed Europeans to travel in the country with little restraint. The White Nile was reasonably navigable for a considerable distance above Khartoum (from Berber, the sixth cataract), with only a single area of difficulty, at the Abu Zaid ford and the Zalait rocks, just upriver from Aba Island, about 200 miles south from Khartoum. These could be passed without much difficulty. The main problem was that 400 miles further south, the river emerged from a huge area of swampland, the Sudd, but at least this was water and the area was sometimes navigable, if with varying degrees of difficulty. But from Berber south there was therefore a stretch of about 700 miles of the river that was more or less clear for steamboats to use.

The Sudd was unknown territory, as was the land beyond (south of) the Sudd, at least to those who did not live there. It was inhabited, as was known, by Blacks of the Shilluk and Dinka tribes. Muhammad Ali certainly scented profit in the area, and characteristically he became interested in finding out what was there. In the late 1830s, he set up an expedition that, after two changes of commander, was led by Salim Qapudan, an Egyptian naval officer.[16] Three exploratory voyages were made. The first part of the journey, as far as the northern boundary of the Sudd, was already known, for it had been raided for loot and slaves by governor General Ali Khurshid in the 1830s, and merchants had travelled them.[17] The real exploration therefore began as the Sudd was reached.

Salim Qapudan had a small group of soldiers and several Europeans on board. The first expedition, in 1839, penetrated through the swamps as far as the village of Bor, 700 miles from Khartoum, where further progress was stopped by an impassable blockage of vegetation across the stream.[18] A second voyage, in 1840, reached beyond Bor to the future site of Gondokoro, 100 miles further on. The third attempt, hampered by the new governor's lack of interest, and by a shortage of supplies, did not get any further. It was further hampered by the hostility of the native inhabitants, who had been alienated by the earlier expeditions, whose soldiers had attacked and kidnapped their fellow tribesmen, to sell them into slavery. It was discovered that beyond Gondokoro, the river ran through a series of rapids as it descended from the Central African Highlands. The solution to the problem of the source of the White Nile thus eluded the Egyptians, but Salim had explored about 1,000 miles of the river, far more than any other single explorer.[19]

It had taken some time for the Sudan to begin to recover from the conquest and rebellion of 1820–3, if it ever did. (This was the period in which al-Hajj Umar from Futa Jalon in the west travelled through Sudan on his pilgrimage.) The heavy taxation, which was partly a cause of the later revolt led by the Mahdi, continued for a time. The governor after Ismail and the founder of Khartoum, al-Birinji, who was a former Mameluke and a soldier, continued the collection of taxes with some brutality, but came to realise that a reduction in taxes would be the obvious first step to encourage recovery, and only this would therefore expand the tax base. His successor as governor general, the former governor of Berber, Mahu Bey Urfali, after a conference with local notables, which itself was something of an innovation, agreed to a suspension of taxation for three years to assist recovery.[20]

It was also the army of the governor Khurshid that provided the soldiers for Salim Qapudan's expeditions along the White Nile, the inefficient gold washers at Fazoghlu and their guards, the slave-raiding expeditions that brought in reinforcing recruits for the army itself, and, more appropriately, also for the force defending the conquests against attacks from outside. The preceding Sennar kingdom had at various times attacked all its neighbours – Darfur and Kordofan, the Nuba Hills south of the latter, and Ethiopia – usually in search of slaves, so in this respect the Egyptian conquest was not much of a change, though Muhammad Ali's governors do seem to have been more determined to seize slaves than the kings in the latter years of the failing Sennar regime.

The result of Salim Qapudan's explorations of the upper White Nile was to open up the far south – Equatoria it became called – to trade and slave hunting. The governor after Khurshid, Ahmad Pasha abu Widam, conducted a ferocious campaign along the Ethiopian frontier, where the inhabitants had already been driven to build forts on the hills in defence; Ahmad Pasha, however, not only had efficient firearms but also artillery, and could breach their defences. His men did not always succeed, but he certainly left desolation and depopulation in his wake.[21]

Beyond the Sudd, the way having been opened by Salim Qapudan's voyages, trade was developed, largely by private enterprise conducted by Europeans, of whom the Savoyard A. Brun-Rollet seems to have been the pioneer – one of a large number of Italians who moved to the Sudan in this period; the Italians were the most numerous of the European nationalities in the country. Brun-Rollet established a successful trade in equatorial products from the time of Ahmad Pasha's campaign.[22] Gondokoro developed as a commercial centre. It was located at the foot of the falls where the Nile came out from the highlands into the low country, a typical position where commercial exchanges would take place between contrasting but complementary economic areas.

The region was also a new source of slaves. The exploration of the Bahr al-Ghazal, a major Nile tributary flowing several hundred miles from the west, whose own tributaries drained a wide area of 40,000 square miles, revealed yet another lucrative slave source.[23] The expeditions of Salim Qapudan had been greeted with friendship by the people of Equatoria at first; the brutal behaviour of the Egyptian soldiers who were part of the expedition, larded as they were with contempt and racial scorn, soon ended that phase, and the potential slaves took refuge in the forests, and sharpened their weapons. The trade in other goods, particularly ivory, stalled, therefore, amid this new animosity, but in the process, the governmental system of the Sudan, with all its cruelty and greed, was extended into the south.

The expansion of Egyptian authority into Equatoria would hardly be unexpected by anyone who had been watching the actions of Muhammad Ali's regime. Greece, Syria, Anatolia and Arabia had all been subjected to his imperialist intrusions, as well as the Sudan, and there were items he must have regarded as unfinished business, such as Darfur. On the other hand, apart from Sudan, none of his empire-building ventures had succeeded. The Ottoman sultan had recovered Anatolia, Arabia and Syria, and Greece had become an independent state, despite Muhammad Ali's armed intervention on the Ottoman side.

To east and west his new Sudanese empire faced powerful enemies. In the aftermath of the 1822 rebellion, some refugee groups had taken refuge over the ill-defined border with Ethiopia. This was a land that was emerging from an extended state of chaos, and had suffered from continuous civil warfare since the 1770s – the 'age of the princes', it has been called, all of whom busily fought every other 'prince' they could reach. The succession of emperors had long been broken, with pretenders and royal heirs pushed on and off the imperial throne by over-powerful subjects – one man held the throne six times, and in the 1830s and 1840s, three men alternated in theoretical power irregularly. As a result, many of the provinces had shifted into an effective independence of the imperial system.[24]

The Ethiopian governor of the borderland where the Sudanese refugees crossed to escape the Turkiyya was Kanfu Hailu, a well-born aristocrat (the province was called Kwari, or Qwari). The mopping-up operations on the Sudanese side captured an Ethiopian priest who was a relative of Kanfu; he came out of the hills to the rescue, with a large army, said to have been 20,000 strong, and defeated the Egyptian commander twice; by then, Kanfu was 100 miles inside Sudanese territory. Some of this territory had already been in dispute with the Egyptian invaders, and had been occupied ten years before by the Egyptians – the border was never marked. Kanfu appears to have been intending to retake that territory that had been seized by the Egyptians as well as rescuing the priest. The problem went to the governor general, Khurshid, who referred it up to Muhammad Ali. Plans were made for a full-scale war, but Muhammad Ali was involved in the Syrian crisis at the same time, and was advised by the British consul that it would not be a sensible move to attack a Christian state at the same time as being in dispute with Britain (though Muhammad Ali found himself at a quasi-war with the British a year later, so his restraint was of no value). Perhaps more compelling in his decision not to embark on an Ethiopian war was the possibility of finding himself at war with four empires all at the same time – Britain, France, the Ottoman Empire and Ethiopia. The Ethiopian problem was allowed to fade away, but was not forgotten; it was the first of a series of border disputes over the next fifty years.[25]

The occupation of what became the Sudan was as yet incomplete, and considerable regions inside the territory were outside Egyptian control. Apart from the stalled conquest of Darfur – the sultanate was now fully alert, but was subject to an arms blockade – there were large areas between the Nile and the Red Sea that were also independent of any Egyptian authority. Ahmed abu Widam, the vigorous slave-hunting governor who succeeded Khurshid as governor general, attacked the region called Taka, a fertile area not far from the Ethiopian frontier, whose inhabitants and wealth were coveted. An eight-month campaign resulted in its eventual submission, and the installation of a garrison at Kassala, which, like Khartoum and al-Ubaiyid, grew into a major local centre as a result.[26]

The conquest of Taka had other consequences. The governor general wrote to the *wali* of the Hejaz in Arabia, suggesting, in rather peremptory tones, that Suakin and Massawa should become part of Muhammad Ali's province; on his part the Hejazi *wali* passed the project up his own chain of command to the sultan in Constantinople. Negotiations followed, and in 1846, several years after the original 'request', the two ports were leased to Egypt, in return for an increase in the annual tribute paid to the sultan. This was not only a desire for territory on Muhammad Ali's part, it was, so it was said, aimed at preventing the Taka people from evading their tax responsibilities by moving away and into the lands of the ports then under Hejazi, and hence Ottoman, control. The lease did not last long, and lapsed with Muhammad Ali's death in 1849; no doubt the people of Taka had by then been brought to their responsibilities over taxes.

The Ethiopian border at Kwari saw trouble again in 1846. Perhaps in pursuit of the same quarrel as before, Kanfu's nephew, Kassa Hailu, who had inherited the governorship after Kanfu's death, brought an army over the border into the country of the Rufa'a Arabs. (Possibly, it was a minor quarrel with this tribe that occasioned the Ethiopian attack; the Egyptians had had trouble with them also.) Kassa marched over 90 miles into Sudanese territory, but was then confronted by the governor general Khalid Pasha Khusraw's army. For once, this was an Egyptian commander who knew his business. He formed his men into a defensive square in the classic manner of European warfare, and deployed two field guns, firing grapeshot. Kassa's army was soundly defeated and retired into Ethiopia.[27] No doubt, this victory over Kassa further along the frontier will have helped persuade the people of Taka to accept their new lot.

These conflicts, together with a campaign against the Hadendowa Arabs in the steppes north of Taka, were clear instances of the continuing Egyptian expansionism. In 1843, Nasir, a dissatisfied claimant to the throne of the Sultanate of Taqali in the Nuba Hills, persuaded the governor of Kordofan to help him seize the throne from the incumbent; this was done, and Nasir became *makk* (king). But he soon became weary of paying the tribute that he had agreed to send to the governor and massacred the Egyptian garrison imposed on him. He then defeated a new Egyptian reprisal attack. The Nuba Hills returned to their status as an independent region outside Egyptian reach.[28] Nasir was later expelled by his new subjects, and was replaced by his nephew, Adam wad Umar; Nasir in 1864 once again appealed for Sudanese help, but again the task proved too great for the governor's army, and the new attack was repulsed.

After Muhammad Ali's death in 1848, he was succeeded by his son Ibrahim, who very soon himself died, then by his successors, his nephew Abbas I (1848–54) and then his son Said (1854–63), neither of whom were interested in further Egyptian expansion in the Sudan. The size of the army in Sudan was reduced to three regiments, plus the Shaiqiyah irregular cavalry, which was enough soldiers to carry out slaving raids, but not really enough to start conquering new territory, as the failures against the hillmen of Taqali had demonstrated. There was thus a decade and a half with a semblance of peace during the reigns of Abbas and Said, but no abandonment of neighbourly hostility nor, fundamentally, of Egyptian ambitions. (This was also the time when al-Hajj Umar campaigned in his *jihad* west of the Sokoto Caliphate; he died the year after the Khedive Said.)

Said's successor, Ismail (1863–79), a son of the conqueror Ibrahim, had more vigour, and his reign saw determined and often successful efforts to expand the Egyptian Empire. All round the frontier, from Darfur to Equatoria to the Red Sea, neighbouring territories were invaded, though not all of his ventures succeeded in holding on to their conquests. The frontier could be divided into three parts – in the west, that over against Darfur, which was now closely guarded by the forces of both sides, though tensions had relaxed a little; in the east, that over against Ethiopia, where clashes had broken out more than once in the past thirty years (and this will be dealt with in a later chapter, as will the associated expansion along the Red Sea); and, third, that in the south, the new provinces of Equatoria and Bahr el-Ghazal, which had gone through some disturbing changes since Salim Qapudan had opened up the way to reach the region.

The exploration phase in the south revealed the size of the area, the trading possibilities, the prospect of netting more slaves, the transport routes (along the rivers), but also the difficulties the Egyptian government had in exerting its own control over the whole huge region, particularly in view of its preoccupations elsewhere. The early military slaving raids soon gave way to well-organised quasi-military private enterprise trading companies who did the raiding in place of the army, which was now not big enough for the task. They initially searched for ivory – that is, for elephants to kill for their tusks – with the acquisition of slaves a secondary activity. These priorities then changed round with the decline in the elephant numbers, and the companies became primarily slaving organisations, basing themselves at fortified locations called *zeribas*.

Ismail's expansionary probes succeeded in pushing back the Sudan frontier in several places, but not against Ethiopia, nor against the Nuba Hills, nor Darfur. The south was the major success region, but even there the government's lack of grip, and the shortage of soldiers, left the country in the hands of the private slaving companies, who went through a characteristic capitalistic process of takeover and acquisition and monopolisation, so that in the end, one slaver became dominant, having driven out, taken over or killed most of his competitors. Meanwhile under Said and Ismail, the major preoccupation of the Egyptian government swung round to the issue of the construction of the Suez Canal.

The canal brought with it the dynasty's entanglement in European finance, which was made more problematic by Khedive Ismail's own extravagance. The Europeans, particularly the British, became evangelistic about ending the slave trade and the abolition of slavery, and this became one of the new conditions on which Ismail would gain financial assistance. In the last phases before 1880, a series of prominent Europeans, including Sir Samuel Baker and General Charles Gordon, were appointed to govern in the south with the joint purpose of establishing government control in the face of the hostility of the slaving companies, and ending the slave trade itself; they were just as unsuccessful at both attempts as the Egyptians.

The first key figure here was Sir Samuel Baker. He had made his name when he had travelled along the White Nile in 1860–2, thirty years after Salim Qapudan's explorations, to meet J.H. Speke, who had explored inland from Zanzibar and had 'discovered' Lake Victoria and the kingdoms around it. When he got to that region, Baker added Lake Albert to the roster of discoveries (and so claimed to have been the discoverer of the 'true' source of the Nile). The question of the source of the Nile was now thus more or less solved, wherever it was precisely. Baker returned to the Nile in 1871 with a remit from Khedive Ismail to explore the possibilities of extending Egyptian power further south as far as the Great Lakes – and so to control the whole line of the White Nile; and he was to suppress the slave traders at the same time. At that point, the power and recalcitrance of the slaving companies in Equatoria was finally fully understood in Cairo. In the furthest south, Baker came up against the organised and populous kingdoms of Bunyoro and Buganda (and several others) as he penetrated to the Great Lakes; these kingdoms, well established and centuries old, were strung along the west side of Lake Victoria and onwards for 500 miles. In the usual arrogant fashion of British explorers he proclaimed them to be Egyptian protectorates, but this was an offer they could and did refuse; Baker interfered in the kingdoms' internal problems, and had to escape betimes, being lucky to live to publicise his claims.[29]

The next phase in the history of the south was an attempted Egyptian campaign to establish the khedive's authority in place of, and over, the slave-trading companies. These had, necessarily, given their purposes, established their headquarters in a series of fortified *zeribas* where they housed their staff, mainly soldiers, and held their captives until they could be moved north to the markets in Sudan and Egypt. The greatest of these slavers was al-Zubayr Rahma Mansur, whose ruthlessness and ability had brought him, in effect, to the position of the ruler of a large trading empire, which consisted of an archipelago of *zeribas* spread from the Nile westwards. When the Egyptian government sent an officer, Muhammad al-Hilali, to establish Egyptian rule and a permanent provincial organisation in Equatoria, inevitably he and al-Zubayr clashed. Both were well armed, and in a battle that they fought, al-Zubayr was victorious and al-Hilali was killed. Al-Zubayr, in fact, as a slaver, had copied the Egyptian methods of Muhammad Ali and had created his own slave army, partly with the intention of using it to capture yet more slaves. It was larger than al-Hilali's forces and had thus been able to challenge him. As a result of this it could hardly be said that the southern provinces were part of the Egyptian Empire, except in Egyptian claims.

Samuel Baker had been employed by the Khedive Ismail to develop an administration along the Upper Nile, but had turned his office into a failed attempt to conquer in the Great Lakes region; his assigned task to suppress the slave trade had turned into a series of battles with the local slaving companies, the fellow slavers of al-Zubayr. Even for the extravagant Ismail, the whole process had been hugely expensive and wasteful – and essentially a failure. So when al-Hilali had been defeated, the whole of the Egyptian Equatorial region was still only tenuously, even only theoretically, under Egyptian rule.

Al-Zubayr, an inveterate slaver, began looking for a new source of slaves. He had earlier clashed with the Azande to his south-west, who were well organised and resisted him with effect; his trading competitors meanwhile operated in the Nile area, and would resist his poaching into 'their' territory. He succeeded in breaking up the Azande resistance by intriguing with the various princes of the tribe, but then turned his attention northwards. Unable to suppress him, Ismail instead appointed him as governor of the province of Bahr al-Ghazal, no doubt expecting this to bring him to loyalty and settle the area down into peacefulness and tax production. But al-Zubayr was already essentially an independent ruler, based on his victories, though he was gratified at the recognition.[30]

To his north was Darfur, where the old Sultan Muhammad IV Husain died in 1873. This clearly rendered Darfur vulnerable and al-Zubayr scented profit; in Khartoum, the governor general Ismail Aiyub similarly showed interest. Al-Zubayr was keen on acquiring a new source of slaves, the governor more generally in acquiring fame, loot, conquest and the favour of the Khedive Ismail. Both set out to invade their victim. Zubayr did the hard work. He defeated the new Darfuri Sultan Ibrahim Qarad's *vizir* and his army, and then defeated and killed the sultan himself.

This record of success alarmed Ismail Aiyub and he marched to reach el-Fasher, the Darfur capital, first. He failed; al-Zubayr was in control when he reached it, and since the Sultan Ibrahim had been killed in the fighting, al-Zubayr was busy ruling the country, his legal authority being his governorship of Bahr el-Ghazal. He had proved himself a formidable military commander, but he was now outmanoeuvred by the more politically astute Ismail Aiyub, who had been tasked by the khedive with organising Darfur as an Egyptian province. Al-Zubayr saw that this meant that his conquests were being removed from him, and, relying on the praise of the khedive (who had appointed him to the rank of *pasha*), he went to Cairo to protest. This was a surprisingly naïve move for a man who had so successfully made his way by intrigue and conquest for the last twenty years; perhaps he relied on Ismail's expressed approval of his successes, and believed the khedive's sincerity. Instead of further praise, he was detained in Cairo under house arrest.[31]

The dispute between al-Zubayr and Ismail Aiyub, together with the distraction of the khedivial government over its financial problems, left Darfur's incorporation incomplete. The reigning dynasty survived, though four successive sultans died in 1873–4, and the next sultan retreated westwards to the Jebel Marra, and kept up a guerrilla campaign of raids and killings for the next quarter-century; as a result, the sultanate itself disintegrated into tribal sections. The result was a constant state of subdued warfare for years, and, for the Egyptian regime, a constant drain on its resources.[32]

Baker's successor as governor in Equatoria was General Gordon, a soldier of fortune who sought out wars to fight and provinces to rule, a restless man with an unsustainably high opinion of himself. He arrived at Gondokoro in 1874, just as al-Zubayr and Ismail Aiyub were cheating each other in Darfur. His associate, Romolo Gessi, a vigorous and effective Italian commander, then campaigned for several years in Equatoria to suppress the slave-trading companies, beginning with Suleiman ibn al-Zubayr, who had inherited his father's trading empire and army, and could deploy an army of 9,000 soldiers. But Gessi had the better army this time, including weapons such as Congreve rockets and field artillery, and it was he who was militarily successful. Yet his success was, as usual, achieved at the cost of a devastated and depopulated land. The slaving companies merely moved on, beyond the range of Gordon and Gessi, to plunder the Azande and sell their slaves into Sudan, while Darfur also proved, as al-Zubayr had assumed, to be a profitable place to raid, especially since the continued existence of the old sultanate provided a worthwhile target for the slavers.[33]

The movement of the slaving frontier ever deeper into Africa as it was pushed onwards by the slow establishment of a more or less organised government, with the slaving companies and their *zeribas* as the advancing slaving frontier, would continue so long as the market for slaves existed in Sudan and Egypt. Egypt was technically no longer a country to which slaves could be legally sold, but ways were always found, and the royal plantations and estates were still operated by slave labour in both Egypt and Sudan. The market for slaves in Sudan was hardly affected by the industrial revolution that Muhammad Ali had set in motion, and this was the basis for the continued profitability of the slaving companies. The only solution, as anyone could see, and as had been revealed in the Atlantic slave trade earlier in the century, was to abolish slavery itself, but neither the Egyptians nor the Sudanese were prepared to go so far.

For the khedivian regime in Egypt, the result of all this was a considerably extended empire, which now included part of the old enemy Darfur, and reached far to the south almost to the Great Lakes; if the advance of the slaving frontier was followed it would soon reach into the Congo basin. But the extension had been so expensive that it helped towards the ruin of the Egyptian finances, and, while the Sudanese regiments had received a constant supply of new slave recruits, the pressure from Europe to end the slave trade was becoming increasingly difficult to resist. Soon it would be necessary to find some better reason to justify the actual Egyptian control of Sudan than enslaving its population.

Chapter 5

An Empire of the Red Sea

Muhammad Ali attempted to extend his rule in all directions, but only his conquest of Sudan could be said to have been successful. He had also shown interest in the lands beside the Red Sea from early in his rule. He had campaigned seriously in Arabia once he was safely in control in Egypt, but this was on behalf of the Ottoman sultan, who had lost control of the Ottoman part of Arabia, particularly the holy cities of Mecca and Medina, to the Wahhabis of the interior, who were regarded as heretics by the Ottoman sultan and by the Egyptians. Muhammad Ali sent his son Tussun to command in the war, but eventually had to go himself to devise suitable tactics to defeat the enemy. Success eventually came in 1818, when the Wahhabis' centre, Dariyya, was captured and destroyed, and the surrounding Arabian tribes were persuaded into his alliance with gifts.[1]

The result was not an extension of Egyptian power, but in that year Muhammad Ali secured control of Suakin and Massawa as part of his campaign, though once the Hejaz in Arabia returned to Ottoman rule, so did those ports, which were administered as part of the Hijazi province. One of the aims of the Arabian war was to combat the Wahhabis' blockade of trade in the Red Sea, which had hurt Egypt as well as the Arabian ports. After 1818, and the Wahhabis' defeat, this trade revived. Suakin and Massawa were part of the Arabian governorship of Hejaz because their main purpose, for the Ottomans, was to link the two sides of the sea, east and west, and enable the *hajj* pilgrimage traffic from Africa to cross without impediment. It was a point Muhammad Ali will have noted.

In 1846, as related in the last chapter, on the initiative of the Sudan governor general, Khalid Khusraw, the Egyptian ruler leased the ports from the Ottoman sultan once more, but that lease expired soon after his death;[2] his successors, Abbas and Said, were not so keen on empire-building, and the antagonisms that activity caused, for the next decade and more. Indeed, the lease of the ports, which had been part of the *vilayet* of Hejaz, were more a means to prevent Muhammad Ali's Sudanese subjects from escaping the heavy Egyptian taxation by fleeing to the shelter of the Hejaz governorship, yet remaining in the Sudan. Thus, there had been good administrative sense for the leased ports to be under the head, the Hejaz governor – and good sense for Muhammad Ali to want to control them. Apart from their traditional attachment, they were part of a pilgrimage route and the pilgrims came under the Hejaz once they were across the Red Sea.

For some decades, as Ottoman power in Arabia faded, the eastern part of Sudan, the lands of the Hadendowa tribe, and the Taka region, were under neither Egyptian nor Hijazi control. By 1850, however, eastern Sudan had been conquered by the Egyptians, and the ports had become Hijazi intrusions into the Sudan.

The attention of the Egyptian government was thus, for the present, after Muhammad Ali's reign, directed inland. At Massawa, which was a fort on an island, the Egyptian governor Ismail Haqqi spent his energies on suppressing the chief of the village of Arkiko on the mainland, who intrigued to displace the Egyptians – no doubt the problem of heavy Egyptian taxation was at the basis of the dispute. The governor's garrison managed to destroy the village in the process, and Ismail Haqqi then proclaimed that Muhammad Ali intended to possess the coast as far as Cape Guardafui (the easternmost point of Africa), though nothing actually resulted for the moment. When the lease on the port of Massawa expired, the claim vanished along with the ports. But the claim had caused some alarm to the British, who declared a longstanding interest in the area (though that interest had existed for only a generation, in fact). The British did control Aden from 1839, however.

The two disputed ports were well placed for development in the future. Suakin, the main *hajj* port, was the obvious place from which the connection with Khartoum and the developing towns along the Nile might be organised. There was a suggestion, by Muhammad Ali, that a railway could be laid for the traffic along that route, as a cheaper alternative to the line that was projected along the Nile.[3] And by 1859, Suakin was connected with Cairo by telegraph in a British scheme to extend the Mediterranean telegraph system to India, though it had a very poor connection at Suakin.[4] Massawa benefited from its proximity to the Ethiopian trade (and from *hajj* traffic from lands to the south and out of Ethiopia, which, though officially a Christian country, had plenty of Muslim subjects). Another source was the rising town of Kassala, which, under the stimulus of the Egyptian garrison as well as the surrounding fertile land, had become the commercial centre of the Taka lands. The emergence of steamships was, however, the real stimulus to both ports, and the 1850s saw both of them begin to grow.

Steamships had reached the Red Sea from India by the 1820s, and Egypt and the Mediterranean from Britain even earlier. By the next decade, the 'overland route' from Alexandria to Suez was organised to connect the Mediterranean traffic with that in the Indian Ocean.[5] When Muhammad Ali acquired some control in Sudan, Suakin and Massawa therefore, these ports were usefully placed along the west coast of the Red Sea for such ships to call at. A coaling depot had been established at Jeddah in Arabia by the East India Company, just across the sea from Suakin, and Suakin might well have become a safer place for them to call at than Jeddah.

There was a warning, however, in events of Aden, where the East India Company had wanted to establish another coaling depot. The Emir of Lahej, Aden's suzerain, objected to this, and the East India Company used force, bombarding Aden and landing an armed force, to convince him to agree. Note was taken all round, and in particular at the isolated forts of Suakin and Massawa, which might well be the prime candidates for similar treatment by the British.

By the 1830s, therefore, there was an effective alternative to the passage to India to that by way of the Cape of Good Hope, by going through Egypt. This cut several months off the time taken for the journey, and was even quicker for messages – the East India Company stationed one packet boat at Suez, which was available to collect messengers and some passengers, and another at Basrah, for the use of those travelling by the Euphrates route. The journey between Alexandria and Suez, at first accomplished slowly by camel, was repeatedly improved over the next years, until a successful railway was built in the 1850s.

And in 1859, after several decades of argument, discussion, disinformation, obstruction, planning and disputes, the construction of a canal through the Isthmus of Suez was finally begun. Since the British already had a more or less efficient connection with India through Egypt by the overland route, they naturally opposed the canal's construction. A canal would also allow other armed ships than those of the Royal Navy to reach the Indian Ocean, which was effectively a British preserve at the time. This would be a menace to their Indian Empire, though it would take a large fleet, carrying a large army, to be a real threat. Furthermore, the canal was a French project, engineered by a Frenchman and financed in France, and this increased British fears. The planner and organiser, Ferdinand de Lesseps, had a family connection with the wife of Emperor Napoleon III, which was yet another good reason for British opposition – just as British opposition stimulated the French to go ahead anyway.[6] A naval scare in the English Channel in 1860 saw the French humiliated; the British concerns subsided.

The slow construction of the canal was the background to events in Egypt, the Sudan and the Red Sea for the next ten years. The old assumption that the canal was impossible to construct or to operate because the waters of the Mediterranean and the Red Seas were at different levels had been dismissed, after a more accurate survey was undertaken. A practical plan had been produced for a British and Egyptian canal in the 1840s, but there were numerous difficulties, financial and political, which got in the way, as well as that of constructing a canal through a desert.

There had been earlier canals, one built in the time of Dareios I of Persia before 500 BC, another, a refurbishment of that, by Ptolemy II in the 270s BC, and a third in the name of the Emperor Trajan in the first decade of the second century AD, which remained in use, no doubt with repairs and dredging and refurbishment, until the eighth century. But these canals connected the Red Sea by way of the Great Bitter Lake and a natural and improved channel with the Nile near to the site of Cairo, and not directly with the Mediterranean. They were fairly narrow, being constructed for ships the size of Greek triremes, but capacious enough to be used by merchant ships – even ships carrying elephants. They were used by oared vessels and, if the wind was right, by sailing vessels.

The new plan was to drive a canal due north from the Great Bitter Lake to the Mediterranean. This was already connected to the Red Sea by a channel, which would be both greater and wider than the Nile–Red Sea canal, and capable of being used by steamships. As the plans were made, all sorts of problems emerged, such as the shallow seas at both termini, which were difficult to keep clear of mud and sand. At the northern end, long jetties, or rather embankments, had to be built to preserve an available approach with a sufficient depth of water for the ships.

A railway was added alongside the canal, and at least two new towns, Ismailia and Port Said (named after the two khedives in office while the building went on), were founded and built. Suez, which had already begun to develop as a station on the overland route, also grew. These new towns, and the men building the canal itself, required an additional canal, the Fresh Water Canal (or Sweetwater Canal), bringing water from the Nile. (The Suez Canal itself is salt, which helps in reducing the depth of water that ships need to float.) This canal was also able to supply water for irrigation, and followed more or less the same line as the earlier canals dating back to that of Dareios the Persian – which also had provided water for irrigation.

In a process that has become familiar with many other expansive construction projects in the years ahead, the cost was much greater than the first estimates, though this was known by de Lesseps from the start and was deliberately concealed by creative accounting, but even in the Suez Canal Company's published accounts, it was clear that no more than half of the cost was covered by the subscriptions when the company was incorporated. The essential thing was to get the project begun, and it was assumed that more money would be forthcoming to finish it. (The engineers were optimistic beings.) The cost was not just in money: the labour force for the canal was conscripted; since the men were paid, the term 'forced labour' is not wholly accurate, though it was widely used. Casualties among the workforce were considerable. However, this was the time of the Industrial Revolution, and mechanisation was applied with some success. In this, one can see why it was regarded as the epitome of the success of 'Industrial Civilisation'.

The construction of the canal was also an episode in the imperial rivalry between Britain and France, as was shown by the dispute over its viability before it was built. On completion, the canal was 'opened' by the French Empress Eugénie, but the first ships through were British, and included a Royal Navy warship. This was hardly surprising given the preponderance of British merchant and naval vessels at sea.

Another example of this ongoing rivalry in the area was taking place at the southern end of the Red Sea at the same time; from Aden, seized by the East India Company in 1839 as a coaling station for steamers, the British had been investigating the possibility of taking control of Perim Island at the very mouth of the Sea, whence they could dominate the Bab el-Mandeb, the southern entrance to the sea, almost as strict a chokepoint as the canal itself. In reply, or in competition, or as a precaution, the French took a lease on the town of Obok on the African mainland, below Ethiopia; it give French merchants access to that empire. This was a means of ensuring that they could have a base in an area where it seemed that the British were going to attempt to establish exclusive control. (Perim Island proved to be waterless and was abandoned; Obok remained in French possession and was the basis of the later French colony and present Republic of Djibouti.)

The Red Sea thus had, in only ten years, become a thoroughfare where it had been a cul-de-sac, and had become an arena of imperial competition. This had happened even before the completion of the Suez Canal, but the canal increased traffic enormously. Steamships were much more able to use the canal than sailing ships, and the peculiar climatic conditions of the northern part of the Red Sea, which for several months each year was windless, or received only northerly winds, was now no longer an obstacle. But the new ease of access to India by way of the canal soon brought the British government to execute a financial coup to acquire financial control of the Suez Canal Company; not long after, they took military control of the canal itself. (See chapter 8.)

In the southern part of the Red Sea, the policy of the emperor of Ethiopia, combined with British militarism and imperial arrogance, brought on a crisis (to be discussed in detail in the next chapter), as a result of which British Indian power was exerted at Ethiopian expense in 1868, the year before the canal was opened. A quarrel between the Emperor Tewodros (1855–68) and Britain had developed, in which the British envoy to Tewodros was detained at his court and not allowed to return to Britain, along with several other men whom the

British insisted on regarding as hostages. They joined a number of Tewodros's internal enemies and rivals, most of whom were kept in his stronghold at Magdala, living in comfort, not under serious threat, but not allowed to leave.

(Tewodros's personal name was Ras Kassa – 'Ras' being a title, translated as king – and he was the son of Kassa Hailu, who had been in conflict with Egyptian forces in the Sudan twenty years before; the son had used his military skill to hoist himself to imperial power; in Ethiopia, however, such a position was dangerous to the holder, as later chapters will demonstrate.)

The dispute with Britain was essentially between differing ways of establishing control without violence, to which both parties all too readily resorted. It seems that Tewodros was quite reasonably annoyed that messages he had sent to Queen Victoria had not been answered, though he had received presents from the queen, and this was his way of demanding that a reply be sent. What he got was a large armed expedition from India, which was determined to free the 'hostages' by force. Had he had more experience of British attitudes he might well have ignored the discourtesy, based as it was on disdain for the fact that he was a mere African 'potentate'; his new and self-achieved dignity, of course, also made him sensitive to insults, as the British should also have understood, had they had any imagination. As it was, Tewodros found himself at the hostile end of a British naval and military force enjoying itself at his expense, and invading and looting an antique (Christian) land.

The British expedition came in 1867–8, a year or so before the Suez Canal was completed.[7] It was thus also a warning to other Red Sea states that they were well within reach of British Indian power – but Egypt knew that already, after the defeat of General Bonaparte's invasion. There was to be another such lesson in a few more years.

Geography dictated that, in order to invade Ethiopia, the British must land in the area of Massawa. This was the most obvious port from which to gain access to the Ethiopian interior, if one was to avoid the desert coastlands. By landing in the Massawa area the British were taking advantage of Egyptian 'neutrality'. The Khedive Ismail, remembering no doubt the several collisions his predecessors had had with Ethiopian power, offered to join in the British invasion. The offer was declined, but he still provided plenty of help, starting with occupying Massawa as a sort of rearguard for the British. This was hardly a neutral act, but Ismail was also contemplating his own invasion of the Christian empire, perhaps assuming that the British attack would cause sufficient damage, that the victim could then be easily defeated. In addition, of course, the Egyptian regime in the Sudan had had a whole series of quarrels and fights with various Ethiopian governors in the past thirty years (including Tewodros's father), so Ismail might reasonably have considered that he was already potentially at war with Ethiopia. In fact, these collisions had never provoked a formal declaration of war by either side, mainly because the Ethiopian commanders had normally been near-independent provincial governors, and on the Egyptian side were independently minded governors general and governors, so the conflict had been, in a sense, largely unofficial; both sides had been able to downplay the fighting and ignore the results, while storing up the clashes for later diplomatic use.

Certainly, the British invasion pummelled the Ethiopians. The British had found Massawa harbour too restricted to accommodate their numerous naval and transport forces, so the army was put onshore 30 miles away at Annesley Bay. They brought 13,000 soldiers, and twice as many followers and servants, carried in 280 ships. This was, of course, the Indian Army, and the 13,000 soldiers included only 4,000 British, with 9,000 Indian troops. The Indian Army was well used to elaborate expeditions, with much of the baggage being luxury provisions for the officers and elaborate tents for their accommodation. (This had been the case in the Egyptian invasion in 1801 also, to the astonishment of the contingents sent out from Britain.)

The result of the invasion was that Emperor Tewodros, beset by internal rebellions and defections, was defeated at his stronghold at Magdala, and committed suicide (with a pistol sent to him as a present by Queen Victoria) as the gates of his fort were blown in by British artillery. They had also used Congreve rockets, just as Romolo Gessi did in the Bahr el-Ghazal in the same decade; victory was normally the result of superior technology in these African wars.

Given the immediate confusion that followed the death of the emperor, brought about by a foreign invader inside Ethiopia, Khedive Ismail no doubt reckoned that his own invasion would be easy; certainly, he sent a force of no more than 2,500 men to conduct the campaign, where the British had used more than four times that, and without any intention of remaining in the country. Ismail chose as his commanders Arendrup Bey, a Danish officer with no experience of command who was also ill, along with the governor of Massawa, Arikel Bey Nubar. This force was destroyed by Ethiopian defenders without any difficulty, and both commanders were killed.[8]

Khedive Ismail followed up the destruction of this small army by sending one that was more likely to be adequate – 12,000 men under a more experienced set of commanders, the chief of whom was the *sirdar*, the commander-in-chief of the Egyptian army, Muhammad Retib Pasha. Again, however, the *sirdar*, like Arendrup, was an administrator, and had never commanded in the field. He had as his second-in-command William Loring, who had risen to be a major general in the Confederate army in the American Civil War, but had no experience of command in Africa; furthermore, the two men could not communicate with each other. This invasion was also defeated, with great loss, and the *sirdar* was compelled to negotiate with the victors, and to buy peace.[9] Khedive Ismail was, of course, annoyed, but took the point and did not attack a third time.

There was clearly no possibility of expanding the Egyptian Empire out of Sudan into the mountains of Ethiopia. The Egyptian army had been fully capable of defeating moribund states such as Sennar and the Mameluke survivors fifty years earlier, but since then it had languished in garrisons, or had taken part in slave hunts against essentially unarmed and unorganised victims. In the more serious attacks on Ethiopia, and against al-Zubayr in the Bahr el-Ghazal, or the surviving sultans in Darfur, it had been beaten all too easily. The Egyptian army was thus scarcely fit to campaign, and certainly not to fight a state such as Ethiopia, which had been conducting a civil war with itself for the previous two generations; and if a civil war does nothing else, it produces skilled soldiers by the thousand. A single Confederate general (from a defeated army in a Civil War) who was unable to communicate either with his superior officer or with his troops was unlikely to make much difference on the Egyptian side.

On the other hand, as the acquisition of fragments of eastern Sudan, of the Equatorial provinces, and of Darfur at the same time showed, the Egyptian army was fully capable of expanding the empire by campaigning against the weak and disorganised areas and poorly armed peoples on and beyond its borders, and there were still such areas available to the west and the south. The army was essentially the same in organisation and in much of its equipment as that developed by Muhammad Ali in the 1820s and 1830s, and which had been commanded in action by Ibrahim in Greece and Arabia. Ismail was beginning to adopt German military methods instead of the French, as a result of the Franco-Prussian War, but this was as much display as substance. Even before the Ethiopian disaster, and perhaps in view of the efficient conduct of the British in their Ethiopian war, he had begun to reform his forces by developing a competent staff, employing for the task a group of discharged American officers, of which, Loring Pasha, defeated by the Ethiopians, had been one.[10]

One of the regions that was evidently available for acquisition was the Red Sea coast south of Massawa as far as Cape Guardafui, the area now known as Somalia, as projected by Muhammad Ali in the 1840s. Ismail had posted a considerable force at that port – which he already possessed – during the British invasion, and this was the base from which his own invasion of Ethiopia had been launched. From there in 1874 (the same year as his invasion and the conquest of Darfur), a fleet of Egyptian ships sailed through the Bab el-Mandeb at the mouth of the Red Sea, to campaign along the Somali coast. This was an Egyptian intrusion into an area of international competition; the French had staked an interest there several years before at Obok, and the British were also present across the Bab el-Mandeb entrance to the Red Sea at Aden. These places were carefully chosen to be both along the steamship route to India and at the mouth of the Red Sea.

The rebuff of the Egyptian invasion of Ethiopia had actually only stimulated Ismail's acquisitiveness. The opening of the Suez Canal had converted the Red Sea into a major international waterway, and control of the coasts, or at least ports along them, would be a strategic asset. Ismail had stated a claim to Berbera on the Somali coast beyond Obok. In 1874–5, the Egyptian fleet landed a force at Zeila, between Berbera and Obok, and established Egyptian authority there. Zeila was at the seaward end of a trade route that connected southern Ethiopia and the principalities there with the sea. The Egyptian commander, Muhammad Rauf Pasha, then moved his forces inland and took control of the ancient city of Harar, a Muslim city that was an ancient enemy of the Ethiopians. This, with Berbera, gave Egypt a considerable new province.

Muhammad Rauf intended to go further, and in Equatoria, Ismail's governor general, Charles Gordon, suggested that the best route for communications out of Equatoria would be to gain a port on the Somali coast, and had suggested Zeila as a suitable candidate. Ismail, however, also had his eye on an extension of his Somali province beyond Cape Guardafui. Kismayu, 1,000 miles along the Indian Ocean coast from the Cape, was seen as a useful acquisition, with a view to exploitation into the interior. Ismail made enquiries as to whether the sultan of Zanzibar, who had a strong claim to a long stretch of the East African coast, had a rival claim stretching so far north. He appears to have been satisfied with the answer, or more likely, he optimistically satisfied himself, and the Egyptian fleet sailed out into the Indian Ocean and made a landing at Kismayu. This was a well-chosen port, at the mouth of the Juba River, which in turn provided a route inland towards southern Ethiopia; it was obviously useful for trade with the interior, but whether it would ever have been useful as a port for Egyptian Equatoria is highly doubtful; Zeila would be even more unlikely.[11]

Amidst all this imperial jostling and claiming, a new player arrived. An Italian shipping magnate, Raffaele Rubattino, had sent a small expedition into this contested, even congested, area, which had planted some placards at a desolate village called Assab, and had left there a group of unfortunate Italian sailors as 'colonists'. This place was just inside the Red Sea on the west coast, a little north of Obok (which was French), but well south of Massawa (which was Egyptian), and across the Bab el-Mandeb from Aden (which was British). It was, however, like Aden and Obok, a strategically well-chosen place, at the southern entrance to the Red Sea, which was no doubt another purpose in the Italian move. The timing was also interesting. Rubattino established his frail little colony in 1870, the year after the opening of the Suez Canal, and the year in which France was preoccupied with the Prussian war; it was also only two years after the British campaign in Ethiopia had drawn wider attention to the area, and amidst the organisation and failure of the unfortunate expeditions by Egyptian forces that were defeated by the Ethiopians.

Rubattino was, on the surface, acting as a private entrepreneur, seeking to tap into the Ethiopian trading possibilities. There was, however, inevitable doubt about his purpose and his precise status. First, Assab was famously exceedingly hot, and completely dry. Its hinterland was the Danakil Desert, one of the worst such places in the world, and not just for its heat and its desiccation; several Italian exploring parties were murdered by the local Afar tribesman during the next decade, when they ventured into the tribal territory. Second, Rubattino had form in such expeditions. In 1860, he had financed Garibaldi's invasion of Sicily and southern Italy during the Italian Wars of Unification, having been subsidised in this by the Piedmont-Sardinian government of Count Cavour. As a veteran intriguer, Cavour was seeking cover for the expedition by pretending he had nothing to do with it while generously financing it, so as to avoid blame for launching an attack on a friendly neutral country (the kingdom of Naples). Garibaldi was thus to be seen as acting on his own initiative and out of his own resources (or Rubattino's). There was reason to believe that the same ruse was being played out at Assab. Rubattino's ships certainly called at Assab with supplies and reinforcements regularly over the next dozen years, and eventually this private company settlement became an official Italian colony.[12]

No one paid much attention to the Italian venture while it struggled on – except, perhaps, the Afars, and the Italian public when something happened to bring it to their newspapers' notice – but the means by which it was supported, whether or not it was realised that Rubattino was financed by the Italian government, implied that it was a less than private and unofficial expedition. This was no doubt fully understood in the foreign offices of Europe, though the connection was unpublicised. The colony certainly stayed in place, producing nothing, costing a good deal in money and lives, and only a government could afford all that. (One may be reminded of the English settlement at Jamestown in Virginia for its costliness and initial difficulties.)

Meanwhile, the Egyptian expedition to Kismayu came to grief. It was commanded by R.F. McKillop Pasha, a former British officer who was now a senior officer in the Egyptian Marine. His arrival at Kismayu brought a protest by Britain to the Ottoman sultan in Istanbul on behalf of the sultan of Zanzibar. The Zanzibari sultan had some sort of a claim on the town, and since he was under British protection it was on his behalf that the protest was being made. Ismail's assumption that he had received a green light for his landing at Kismayu from the Zanzibari sultan was apparently mistaken, or over-optimistic; it was equally, indeed more, likely that the sultan of Zanzibar had been persuaded to decide he had a claim on Kismayu by a British diplomat.[13]

Rather like Rubattino and the Italians at Assab, the British had form in this area. Their conquest of Aden in 1839 had been undertaken to obtain a coaling station for the use of the new steamships, on the route between Egypt and India, but it had involved the bombardment of the town, and British Aden existed amid the continuing hostility of its neighbours around the town. It was, of course, hardly a coincidence that this established a British base at the very entrance to the Red Sea. In a similar way, Muhammad Ali, having gained leases on Suakin and Massawa in 1846, was then credited with making a claim to the whole coast from those ports to Cape Guardafui. It was not, of course, that he stated this personally, but it was stated on his behalf by his governor at Massawa. Everyone in this area was acting remotely – the British through the East India Company, the sultan of Zanzibar, and the Ottoman sultan; France through the Suez Canal Company, Italy through Rubattino, and Egypt through a governor who could be disavowed. The British protest to the sultan in Constantinople over Ismail's claim resulted in a general lapsing of the various Egyptian leases and claims, either because of Ottoman or British pressure, or because, as in 1849, the new khedive in Egypt was uninterested in the venture, or, more likely, all of these.

The prospect of the Egyptian claim to the Somali coast being revived – and implemented – had brought instant alarm at Aden, and then in India. One of the places seized by Muhammad Rauf Pasha was the port of Zeila. This was the main port for trade with southern Ethiopia; under Egyptian control it was likely to be less amenable to foreign traders – read 'British' – and probably a more expensive place in which to operate, if the Egyptian customs rates were imposed and collected (and bribes expected). So when the Egyptian expedition was extended even further, as far as the Juba River at Kismayu, and therefore far beyond Cape Guardafui, the original limit of the Egyptian claim, and implying an Egyptian claim to the whole coast from Suakin to Kismayu, it brought the British to protest on behalf of the Zanzibari sultan by way of Constantinople, and there they made it stick. The fact that the Egyptian naval commander was an expatriate Scot rendered the British protest even more effective; he would be unlikely to defy his home government if he wanted eventually to return to Britain.

All was not lost for Ismail, however. Having stretched beyond his capacity as far as Kismayu, he negotiated a settlement with the British, in which the latter provided a recognition of Egyptian claims to the Somali coast as far as Ras Hafun (somewhat south of Cape Guardafui), by way of the sultan in Constantinople once more. As yet, it was a conditional agreement only and so only tentative. The Italian seizure of Assab was certainly intrusive, since it was technically a piece of Italian private enterprise. Such conditional and tentative moves have a way of solidifying.

For the moment, however, and for several years ahead, the Egyptians had established a viable and public claim to the northern Somali coast, had involved the British and the Ottoman sultan in doing so, and had established actual control in the city of Harar and the ports along the coast from Zeila to Berbera. This took place in the same period that Darfur was being conquered, and the Bahr el-Ghazal province was being expanded south-westwards into the Azande country. Since the 'Scramble for Africa' had yet to begin seriously (with the German intervention, the first example of which was, coincidentally, on the coast just south of Kismayu), one may note that Egypt was well ahead of the game yet again, and had succeeded in producing an extensive empire at minimal cost, commanding substantial potential resources. But the Egyptian expansion had been stopped at Kismayu, and had then receded, just as it had in the Great Lakes region, where Baker's bluff about an Egyptian protectorate had been called; further moves west from Darfur now looked very unlikely, and the resistance in Central Africa was bitter. The increasing pressure from Europe to halt the slave trade, and even abolish slavery, was providing a major internal problem, while the defeats in Ethiopia, and the control problem in Central Africa, were all harbingers of future problems. The empire of Egypt in the Red Sea was, like the other imperialist ventures, based on exerting minimal force; its foundations were thus shallow and vulnerable. The next decade would demonstrate its weaknesses.

Chapter 6

Ethiopian Revival

Ethiopia has already appeared more than once in this account, especially in the last chapter. It is time to discuss it and its significance for events in the Sudan.[1] Its basic characteristic is that it is a Christian country, surrounded by Muslims and pagans – in fact, it includes communities of both of these within its borders. It has a history as a Christian country for almost 1,700 years, becoming Christian at the same time as the Roman Empire converted officially, and under the urging of the first Christian Roman emperors. It had been an organised society for several centuries before then, and archaeologists are finding increasingly early signs of this; it is, that is, a society very old, very proud of itself, and more than happy with its differences from its neighbours.

The neighbouring Muslim states put it under serious and continual pressure several times, notably in the sixteenth century when Portuguese explorers and traders and priests reached it – and claimed to have rescued it from Islam. Its survival, however, was mainly by its own efforts, as always; it has since suffered similar pressure from the European imperialists, notably the Italian fascists. In the late nineteenth century it was invaded by Egyptians, British and Italians, and by the Mahdists.

The Portuguese interference in the sixteenth century helped the country to survive the Muslim attacks at that time, but the Portuguese became too insistent – their Catholic Christianity clashed with Ethiopian Monophysitism – and the Ethiopians found their rescuers from the Muslims had become their annoying would-be persecutors and controllers. The Portuguese were eventually shut out. It was a not dissimilar situation in the nineteenth century. It had been Italian interference and arms supplies that enabled Ethiopia to survive a later Italian attack, and it was British interference in 1941 – on the Portuguese pattern, as rescuers, though principally in their own interests – that helped to oust the Italian fascist regime. The Ethiopians are thus past masters at accepting just sufficient help from outside to overcome their current problem, but they would then go their own way regardless. This history has made the inhabitants tough, independent and resilient, unwilling for the most part to accept outside authority of any sort, except in a dire emergency.

Ethiopians live on a high mountain plateau, on average, 7,000–8000 feet above sea level, with mountains even higher. It is intricate, much fissured, beautiful and fertile. Its intricacy, however, promotes division and disunion, which are accentuated by religious and deep-seated tribal divisions. It has a regrettable tendency to divide into autonomous regions, and to see parts of the country secede into independence, usually only temporarily. It is, thanks to its high plateau nature, and the steep approaches this mandates, generally very difficult to enter if one is not wanted, and is therefore not easily to be invaded, and if invaded it is defensible and very difficult to conquer. And yet, invaders, with any sense, will begin by exploiting the internal divisions, even before making an attack. Altogether, it is a formidable local power when united, and even when divided; each province is fully capable of a strong defence, against other Ethiopians or against intruding outsiders. At the same time, Ethiopian aggression against its neighbours is as difficult to accomplish as are external invasions, since the Ethiopians, from a high and wet mountain country, do not like the low-lying dry deserts or the hot lowlands.

When Muhammad Ali's armies conquered Sudan in the 1820s, they reached the foot of the mountain massif of Ethiopia and came to an abrupt halt. They were able to move easily into eastern Sudan, to Kassala, Massawa and Suakin, and to campaign into Equatoria and the Bahr el-Ghazal, but the mountain region proved to be an impassable obstacle. Apart from the difficult climate, which is of the monsoon variety, and so can be oppressively wet and cool for the lowlanders in the rainy season, access is through long, steep and difficult passes, where, as Egyptians and others have discovered and Ethiopians have long known, ambushes are easy to mount. The first Egyptian encounter with the massif, when they were searching for gold at Fazoghlu, found that the main access into the country was by the exceedingly difficult, or impossible, Blue Nile gorge, several thousands of feet deep. The Egyptians were held up even by Darfur; they never managed to conquer the Nuba Hills permanently, and only got their forces into those hills when a pretender to the throne invited them in. They never penetrated more than a short distance into Ethiopia, in brief invasions. They could conquer the lowlands, and even make progress in the sparsely populated desert lands beside the Red Sea, but they never had any permanent success in the hills. It was even more humiliating that the Egyptian invasions were defeated by provincial forces, for not until the 1890s could an Ethiopian ruler mass an army from the whole country.

The empire of Ethiopia, even so, was divided into independent provinces and regions and societies during the time the Egyptians were campaigning in the lowlands, and for a century and more beforehand; an emperor existed, but scarcely ruled anywhere outside his camp or palace. Ethiopian historical theory counts the imperial power back to the seduction of King Solomon by the Queen of Sheba (or vice versa), supposedly about 1000 BC. Their union, in Jerusalem when the queen was visiting, according to the myth recorded in the Bible, produced the first member of the imperial dynasty. This myth is accepted as correct, and the dynasty or rulers that emerged in the thirteenth century, replacing an earlier one, is called the 'Solomonic'.

This supposed origin was vigorously promoted as a unifying national myth; in turn, this deliberately lent emphasis to its Christianity in a land threatened by Muslims. The dynasty retained its charisma for four centuries; a series of energetic emperors successfully defended the country against assault by the nearby Muslim powers in the fifteenth and sixteenth centuries (assisted by the Portuguese). This prestige was retained by the emperors through to the mid-eighteenth century, even as the imperial system collapsed into a century and more of intermittent civil war, leaving the emperors with no more than the name. In turn, needless to say, this attracted foreign invasions. The civil warfare was partly a quest for independence by many of the provinces, and partly a quest to establish control over the Solomonic imperial dynasty, which continued until the 1850s to provide the occupants of the imperial throne. Ultimately, of course, the imperial house faded into powerlessness – by about 1770 – and the civil warfare from then on became contests to establish a new ruler, and if possible a new dynasty for the whole country.[2]

This was the situation within the country when Muhammad Ali's armies were able to conquer the Sudan lowlands with no difficulty and so arrive at the foot of the Ethiopian mountains in the 1820s. They extended their operations south along the White Nile, and east to the Red Sea, conquering, amongst other areas, the Taka country, an Ethiopian neighbour, and gaining intermittent control of Massawa, a port through which Ethiopian merchants habitually gained access to the sea and its trade. By about 1850, Egyptian power was lying up against the Ethiopian borders on the west and the north; the borders, of course, were vague, and conflicts had taken place between the governor of the Ethiopian province of Qwari and Egyptian governors, and along the Ethiopian western borderlands, especially in the great slaving campaign of governor Ahmad Pasha abu Widam in the 1840s (see chapter 4).

Within Ethiopia, the internal contest had begun to throw up non-Solomonic pretenders aiming to replace the moribund old imperial dynasty, but emperors of the Solomonic line were still there. They only existed as *rois fainéants*, always dominated by powerful regents. Behind their powerless position the provincial lands separated from one another into effectively independent principalities. Between 1770 and 1850, there were twenty-six emperors, but of these some held office several times – one of them six times, one four times, several others more than once – such was the instability. But the civil war, as such wars do, ended with a single powerful soldier defeating all the other pretenders and powers, and making himself emperor; he was in fact not the first to take the throne away from the Solomonic line, but his power and his comparative longevity as emperor cleared the way for others to do the same after him.

The victor in the civil wars was Ras Kassa, whose throne name was Tewodros, and who has appeared in this account earlier, first as Kassa Hailu, the son or nephew of the governor Kenfu of Qwari; both of these powerful provincial rulers had campaigned into Sudan in the 1840s. Tewodros was, to traditionalists, a usurper. He built up a new army, no longer a levy of his followers and the peasants on his estates in the usual way, but a larger and professional force, such as he had faced in his forays into Sudan. His new, disciplined, army was better armed than a group of untrained feudal followers (partly armed with guns acquired from the Egyptians) and loyal to him personally because of his successes and the rewards he could provide.

Tewodros's victory, of course, was what was necessary to end the civil warfare, but the political divisions of the country ran very deep, and when his force met an even greater and more professional army – the British Indian invading army in 1867–8 – those in Ethiopia he had earlier defeated quickly broke away again. Hence, in part, the ease of Tewodros's defeat by the British.

Tewodros had successively defeated the several provincial rulers, partly by superior generalship, and partly by his efficient army. He then reformed the administration of the provinces, and in most cases installed his own men as governors and administrators, turning out the local elites. This, of course, created an excluded class, resentful, and with much local influence; in one major province, Shoa, in the south, he used members of the local elite as his governors rather than impose new men, but this did not prevent rebellions any more than the alternative he used elsewhere. As a result, his reign (1855–68) was largely a continual series of campaigns to suppress rebellions. By 1865, three major provinces were in full rebellion, Tigray in the north, Lasta in the centre, and Shoa in the south, whose *rases* had emulated Tewodros in professionalising their armies and gathering modern weapons. Tewodros could still win the battles, but that was now no longer enough. The political significance of his career is perhaps that he was the only man who seemed to see Ethiopia as a single polity, where his opponents saw it as a set of independent kingdoms.

Tewodros's supplies of weaponry came by imports, some from Egypt, some from local manufacture, and others from wherever he could find them. He had established diplomatic contact with the British, whose East India Company was active in the Red Sea and along its coasts. Above all, he appreciated that as his was a Christian country; another Christian country was most likely to be of assistance to him. But he mishandled the relationship, as did the British on their side. Tewodros's practice was to take prisoner a select group of the elite from each conquered province and to hold them as hostages at his mountain fortress at Magdala. He attempted to use this method to control his relationship with the British, but they had come up against similar methods in their Indian Empire, and refused to give in to what was seen as blackmail. (Most of the Ethiopians similarly refused in the end, but by that time, Tewodros's power was failing.) From India came the expeditionary force briefly discussed in the previous chapter: 13,000 troops, 20,000 followers and servants, batteries of efficient mountain artillery, elephants, camels, all carried in the fleet of 280 ships; an armed force capable of constructing roads and bridges and campaigning in mountain country. Ethiopia's mountain defences were not sufficient this time.[3]

General Robert Napier, one of a family of military and naval commanders busy in the British Empire in the mid-nineteenth century, efficiently moved his force from Annesley Bay, the landing place near Massawa, then on into the mountains, constructing a road along the way. He contacted the rebel leader in Tigray, Kassa Mercha, through whose territory he had to march to get to Magdala, and arranged an undisputed passage for his army; in Lasta province, a leader emerged to take command of the local army in place of Tewodros's appointee and removed it from the resistance; the *negus* Menelik of Shoa escaped from Magdala and his country was thereupon effectively independent of Tewodros's authority. The pressure of the British invasion, and its unstoppable advance, exercised a major influence on the disintegration of Tewodros's empire, though this was already in process before the British arrived.

Tewodros scarcely used his 'hostages' in any attempt to begin negotiations, and when the British forces – two-thirds of whom were Indians – arrived at Magdala, he despaired. He sent many of his Ethiopian prisoners away unharmed, and dismissed most of his soldiers – he was regarded as mad by his opponents, but he was more stressed than incapable, and not vindictive. The British artillery bombarded the great gates of the fortress and broke them down, and when they moved into the fort, Tewodros shot himself. The fortress was then sacked and looted by the victors, as would be expected.

The fortress of Magdala, having been bombarded, ruined and captured, the emperor's body was located and identified. General Napier had completed his main task and began to withdraw his forces, taking the rescued captives away, and released any remaining Ethiopian prisoner/hostages. He made no attempt to set up a new regime, judging that the Ethiopians could and should sort out their own affairs, a remarkable abnegation, but one that made sense. To involve himself in Ethiopian politics would cause him escalating complexities. In any case, his army was scarcely large enough to make the attempt. A former emperor, Yohannes III, was released, but his two terms on the throne, each less than a year in length, had impressed no one; he was ignored. The one gesture Napier indulged in was to thank Kassa Mercha, the local strongman in Tigray in the north, whom he had contacted earlier, and who now mustered an escort for the retiring British. As a reward, Napier handed over a selection of modern weapons – a battery of field guns, a large quantity of rifles, and ammunition. A British soldier, John Kirkham, who had formerly been General Gordon's adjutant, was hired by Ras Kassa Mercha to train his soldiers in these weapons, and to organise his army on more effective lines – as Tewodros had done also. It will be noted that here is a classic example of foreign interference in Ethiopia – brief, effective, but soon over – and with a decided effect on the future development of the country's internal affairs.

Kassa Mercha was attacked by another survivor of Tewodros's reign, Wagshum Gobeze. He had taken over the army in Lasta that had been gathered by his mother and her second husband. (Her first husband, Gobeze's father, had been executed by Tewodros.) He had used this force even during Tewodros's reign to drive the emperor's governor out of Tigray, the northernmost province of the country, one region that has aimed at independence, or at least autonomy, for centuries.[4] With Tewodros's death, Gobeze carried out a series of symbolic acts in pursuit of his aim to become the next emperor. He brought the body of the last *abuna* – the head of the Ethiopian Church – to Gondar for ceremonial burial. Tewodros had quarrelled with the *abuna* and jailed him, and there he had died. He had not been replaced, which was a complicated and intricate process, for he had to be nominated and consecrated by the head of the Coptic Church in Egypt, which involved negotiations with Egyptian authorities, and the payment of a large tribute. In the course of a theological dispute between Tewodros and a group of priests at Gondar, the nearest thing to an imperial capital, much of that city had been burned; Gobeze repaired the churches that were damaged. Having thus made his point, Gobeze had himself crowned as the new emperor, taking the name Tekle Giyorgis.[5] (The first emperor of that name had been the one who had held the throne six times between 1779 and 1800, but only for a total of thirteen years – perhaps not a good omen.)

Tekle Giyorgis II was, despite his ceremonies, somewhat premature. He had married Kassa Mercha's sister, but this relationship of the two men did not produce an alliance. Kassa Mercha quietly developed and extended his own power, helped by the British arms given him by Napier. In this, he was acting in the same way as the new would-be emperor. Then, when he was strong enough to attack Tekle Giyorgis, there was another civil war. The new emperor was defeated and killed, having reigned for only three years (1868–71). Significantly, he had commanded the larger army in the battle, which took place at Adowa, but Kassa

Mercha had a better trained force, thanks in part to Kirkham's training regime. During his rival's reign, Kassa Mercha had deliberately entrenched himself in Tigray, and had extended his boundaries, in particular by annexing Hamasien, a highland region inland of Massawa, and the most northerly Ethiopian province. It had been the target of the Egyptian forces earlier.

He then went one better than Tekle Giyorgis. The latter had buried the last *abuna*; Kassa Mercha negotiated with Khedive Ismail and the Coptic Church in Egypt for that *abuna*'s live replacement. It cost a substantial sum in tribute but in 1872 the new *abuna* Atnatewos had arrived and one of his first acts was to crown Kassa Mercha as the Emperor Yohannes IV; the ceremony took place at Axum, the ancient imperial centre, amid the great monuments from the time of the first imperial dynasty that had accepted Christianity.[6] The past casts a long shadow in Ethiopia (starting with the Queen of Sheba), but it could also be harnessed to the benefit of the present and future.

There was another Ethiopian state re-emerging from the blanket of violence of Tewodros's conquests. In the south was the kingdom of Shoa (or Shewa), which had been growing in power and extent before Tewodros's emergence. It was ruled by a line of capable kings, holding office by direct hereditary descent, for over a century and a half – an unusual achievement in Ethiopia in that period of violence. The king in 1855 was Menelik, the eighth in that succession, who inherited the kingship at the age of 11 years; he had been captured by Tewodros, imprisoned at Magdala, and was one of those released in Tewodros's last days.

The position of Shoa was on the southern frontier of the territory that was reckoned to be Ethiopia, facing south towards a series of smaller and weaker communities, mainly pagan, and mainly Galla. Under the dynasty's vigorous leadership the kingdom had first survived the raids of its pagan neighbours – the sort of thing that inevitably happened when an empire such as Ethiopia became unstable – but then, having beaten back these raids, instead of mixing it with the other Ethiopian states, Shoa's kings' attention was directed at conquering and incorporating those local and southern enemies.[7]

The kingdom's centre was the town of Ankober – another of the frequent steep hills like Magdala (*ambas*, often the eroded plugs of extinct volcanoes) – and its surroundings. King Sahle Selassie (1813–47) had campaigned to secure his northern frontier, and, having done that, he then turned southwards. His victims were a series of small Galla states. Their territories were divided, but were wealthy, productive of goods to be traded, and of food. In part due to Sahle Selassie's imposition of peace on the region, and partly due to a revival of trade in the Red Sea thanks to Muhammad Ali's work in Egypt and Arabia, commerce developed and increased, usually in the hands of caravan masters conducted by Ethiopian Muslims based in Adal, the country of Harar, using Zeila as their main trading port.[8]

The original route for such exports from Shoa and the Galla country was northward, heading for Massawa through Tigray, but Sahle Selassie's conquests helped to open up the new route (or revive an old one) that reached the coast at Zeila in the Somali lands. Sahle Selassie, of course, profited by taxation on the goods traded, which included ivory, gold, coffee, gum arabic and other products. This export trade was built on a gradually increasing internal trade within the kingdom and the empire, which connected Shoa with Harar and the Afar lands to the east, and the semi-Ethiopian regimes of Sidamo and the Galla states to the south. Behind the political chaos and imperial instability of the early and mid-nineteenth century, Shoa was gradually increasing in power.

Into this relatively smoothly developing situation, where Shoa was increasing in wealth (Sahle Selassie had a great store of gold, the product of his taxation regime), and expanding in territory, came the Emperor Tewodros. It was inevitable that he would see Shoa as a major rival to be crushed. In the war that followed, Tewodros was victorious, thanks to his disciplined army, part of which was armed with muskets; Sahle Selassie's son and successor, the *negus* Haile Malakot,[9] died of illness and despair as a result of his defeat.[10] He left an 11-year-old son, Menelik, whose preservation was the object of the next phase of the war. Tewodros's superior strategy resulted in the Shoans who were attempting to move the king into shelter being trapped and either killed or captured. They surrendered Menelik as a hostage, and the prince was taken, along with his mother and several prominent Shoans, to be lodged at Magdala for the next ten years. Despite the clear evidence of Shoan loyalty to him, Tewodros kept Menelik safe.

This conquest had been relatively easy for Tewodros's forces, and it would seem that Tewodros as a result became over-confident. In contrast to his normal practice, he appointed a son of Sahle Selassie, Haile Mikail, as his governor of Shoa, and one of the former generals of that king, Ardagatchew, as the frontier governor (though this task was recognised as normally needing three or four men, one each for the several sections of the frontier). The continuation in power of these men from the former regime perpetuated the loyalty of the population to the local dynasty, but hardly reconciled them to Tewodros's rule. In other conquests, Tewodros had deliberately removed the old dynasties and their prominent adherents and replaced them with his own men, and while he did this also in Shoa, there he chose prominent dynastic loyalists as his governors, presuming that by their appointment they had become loyal to him. The failure to remove such loyalists in Shoa may be, as suggested, the emperor's over-confidence, but it may also be a recognition that Shoan loyalty to the old dynasty was so strong that to attempt to replace it would cause continual trouble. Either way, the old dynasty and the Shoan elite remained in power; also it was known that Menelik was alive and well, and was growing up to adulthood at Magdala. The political balance was clearly very delicate.

Whatever Tewodros's precise aims in Shoa, which were presumably to establish the kingdom as a peaceful and loyal region, they failed utterly. As soon as, in 1856, he set off to return to the north with his army, a rebellion began, led by Haile Malakot's younger brother, Seifu Selassie. He repeatedly defeated the imperial forces over the next four years, and eventually, Tewodros removed the governor Haile Mikail and imprisoned him at Magdala, with all the rest, thereby acknowledging that his loyalty was to Menelik. The rebels had by then recaptured Ankober, the Shoan royal centre. Appealed to by his new governor who was unable to take the place, Tewodros himself came to attack it, but also failed. He began to withdraw, and part of the Shoan forces came down from the city to pursue; Tewodros at once reversed course and the pursuers were destroyed. (Whether this was a deliberate ruse by Tewodros or only his quick tactical thinking is not clear.) The remaining garrison, composed of the men who had not fallen for the trick, was too small to resist further, and the city was thus captured and sacked; as at Gondar, the churches were a particular target due to a theological dispute in which the local clergy took the view opposed to the emperor's.[11]

Prince Seifu Selassie had thus lost his army, and the kingdom fell once more to Tewodros. Seifu himself escaped from the final massacre, but the province he had ruled, Marabiete, was systematically devastated by Tewodros's army. When Seifu attempted to organise its recovery he was killed in the fighting. Despite the new crisis of the rebellion against him, led by chieftains loyal to the old dynasty, Tewodros persisted in appointing more Menelikan loyalists, Aboya as governor, and Bezabeh as frontier governor.

The new governors had to rule over a badly damaged state, but knew full well that the population remained loyal to the absent Menelik. Eventually in 1864, when Aboya left to take the annual tribute to Magdala, Bezabah rebelled and proclaimed himself *negus* (king), but made it clear that this was mainly intended to deter other pretenders, and announced that if and when Menelik returned to Shoa he would surrender power to him. Tewodros came south again to suppress this new rebellion, but failed. Shoa's neighbour, the Wallo Gallas, were also attacked by the imperial army; the people withdrew to a series of those impregnable hill forts and sent guerrilla bands to harass Tewodros's forces, a form of warfare that disconcerted the imperial forces and wearied them. When the army came to Shoa, therefore, it was able to plunder the lowlands, but was not strong enough to capture the fortress of Afqara in the north of Shoa, close to the Wallo territory, which the rebels held as their base.

In effect, therefore, both the Wallo Gallas and the Shoans had established their independence of Tewodros's regime, subject to repeated unpleasant, but unsuccessful, attacks. In addition, the harassed emperor faced rebellions in many other provinces, including Tigray and Lasta (the lands of Kassa Mercha and the future emperor Tekle Giyorgis respectively). Clearly, the success of the Shoans had persuaded others that Tewodros was beatable. In 1865, Menelik, with his mother and some of the Shoan elite who had been imprisoned with him, escaped from Magdala. They were welcomed by Queen Warquit, who was ruling in Wallo Galla in place of her son, who was another of the prisoners at Magdala. (Again, Tewodros's restraint in merely imprisoning Menelik and the queen's son is remarkable – though they were, of course, only valuable as hostages while still alive.) Despite the danger to her son, she gave Menelik support and an escort. But Tewodros, when he found out, caused the queen's son, and over thirty of her and Menelik's people, to be killed; there were limits to his restraint.

The escapees were welcomed by the first guards they met on entering Shoa. The local governor joined Menelik, and he was followed by the governor of Efrata province. Some opposition came from men loyal to Bezabeh, which was overcome fairly easily, and the forces of the defeated joined the royal party. Bezabeh did not, as he had promised, surrender to the arriving prince; instead he apparently put it about that the invaders were in fact being led by Tewodros. But when the army he sent to meet Menelik's forces did so, the troops realised it was really Menelik and refused to fight him. Bezabeh fled for refuge to a hill fort, and in August 1865, two months after escaping from Magdala, Menelik was installed as *negus* at Ankober. Bezabeh surrendered and was pardoned, but he soon rebelled, and then he was captured and executed.[12]

In 1871, therefore, by which time both Tewodros and Tekle Giyorgis had been removed from the scene, Kassa Mercha in Tigray and Menelik in Shoa were plainly the main powers within Ethiopia. Kassa Mercha became the new emperor, with the throne name of Yohannes IV. Between Tigray and Shoa was the old central region of Ethiopia, including Gondar and Lasta, which was not part of either man's territory, and for a time they both campaigned in these parts, but separately. Menelik looked north and campaigned vigorously to extend his kingdom over the Wallo Gallas, who had helped him gain the throne. Yohannes used his military energies to establish his control in the northern regions and his dominance over other lands between the kingdoms, notably Gondar, the old imperial capital.

It was Yohannes, therefore, who had to face the invasions of the Egyptian forces from outside, though all Ethiopia was affected by the Egyptian fleet blockade of the Red Sea and Somali coasts. Menelik made contact with the French at Obok and acquired the services of several French advisers, and benefited from the French traders' willingness to sell him weapons. The traders made notoriously high profits from their deals, but for Menelik the bargain was worth it as he saw his kingdom became steadily better armed. Yohannes, by contrast, who was also arming, faced the Egyptians, the Italians, the British, and perhaps the French, who favoured Shoa. It was his territory that was the object of the Egyptian invasions in 1875 in 1876, from their base at Massawa.

The Italians had taken control of Assab and, though they had not succeeded in expanding their territory to any degree, they were still there, in a port that had been one of Ethiopia's prime export routes. Maybe Yohannes was fooled by the Italians' pretence that the colony was an episode of private enterprise, but Menelik made contact with them as well as the French at Obok. Neither the French nor the Italians recognised or accepted the Egyptian naval blockade, which Ismail could not therefore enforce totally. The Egyptians in the same period, with their moves into Equatoria, into the Somali lands, and their naval blockade, had extended their control of the Ethiopian surroundings from the western and northern boundaries to the Red Sea coast, and as far as the Great Lakes region of Central Africa, aiming to take in the Somali coast as far as Cape Guardafui, and threatened to close off any possible trade routes south by taking control of Kismayu. It seemed that the Egyptian Empire was succeeding in surrounding Ethiopia.

It was therefore the Egyptian Empire of Khedive Ismail that seemed to be the main foreign problem for the Ethiopians, and the division of Ethiopia between its princes could be a serious disability if a war with Egypt began. Egypt's, or rather the khedive's, financial difficulties had been relieved to some extent with the opening of the Suez Canal, which generated income, and then in 1874 by the British purchase of the Suez Canal Company shares assigned to the khedive. This was also the year when Ismail's armies took over Darfur, Bahr el-Ghazal, and the Somali coast, so the khedive's financial problems had not held up the expansion of his empire. His army had been reformed and beefed up by the recruitment of expatriate American officers, both former Union and former Confederate, though if they were as hopeless as Loring, they were not much to worry about. (Most unemployed United States officers were, of course, essentially amateurs; what Ismail needed most was actually a trained staff.)

Yohannes had settled the issue of a new *abuna*, and he could ignore, or even support, Menelik in his advances in the south, neither being a real threat to the other, at least for the moment. But the Egyptians had been a threat to both ever since Tewodros was killed, and Yohannes will have known that Ismail was likely to invade. The attack came in 1875.

This war has been discussed from the Egyptian side in the last chapter. From the Ethiopian side it was somewhat more complicated. In preparation for the attack the Egyptians had begun diplomatic moves almost as soon as the British had withdrawn in 1868. One of their Egyptian agents was J.A.W. Hunzinger, a Swiss who was a commercial agent at Keren in the hills in the disputed northern borderlands. He was appointed by Ismail as governor of Massawa, and then as governor of the Red Sea coasts. He had attempted, in 1873, to contact Menelik in Shoa. The purpose was clearly to ally Egypt with Shoa, presuming that both were hostile to Tigray; then they would jointly attack Emperor Yohannes. This was early in the period after the coronation of Yohannes in 1871, when the relationships of the Tigrayan emperor with the Shoan *negus* were still uncertain. There was in the event no success for Hunzinger's project; no doubt Menelik's French advisers had something to do with that, but Menelik was a king who knew his own mind.

When Ismail sent his forces to invade Ethiopia, in 1875, Hunzinger led another force out of Tadjoura, close to French Obok, aimed directly at Shoa, while the main force, under Arendrup Bey, invaded from Massawa aimed at Yohannes's forces. Both attacks failed, but for different reasons. The Massawa force was destroyed by Yohannes's army in a battle at Gundet on the Mareb River on the northern border of Tigray, having penetrated through the northern area of Ethiopia. (That Ismail sent an army of only 2,500 men on this campaign is a good indication that Egyptian intelligence on Ethiopia and its capabilities was poor, and that recent easy successes had built up Egyptian self-confidence to a dangerous degree.) Hunzinger's force aimed at Shoa was ambushed and destroyed by the Danakil inhabitants of the region between the coast and the Ethiopian highlands, through whose territory he was advancing. It thus failed even to reach Ethiopia, falling victim, like many Italian parties, to the local inhabitants, who objected to their lands being used in such a way. Ismail tried again the next year, with an army under the *sirdar*, with Loring in operational command, this time only from the north but with the much larger army of 13,000 men, and this attack was also defeated, in a battle at al-Jira, having advanced no more than 100 miles from its base at Massawa. The Egyptian *sirdar* then made a peace agreement with Yohannes, but there were plenty of disputed regions and issues, which could be made an excuse if Ismail wished to renew the war – if he ever felt he needed an excuse. The naval blockade remained in place.[13]

The threat from outside was therefore lessened, but Yohannes could not be certain that it would not be renewed. He and Menelik had bickered over their mutual frontier, and each had campaigned to secure parts of the territories between their kingdoms. Yohannes had campaigned to secure Gondar, the traditional imperial centre, and the areas of Begemdar and Gojjam around Lake

Tana; Menelik campaigned to gain control of the Wallo Galla territory to his north, and in particular to secure Magdala as a northern boundary fortress. Menelik's grip on Wallo was much firmer than Yohannes's hold on his own conquests, where he had accepted the submission of the existing chieftains; Menelik had imposed a major garrison in Wallo.

Both rulers therefore succeeded in securing extensions to their kingdoms, but then, in 1875, they clashed when Yohannes attacked Shoa. It was no doubt this quarrel that encouraged Ismail, and in particular Hunzinger, in the campaigns later in 1875, and then in 1876. But the Egyptian threat was clear to both Yohannes and Menelik. They had both seen the establishment the year before of Egyptian power that was evidently aimed at surrounding Ethiopia. Rather than solve their dispute by allying with the outsider (as the outsiders hoped and aimed for), the two rulers agreed to a peace in which Menelik accepted a subordinate position to Yohannes and agreed to pay him tribute. They continued to bicker for the next ten or more years, but most of the time each left the other free to govern at home and extend their territories.

A serious dispute came in 1877, when Menelik invaded Gojjam. He had already seized control of Wallo (including Magdala); his aim in Gojjam, which had been brought under Yohannes's control earlier, is not clear. It seemed at the time that he was aiming to gain control of Gondar, the old imperial capital, and perhaps have himself proclaimed as *negusa nagast* there. As it happened, he had chosen a time when the pressures on Yohannes from Egypt were much reduced. The Khedive Ismail had sent part of his forces to assist the Ottoman sultan in the Russo-Turkish War in the Balkans, which began in 1876 (and he had been compelled to withdraw from Kismayu the year before). This allowed Yohannes to campaign in safety southwards against Menelik, and Yohannes now had a much larger and very efficient army. He penetrated through Wallo and into Shoa's northernmost province of Manz before Menelik, who was facing imminent defeat, and whose people were rushing to take refuge in their fortresses and on mountain tops, asked for negotiations.

Both rulers had good reasons for making a new peace agreement, one that was more definitive than before. Menelik needed to do so because he faced only defeat if he fought on, and possible deposition; Yohannes needed peace, a definitive peace, with Shoa, because the pressure from the north would soon revive since the Russo-Turkish War was likely to end soon, allowing Ismail to turn his attention again to Ethiopia. The Tigray-Shoa war thus ended in another compromise. Menelik agreed to his subordinate status once more, and Yohannes accepted Menelik as the hereditary ruler of Shoa, and crowned him as *negus* in a public ceremony, which effectively recognised him as an independent ruler.

The Egyptian animosity was not restricted to military action. The Egyptian fleet still, largely ineffectively, had been blockading many of the ports used by Ethiopian trade. Massawa, for example, was closed to Ethiopian merchants because it was under Egyptian occupation, and neither Egypt nor Ethiopia had agreed to make peace – the *sirdar*'s agreement with Yohannes had simply been a disengagement of their forces.

The Egyptian occupation of Zeila and Berbera on the Somali coast, and of Harar inland (by Muhammad Rauf's expedition), blocked Shoa's main outlets to the sea. But there were two other ports that could be used – French Obok and perhaps Italian Assab. Menelik in particular was very anxious to continue purchasing further weapons, and usually it was French merchants who could supply them, operating through Obok. The weapons they were selling were not usually the very latest in guns; instead, they were weapons discarded when European armies rearmed with the latest versions. Enough, however, were acquired to enable Menelik to field a powerful force with which he could defeat his neighbours to the south of Shoa, and subdue the several Galla communities along his frontier. This success, of course, drew his attention away from Yohannes, and at the same time built up his military forces and expanded his territory. And as will be seen, the Egyptian blockade ceased to be effective from 1882.

The period since the destruction of Tewodros's attempt to unite the Ethiopian sections into a renewed united empire had therefore seen the emergence of two predominant Ethiopian powers, Tigray under Yohannes, Shoa under Menelik; further, though they argued and disputed, these two had enough to preoccupy them each elsewhere to keep them from actually fighting each other too seriously – and perhaps both were conscious of the threats they both faced. In effect, Tewodros's project had come close to achievement by the activities of his enemies and successors.

Chapter 7

Egypt: The Limits of Empire

The Egyptian Empire was essentially the lands through which the river Nile flows. Of the lands that the khedives took over, only the Sudan, south of Egypt, remained under Egyptian control for more than a few years: Greece, Syria, Arabia, and the Red Sea coasts were all merely temporary conquests, and in none did Egyptian control last more than ten years. But the empire defined by the Nile Valley, from Alexandria to Lake Victoria, was still growing when the whole imperial structure collapsed. In the 1870s, Darfur and the Red Sea coast were added, and attempts were made on Ethiopia and Somalia, and into the Great Lakes region, but none of these ventures lasted for long.

The river provided the obvious route for conquest but its course was not understood at first. For a long time it was unclear where its source or sources were. The inhabitants of Egypt treated it as a force of nature, and had long adapted their agricultural system to its regime of flood and fall, and came to depend entirely on that regime, which replenished their soils with rich deposits every year, so that Egypt was reported to be a wealthy country, despite being mainly desert and populated by peasants living in poverty. One result of the country's total dependency on the river was that a single 'low Nile' season brought famine to the whole country.

It was necessary to gain access to the Sudan and country beyond – Ethiopia, South Sudan, the Great Lakes region – in order to disentangle the nature of the river's course, though this was hardly the main purpose of the conquest. The Blue Nile seemed for a time to be the main source, and it was clear that the floodwaters came from there, although it took time to be understood that it was the monsoon climate of the Ethiopian Highlands that was the source of that regime. In the 1770s, James Bruce described for Europeans that the source was in Lake Tana; he was, of course, for long disbelieved, but in general terms the Ethiopian origin of the flood seems to have been long understood in the Nile Valley, if only because it was the Blue Nile that produced the floodwaters. But the Blue Nile proved to be no more than an equal tributary with the White Nile; when the confluence of the waters at (the future) Khartoum was visible, it was seen that the two rivers, White and Blue, were equal, but had different regimes – and from Khartoum, where they joined, their waters remain visibly separate for some distance before mixing into one flow.

The search was therefore on, for those who thought the source of the river important, to locate the White Nile's origin. This was, above all, one of the obsessions of nineteenth-century European scholars, explorers and theorists. It was a search hindered by the Sudd vegetation, a barrier to navigation – 'Sudd' means 'barrier' – but also by conflicts in the lands through which the river flowed, and by the river's separation into distributaries in the Sudd. This was, apart from everything else, an inland delta system, with several rivers branching and rejoining, and by the existence of large tributaries joining the main stream, such as the Bahr el-Ghazal. Salim Qapudan, the Egyptian explorer of the White Nile, was the first to sail into what became the Equatoria province along 800 miles of the unknown section of the river, though he is never credited in any discussion of the exploration of Africa, which is too easily considered as an almost exclusively European enterprise.[1] He explored the river, and the Sudd, and eventually reached a part of the river's course where a series of rapids blocked any further access southwards along the White Nile, and which therefore evidently flowed from East Africa – meaning those Great Lakes that were 'explored' or 'discovered' by expeditions from the Congo basin and from the Zanzibari coast.[2]

The Sudd was a region where the predominant vegetation was the water hyacinth, which was often a floating plant, and which could collect into great rafts of linked plants. These occasionally joined together, and the vegetable rafts were often seeded with papyri. Once joined, the great rafts could hold together for years, forming huge hindrances to navigation. The plants provided food for a large population of hippopotami; crocodiles were another major inhabitant; both of these could be hostile to men, and both were particularly liable to attack boats, no doubt regarding them as competitors. The quantity of insects in the region was astonishing.

The Sudd had been traversed by Salim, but it remained a major barrier, impassable when the plants joined in the great vegetation rafts, so that most traffic did not attempt to penetrate it, and Fashoda was often the terminus of a river voyage. The first of Salim Qapudan's voyages was blocked by the vegetation, and as late as the 1960s, when Arnold Toynbee sailed on a houseboat through the Sudd he was held up for several hours by one of these rafts, despite previous operations to open the waterways. It took two days for the boat to get through this *barrier*, which is a precise and accurate description of this part of the river.[3] In 1897–8, the Marchand expedition took nearly a year to get through.

After Salim Qapudan's successful second voyage it was another forty years before new explorers, Speke and Baker notably, sorted out the various channels, lakes and sources between the Great Lakes and Equatoria, and determined where the Nile had its ultimate source. It is hardly surprising that such a great and complex river proved to have more than one source in Central Africa, just as at Khartoum it clearly had two main sources, the White and the Blue, more or less equal tributaries, and that its course should be so varied, with cataracts, rapids, lakes, waterfalls, Sudd barrier, and all.

By flowing through a series of lakes – Victoria, Albert, Edward, Kyoga – which helped to regulate its flow, it was clear that nature had produced the same sort of barrage system on the White Nile that later was constructed artificially at Aswan in Egypt to do the same task, and there to eliminate the flood regime for Egypt and provide instead a constant and dependable flow. The White Nile was thus a river with a regular and predictable flow, whereas the Blue Nile produced a flood almost every year. This condition in the White Nile's source area produced in some imperialistic minds the possibility of 'controlling' that source of the river, and so if the source could be controlled this could be translated into political control of the lands downstream, presumably by some sort of blackmail. The concept was woolly, since the regime of the White Nile was barely understood, but the late nineteenth century was rife with imaginative imperialist schemes.[4]

It is odd that the Nile should have provoked such ideas, where no similar thoughts of controlling the sources of the Rhine or the Danube or the Mississippi or the Amazon had developed; it seems to have been a product of the imperialist impulse combined with the Industrial Revolution's exultation at the possibilities of engineering, together with the river's course through a desert land, which might be used to impose starvation downriver. Of course, in the end, familiarity with the river made it obvious that such a wide-ranging plan was physically impossible. Since 'control' of the river implied the ability to prevent it from flowing north, the sheer size of the river would tend to preclude that. But the whole notion stimulated attempts at exploration and drove forward schemes to gain political control over Central Africa.[5] The land between the Sudd and the Great Lakes became one of imperial competition.

So the idea of controlling the Nile existed, and was one of the motives behind the pressure in the 1870s and 1880s to explore and seize the lands that became the Egyptian province of Equatoria, and was a spur to reaching the Great Lakes region and gaining political control in that region. The approach had been pioneered by the advances of the Egyptian explorers and slaving companies, but it also attracted men coming from the Congo basin and from East Africa: Belgians, British and Germans were involved, as well as Egyptians, Ethiopians and East Africans. In the process the most unanticipated discovery – at least by Europeans – was the well-organised system of states west of Lake Victoria, which Baker had bumped into in the 1870s and which Gordon contacted – Bunyoro,

Buganda, Toro, Rwanda, Burundi, and others. It was, therefore, the expansion of the Egyptian Empire southwards that was the stimulus for the imperial encroachment into the Upper Nile area and East Africa. The expansion of the Ethiopian Empire, and the greed of King Leopold of the Belgians, together with, more distantly, the approach of the French from West Africa, were all of them sources of active involvement in the area between 1870 and 1900.

In 1870–2, Sir Samuel Baker, as governor of the Equatoria province, made contact with the kingdom of Bunyoro. Its king, Kabalega (1869–99), rebuffed his attempt to make Bunyoro a protectorate (presumably of Egypt).[6] And Bunyoro was by no means the most powerful of these states.

Baker was a tough and energetic man, but not much of an administrator or diplomat. He spent his time as governor exploring the gap in geographical knowledge south of Equatoria in order to link the Egyptian lands there with the Great Lakes region, an extension of his exploratory work earlier. He became entangled in the conflict with the slave traders, the suppression of which, to be sure, was part of his remit as governor, but he tended to stir up disorder rather than solve the problems, and he did not stay in office long enough to have a serious effect on the trade in slaves, which was more deeply rooted than he seems to have realised.

Baker noted the hostility between Bunyoro and Buganda, and attempted to use this to secure control of both. He failed, but his reports, and those of his competitors, drew attention to the existence of these kingdoms, which were exercising some power in the area. In the usual way, the competition between them was another reason for the region as a whole to be vulnerable to imperial interference and manipulation.

Baker's successor as governor, after a year or so, was General Charles Gordon, recruited by Nubar Pasha, a high Egyptian politician, at an embassy party in Constantinople. It took Gordon a year to take up his post, and when he did so, he pursued a similar course to that taken by Baker. He moved south along the upper White Nile to attempt to establish Egyptian authority in the Great Lakes kingdoms, and spent much of the rest of his time marching about combatting the slavers. He attempted to intervene in the affairs of the kingdoms, and established a number of his men in posts in Buganda. He planted another series of posts along the river north of Buganda, and so partly opening it up to traffic – but there were five rapids and two major waterfalls between Gondokoro and Lake Victoria, so it would take more than a brief foray and a few posts to have any serious effect. He eventually withdrew the posts he had placed in Buganda, and in effect abandoned the attempt to extend the Egyptian Empire into Central Africa.[7] He must have known that one of the primary objects in Cairo for gaining control of Central Africa was to gain access to a population that could be raided for slaves; perhaps Gordon finally perceived that he was inadvertently making himself an accomplice in the extension of the trade he was supposed to be acting to destroy.

Anti-slavery had become official Egyptian policy by this time, partly under the pressure of the European states, particularly Britain, but just as much because it had become understood that free labour that was paid regular, if not necessarily generous, wages was more effective than slaves, whose labour was thought costless, but wasn't, and was certainly always inefficient. Khedivian estates in Egypt were still nevertheless being operated by slave labour, and slavery continued in use in Sudan. It was the continuation of slavery that provided the market for the slave traders, and only the ending of the practice of employing slaves would end the trade; it had taken the British at home a full generation, between 1807 and 1838, to understand that and legislate to abolish the practice; one could hardly expect the Egyptians and Sudanese to learn the lesson more quickly, especially when slavery was embedded so much more deeply in their societies, and was not something as distant as across the Atlantic in the Caribbean. Its abolition would be enormously disruptive to both countries; permitting it to fade away would certainly be preferable, and fitted best into British colonial bureaucratic attitudes.[8]

The depopulation and devastation left by the slave raids and the violence of the slave traders in the southernmost provinces of Egyptian Sudan produced an unproductive territory. All in all, Gordon may have felt that he was accomplishing something, but he was so busy with his exploring and anti-slavery campaigns that the ordinary administration was neglected. He was very liable to shoot off in pursuit of a new task, leaving other tasks half finished.

The aftermath of the conquest and the military campaigns against the slave traders should have been a period of quiet recovery, not of more frantic activity. Gordon was, after all, a Royal Engineer officer and campaigning soldier, not an administrator – and Baker had been lacking in administrative skills as well. Gordon collected a large staff, officials, soldiers, and others, but the poverty to which the region had been reduced could hardly support the numbers he recruited. After two years, exhausted, Gordon resigned and left for Britain. Again, like Baker, his tenure of office was partly misdirected, and was far too brief to have any permanent effects in the anti-slavery policy.

By this time, the Khedive Ismail was enmeshed in the financial crisis that eventually brought him down (to be discussed later in this chapter). In 1877, he reappointed Gordon to the Sudan, having apparently been impressed by his energy, if not his achievements. This time he was governor general of the whole region, but, when the financial crisis demanded peace, economic development and financial retrenchment, Gordon spent his time as governor general pursuing the same policies as he had in Equatoria. (One of his successors in Equatoria, the German Emin Pasha, was to prove a more effective governor, above all because he was a competent linguist, knew Arabic, and could speak to the people and be understood; he even learnt some of the African languages.)[9] Gordon concentrated on the elimination of the slave traders; in part, this was because he was expected to do this by the British government, whereas it was only one of the items in his instructions from Ismail. It seems clear that he had acquired a conflict of loyalties; on the one hand, he admired Ismail, who was in many ways an admirable man and ruler; on the other hand, he was a British subject, always remained so, and was thereby vulnerable to British expectations, and even instructions, which bypassed the Egyptian government, his official employers.

It is clear that administration was not his strong suit, nor was the selection of subordinates, who were often placed in unsuitable posts, and too often moved about or abruptly dismissed. He does not seem to have understood that it took time for an official to work himself into a post and understand what it required of him. His period as governor general was no more a success than his earlier stint in Equatoria. Inevitably, however, amongst the frequent appointments and dismissals he did have some successes, though too many able men failed to rise to Gordon's own hopes – not always clearly articulated – and were moved on or removed after only a short time.[10]

In the end, Gordon resigned his post in 1880 in sympathy with the forced abdication of Khedive Ismail, who had appointed him, and whom he admired – and possibly seizing that as his excuse to leave at that point. It cannot be said that either man had been successful as a ruler, but at least Ismail was consistent in his work; one could hardly say that of Gordon, except in the intermittent pursuit of the slave traders. In Bahr el-Ghazal he employed Romolo Gessi to suppress the slave traders, which required repeated campaigns to destroy their *zeribas*, but this left the province in a devastated condition, and its effect on the slave traders was not to suppress them, nor stop them from pursuing their avocation, but to drive them out; in practice, the traders and the slave hunters simply went elsewhere, and were liable to return to their old territories when the armies had moved on. That part of the population of the Bahr el-Ghazal province that had survived emerged from hiding when it was, or seemed, safe, and began to reclaim their lands and restart their lives, though they were inevitably distrustful of strangers and much reduced in numbers. And the slave traders themselves had only been driven away, not eliminated. Some of them went on to destroy the society of the Azande, south-west of Equatoria. Rabeh, who had been one of al-Zubayr's slaves, emerged to take over command of a section of his forces. He was able to go on further raids against societies to the west, in a freebooting career lasting twenty years; he eventually ruled his own kingdom, in a rough and ready way, a state occupying a territory between Wadai and Bornu, both of which he damaged in the process. Pushing the problem into another area was hardly a solution.

Ismail had, as noted, encouraged the development of modern infrastructure communications in Sudan, railways and the telegraph system, steamboats on the Nile, while sea communications along the Red Sea were left to private enterprise, with Suakin used as the main port, though it was a difficult harbour. Soon after the conquest of Darfur, for example, the telegraph was strung first to connect Kordofan with Khartoum, and then a start was made to extend the line to el-Fasher, the Darfur government centre, though it had not reached so far in Gordon's time. Khartoum was also connected to Cairo by a line that had taken six years to set up (1864 to 1870); this was ready in time for Gordon to use it to send a series of contradictory messages to the government in Cairo, to the puzzlement of the ministers there. A separate line linked Suakin with Kassala, set up with some difficulty by the local provincial governor of the Taka area – the Beja nomads stole the wire, and took the poles for firewood – that line was then linked to the Khartoum station. Gordon was thus the first governor general to be able to communicate by telegraph with his subordinate officers in Darfur, Kassala, Suakin, and so on, and able to report directly to Cairo; equally, of course, Cairo could send him orders more easily.

This was a revolutionary development for the region. When it might have taken a month for a message to go from Khartoum to Cairo in pre-telegraph days (and another month for a reply to be received), now the whole process could take only a few hours. The government in Cairo could hear the fate of the Egyptian Ethiopian expedition, or the successes in Darfur and Kordofan, almost as soon as they were completed. And the governors of provinces could be controlled much more closely than before.[11]

Railways were much more difficult to construct. Egypt had 1,000 miles of track by Ismail's reign, but this did not extend into Sudan. Some progress had been made in the 1860s with a line along the Nile, which had reached Wadi Halfa by 1875, so passing two of the cataracts. Several alternative possibilities for new lines were aired during the previous decade also. Gordon, an engineer by training, and perhaps by instinct, recommended the construction of a series of tramways around each of the cataracts, while riverboats would operate between cataracts in the navigable parts of the river. This suggestion was not generally liked, in part because it meant repeated loading and unloading of cargoes. An alternative suggestion was for a line from Suakin to Berber on the Nile, which would link the navigable Red Sea with the navigable section of the White and Blue Niles (Berber was just south of the fifth cataract). The port at Suakin was already being well used, and the route was well known to travellers

– in 1872, Samuel Baker and his wife returned to Egypt that way, rather than along the Nile. The advantage of such a line was that it would be cheaper than constructing a line along the river and/or through the desert. The original proposal had been for just that, a line all the way along the river, and this was in fact the favoured proposal all along, since it would tend to unite Egypt and Sudan, whereas the Suakin line would imply Sudan's separation. There were several reports on progress and prospects during the 1870s, but not much in the way of construction in the absence of a decision, and the heavy cost that would be involved. As a result, the Nile line advanced only 30 miles south from Wadi Halfa, and the Suakin line was not even started. Then the dead hand of the International Commission (to be discussed later) descended on the project and construction was suspended in 1879, still no further south than that short distance beyond – south of – Wadi Halfa.[12]

Gordon's tenure of office as governor general (1877–80) overlapped with the extension of the telegraph and the arguments over the railway. It also overlapped with the growth of the Egyptian Empire to its greatest extent, and then the beginnings of its retraction. The recession of the empire was partly due to its over-extension by sea and by land, and partly due to the restrictive activities of the International Commission. The failure to push on with the Sudan railway, which was obviously a necessity for holding the empire together, was a serious blow. In a sense, this must be counted as one of the several regions and projects that were surrendered in the last years of Ismail's reign; geographically, in 1876 Gordon withdrew the posts he had planted in Buganda. The invasion of Ethiopia in 1875 was a conspicuous failure. Equatoria and Bahr el-Ghazal were held, but were in such a devastated condition after the wars with the slave traders that this could hardly have been the intended result, and the region was scarcely an asset. The greatest acquisition was Darfur, which was retained, but a superficial investigation would demonstrate that its conquest was the work of al-Zubayr's military activity, not that of the Egyptian army – and there was a continuing guerrilla campaign led by the displaced Darfurian dynasty. All this was expensive, as empires always were.

Egypt's attempted expansion along the Somali coast, first from Massawa to Berbera, and then along the Indian Ocean coast to Kismayu, in the same period, was similarly unsuccessful, when the British had supported the sultan of Zanzibar over the question of Kismayu and the neighbouring towns. The Egyptian extension along that coast came in 1874–6, and the Kismayu expedition was abandoned in the latter year. At much the same time, Gordon in Equatoria was suggesting the development of a route of communication for Egyptians from Central Africa to the Somali coast at Kismayu, which had been seized in 1874. It was intended by the naval commander, McKillop, that a force sent by

Gordon from the Equatoria province would meet the navy there, but this did not happen, and the British scotched the project even as it began.[13] This was another imperialist scheme that never got started; it was also impractical from the beginning, at least with the technology of the time. Not only did the Egyptians withdraw from their most extended foray along the Somali Indian Ocean coast, but they were also incapable of advancing further in Central Africa in the face of the determined resistance of the Bunyoro and Buganda kingdoms. Gordon was as decisively rebuffed there as Baker had been; the next governor, Eduard Schnitzer (alias Emin Pasha), successfully negotiated with King Kabalega of Bunyoro, and withdrew the last few Egyptian posts that had been placed in Buganda by Gordon. Both on the Somali coast and in Central Africa, the Egyptian reach had been too far.

These retractions were not necessarily the beginning of a decisive decline; it could have been a matter of calculation and in preparation for a further advance. But one of the reasons the Egyptian government began to withdraw from its most extended ventures was that the Khedive Ismail's extravagance had finally brought him to a financial crisis from which he could not escape. The count against him was formidable. He had enlarged and re-equipped his army, always an expensive undertaking. He had expanded his empire, always a costly business, from which returns were slow to appear. He had waged a costly war against Ethiopia without success, in the process losing several thousands of men and their equipment. He had agreed to the installation of the Sudan railway, whose cost was enlarging by the day.

Perhaps the most costly of his investments, however, was that he had employed large numbers of Europeans. There were perhaps 100,000 Europeans in Egypt and Sudan during his reign, and while not all of these men were employed by the Egyptian government, many of them were, and many of them were corrupt, all were greedy, and all those whom Ismail employed were routinely paid more than the equivalent Egyptians; Gordon in the south was especially thought to have favoured Europeans over Egyptians.[14]

The finance for much of this had been borrowed from European bankers and financiers at increasingly exorbitant rates of interest, and discounts and charges had substantially decreased the expected product. The financiers eventually realised that Ismail had overreached himself in this area, as he had in his empire, and that the financial system in Egypt was about to be overwhelmed with government debt.[15]

In the quarter-century after the death of Muhammad Ali (i.e., 1849–75), substantial developments had taken place, in Egypt particularly, if less so in Sudan. It was based, of course, on Muhammad Ali's own work, though he seems to have kept a firmer grip on his treasury than Ismail, who was much more carelessly spendthrift. The population had continued to grow in that period (by 14 per cent), as had agricultural production (by 35 per cent); trade had expanded, imports had grown from £2m to £6.5m annually, and exports from £4.5m to £14m annually, all of which should have ensured that the khedivial treasury was in a healthy condition. Infrastructure had been, or was being, built and expanded: 1,000 miles of railway, 8,000 miles of irrigation canals to expand the land devoted to agriculture, 5,000 miles of telegraph lines; all this had been built or installed; and there was the Suez Canal, modern harbours at Alexandria and Port Said, and the new towns along the canal.[16] Much of this, however, was financed by those foreign bankers who provided the loans to the Egyptian government. By 1876, these loans amounted to £100m, on which the annual interest payment was at least £5m and probably more. This had to be financed out of taxation, paid above all by the Egyptian peasantry, whose treatment by the tax collectors could be brutal, and consequently their readiness to pay grew ever less. So not only was Ismail's treasury in hock to the bankers, the population on whose work he relied was becoming increasingly hostile to the khedivian regime.

Ismail's extravagant ways of raising money were similar to his imperial expansion. Expansion, in or against the Red Sea lands, Ethiopia, Equatoria, Darfur, Buganda and the Great Lakes region, had all been undertaken at the same time as building up his telegraph network, and funding the Sudan railway (though the Egyptian Treasury tried to insist that Sudan pay for that). We may call it the Suez Canal syndrome, where the results of the successful completion of one project leads on to an extravagant process of expanding everywhere else on the assumption that other projects will be financially successful as well. Ismail financed these enterprises by accepting loans at increasingly expensive interest rates, and this included selling his allocation of the Suez Canal Company shares to the British government. This raised £4m (less than a year's interest charges), but two years later he found it was almost impossible to raise any more European finance at any price; the financiers were no longer willing to provide further loans.[17]

Between 1876 and 1879, repeated attempts were made to sort out Ismail's and Egypt's finances, all of which would involve extravagant claims on the Egyptian Treasury and increasing pressure on the Egyptian taxpayers, and none of which proved to be satisfactory. Ismail's last ploy, in 1878, was to appoint two Europeans – a Frenchman, Ernest de Blignières, as Minister of Public Works, and a Briton, Charles Rivers Wilson, as Minister of Finance – the assumption being that they would bring much-needed financial expertise to their task, and would receive the blame from those who suffered from their measures.

But their task was actually to pay Egypt's European creditors, not to sort out the situation in Egypt, and they were as much representatives of their home governments as they were Egyptian ministers of Ismail. Despite being appointed by the khedive, therefore, they were not responsible to him. The system was, in fact, a form of imperialism.

The measures taken by this 'international government' quickly angered a whole series of the most influential sections of the Egyptian population. The imposition of economy in expenditure included a reduction in the roster of army officers, and in the numbers of officials of the civic administration, many of both being dismissed, but they did not receive their due back pay. A large group of landowners were angered by the arbitrary alteration of the rules of a loan they had made to the government some time before; the change reduced their income drastically. Resentment at the fact that the two European ministers were Christians developed quickly, the assumption being they were therefore instinctively hostile to a Muslim country, which their measures clearly did not refute; and Nubar Pasha, an Armenian Christian (who had hired the Evangelical Christian General Gordon to govern Sudan), was quickly sacrificed by Ismail and forced to resign. The new European ministers' refusal to conform to Egyptian customs, such as wearing official dress, provoked considerable anger, and were taken to be the outward sign of their priorities (Europeans over Egyptians), quite likely correctly.[18]

It seems highly unlikely that the Europeans appointed as Egyptian ministers rarely understood the damage they were doing to Egypt and the khedivial regime by their narrow-minded financial measures. And, of course, the key man they were angering was Ismail. Complaints by his subjects to the khedive only produced the answer that the ministers were those who were responsible. Ismail was thus abdicating responsibility, and therefore he was blaming the ministers' home governments, and the bondholders; but this deflection of blame was also partly a ploy to prepare the ground for his own measures. Eventually, after a popular demonstration – which had actually been organised by Ismail himself – he dismissed the two ministers, saying they were too unpopular (which was no doubt true enough).[19] This amounted to Ismail's own resumption of control of the country's finances. And yet Ismail had apparently no idea what to do to get out of the financial fix he was in. It seems clear from what he did next that he intended to evade the problem, just as he was trying to evade the blame.

The pressure on Ismail now came from the governments in London and Paris, who had to proceed carefully, to avoid upsetting the whole system. But then Chancellor Bismarck in Germany intervened. He had not shown any interest in the issue earlier, but now he threatened to take steps himself to deal with the loan crisis, but without specifying what he intended. He had been prompted to do this by the Rothschilds, one of the major bondholders, who had heard that it was intended to cease paying interest on one of the loans they were involved in. Bismarck had also quickly grasped that the issue would be a most useful way of sowing discord between Britain and France. He always feared the conclusion of any agreement between these two which would endanger the settlement he had imposed on France after the Franco-Prussian War; keeping Britain and France arguing over financial and colonial matters was a perfect way to protect his achievement from any joint action on their part.[20]

The British and French, in order to prevent this German intervention, now turned against Ismail when he dismissed the European ministers and urged him to abdicate in favour of his son Taufiq, who was believed to be much more manipulable;[21] Ismail, who could only be deposed by the sultan in Constantinople, refused to abdicate, and reacted by spending plenty of money in bribing various people in Constantinople to prevent his deposition.[22] He repudiated some of the earlier financial measures that had been taken by the dismissed ministers, and reversed the reduction in the army, aiming to increase the establishment to 60,000 men.[23] This was effectively a cancellation of many of the earlier economy measures, and implied a later inability to pay the interest charges. He was gambling that the sultan would not depose him – he had supplied him with Egyptian troops in the recent Russo-Turkish War – and that his army would be sufficient, and sufficiently loyal, to maintain his control over the empire and defend Egypt. It was in effect a royal *coup d'état*, as Lord Cromer later pointed out, bringing his own government back under his own authority once more.[24]

It should have been a popular move, but it did not work, though it was a good try (and could have been seen in Egyptian history as a model of sorts for Colonel Nasser's later 'nationalisation' of the Suez Canal). The Ottoman sultan was persuaded by the British and French, on whom he relied for international support in other areas, such as against Russia in the Balkans. Only a few years before, the British Mediterranean Fleet, together with a French military contingent, had intervened to prevent Constantinople from falling to a Russian conquest. He accepted that Ismail had to go, and perhaps it was the implied threat of an increased Egyptian army that was the final gesture. A possible next move by Ismail might well have been a declaration of Egyptian independence, or even a new invasion of the Ottoman Syrian and Arabian provinces. Ismail's *coup* against the 'international government' could have been his initial move towards formal independence. In June 1879, the sultan's *firman*, his order of deposition, was delivered, and was followed by a second *firman* appointing Taufiq as his successor. Ismail's further measures, whatever he intended, were at once stopped; the sultan had thus mounted his own *coup* to stop Ismail's *coup*.[25]

The new khedive, Taufiq, was, by the method of his accession, rendered no more than a figurehead. The Egyptian government fell into the hands, after a period of negotiation, of an International Commission of Liquidation, which was to deal with the problem of the Egyptian debt. The commissioners were two British, two French, and one each from Italy, Germany and Austria (the inclusion of a German delegate thus achieved Bismarck's disruptive aim). The commission calculated the needs of the Egyptian administration, and the 'surplus' was to be directed towards the payment of the interest to the bondholders. Any increase in revenues was to be directed into a sinking fund to begin the repayment of the debt. The result was that the Egyptian economy was to be wholly subordinated to the debt.[26]

It will have chagrined Ismail to see that the commission was able to systematically reduce the interest payments on the various sorts of debt, and also virtually abolished payments of interest on internal loans; the foreign creditors were thus favoured at the expense, once more, of the Egyptians. The conclusion to be arrived at was that, with proper financial expertise and rather more disinterested advice than the commission had provided (plus more international support), Ismail could have achieved the same result without losing his position. But he had got himself into the financial mess and that meant that no one trusted him to take the required measures to get out of it. His deposition looks very like the result that had been desired by the European bondholders and governments alike; probably nothing Ismail could do would have satisfied them. The necessary expedients to deal with the debt burden clearly existed, but they were only applied when Ismail was out of the way. The installation of Taufiq was the replacement of a strong ruler by a weaker.

The commission, though it was without a clear remit, could be trusted by the creditors – at least those outside Egypt – since it was backed by the commissioners' home governments. In large part, Ismail had been duped by those to whom he had turned for the loans, who had taken excessive fees and discounts for themselves. Having gained such rewards, they were now perfectly satisfied with the new system, even if it promised lower interest payments, since it was under international control and was not therefore going to be able to default, which had always been a possibility they had feared from Ismail's regime.

Not given any serious consideration in this settlement was the possible Egyptian reaction. The British representative on the commission, Major Evelyn Baring (later Lord Cromer) insisted that the burden on Egypt be limited, when the bondholders had wished to squeeze the country for every penny it could be made to produce. But the settlement was as bad for them as the Egyptians can have expected. Where the early 'international government' had angered several groups of Egyptians, their anger had been deferred by Ismail's *coup*, which seemed to put him back in charge. Now this new 'international government' had removed Ismail, and had fixed its grip even more firmly on Egypt. The new khedive was essentially powerless, and could no longer be used as a shield for the foreigners, or for the Egyptians; the anger in Egypt developed once more, and there was now no further means of defusing it.

The financial crisis in Cairo had therefore spread to European capitals, and was about to affect the Egyptian army and the Egyptian Empire, though rather more seriously. There was no real reason for the expansion of the crisis into these areas, however. The financial issue had proved to be relatively easy to solve, though at a serious cost to the Egyptians. But the Egyptian army survived, as did the empire. Yet these three – the population, the army, the empire – were intimately linked, though it seems likely that by focusing on the government debt, those who manipulated Egyptian affairs did not realise it. They were soon to be alerted, and found that they had taken on new financial burdens that they could not charge to their Egyptian account.

The period of the financial crisis, say, 1874 to 1879, was also the period in which the expansion of the Egyptian Empire halted and began to go into reverse – in the Red Sea, in the far south, in Darfur – and so the remainder became vulnerable to internal uprisings and external attacks. Like many other aspects of the general crisis in Egypt at the time, the responsibility of the Europeans, who had so carelessly intervened, was also involved in the future of Egypt's empire. It was one other item, among many, that only became clear to them as time passed.

Chapter 8

Revolutions and Invasions

The deposition of Khedive Ismail in June 1879 simply replaced one khedive with his son, Taufiq, at least in theory. In fact, it did much more, for it replaced the government of the khedives, which had at least a claim to be quasi-Egyptian, with a joint Anglo-French 'Dual Control', that is, government by foreigners. This regime lasted for about eighteen months, a period of increasing unpopularity for the controllers, for the Egyptian government, and for the Khedive Taufiq. As a system, it was confusing to everyone, above all because it was not clear to Egyptians, or to foreigners for that matter, precisely where responsibility lay. The khedive issued decrees and so on, but this was at the behest of the Dual Control, yet these *éminences grises* did not accept responsibility, while the khedive, largely a puppet, could obviously pass the buck. It was a replay of the situation under Ismail.

What was quite clear was that the employment of Europeans increased greatly at the expense of Egyptian officials, who were pushed into unemployment. This was certainly the responsibility of the Dual Control regime, but the Europeans were paid out of Egyptian tax revenues – another piece of the Dual Control failure of responsibility. The process not only put the administration into the hands of Europeans who were generally ignorant of Egyptian processes and customs, but, as before, these Europeans were paid more generously than their Egyptian predecessors or contemporaries. Individual efficiency and effectiveness was not the primary concern to those who made these appointments, or those who were their appointees. At the same time, further economies in the administration were introduced and enforced. In particular, the army strength was to be fixed at 18,000 men, a huge reduction from Ismail's intention to increase the strength to 60,000; this was soon recommended to be further reduced, to 12,000.[1]

Sudan was also directly affected by all this. Gordon resigned as governor general early in 1880, citing his sympathy for Ismail, but he also did not like Taufiq and was weary of Sudan. His stated reasons may actually have been merely excuses, since he must have seen by then that his administration was in a mess, a large part of which was due to him.[2] His replacement was Muhammad Rauf, who had gained a considerable reputation as a subordinate commander (*qaim maqam* or *kaimakam*), under Baker in Equatoria, and as the commander of the brief campaign in 1875 that took control of Zeila and Harar; he had served in Gordon's governor generalship and had been dismissed by him, twice.[3] This last experience did no harm to his reputation, since Gordon's hirings and firings were notably erratic and thoughtless; dismissal by him was usually just a brief interruption and gained sympathy rather than blame; to be dismissed twice by Gordon might be considered a mark of honour.

The replacement of a European (Gordon) with an Egyptian (Muhammad Rauf) as governor general was no doubt approved by the increasingly vocal nationalist groups in Egypt. It is even possible that it was greeted with pleasure by the Sudanese, since Rauf was only half-Egyptian; he was actually a Nubian with an Ethiopian mother.[4] But he was calm and a reasonably efficient administrator, and his character and his instructions both aimed at sorting out the mess Gordon and Gessi and others had left, particularly in the south. He would have been an ideal governor in a period of political calm, and the contrast he made with Gordon would, given time, have had a beneficial effect; it was unfortunate that he came into office just as the storm was approaching.

He did not get much chance to implement his policies, despite his evident good intentions – which have gained him the reputation for being 'weak' amongst the more muscularly minded historians, especially British. Appointed in March 1880, it was not until June that he reached Khartoum. His unwillingness to create even more disturbance after Gordon's hyperactivity led to him being accused, in the contemporary British press, of reversing some of Gordon's anti-slavery policies. That press was in a state of even greater irresponsibility and nationalist uproar than usual. Rauf had the spirit to argue that these accusations were unjust, but this, of course, would carry no more weight in Fleet Street than any other refutation of inaccurate or invented newspaper reports, even if it had been published rather than merely stated in letters and reports. It is interesting, though, that he saw some of these British newspaper attacks while in Khartoum, meaning he was up to date on international affairs to a considerable extent. He was certainly kept in office, despite – or perhaps because of – the press attacks, which were all too clearly based on ignorance and prejudice.[5]

Rauf had been in occupation of his office for only six months when the next calamity arrived. In January 1881, three of the four colonels of the reduced Egyptian army made a major political move. They had seen the army reduced to 18,000 men by order of the new khedive, though it was well understood that in this case he was merely passing on the policy, even the instructions, of the Anglo-French controllers. Then the further reduction was ordered, to 12,000, and the Minister of War, Uthman Rifqi, drafted a new law that would have had the effect of restricting the appointment of officers in the army to the Turks and Circassians, men who were rich enough to attend the military academy; this would cut out the native Egyptians, even those who were already in the army, or who had already been commissioned as officers. Since three of the four colonels who were in command of the army's regiments were of *fellahin* origin, this was, in a time of nationalist agitation, insulting to all the *fellahin*, and even inflammatory to those who might seek their status. That Uthman Rifqi himself was a Circassian made the proposals even worse.

To restrict the ranks of officers to Turks and Circassians was also to hark back to the days of the Mamelukes, who were often recruited from exactly those ethnic groups, and were associates of Uthman Rifqi and his like. (It is evident that Muhammad Ali's clear-out of the Mamelukes had been less than complete.) The three colonels presented a petition arguing against the measure; the response of the Council of Ministers (and the khedive) was to decide to court-martial them, which, apart from being unjust, would no doubt be a rigged trial, and which, politically, looks very much like a response designed ultimately to remove any *fellahin* officers who had already risen through the officer ranks in favour of Turks and Circassians, who would no doubt replace them. Native Egyptians were evidently expected to remain in the lower ranks, presumably as cannon fodder.

The three colonels had expected that some measure such as a court martial would be used against them, and they had left contingency orders with their regiments. Uthman Rifqi, the man who was drafting the new law, commanded the three men involved to meet him at the barracks and there he intended to put them under arrest. Their regiments, when the colonels did not appear at the expected time stated in those contingency orders, marched to the barracks and released them.[6] This, of course, was mutiny.

The senior of the three colonels was Ahmad Urabi, and he now emerged as a major political figure, standing for a nationalist regime as against the foreigners, and an inclusive policy of both *fellahin* and Turks. The colonels, having demonstrated clearly where the army's loyalty lay, forced the replacement of the Minister of War by their own nominee, Mahmud Sami al-Barudi, a successful commander, and a poet. Later, they forced the replacement of Prime Minister Riaz Pasha by the leader of the 'constitutionalists', Sharif Pasha, who had been in that office before Riaz, but had resigned because of the khedive's pro-Turk policies. Now he advocated a parliamentary system, and insisted that the Assembly of Notables (one of Ismail's innovations) be called to discuss matters. The result was a very public demonstration of the drastically weakened position of the khedive.[7]

The movement that had compelled these changes was partly military, but mainly nationalist – the party that gathered under Urabi's leadership was called 'Nationalist'. Sharif Pasha, however, supported the Dual Control system. The Nationalists' activities were directed at first at removing the Circassians from the officer corps, the group that had been intended by Uthman to be established in more or less permanent, even quasi-hereditary, control of the army. The Nationalists were also vociferously anti-foreign, in which, of course, they had considerable justification. By reducing the authority of the khedive, these events also threatened the position of the Dual Control system, which had been installed at the behest of France and Britain.[8]

How much of all this was known or understood in Sudan is unclear, though it is reasonable to suppose that the governors, and the foreigners holding the senior offices, were apprised of events by the reports, by Egyptian messages, by the telegraph, and by letters, and probably understood something of what was happening. Muhammad Rauf's appointment as governor general, which took place in the midst of the crisis, was possibly a mark of the Nationalists' growing importance in Egyptian politics, but one result of the events in Egypt had been the order to further reduce the size of the army, and Rauf was instructed to reduce the expenses of the Sudan government. This he did by disbanding several military formations.[9]

The army in the Sudan was, even after this, still double the size of that in Egypt, at about 35,000 men, but the units were spread from the Ethiopian border to Darfur and from Dongola to Equatoria, and most of the units were in garrisons in potentially restless regions. These troops, moreover, were poorly trained, largely inexperienced in any serious form of warfare, and the officers were generally inattentive to their duties. Corruption was ubiquitous, and included withholding, or confiscating, their soldiers' wages. The garrison stations were unfortified, even on the Ethiopian border, where attacks might be expected.[10]

The reduction of his garrison forces also reduced Rauf's ability to exercise control over the huge province that he ruled (Sudan is the size of several West European states put together). Much of this territory had only recently been conquered, though he did have the advantage of the expanding telegraph network. It did not help, however, that the administration mandated for Sudan was repeatedly altered during his time.

There was also another problem in Sudan that emerged in Rauf's period as governor general. For many years, the reputation of Muhammad Ahmad Abdallah had been growing amongst the Muslims, particularly the poor. He had been born in 1844 at New Dongola in northern Sudan, and his family had moved south to Karari, a little north of Omdurman, and near the confluence of the two Niles, when he was five. His father was a boat-builder, and the growth of prosperity along the Nile rivers clearly gave him a market. For thirty years, from his early teens, Muhammad Ahmad studied with a series of Islamic teachers, becoming highly educated in the Islamic mode, steeped in Islamic doctrine and belief. In 1870, aged 26, with his family, he settled at Aba Island in the White Nile, 150 miles south of Omdurman, where his followers gathered to join what in the western Sahara and West Africa would have been called a *ribat*. He had emerged by 1880 as the head of his *tariqa*, or school of philosophy, when its earlier head died.[11]

This community, gathered principally from nearby rural tribes, lived in an atmosphere of intense religious study and devotion – one might say, indoctrination – with Muhammad Ahmad as its chief, moderator and teacher, his authority growing and his local influence considerable. In troubled times it is not surprising that he developed the conviction that he was called to rescue the faith from contamination, as Christians populated the government of Sudan. He was also repelled by the corruption in government and angered by the continuing misery of the population. This could easily be blamed on Egyptian rule, though there is no real evidence that conditions were significantly worse than before the Egyptian conquest. This conviction of an inner call had happened to holy men of his type numerous times in West Africa, in Sokoto, where a caliphate had developed, in the Futa kingdoms in Senegal (see chapter 1), and a particular version had emerged in Cyrenaica as the Sanusi brotherhood, which had had influence in Sudan for some time. Perhaps more relevant was information about the developments under al-Hajj Umar in the west. His career of conquest happened during Muhammad Ahmad's lifetime, and news of it will have arrived by way of the pilgrims who passed through Sudan on the way to Mecca.

The initial fervour of most of these movements had usually faded with success and the need to devote their attentions to governing – as with the mediaeval Almohads and Almoravids – but the early fervour could be revived under pressure or threat, or with the emergence of a new charismatic teacher. Many of these movements of African Muslims eventually adopted war, as mandated in the Koran, as a means of breaking the grip of earlier powers on their chosen field of activity, and so of extending their beliefs over those who needed to be purified or converted. (Usuman dan Fodio spent thirty years teaching and preaching before calling a *jihad*; al-Hajj Umar was over twenty years travelling and working as a merchant before his rising began; Muhammad Ahmad spent about twenty years in the same condition; the precise timing would depend on local conditions.) Muhammad Ahmad, as his later history shows, was well aware of the processes of the earlier African Muslim developments.

The pattern of these men's careers – preparation over two or three decades, then calling a *jihad*, and then success in war – is so similar that its roots call for investigation. In fact, of course, they were patterning themselves, probably quite consciously, on the life of their prophet, the original Muhammad, whose uprising came in his fiftieth year after a career as a travelling merchant. In each case also there came an event where they were driven out of their home or base – Usuman was forced by King Yunfa of Gobir to evacuate to Gudu, Umar was driven out of Futa Jalon to take refuge in Dinguiraye, the Prophet's expulsion from Mecca to take refuge in Medina had been a political move by the Meccan merchants. Usuman and Umar were expelled because of their teaching, which was disturbing their home societies, and they do seem to have acted in such a provocative way as to earn their expulsion as a reward. They could then claim kinship with the Prophet's experience, his *hijra*; the repetition of the Prophet's experience was their valediction.

The development of the authority of Muhammad Ahmad had taken place during the rule of the Egyptian khedives and their governors general, a period referred to at times as the Turkiyya, since the governors were usually, like the khedives themselves, arrivals from parts of the Ottoman Empire, and were regarded collectively as Turks, whether Albanians or Circassians or others. The community on Aba Island was no doubt known of amongst the governors, and since they were Muslims and appeared quiet, it would be regarded favourably; an Islamic settlement of the sort was not necessarily deemed dangerous – unless the governors were familiar with other instances of insurrections emerging from the *ribats*. Of course, the Aba Island group did represent an alternative source of authority to that of the governors, and some may have seen this as suspicious. The widespread misery in the region, and the heavy taxation system administered by the Turkiyya, encouraged Muhammad Ahmad to think in terms of a cleansing rising to drive out the Egyptian tyranny. Umar had aimed to cleanse the Segu communities, Usuman the Hausas and Fulanis; the Almohads and Almoravids cleansed Morocco and Islamic Spain; none of the *jihads* reached beyond the Islamic lands to convert non-Muslims.

In 1880, shortly after assuming the leadership of his *tariqa*, Muhammad Ahmad went on a tour of Kordofan. He perceived two particular advantages in the condition of affairs there. First of all, politically, the elite of the region was divided. Muhammad Ahmad made contact with one of the political groups, which was in dispute with the group that was in power; he preached to the poor; it is clear that he was already known to them by reputation, probably from messengers he had sent out in advance to explain his purpose. He quickly attracted a considerable crowd, and when he left, he promised to return. It will have been clear to him that he could count on considerable support in the region, both political and popular, and that he could use the political division of the ruling elite to secure that support from a large part of the population. This contact was evidently his purpose. His successful tour appears to have been decisive for his next move.[12]

He was seeking out possible areas of support on the fringes of Sudan. The region of Kordofan was geographically somewhat distant from the central authority in Sudan, located at Khartoum. He had evidently decided that he found in the Kordofani population a useful basis for his intended insurrection. If opposition to him arose, it would no doubt appear from Khartoum, at a distance; from Kordofan, he would have ample warning of it. He was apparently fully aware of the political condition of the Sudan generally under Egyptian rule, and of the potential that existed in the discontent of many parts of the people for his purpose. He was to prove himself a political player of considerable skill in exploiting these conditions.

By March 1881, he judged the time right to announce his mission. He privately informed a group of his associates at Aba that he was the Mahdi, the promised one, who would bring unity and purity to the faith.[13] This was not a sudden decision, an abrupt revelation. He had been convinced of his mission for at least three years, for it had been the cause of the quarrel he had had with his colleague Muhammad al-Sharif, who had warned the governor Muhammad Rauf; but Rauf discounted the warning because of the quarrel, which led to al-Sharif being regarded as a discontented rival. It was obviously an intention long contemplated in Muhammad Ahmad's mind, and so it follows that he had been preparing the ground, both among his own followers and geographically, for years. His visit to Kordofan was aimed at recruiting further political support to be activated once he made his declaration public. His encampment at Aba Island had become his political base, not simply a matter of a comfortable residence and an Islamic school; it was, for example, like Kordofan, safely distant from Khartoum. He had recruited a band of active supporters, the young men of whom had weapons, and he had indoctrinated them with his intentions and established his authority over them.

His announcement as Mahdi was made in two stages, first to his closest followers,[14] who were perhaps expecting it, and then publicly. His colleagues were thus prepared for future action, and Muhammad Ahmad then went again to Kordofan (July and August 1881). There he revealed his new status to another select group of his supporters, preached again with success to the population, then travelled south to the Nuba Hills, where he explained his status to the *makk*, Adam wad Umar, of the Taqali kingdom. This was an autonomous state that, from its natural fortress in the hills, had defied Egyptian attacks in the past. The *makk* (the local term for *malik*, Arabic for 'king') was privately supportive, but publicly neutral, which was quite enough for the Mahdi for the moment.[15]

In this three-month tour the Mahdi was acting once more as a very clever politician and military strategist. He knew how to arouse the population, and at the same time, he could negotiate as an equal with the powerful. He could also, as with the *makk*, be pragmatic. He had become reasonably familiar with Kordofan and its political condition and had evidently sized up the strengths and weaknesses of Taqali, a kingdom that had successfully repelled every invader in the past. If Taqali was hostile, its geographical position on the flank of Kordofan would render it dangerous; it was necessary to, at least, neutralise it at the start.

A considerable number of people by this time knew of the new revelation, and it was presumably reckoned that the secret would soon leak out more widely, though none of those he spoke to on the subject retailed the secret to the governor general or to his officials. Muhammad Ahmad made his public announcement on 29 June 1881 at Aba, and then wrote to a number of notables announcing this.[16] It may be stressed that this was only the announcement of Muhammad Ahmad as the expected one; it was not a summons to *jihad*. His initial purpose at this stage was to withdraw his purified followers from contamination by those who were not his supporters; he was setting up a community of the faithful, as an example, perhaps, for the rest of the population to emulate, in the hope that the change would spread easily. On the other hand, he had clearly understood that such a move – he had already chosen the destination for his withdrawal (his *hijra*) – would be most unpopular with the Egyptian administration. It was, first, the withdrawal of his community out of reach of the tax collectors; it would set up an example beside which the violence and corruption of the administration would be judged and found wanting; he would summon his followers to join him. The government would not tolerate these challenges. Others would move to join the Mahdi's group, and other communities like his would probably emerge to emulate him. He surely expected to be challenged, and when he rejected the secular authority of the governor general as illegitimate, to be attacked.

The news of his public declaration reached the governor general, Muhammad Rauf. He had been warned earlier about the possibility, but since this warning came from the man with whom the Mahdi was known to have quarrelled, Rauf had reasonably concluded that it was worth little attention, being a personal dispute. This reaction argues that Rauf was well informed about both men, their aims and their quarrels; indeed, he had been in correspondence with Muhammad Ahmad earlier, for he had been one of those to whom the new Mahdi wrote announcing his mission. The Mahdi's announcement may therefore not have been much of a surprise to the governor general. But now the news from Aba apparently confirmed that warning, and it had at last become worth his full attention.

The governor general sent an emissary, one of his assistants, Muhammad Abu al-Suud, to investigate, and to summon the Mahdi to Khartoum for investigation. Al-Suud reached Aba on 7 August 1881. Muhammad Ahmad refused to go.[17] Rauf had already consulted the *ulama*, the assembly of religious officials in

Khartoum, who (not surprisingly) decided that the Mahdi was propagating 'false doctrine' – that is, he was a heretic – and they understood that he plainly threatened their own religious authority. Rauf, with this religious backing, now ordered his arrest. He had plenty of justification for this, what with the Mahdi's religious declaration, which implied a rebellion, or at least disturbances, his defiance of the secular summons, and the condemnation by the *ulama*.

The Mahdi had meanwhile issued a call to his followers for *hijra*, which is to say, they should come to join him and so form a pure society separate from the infidels and heretics, with whom he would then set out to establish himself at his chosen destination. His recent journeys in the west had led him to choose that eventual new base. But the report by Abu al-Suud to Muhammad Rauf, and information about the Mahdi and his followers, led the governor general to decide to use force at once. The *ulama* condemnation and al-Suud's report evidently convinced Rauf that persuasion and diplomacy were going to be insufficient. Rauf had enquired of Muhammad Ahmad, after seeing some items of propaganda from him, as to his intentions; the reply is said to have been threatening, promising violence against unbelievers. Exactly when this letter was written is not clear, nor is exactly what it said, but it does not fit before the attack that Rauf sent against Aba in August 1881. Until attacked, Muhammad Ahmad had made no threats, only summonses to the faithful. The letter is best located after the attack, or possibly it was invented somewhat later as an explanation for Rauf's new policy.

Rauf's decision to use force was reached as soon as al-Suud returned to Khartoum; he was not wasting any time. Al-Suud was sent from Khartoum back to Aba with two companies of soldiers, carried in two steamers, to perform the arrest he had failed to make on his own earlier.[18] The Mahdi knew that the likely result of his defiance would be an attack of some sort, and had collected an armed force, roughly equal in numbers to the soldiers, but armed only with spears and swords, not muskets and rifles.[19]

The troops landed at Aba on 12 August, only five days after al-Suud's original visit; he had sailed 300 miles (150 each way) and collected his armed force in that time. This was indeed a rapid response, suggesting that Muhammad Rauf appreciated the danger, and had made preparations even while his emissary was negotiating: the two companies of soldiers were evidently ready in anticipation of Muhammad Ahmad's defiance. Having landed on the island, they attempted a march by night, but the two companies became separated, and were then ambushed separately and in the dark (in which the soldiers' muskets would be less useful than the swords of the defenders). The Mahdists' surprise was successful – the soldiers probably did not expect such a rapid and fierce response to their arrival, nor a night attack. The survivors of the soldiers fled back to the steamers, which took them back to Khartoum.[20] The Mahdi's forces suffered only twelve casualties. The governor general's speedy response and attack had failed, probably because Muhammad al-Suud had tried his night attack. If he had waited until daylight, he would most likely have won his fight and the Mahdi would have been suppressed; this was the essential mistake; the Mahdi was now on his way to fame and success.

Then, next day, with all his followers, the Mahdi set out on his *hijra*, leaving the camp at Aba deserted. Clearly, this had been his intention all along; the attack had not deterred him or changed his plan, but by waiting to defeat the attack he had displayed great confidence in his mission, and, more probably, he had gained time to get away to his chosen new camp.

Muhammad Rauf now organised a bigger contingent of 500 soldiers, which he sent to Kawwa, a short distance north of Aba Island; at the same time, he sent instructions to the governor of Kordofan, ordering him to bring in reinforcements from his own forces. (It is evident that Muhammad Rauf in Khartoum did not have a large force under his own hand; probably also he did not dare reduce the force he left in Khartoum too drastically; in addition, he obviously had no idea that his quarry had moved out.) This was perhaps over-insurance, putting at least 1,000 soldiers against perhaps 250 fully armed men, but it was evidently a sensible reaction to his earlier mistake of underestimating the enemy. Before the two forces could join, the contingent at Kawwa reconnoitred Aba and found that the enemy had left. The troops attempted to follow the fugitives, but heavy rain prevented them from doing so, and the Kordofan contingent was also thwarted.[21]

The Mahdi was headed towards the Nuba Hills, but chose a new camping ground rather to the south of the main set of hills, at Jabal Qadir. This was the location where the Taqali kingdom had successfully fought off earlier attacks; his choice was evidently a result of his visit to the hills earlier, and of his conversation with Makk Adam. It was a chosen refuge that was based on a good understanding of military and political affairs. On the way, he and his forces met and defeated a tribal force led by a local chief. They were welcomed by the chief at Jabal Qadir, again suggesting that this was another pre-arranged move, and they rested there to recover.[22]

The military achievements of the Mahdi's people, even though minor, being little more than two victorious skirmishes, were exactly what was required to convince waverers that the Mahdi was indeed the rightly guided one, favoured by Allah. He did not fail to emphasise that his own forces were inferior to his opponents, which may not have been true in either case, given the accumulation of his followers at Jabal Qadir, but these claims made it evident that he could claim with conviction that Allah was on his side. His activities so far had been deliberately copying the actions and movements of the Prophet Muhammad at the start of his own mission, and this became obvious as well as he went along. His forces came to be called the Ansar, and he renamed Jabal Qadir as Massa, both names taken from the career of the Prophet.

The destination of the flight from Aba, Jabal Qadir, was about 150 miles south-west of the island,[23] and their arrival there brought them within range of the governor of Fashoda, Rashid Bey Ayman, who had been specifically forbidden to attempt anything by Muhammad Rauf. Rauf realised by now that the enemy was more formidable than expected, and that defeats of individual governors would only strengthen the movement. Nevertheless, Ayman mounted an expedition against the arrivals, presumably hoping that a victory would lead to great things for himself. He had been informed that the Mahdists were suffering from sickness – which always spread in this area during the rains – and he assumed that they were therefore especially vulnerable. He brought a force of 400 regular soldiers and 1,000 Shilluk tribesmen as irregulars to the attack, travelling clandestinely to attack by surprise. The Mahdi, however, was fully informed of their approach – he had widespread support among the tribes, and it was a woman of the Kinana tribe who brought the news of the approach of Ayman's forces. Forewarned, therefore, the clandestine approach by the Mahdi's enemy failed (as it had at Aba Island), and on 9 December 1881, Rashid Bey Ayman's force fell into an ambush and was destroyed. A large quantity of arms fell into the Mahdists' hands.[24]

All these defeats – three in a row within six months – were essentially the result of underestimating the determination of the Ansar by the Mahdi's enemies, and not just by Muhammad Rauf. Rauf had certainly done so at first, though then he seems to have veered round to over-estimating their strength. His later attack was intended to be made with a much stronger force, but it was thwarted by the enemy's disappearance. Rashid Bey Ayman certainly also underestimated the enemy. No doubt the Mahdist forces were inspired, but the government forces tended to be careless, repeatedly allowing themselves to be ambushed, implying a lack of intelligence information, failures of command, and a failure to reconnoitre.

Muhammad Ahmad had been able to march to his chosen refuge at Jabal Qadir, which was his Medina, his version of the Prophet's destination in the *hijra*. He faced only a minor intervention by an enemy, and his rising was already being seen as a success, for each victory was proclaimed as one against the odds. To Muslims of all sorts this was fascinating, but also terrifying. Muhammad Rauf's own new caution may have something of the fear of a devout man operating against a god-chosen man. He certainly did not mount another attack – no doubt his 500 men at Kawwa were demoralised and probably afflicted with sickness. Instead, he appealed to Cairo for reinforcements.[25]

The fame of the new Mahdi spread rapidly through Sudan. On the one hand, he had attracted many new followers who arrived to join him at Jabal Qadir. On the other, it inspired risings elsewhere, notably in the Jazira, the fertile land between the two Niles, south of Khartoum, where an insurrection drove the garrison of Sennar to take refuge in the government buildings, and besieged the men there.

With his new, wider responsibilities the Mahdi had to impose a military organisation on his people. He appointed three *khalifas*, 'successors', though in this case it clearly meant military divisional commanders, each of whom commanded a division of the forces who had been gathered. The overall military commander, the 'Commander of the Armies of the Mahdiya', was Muhammad Ahmad's elder brother, also called Muhammad. The three *khalifa*s were Abdallahi al-Taisha, an early supporter from that Baggara tribe of southern Kordofan; Ali wad Helu, and Muhammad al-Sharif (the Mahdi's old opponent). Their contingents were recruited from particular tribes – the Baggara, the Kinana and the Digham, and those of the Jazira and north along the Nile. There was intended to be a fourth *khalifa*, which was offered by the Mahdi to the head of the Sanussiya, Muhammad al-Sanusi, who lived in Libya and who did not attempt an uprising. This offer was refused, and Muhammad Ahmad was described by al-Sanusi, in a letter to the Khedive Ismail, as an 'apostate in religion and a renegade', which seems a clear enough rejection of the Mahdi's pretensions.[26]

The appeal for reinforcements sent by Muhammad Rauf arrived at Cairo in the midst of the continuing political crisis in Egypt originating with the army mutiny. In September 1881 (while the Mahdi was moving towards the Jabal Qadir and defeating the local tribe), the khedivial government in Cairo attempted to disperse the regiments of the colonels whom it had failed to arrest earlier; orders were given to three of the colonels to remove their regiments from the city to various parts of Egypt. The colonels scented a plot against them personally, in which they were undoubtedly correct. On 11 September, the regiments headed by the colonels assembled in Abdin Square, facing the khedive's palace, and Urabi presented to Khedive Taufiq, who came out to meet them, a set of demands – to replace the present ministry with a Nationalist one, and to return the army to an establishment of 18,000 men as had been mandated in the original *firman* from the Sultan in 1841. Taufiq was scared by the sight of the force arrayed against him, and agreed to their demands, but insincerely. A new government of Nationalists was formed by 14 September, and gathered considerable support among the notables, both 'Turk' and *fellah*, in the next month.[27]

In London and Paris, changes of government had also taken place during this prolonged Egyptian crisis. These had brought to power a government under Leon Gambetta in France, which favoured a strong response to the new Egyptian regime, which was seen to be dominated by the Egyptian 'mutineers'; in Britain, the first Gladstone administration had taken office, in which Lord Granville was Foreign Secretary; he made no pretence at understanding the Egyptian situation, which left him essentially at Gambetta's mercy.[28]

The French distaste for the new situation in Cairo was based on the fear that the new government was intent on reducing the powers of the Dual Control system, which guaranteed interest payments to French bondholders. The British response was less forceful than the French, and the latter could take no decisive action without British support. The French premier, Gambetta, concocted a note to be sent to the new Egyptian government in the name of both France and Britain, which was interpreted by the Egyptians, rightly, as interference in their affairs. This inflamed the anti-foreign sentiment that was already held by the government and its supporters. The British government had gone along with the Joint Note, though at first Granville did not believe it was really intended to be inflammatory. The note was delivered on 6 January 1882.[29]

In Egypt, the arrival of the Joint Note precipitated a further stage in the ongoing crisis, while in Sudan the defeat of Rashid Bey Ayman and his army at Jabal Qadir made it clear that the Egyptian position in Sudan had now come under serious threat. For the next year, therefore, the two crises ran in parallel, but remained curiously separate as well. It must certainly have been difficult in Cairo to understand and respond to Sudanese events, which seemed more like minor uprisings than anything serious. Meanwhile, the new government was having to cope with the problems raised by its own army, with the Dual Control system, and with the enmity between the khedive and the Assembly. On top of these issues (and the rising in the Sudan), the threats from Britain and France seemed much more serious and threatening than anything else; in Cairo, these problems seemed to be much more threatening than the minor events in Sudan. They apparently had so much to concern them that a minor fight in the distant Sudan was low in their priorities for discussion or action. It would be difficult to send reinforcements to Sudan in the face of a likely refusal by their soldiers to go – they would inevitably presume that the order was another attempt to divide them from their comrades. The problem in Cairo stymied any possible action everywhere.

The Assembly of Notables was in session in Cairo after the khedive had succumbed to the military's pressure. It was largely composed of Nationalists by this time, and they expressed dislike of the terms of the budget imposed by the Dual Controllers. The Assembly made it clear that they upheld the country's international obligations – that is, the payments of interest to the bondholders – but that they intended to consider and vote on the budget anyway, and to insist on controlling that part of the monies that were not directly already assigned – that is, the surplus that had been intended for a sinking fund. This was the issue on which the Assembly chose to exert pressure on both the khedive and the Dual Control system. To the French, and soon to the British, this looked less like a constitutional problem and more like an assault on the Dual Control system – and there was no doubt that the Egyptians would be happy to be rid of it. The result was a change in the personnel of the ministry, when Mahmud Sami al-Barudi became Prime Minister, and Colonel Ahmad Urabi became Secretary for War, promoted from Undersecretary (3 February 1882).[30]

It was clear to observers and to Egyptians that this was a government in which the military had the whip hand. The Controllers were unable to exert any authority, and had no influence with the new government; de Blignières resigned. (In France, Gambetta had fallen from power in January 1882.) Urabi arranged for the Egyptian army to be refreshed with more recruits, particularly of officers, and all ranks were given an increase in pay. In some areas, however, the soldiers, all too confident in their power, behaved as tyrants and thieves.[31] It was clear that the khedive and even the Assembly were no more in control than were the Dual Controllers. The British and French suggested to the Ottoman sultan that he intervene, but he did not like Taufiq, and to some extent, he sympathised with Urabi, whom he promoted to pasha, and with whom he was in friendly contact.

In Sudan meanwhile, no immediate response to the request for reinforcements had arrived. Eventually, two measures were taken. A new ministry, for Sudan specifically, was set up (21 February 1882), and a month later, Muhammad Rauf was recalled, and replaced by Abd al-Qadir Pasha Hilmi, who became both the minister and then also the next governor general.[32] In the interim, Carl Giegler, who had been Muhammad Rauf's deputy, as he had been Gordon's, acted as temporary governor general. He organised a new, larger force, collected from the garrisons of Khartoum, al-Ubaiyid, and Sennar. They gathered on the White Nile, where Yusuf Asher al-Shallali took command. Al-Shallali had served in Bahr al-Ghazal under Romolo Gessi and so had some experience of war in Sudan, but not against Muslim fanatics; one of his regimental commanders, Colonel Muhammad Bey Sulayman, also had experience of action, this time back in the Mexican War. As soon as permission for the offensive against the uprising arrived from Cairo, they began.

There were in fact three government forces: that under al-Shallali on the White Nile, that coming to join it from al-Ubaiyid; and that commanded by Giegler personally, which was marching along the Blue Nile southwards to deal with the situation at Sennar. They were intending to meet and attack the Mahdi's forces at Jabal Qadir. This was a long march away, and first Giegler had to recover control of Sennar. Giegler's force actually first met and defeated a force of the Sharif Ahmad Taha at the latter's village of Faqir Sharif. Giegler sent an emissary to bring Taha to the ship in which he was travelling, but when the villagers heard that the emissary had actually arrested Taha rather than escorted him to the ship, they turned on him. Giegler then brought up his forces and attacked the village. It is less than clear if the *sharif* was actually a rebel, or if his arrest was simply Giegler's emissary being arrogant.

The Mahdi, however, when he heard of the events at Faqir Sharif, was publicly furious, and railed at his own people that they should get revenge. This rather suggests that the *sharif* was already an ally and that some sort of rebellion in the Blue Nile area had been intended, or perhaps the Mahdi was opportunistically intervening, scenting possible support. Giegler had recruited a band of Shaiqiyah from those who had been settled near Khartoum long ago, and brought up other forces from Khartoum and Kassala. This was enough to drive the insurgents from Sennar, but it had all taken so long that the army commanded by al-Shallali on the White Nile was well on the way to attack Jabal Qadir by the time Sennar was secured.[33] The problem at Sennar was, moreover, only temporarily solved. Giegler's force had to move on, at which point the town was put under siege again by the original attackers. They cut the telegraph wires and settled down to a long blockade.[34]

Al-Shalali's main force on the White Nile and the al-Ubaiyid contingent did finally link up and jointly marched to attack the Mahdi's base at Jabal Qadir. After a difficult and exhausting march, they camped close under the mountain. At dawn the next day (30 May 1882), they were awakened by the screams of the attackers. A *zeriba* of thorn bushes had been erected to defend the camp, but possibly because of the troops' weariness, it had not been well done, and anyway, the hyped-up attackers simply charged through it. The government force was overwhelmed. Some men escaped through the rear of the *zeriba* only to be hunted down and killed by the pursuers. Those inside the *zeriba* were generally killed in the fighting.

The discrepancy between casualties demonstrates the result – the Mahdists had about 200 killed; the government army was totally destroyed. The exact numbers involved on either side are unclear, but al-Shallali's force was between 4,000 and 6,000 inside the *zeriba*, and most of them, including the commanders, were killed. The Mahdi is said to have put an army of 8,000 men into the attack; a year before, he had commanded only 350.[35]

Both of these fights took place in May 1882, Giegler's victory over Taha at Abu Haraz on 7 May, and that at Jabal Qadir on 30 May. In Egypt at the same time, matters were slowly moving towards conflict. The British and French sent a joint squadron of naval ships into the area, which anchored at Suda Bay in Crete, and then each sent a battleship and two gunboats to lie off Alexandria, where they arrived on 19 May. The two admirals, however, had diverging instructions. The French admiral's instructions were that he should give support to the khedive, but only fight if attacked, and what support he was to provide for the khedive was not specified – presumably moral, since direct military support was excluded. The British Admiral Sir Beauchamp Seymour was likewise to support the khedive's authority, but he was also to look to the protection of the European residents, and he could land armed sailors if necessary.[36]

The political position in Cairo became steadily more confused. Eventually, on 26 May, Prime Minister al-Barudi resigned, and after that, no new government could be formed. Taufiq attempted to find a new prime minister, but then took over the sole authority to himself; the presence of the battleships, therefore, made it appear that the Europeans were supporting Taufiq in an attempt to restore the old despotic khedivial rule. Rumours and mistaken information made the situation still worse, compounded by Taufiq's inability to exercise any real control. He also feared that the sultan would depose him in favour of his great uncle, Halim; this was certainly the intention in Constantinople, and it was quite in accord with the Ottoman Law of succession. Two Turkish diplomats were actually sent, with instructions that one of them was to contract Urabi, while the senior man should negotiate with Taufiq, though this was hardly a decisive intervention.

Urabi had been reinstalled as Minister of War, by request of a delegation from the Assembly of Notables, and Taufiq made him responsible for public order, a reasonable decision since Urabi had effective control of the army, which was the only force available for such a task. But before the Turks or the khedive or Urabi could reach any sort of conclusion on a way forward, Alexandria exploded in riots.

Chapter 9

The Destruction of the Egyptian Empire: I – Egypt

The riot on 11 June 1882 in Alexandria, which set off a much wider international crisis, began with a quarrel between a drunken Maltese and an Egyptian donkey boy, which ended in the boy's death.[1] Under normal conditions, such a quarrel and its result would scarcely be noted except in a police report and possibly in the courts. By June, however, Alexandria (and Egypt) was not in a normal state. For a start, the two battleships, HMS *Invincible* and the French *La Galissonnière*, had been lying off the port for the past month, each attended by two armed gunboats, their mere presence being a manifest threat to the city. The British Admiral Sir Beauchamp Seymour had instructions to protect European civilians, a standard inclusion in British colonial naval warfare instructions, and this implied his right to employ force; the French Admiral Conrad's instructions did not permit him to use force, a crucial difference.

Alexandria was effectively a new city, having revived from its long slow decline during the Mameluke period with the increase of Egypt's overseas trade in recent decades. Its harbour was hospitable to all ships, and it was the obvious port for trade with Egypt. Its inhabitants, as a result, were a wide variety of people of varied ethnic origins, British, French, German, Greek, Maltese, Italian, Turks, as well as Arabs, Syrians, Sudanese (some of them slaves) and, in an overall minority but the largest single contingent, Egyptians, mainly poor; it was thus the most extreme example of a cosmopolitan Mediterranean city.[2] The Europeans tended to be comparatively wealthy and prone to arrogant behaviour as well as vulgar displays of their wealth. Apart from ethnic tensions and political disputes, there was clearly also a problem of the antagonism between social classes.[3] There were plenty of tensions – social, religious, ethnic, nationalist – in the city; an ethnic or religious killing was hardly unexpected, and, perhaps was not really news at first; the murder of a Muslim boy by a Christian Maltese did, however, encompass several categories of the tensions in the city.

Those tensions in the city, which were echoed in Cairo, and more distantly in the country, had been increased over the previous months by the changes of government in Cairo; Colonel Ahmad Urabi Pasha had been moved in and out of office, a process accompanied by his increasing popularity. The weak Khedive Taufiq was acting essentially at the behest of the British and French, he could be seen to have been rendered virtually powerless, and received barely concealed threats from both British and French officials.[4] In Alexandria, which was separate from and somewhat distant from Cairo, the difficult atmosphere in the city had become intensified. Nationalist politicians and Muslim preachers were busy making inflammatory speeches; Europeans, particularly Greeks and Maltese, whose governments were less able to protect them than those of the Western Europeans, were arming themselves, and preparing for defence. Underlying it all was the constant tension between Muslims and Christians, which only partly overlapped with that between Europeans and Egyptians. The fight between the drunken Maltese (Christian, European) and the (Muslim) Egyptian donkey boy brought out several of these contingencies of cause; with the preceding tension, this brought on the riot.

The riot may be described as anti-European, but the majority of casualties were Egyptian; the generally accepted number of casualties among Europeans is about 50 killed, though claims vary between 40 and 200; the latter figure was clearly too high; they included 3 British sailors on shore leave. The number of Egyptians killed is equally vague, but at least 150 seem to have died, and probably more.

Other similar riots and killings took place in other towns in Egypt but on a much lesser scale.[5] In Alexandria, many of those who felt threatened fled to the civilian ships in the harbour, or to other parts of Egypt; 20,000 were said to have left the city, or were planning to do so. By this time, there were many more than the two battleships and four gunboats present in the harbour – another indication that trouble had been expected; warships of other navies, as well as more British and French ships, had arrived. When the news of the riot reached Urabi in Cairo, he at once sent troops with orders to halt the rioting, then arrived himself, as did the khedive, who moved into the Ras el-Tin palace, which was in a very vulnerable place on a peninsula (the former Pharos Island) between the open sea and the harbour. By 5 pm next day, the Egyptian army had quelled the riot.[6] It had been noticed that the police had not attempted to intervene to stop the rioting, and in some cases had joined in the subsequent looting.

A good deal of energy was subsequently devoted to laying blame for the riot. It was generally believed amongst the Europeans that the violence had been instigated deliberately, and Urabi, as the leading Nationalist politician, was their popular choice as the instigator; alternatively, the khedive could be blamed; this despite both being in Cairo when the riot began and despite their very obvious joint efforts to quell the rioting. Those on the spot could see that it was mainly spontaneous, but the consuls in the city generally took the opportunity to cast the blame on Urabi, whom they had not liked in the first place. The British and French consuls' reports were generally somewhat misleading at this time, written with a subtext in which they were urging intervention, particularly against Urabi. Several politicians, among them Sir Charles Dilke, were at first persuaded that the riot had been instigated from above, but came later to accept that it really had been spontaneous; Cromer later described it as 'the natural outcome of public effervescence',[7] but these opinions only developed later; Urabi received blame at the start, and this preliminary inaccurate accusation stuck.

For the next month, there were talks, conferences, disputes and arguments over what to do. Foreign interference, such as the Dual Control system, had so sapped the khedive's authority that it was now up to the British and French to deal with the problem. The British Cabinet was gradually pushed by its more militant members into a belligerent stance; the French government, much more subject than the British to criticism by its Chamber of Deputies and public, refused to contemplate offensive action; in Alexandria, the Egyptian soldiers were deployed to develop defences, but this largely stopped when Admiral Seymour protested, though the forts and batteries were still manned and some work continued out of British sight and range. The British Cabinet was told that the work continued, but not that this was taking place in forts that did not threaten the ships.[8] Partial, inaccurate and biased information was rife in this crisis, together with the personal agendas of many participants. It is no wonder it produced violence.

Then, on 10 July 1882, Seymour, who now had eight major warships in his command, and several gunboats, sent an ultimatum to the khedive demanding that the fortifications be dismantled, which was evidently a step further than had been originally intended. This had been suggested as a pretext for action already, but so far only informally in London, though the idea may have got through to Seymour; it seems that the admiral did not want to wait for orders but simply interpreted his instructions rather broadly. British admirals were, of course, expected to act on their own initiative in difficult situations, but this was normally in more distant posts that were out of touch with London.

The Egyptian government attempted a compromise, but Seymour rejected anything short of surrender, which was certainly going well beyond his instructions. The consuls of foreign states were warned what was intended by Seymour, and through them their governments, and he presumably expected the consuls to warn their people in the city as well, hence the departure of several thousands of Europeans, who often went elsewhere in Egypt. The ships in the harbour that had received refugees, often non-British vessels, now left, as did most of the other foreign warships.

More importantly, the French ships collected the French consul and his staff, and also sailed away; what happened was to be an entirely British responsibility. Admiral Conrad took up a new anchorage off Port Said, which, with the Suez Canal, the French were most concerned to protect. Seymour was thus left to make his own decisions. It was clear after these maritime movements that he would have no international support for his actions. No one on the British side could say if he had been given contingency instructions about attacking beyond those in his original instructions, so it looks as though he was making a very liberal, indeed aggressive, interpretation of them. As was usually expected of a naval commander in the Royal Navy facing a difficult decision, he had held a council of war with his senior officers, who apparently accepted his plans. On 11 July, having received no 'satisfactory' reply to his ultimatum, as he would have put it, he began to bombard the forts.[9]

The British ships that had been assembled included four ironclad battleships, four 'iron screw ships', which were smaller than the battleships and less well armed but more stable as gun platforms, and four gunboats. The bombardment began at 7 am, but the shooting was neither very accurate nor very effective, largely because the ammunition proved to be defective and erratic; the shooting went on, however, long enough to cause considerable destruction by sheer persistence. Whatever return fire was directed at the ships in reply ceased after a time, not usually because of the destruction wrought by the bombardment, but because the Egyptian soldiers were either driven out of their forts or ran out of ammunition.

Some destruction of the forts, which were, of course, the primary targets, was achieved, but rather less than was assumed at the time. The officers of the Royal Engineers who examined the forts later were clear that they were still fit to fight, had they been manned and supplied. Several of the British ships suffered damage, either from Egyptian return fire, or from the premature explosion of their own shells; all had received numerous hits from the shore batteries.[10] Thirty-three British sailors were killed or wounded; on the Egyptian side the casualties were certainly greater, but the totals were, as usual, wildly uncertain; varying suggestions go from 300 to 2,000 in various British sources – though all these figures were pure guesses, and the higher figures were considerable and unjustifiable exaggerations.

Next day, Urabi, who had been with the khedive in the Ras el-Tin palace (which was damaged), during the bombardment, ordered his troops out of the city to take up a defensive position at Kafr el-Dawar, about 10 miles south-east along the line of the railway and the canal from Alexandria towards Cairo. This was the strategic key along that route, where a relatively small force could block an attack. Clearly, Urabi assumed that the bombardment was the preliminary to an armed invasion, not unreasonably. Instead, Seymour, who did not have any troops on his ships, other than the usual contingents of Royal Marines, did not feel that he had sufficient strength to make an invasion landing, and assumed that the city would be defended. His plan, that is, had not gone beyond the bombardment, an inexcusable omission by him and his staff. At dawn next day, the city was seen to be on fire, and neither the Egyptian army nor the British fleet was prepared to do anything about it, each fearing to fall into an armed trap. The fire was variously blamed on British fire, on Egyptian forces as they withdrew, and on a group of convicts who escaped, or were released, from the local jail. In fact, it may have been a combination of all of these, to which may be added the carelessness (or deliberation) of looters who became active when the Egyptian army withdrew.

A party of sailors and marines did land on the 13th, once Seymour had gained permission to do so from London, primarily to occupy some of the forts, and more were landed in the next days, under the command of Captain Jacky Fisher of HMS *Inflexible*. They gradually took control of the centre of the city and the most prominent buildings there. In addition, a military force from the Mediterranean garrisons was being collected at Cyprus. The commander designate, Major General Sir Archibald Alison, reached that island on the 14th. He commanded two infantry battalions – of the Stafford Regiment and of the King's Royal Rifles – and the 17th Royal Engineers Company; a Royal Marine battalion was added. He moved with this force first to Port Said, and then, when he heard of the situation at Alexandria, he moved them to the city. The seamen and marines on shore, commanded by Captain Fisher, were now relieved by the troops as they arrived. By the 18th, there were nearly 4,000 troops, seamen and marines, in the city, with artillery; a squadron of mounted infantry had been organised (mounted on horses donated by the khedive from his own stable), and this force patrolled towards the Egyptian position at Kafr el-Dawar. There, both sides fortified their positions.[11]

Seymour's decision had been made without any clear authority from London, and without considering what to do beyond bombarding the forts. It is not known what he expected, but he had probably presumed that the bombardment would produce a swift Egyptian surrender. So the key to what happened after the bombardment was that he was improvising, as was the government in London, hence the fire, the delayed landings, and so on. On the British side, of course, all involved conspired to claim success afterwards, but an unoccupied city in flames was not a success. The bombardment was the first move in the war to conquer Egypt (not a term usually used by the shamefaced British) and its improvisatory nature set the pattern for all that followed. The French policy of, in effect, letting the Egyptians sort out their own problems, was much more intelligent.

The khedive had been in his palace in the city during the bombardment. Admiral Seymour had already offered him protection, which had been refused (and the Egyptian soldiers had been authorised to return the British fire), but with the fire raging, looting beginning, and the withdrawal of the Egyptian forces, he had at last accepted the offer. He had lost all support in Egypt by this time, and must have feared for his life, or at least for his throne. On 22 July, now under protection from the British forces, he had decided that their support for him was his only hope of regaining a semblance of authority in Egypt, and he publicly branded Urabi as a rebel. This was to be the legal basis, such as it was, for the British campaign that now began – the object ostensibly being the restoration of the legitimate sovereign; improvisation again. Urabi, on the other hand, had plenty of support in Egypt. Since he was now branded a rebel, so presumably were his supporters, which was most of the army and population of Egypt. Two days before, the British Cabinet had decided to send a full expeditionary force to occupy Alexandria; the news of this, reaching Seymour, and so the khedive, plus the arrival of Alison's forces, was presumably the trigger for the declaration against Urabi. But in Cairo, a 'National Council' composed of Egyptian notables, now met and gave its strong support to Urabi, as did the sultan in Constantinople, who refused to echo the khedive's declaration of him as a rebel. This, in legal terms, should have prevented any British invasion, for the sultan was the khedive's suzerain, but the sultan was dithering over whom to support. In response, the khedive himself was now being termed a traitor.[12]

(Urabi is said to have been reading up on events of the French Revolution,[13] possibly to find out how to conduct, or improve on, a revolution of his own; the decision of the khedive to flee to the British ships no doubt reminded him of the flight to Varennes; the next stage would be the foreign invasion to restore the king, or khedive; in the French version this invasion was defeated by the cannonade of Valmy, and no doubt this will have heartened him.)

The British felt compelled to go on, using the khedive as their nominal political shield, and with his restoration to power and authority as their object, despite the clear evidence of widespread support in Egypt for Urabi and the sultan's posture. Again, this was an improvisation, without any serious consideration of what they would need to do next, or how to gauge success and what it would amount to. They opted to secure control of the Suez Canal as their first objective. There had been rumours that Urabi planned to destroy the canal, or at least to block it. He had actually only failed to do anything about blocking the canal because its creator, Ferdinand de Lesseps, who was present in all this, had assured him that the British would be unable to use it anyway, presumably because he thought the French ships under Conrad would stop the Royal Navy.[14]

The canal was seized by two maritime expeditions: Admiral Sir Anthony Hoskins came from Britain to land a force at Port Said; Admiral Sir William Hewett, coming from India, landed a second force at Suez. These landings took place on 27 and 30 July respectively – a virtual repetition of the anti-French expeditions of 1801.[15] While this was happening, in Paris the new government fell and was replaced by one even less enamoured of military involvement in Egypt than either of its predecessors. The French ships now withdrew from both Port Said and Alexandria, leaving the field clear for the British, though the withdrawal was an action of disapproval at British intentions. The Royal Navy, as Seymour had shown, was never reluctant to act, with or without specific orders, believing that any mess so created would be sorted out by the politicians and diplomats later, and that success would be obvious when it came about.

Now Taufiq's khedivial authority was used to take control of the Canal. De Lesseps, 'who apparently considered the canal as a sovereign state of which he himself was the dictator',[16] protested in vain, and the Egyptian defences were thus outflanked. De Lesseps' assurance to Urabi that he would prevent such a landing was no more than an idle boast.[17]

The preliminary plan of the military campaign had been set out as early as 3 July by Lieutenant General Sir Garnet Wolseley in London, long before the British Cabinet had decided to intervene with military force (as opposed to naval force); the plan was presumably only a staff exercise at first. The requirements were detailed, down to the provision for the sick to be transported on the Egyptian railways. The campaign was to seize the canal first, then strike at Cairo from Ismailia along the railway and the Ismailia Canal, which had replaced the Sweetwater Canal, originally built to supply the men working on the canal's construction. The only real alternative to a campaign along the canal was to break out from Alexandria. The use of British sea power was well calculated, considering it was an army plan. The landing force was to begin by moving steadily forward towards Cairo, small steps at a time, and was to be constantly reinforced by more landings behind them at Ismailia.

The Egyptian army was expected to occupy and defend the position at Tel el-Kebir, the strategic equivalent to the east of Cairo of that at Kafr el-Dawar in the Delta, which was occupied by the Egyptians to prevent advances from Alexandria.[18] In fact, it became clear by this campaign that the construction of the canal, and its railway and canal adjuncts, had provided an enemy, in this case the British, with a most welcome and clear route into the heart of Egypt, a preferable alternative to fighting its way through the Delta, with its streams, swamps and lakes. The route to Cairo from Ismailia was also about half the distance of that from Alexandria, 75 miles as against 120.[19] (The other military use of the canal was as a moat to prevent an invasion through Sinai, which emerged in the Great War.)

A good deal of public, and obvious, preparation accompanied this expedition, which was centred on gaining control of the canal above all, which by this time was partly owned by the British government, while a wide collection of French investors held the rest of the shares. Rumour had it that Urabi was planning to block the canal with explosives, though he had accepted de Lesseps' assurances that the canal was safe; so that did not happen, even if Urabi had thought of it. It was now obvious that the canal had become a vital British imperial communication link, and so political domination of Egypt was seen as vital to control the canal, since Egypt and the canal went together. The British expedition showed how relatively easy it was to seize control of the canal. De Lesseps' notion that he could prevent the use of 'his' canal by a military power was self-delusion to a high degree; there had been plenty of argument before 'his' canal was built, centred on its strategic significance; he had no excuse for ignorance on this.

Rather less emphasis was laid on the financial and commercial commitments made in Egypt by British commercial organisations, though this as a cause of the British invasion has become something that has been emphasised in later accounts. (French investments were greater, but this did not bring the French to mount an invasion.) The British by this time knew full well that conquests were expensive, and holding on to them afterwards was a continuous and debilitating expense, both for the conquerors and for the conquered. The formal purpose of the expedition was to restore the khedive to his position and his authority. Having done so, it must have been clear to many observers, even before the invasion succeeded, that it would be necessary to go on propping him up for quite some time, just as it would be necessary to continue controlling the canal. With the khedive restored, then, of course, the British forces really would go home – unless something else happened to detain them – which, of course, it did regularly for the next seventy years. To reach that point of political control seems to have been the essential aim of the operation. And, of course, the decision to withdraw was always Britain's, not Egypt's.

The campaign was, as Wolseley's initial plan showed, straightforward.[20] The canal had been seized by the Royal Navy by early August; Wolseley's expeditionary force arrived at Alexandria on 15 August, but then at once it sailed off again. He seems to have initially decided that Abukir, close to Alexandria, would be a suitable place to land, but then changed his mind, perhaps on hearing that the canal had been secured; the threat at Abukir, however, effectively distracted the Egyptians, whether or not it was a feint – some ships remained off the town for a time, though as they did nothing, it was soon obvious that this really was a feint, or an abandoned plan. The Egyptians perhaps assumed that an offensive by the forces in occupation of Alexandria was intended, and they were certainly surprised that the attack came along the canal. (Urabi was still ignorant of the true situation when interviewed later during his exile.)[21] Ismailia became the main British base; it was halfway along the canal, where the railway and Sweetwater Canal from Cairo reached Lake Timsah, which had room to accommodate the British transports and the supply fleet. The expeditionary force landed at Ismailia and had consolidated its position there by 23 August; more units disembarked there over the next several days.[22]

The new Egyptian government mobilised its forces. At Kafr el-Dawar, Urabi had only about 5,000 men, a number whose total rose slowly. By calling up reserves the army was raised quickly to about 60,000 men, and this could grow further as the Bedouin joined in. But Egypt was vulnerable, particularly to an enemy with command of the sea, and the army had to be divided into forces spread to defend the several mouths of the Nile, and facing the canal. More than half of the army was placed at the ports along the Delta coast from Alexandria to Damietta to face any landing from the Mediterranean. Cairo was held by 11,000 men, as much to prevent any anti-Urabi coup as to defend the city. The main force facing the British along the Ismailia Canal, which was to be the main line of attack, was thus no more than 12,000 men, less than a fifth of the total army.[23]

The British were already in occupation of Alexandria, and it would not be politic to allow that city to be retaken by the Egyptians, so a reasonably substantial British force had to be retained in the city – which, after the riots, was hardly a place that would welcome a new foreign occupation. The British consul general, Sir Edward Malet, was firmly of the opinion that the city must be held. Nevertheless, Wolseley withdrew two of his battalions from the city, but replaced them with men sent from depots in Britain, so making use of his trained battalions in his offensive. The British garrison in the city remained at about 4,000 men all through the fighting, undisturbed by the more numerous but immobile Egyptians at Kafr el-Dawar.[24] Fortifications east of the city at Ramleh were developed, as was an entrenched camp facing the Egyptians at Kafr el-Dawar, thus providing two obstacles to any Egyptian attack; a fortified line was also developed to the west of the city to block any encircling movement by the Egyptians, or an attack by way of the desert. The garrison made frequent raids and threats against the Egyptians camped at Kafr el-Dawar in order to hold them there, but discontinued the practice once it was understood that these movements no longer impressed the Egyptians after they had not been followed up.

The main British invading force had been directed to Alexandria at first and had then threatened to land at Abukir when it left the city, but it was really headed for Ismailia – the Egyptian forces therefore had been thoroughly distracted, and they thus obligingly kept a considerable force at Abukir (though how deliberate the deception was is not clear; if it really was deliberate, it worked). Another Egyptian force was stationed at Damietta, which was also a possible landing place. The Damietta force was later depleted to reinforce the Tel el-Kebir army, which also had to leave forces to hold Port Said and Suez at the canal entrances; they were also withdrawn as the invaders arrived. This widening threat provoked the Egyptian government into conscripting even more men, and the army was raised to 100,000 men fairly quickly, though the last recruits were conscripted with much reluctance and it was rumoured that some of them were brought to the camps in chains.[25] These recruits were in fact very quickly armed, equipped and clothed, the Egyptian government demonstrating much efficiency in this respect, but the fact remained that these latest conscripts were almost totally untrained. Animals for transport were also requisitioned, sometimes at gunpoint, from the *fellahin*. This was dangerous, for the loss of an animal might destroy a peasant's ability to grow food.[26]

Having established themselves at Ismailia, the British forces advanced slowly along the line of the railway and the Ismailia Canal. The Egyptians reacted to each forward movement, but usually soon abandoned their advanced positions. It was August and the temperature was oppressive, particularly for the unacclimatised British; one reason the Egyptians had some confidence in their actions was that the casualty rate among the British, from dehydration and sunstroke, was very high.[27] And yet a number of the British units were from India, so they were already acclimatised. By retreating from their advanced positions, Egyptians were being steadily driven back, a demoralising process, even if in most cases their retreats were deliberate and well organised. By 28 August, the confrontation had reached Kassassin, a lock on the Ismailia Canal, which represented a British advance from Ismailia of about 25 miles in four days. The cavalry – 9th Dragoon Guards and the Household Cavalry – charged the position in the dark to dislodge part of the Egyptian forces, but most of them remained in position.[28] The Egyptian army, now appreciating that this was the main British line of attack, had been reinforced by contingents brought from the various units situated at the Delta ports, including above all a force of Nubian soldiers from Damietta.

The British spent several days bringing forward more troops, including the Highland Brigade (four battalions), and the Brigade of Guards, together with the Indian contingent, mainly grouped into the Indian division, though the great majority of troops involved in the fight were British.[29] The Egyptians launched an unsuccessful attack on 9 September, which was defeated. Four days later, on 13 September, the British replied, having gathered up their full force for the first time. By now, also the two commanders, Urabi and Wolseley, were personally in command of their forces. Urabi commanded about 20,000 men and 75 guns, according to his later statement when he was interviewed in his exile in Ceylon; Wolseley had about 17,000, about as many guns, and also some Gatling machine guns; the guns were concentrated in a group very close to the Egyptian lines.

The British made an approach march during the night of the 12/13th, and launched their attack a little before dawn, at about 5 am. The Egyptians, in a good defensive position, fought hard, but by 6 am, they had been driven from their positions and were in full retreat. The British had 400-plus casualties, killed and wounded; the Egyptian casualties were estimated at anything between 1,500 and 3,000, figures, as usual, that were certainly exaggerated and anyway only approximate. The pursuit was led by the Indian cavalry, and reached Belbeis on the Nile by late on the 14th. By the morning of 15 September, a small British cavalry force had reached the citadel in Cairo, where the garrison of 6,000 surrendered; the British forces then occupied the strategic posts in the city. Urabi had led the debacle and was arrested at his home.[30]

The political situation in Egypt was now, as a result of the British victory, dire. The Dual Control scheme had failed; the Egyptian army had failed; the Egyptian position in their Sudanese colony in the south was in the process of failing as the Mahdi won his early victories (in a couple of months the Mahdi would be in full control of Darfur and Kordofan, and a rising would begin in eastern Sudan (see chapter 9)); the khedivial system had already failed; and the Turkish suzerainty was rendered null by the sultan's dithering over who to support. The popular revolution in Egypt, led by the army, which had evidently been in process before the British invasion, was aborted and its leader was now a prisoner. The Egyptians could not be faulted for feeling utterly depressed and bewildered.

The British had gone it alone, and in theory they were now in sole control of Egypt. But, as usual, they had no plan for the future, for what to do with their victory (shades of Admiral Seymour after the bombardment of Alexandria). They were constrained by a network of international obligations – to the sultan, still in theory the suzerain of Egypt; to the Khedive Taufiq, in whose name the military campaign had been conducted; to the foreign bondholders who were still owed their due interest payments; to the Suez Canal Company and its stockholders, who included the British government; and to the European powers, above all the French, but Bismarck was indicating a German interest as well.

It was, amid these obligations and interests, manifestly impossible for the conquerors to relinquish political control, especially in view of the failure of both the khedivial and revolutionary governments in Egypt. The first results of the British relinquishing of power would be to drive out the khedive, then an Egyptian repudiation of some or all of the financial obligations incurred by the khedivial regime. It could be argued that the khedivial system and its international partners had brought about the invasion and foreign occupation, and so such a repudiation would be seen as justified, at least in Egypt. These obligations had, after all, been undertaken by the khedives, and the khedivial system would have to go if the khedive was removed; the Egyptians could well argue that it was the khedives who had borrowed the money, above all, Khedive Ismail, who was now in exile, not the Egyptians.

So the defeat of the Egyptian army was also the defeat of the revolution. (For Urabi in his study of the French Revolution, the French revolutionary victory of Valmy against the invaders had been reversed.) So the newly imposed British occupation would have to continue; it was impossible for the British to contemplate the annexation of Egypt, though this would have severed several Gordian knots, because of all the international obligations, especially since the war had been fought on behalf of the khedive.[31] This implied that the problems had been brought on the British by their Egyptian improvisations; if they did not like the situation they were in, it was their own fault.

The British had therefore, as usual without intending it, brought themselves to a position where they had taken control of another country, one with enormous financial obligations and with as great internal problems, especially when the khedivate of Egypt stretched as far as the Sudd and Equatoria, the borders of Ethiopia, and the western border of Darfur. They had taken on these obligations and responsibilities, and had to make an effort to solve the problems. Inevitably, given their own history, they would apply British imperial methods to their new quasi-colony, notably those developed in India. They had no reason to assume that such methods would be acceptable to the people of Egypt, still less to those of the rebellious Sudan.

If Britain was to retain any international credibility, it had to ensure that the bondholders' debts were paid, and the only way to do so was to retain control of the country, and use its tax revenue for that purpose; in other words, a continuation of the preceding financial regime. British politicians repeatedly announced that its military occupation of Egypt was only temporary and would soon cease, but those who said this must have known that a military withdrawal would be impossible for some time. (In the end, the military withdrawal in 1952 was soon followed by the Republican revolution of 1953.) There were too many obligations it had assumed by its successful invasion.[32]

In the absence of any clear political solution from the British occupiers, an outsider was drafted in to consider, make a report, and produce a plan. This was Lord Dufferin, sent over from Constantinople, where he was ambassador, and he eventually did make some recommendations. The initial programme of measures to be implemented by the occupation regime was drawn up, and the actual implementation was handed to Sir Evelyn Baring, who had been in Egypt between 1876 and 1879, and now, after three years in India, he was to be Malet's successor as consul general. He had started out as a soldier – Major Baring in India – but his military career had been mainly clerical, secretarial and administrative. He was to remain in post in Egypt for more than twenty years, in effect as viceroy, or to the Egyptians, as a dictator.[33]

Some parts of the new dispensation could be installed fairly readily. A new government was organised by the khedive, selecting, of course, his own supporters, who, with the victory of the British forces, had quickly multiplied. The less than valiant shifted their support from Urabi to Taufiq, deserting the revolution for the safety of the restored khedive's regime. The Egyptian army was disbanded, to be reconstituted gradually, and retrained. Given that the British Army was now in control, the new Egyptian army would not simply be retrained, but commanded by British officers, and the mobile gendarmerie would also have British soldiers in command. This would at least produce an effective army, but its size would be restricted by the continuing financial situation. This would have a dire effect on the situation in the Sudan, just as the previous regime had overseen the contraction of Egypt elsewhere.

The Dual Control system had already vanished. It was to be replaced by a single British financial adviser, a nearly innocuous title for the man who, because he controlled the finances of the country, emerged quickly to a very strong political position. This, however, would only take place when a suitably powerful man was appointed above him – Sir Archibald Colvin was 'financial adviser' under Baring; he was replaced by Sir Edgar Vincent after only eight months. Colvin had been in post when Baring arrived; Vincent was Baring's own choice for the position, a mark of Baring's determination to be in control of the whole administration.[34] Similar officials were to be installed in the Ministry of Public Works, an important organisation since it would be charged with developing Egyptian agriculture and expanding irrigation to ensure the increase in tax revenue with which to pay down, or at least secure, the debt. The old oppressive taxation system would need to be reined in, since it had actually held back increases in productivity, but the Egyptian *fellahin* would still be working to pay the khedival debts.[35]

That taxation regime had been the product of the oppressive despotism of the khedives; collection methods could include flogging the peasants who were perceived as 'cheating'. To lighten the burden, or spread the responsibility, an attempt was to be made to develop a representative authority. Not a democratic one, of course, but at least with a representative element included; it would obviously also be influenced, even controlled, by the British officials, the successor, with much the same members, of the Assembly of Notables. To be fair, it was intended that this would be the eventual successor of the British occupation, which would leave a quasi-democratic system in position when it ended and the troops were withdrawn – which in turn would happen 'soon', of course. (The concept was also to be applied in India eventually.) It was, however, a very long-term project, and was usually accused of being merely a means of extending British rule. In fact, for some time, the British system was no more than the khedivial despotism in a British guise.

Cromer's regime in Egypt was seen as a success by his contemporaries in Britain, but has come in for strong criticism from Egyptian historians. The main purpose, at least at first, of the British imposition of control, was financial. Baring was successful in paying down the debt by 1889, but this came at a considerable cost. One means of raising the necessary money was to sell off the lands of the khedival family, the Domain lands (*Daria Samiyya*) – which until fairly recently had been worked by slaves. This was done in blocks of 50 *faddans*, which were 'equivalent to a large estate', and which could therefore only be bought by those who were already wealthy. The process reinforced the social and political domination by the rich. This solution, again, was to be applied in another part of the empire, when the Irish land problem was solved by subdividing and selling off the larger states in small lots – but in this case the deliberate intention was to avert the perpetuation of the larger estates, so that the lots were sold off to individuals on easy terms. It might have been better to have done that in Egypt also. The peasantry could be counted as supporters of Urabi, so by limiting their easy access to land, the revolution was delayed again; but a large redistribution of agricultural land would count as a social revolution and the British were not in the business of promoting revolution.

The failure to encourage industrialisation – which would compete with British industry – left the *fellahin* with no alternative but to work their own small plots; their product would then be competing with those from the estates of the rich, who could operate by much more economical methods. As a result, the peasants' plots increasingly fell into the hands of the wealthy, whose estates grew steadily larger. The encouragement of cotton production, also for the ultimate benefit of British industry, was a further indication of the British prejudice of Cromer and his administrators. Cotton was certainly an export success, but within Egypt, it was grown on land previously devoted to producing food, so that by the end of the nineteenth century, Egypt, that famously rich land, which had fed the British Army in Spain, had to import food.[36]

The occupation army was more concerned with the defence of the canal and internal control in Egypt, than with the Sudan. The new Egyptian army could not be available for campaigning for some time, and the old army had been disbanded. The result was a neglect of what was happening in the Sudan until it was too late, and the land had been lost to Egypt. The destruction of the Egyptian Empire of the khedives began from within. This was a further consequence of the myopic British vision of concentration on the finances of Egypt.

Chapter 10

The Destruction of the Egyptian Empire: II – Sudan

It has taken eight chapters but at last, we have reached the point at which the Mahdi reaches for control of his country. The point has been that he was not particularly original in his revolution, and that what he achieved had to be put into a much wider political context in order for it to be understood. He operated as a fairly typical Muslim holy man, a species of political activist who were always liable to tip over into violence. He came to power in a country that had been badly damaged by previous conquest and misgovernment. His achievement was considerable, given the quality of the opponents he confronted, but there was a fundamental flaw in his political understanding of those opponents. Nevertheless, it seems likely that only his untimely death prevented him from going on to much greater achievements. Above all, it is necessary to put his career, and his country and the surrounding countries, into an African context, rather than seeing it as a part of an evanescent European conquest.

He can be well compared with Usuman dan Fodio, active in the time of the Mahdi's father, with al-Hajj Umar, his older contemporary, and to some extent with Samori, but he was a nationalist, if anything. All four of these men led revolutions in Africa in the nineteenth century. Their careers were all very similar in their trajectories, they all took advantage of the previous oppression of the general population by the rulers whom they displaced, and they all founded new states that lasted for some time, but which were then destroyed or taken over by European imperialists. To understand the Mahdi and his achievement it is necessary, in other words, to take these other religious revolutionaries into account.

It happened that religion was the motivation of Usuman, Umar and Muhammad Ahmad, but the fourth of the revolutionaries, Samori, was as successful as these others without resorting to Islam – in fact, he rejected Islam, after attempting to use it in his service. It was thus evident that the problems they were tackling were not necessarily of a religious nature, though in several cases they could be best articulated in religious terms. The basic problems in the Sahel region of North Africa were social; and articulating them in religious terms was a distraction that did not solve any of those problems. Imposing a religious regime on a disturbed social problem area only continued the problem without solving it, by replacing the ruling elite. This is not, of course, in any way to denigrate the importance and the achievement of these revolutionaries, all of whom were notably successful and admirable men.

Sudan was one of the problem areas inherited by the new British-dominated Egyptian regime. After the defeat of al-Shallali's army at Jabal Qadir at the end of May 1882 (a month before the riot in Alexandria), the Mahdist advance was directed north and west from the base at Jabal Qadir into the regions of Kordofan and Darfur, both areas only relatively recently conquered by the Egyptian administration, and with which the Mahdi was familiar. In Kordofan, the Mahdi's victories had stimulated a series of tribal risings, combated by the forces of the Egyptian government, who won ephemeral victories, after each of which the tribal armies dispersed only to reassemble not much later. The Egyptian garrison was sufficient to hold the towns, but not to decisively crush the tribes. In June, Muhammad Rauf's successor as governor general, Abd al-Qadir Pasha Hilmi, began to fortify Khartoum.

The victories of the government forces in Kordofan had been so unconvincing that the Egyptian conquest regime there had collapsed at the first test. The problem for the Egyptian governors general in Khartoum was that they had to maintain garrisons in the main centres, and so were not able to deploy sufficient troops to follow up any victory, and from late 1881 the khedivian government in Egypt was similarly in dissolution and under threat, and so had no forces to spare to help out, or perhaps one should say the khedive, given the refusal of his soldiers to march away from Cairo and Egypt, had no forces prepared to go to the Sudan to help out. On the other hand, the problem for the rebel tribesmen was that they might scatter after their defeats and so survive, but the government forces could usually beat them in battle, and they found it difficult or impossible to capture any of the garrison towns. Stalemate followed. The government held the main towns, the tribes the countryside.

This was an ideal condition for an intervention by the Mahdi, which came in August 1882, less than a month before the defeat of the Egyptian army at Tel el-Kebir. The Mahdi commanded a force of several thousands when he moved against Kordofan. This was now possible for him, having a substantial and reasonably well-armed force. The survivors of al-Shallali's army had been integrated into the Mahdi's army, which also collected the weaponry of the dead soldiers, though (for the moment) there was a refusal to make use of the captured firearms, deemed (for the moment) to be un-Islamic.

Muhammad Ahmad could have a decisive effect on the conflict in Kordofan, in part by simply allying with some of those tribes who were antagonistic to the government. He also received a new commander, Madibbu Ali, a dissident from a tribal political dispute among the Rizeyqat tribe in Darfur. He was welcomed, and then at once was sent back to Darfur to stimulate a rising, acting as the Mahdi's man, and with the Mahdi's authority to back him up. There, even if he failed, he would at least distract the Egyptian governor of Darfur, the Austrian Rudolph Slatin Pasha, from intervening in Kordofan. So it became clear that the Mahdi's strategy was to promote political disruption and then to intervene to bring his own peace and his own authority.[1]

In Darfur, Madibbu Ali was able to rally supporters – he had been joint chief of the important Rizeyqat tribe until ousted, and he could call on tribal members who were loyal to him. He now menaced the outlying garrison at Shakka, in the south of the country, and defeated the governor there in July (two days before the riots in Alexandria). At Dara, halfway between el-Fasher (the government centre) and Shakka, the governor was Muhammad Khalid, who, as a cousin of the Mahdi, was a potential rebel; from long residence in Darfur, he was also influential. Slatin was suspicious of him, but was beset by other problems. He tackled Madibbu first, marching from el-Fasher, but, as with the government/tribesmen conflicts in Kordofan, the fight was indecisive;[2] Slatin continued to be beset, and the theoretically defeated enemy forces rallied.

The Mahdi sought an alliance with his old acquaintance Makk Adam in the Nuba Hills, but the *makk* was wary, and still would not commit himself. He did, however, permit the Mahdists to rest up on their journey towards Kordofan at the Jabal Qadir. In August, the Mahdi brought his forces out of the hills into Kordofan, aiming to capture al-Ubaiyid, the provincial capital. As he approached the city, where the governor Muhammad Said commanded, a disaffected tribal group defected from the governor's forces, leaving him with just his reduced garrison and his own household to defend the city. He was fortunate, however, that the deserters had left before the Mahdi attacked, for it meant that he was at least able to rely on those defenders who remained, while his supplies would last longer, and he was relieved of the possibility of further treachery. The attack that came was a wild and undisciplined charge, while the defenders were disciplined and operated from behind the walls. They also had firearms, which the Mahdists had forsworn. It was a disaster for the attackers, with many casualties, including two of Muhammad Ahmad's brothers, and a brother of the Khalifa Abdullahi.

This was the 'Friday Battle', fought on the Muslim day of prayer, and after it the Mahdist forces reeled back to recover at Kaba, several miles away – but they were still there, still numerous, and still menacing; unlike defeated tribal forces, they did not disperse. This, therefore, was different from the tribal battles – the Mahdists did not scatter only to regroup later; instead, they retained their cohesion. The casualties are put at '10,000', which is typically inexact, and probably exaggerated by a factor of at least two or perhaps four, but it was nevertheless a stinging defeat, and the first that had been suffered by the Mahdi.[3]

On the way to Kordofan, the Mahdi had sent out a small group to eliminate a Christian mission station at Dilling to the west of the Nuba Hills. He had two (at least) purposes in this. First, probably, was the wish to eliminate a religious competitor; second, he knew that the mission station was a thorn in Makk Adam's side, and that one of the *makk*'s sons, Umar, had already attempted to suppress them. With Mahdist help, however, Umar was now successful, and he joined the Ansar. The Mahdi was thus gaining points with the *makk*, though it did not have any immediate effect. One of those captured at the mission was Father Josef Ohrwalder, who remained a prisoner of the Mahdists for the next ten years.[4] Ohrwalder wrote his memoirs after his release, but they may not be altogether reliable; they were translated into English by General Sir Francis Reginald Wingate, the intelligence chief in the Sudan, who twisted the story to shed bright lights on British actions, and dark shadows on the Mahdi's.[5]

To the north of al-Ubaiyid, the town of Bara had been captured by a Mahdist faction and then recovered by government forces, but then the town and its garrison were put under Mahdist siege for some time. A relieving force set out from Khartoum in September, after the good news arriving from al-Ubaiyid of the Friday victory, which had built up non-Mahdist courage. This force was ambushed close to its target, and the survivors of the defeat – half the force – took refuge inside the besieged town, so reducing its ability to last out. From al-Ubaiyid, raiding parties came out to scour the nearby villages for food and cattle for the besieged garrison and people; though relatively productive, the land could not supply the necessary food. By the end of 1882, both al-Ubaiyid and Bara were starving. Meanwhile, the Mahdi had learned from his defeat and set about instilling some military discipline into his disorderly forces. He also sent back to Jabal Qadir for the firearms that had been captured from the various defeated enemies and stored there; he discarded the former decision that firearms were un-Islamic, once more displaying an admirable pragmatism and an adaptability in pursuit of victory.[6] The governor and garrison at al-Ubaiyid was thus now both starving and was subject to increasingly accurate sniping.[7] At Bara, a Mahdist sympathiser set fire to the huts where provisions had been stored; now starving, the town surrendered on 6 January 1883; at al-Ubaiyid, the city was surrendered to the Mahdi on the 19th.

The survivors of both sieges were enrolled in the victorious army, on condition of taking the oath of allegiance to the Mahdi. Refusers were killed, as was Muhammad Said, the governor, when he was discovered to have attempted to conceal his hoard of gold, and to have tried to send out intelligence to Khartoum. Such was the Mahdi's discipline.[8] Recruiting the surviving enemy forces was to be the normal practice after his victories – it was the quickest way to increase his armed force; these recruits were trained and accustomed to military discipline, and also proved to be surprisingly loyal.

In Darfur, Slatin Pasha gathered a considerable army to march to succour Shakka; he intended then to use it as a base for controlling the local tribes, but he was ambushed and his force destroyed along the way. He led the survivors on a gruelling march to Dara, where he stood siege; he sent Muhammad Khalid off to his cousin the Mahdi to get rid of him; he was clearly a danger, and probably an agitator for the Mahdist's cause. Slatin's enemies were much encouraged by the news of the fall of al-Ubaiyid, and the Dara siege was tightened. Outside the town, Slatin's province fell away so that the governor was left to govern no more than the place in which he was confined.[9]

When Slatin finally surrendered Dara at the end of 1883, all the western provinces had become the Mahdi's. He had succeeded less because of his victories than because the Egyptian regime was so detested that the arrival of the Mahdi's armies prompted immediate desertions and risings by the local tribes, and risings in both Kordofan and Darfur. These tribes often then revived old enmities against their neighbours, reducing the province to anarchy, and this allowed the Mahdi to impose his own peace. The Mahdi's conquest was thus not really dissimilar from that by the Egyptians, and the resistance led by the Darfuri displaced dynasty did not cease – for them the issue was independence and the revival of their power, not simply enmity to the Egyptians, though they felt that too. The tribes were also probably more interested in independence than in submission, but the Mahdi had the power. Slatin became another of the Mahdi's Christian prisoners, later also writing his memoirs, to be translated and adapted by General Wingate.[10]

These disasters for the Egyptians, at Bara and al-Ubaiyid, Shakka and Dara, coincided with the imposition of effective British control over the Egyptian government during 1882 and 1883, but the khedive's new government was still determined to make a strong effort to defend its existing dominion in Sudan and to recover the lost provinces. The British government did not want to get its own troops involved, and refused to help, but did allow Egypt to use whatever forces it had to make the attempt. In November and December 1883, 10,000 surviving members of Urabi's defeated and demobilised army were re-recruited and sent south to reinforce Khartoum, and to become an expeditionary force of reconquest. (The removal of these men from Egypt was a relief to both the khedive and the British; they could have been a very destabilising group.)

A retired Indian Army officer, Colonel William Hicks, was installed as chief of staff in this expedition, with Sulayman Pasha Niyazi, a senior (and even older) Egyptian officer, in overall command. Hicks had a staff of eight

British officers with him. Neither of the commanders, nor any of his officers, had any experience in Sudanese warfare, or of Sudan itself for that matter. The relationship between Sulayman and Hicks did not work, and in July, Sulayman was removed to become the governor of the Red Sea province; Hicks was given the overall command in his place.[11] Hicks's intrigue had resulted in both men being promoted.[12]

Hicks's expedition was a disaster. The troops began their march in a gloomy mood, and they became steadily more morose. Hicks first succeeded in defeating some Mahdist groups who threatened the towns along the White Nile upstream from Khartoum, but then he turned to recover Kordofan. He chose a longer route towards al-Ubaiyid than that which was recommended, but one that would also take him through territory that was supposed to have more water available. It took him close to the Nuba Hills, and he hoped that Makk Adam would join him, but there was no sign of him – the *makk* was continuing his balanced neutrality, which consisted of maintaining friendly relations with everyone, but without incurring any binding obligations. On the other hand, it was partly due to Adam's evidence that Hicks was taking the southern route. It seems clear that Hicks trusted his vague promises far too much.[13]

Hicks's plan was to establish a series of fortified posts along the way, but it was soon obvious that this would reduce his fighting force from the 5,000 he began with to 3,000 or less, where the Mahdi's forces, according to one rather distant observer, were put at (the usually exaggerated) '60,000'.[14] So the idea was abandoned. More troops were sent from Egypt, and Hicks eventually started his final advance with 8,000 men, served by 2,000 camp followers and 5,500 camels. This was not enough to win a battle, and yet too many for the logistics. The march was through dry and difficult country, and thirst soon afflicted the troops, despite the supposed good water sources, which may have been adequate for a raiding party, or a caravan, but not for such a large force.

The Mahdi had benefited from the knowledge that this was an Egyptian attack, and the tribes of Kordofan had no wish to be subjected to Egyptian rule again. He therefore was able to muster support from many of the tribes, including those who were lukewarm about his own rule. He established a camp close outside al-Ubaiyid, and set up a moderately effective training regime – again demonstrating his pragmatic bent. A wild charge by fanatics was usually sufficient in a fight with equally undisciplined tribesmen, but against an alert and disciplined force, an approximation to a strict military discipline was required. All those who turned up were well supplied with food and water, in contrast to Hicks's force, and the Mahdi and his army could wait in the al-Ubaiyid area in relative comfort, learn the new tactics for meeting Hicks's debilitated forces, and wait to be attacked.

Hicks's force reached al-Radad, 40 miles south of al-Ubaiyid, after a march that had already lasted a month. He waited there for six days, expecting reinforcements, or supplies, or messages, to arrive from the Makk Adam of Taqali, but the *makk* had revived his customary neutrality and no reinforcements arrived, while Hicks's own forces consumed their supplies and suffered desertions. The march was renewed on 30 October 1883, directed at al-Ubaiyid at last. Next day, the Mahdi's army, clearly well informed of Hicks's movements, marched to intercept. For three days, 3 to 5 November, battles took place. The Egyptians faced Mahdist armed fire for the first time, firing volleys like any modern army – indeed, the men with the guns were mainly captured Sudanese soldiers who had been enlisted earlier to avoid summary execution, and, of course, they already had the discipline required. The final battle on 5 November, at Shaykan, saw the Egyptian army surrounded and largely massacred. Out of the 8,000 men who had started out, or perhaps 10,000 with the camp followers, only about 250 are said to have survived[15] – apart from those who had deserted before the battle, of course.

The battle at Shaykan was decisive. Slatin at Dara now soon surrendered, and the Darfuri capital, el-Fasher, was taken by the Mahdists in January 1884. As a result, the whole of the western Sudan was under the Mahdi's control by the beginning of 1884, and he had just got started. He claimed that the Prophet Muhammad had appeared in a vision listing the places he expected the Mahdi to conquer after al-Ubaiyid – Mecca, Medina, Cairo, Jerusalem and Iraq. This may be taken as the Mahdi's own personal programme; it will be noted that this was to be an Arab state, conquered at the expense of the Ottoman Empire; true to the form of such Muslim reformers, it was Muslim states and people who were to be his victims.[16]

Makk Adam in the Nuba Hills had equivocated for the last time. His position, south of Kordofan and partly across the Mahdi's communications back to Jabal Qadir, was now intolerable, as was his neutrality – for to be neutral in a holy war is to be hostile. A combination of military pressure, ideological persuasion, and threatening letters brought the *makk* to surrender at last in March 1884. But this did not mean he was giving up his neutrality, and Adam soon left al-Ubaiyid and returned home. There, at last, he openly defied the Mahdi and distributed arms to the hill people, who included refugees from both Egyptian and Mahdist rule. At last, the Mahdi lost patience and sent the Ansar into the hills. A three-month campaign-cum-occupation wore down Taqali resistance. Makk Adam surrendered for the second time in July 1884. He died in September, near Khartoum, of grief and humiliation as much as anything. The Ansar had already left for Khartoum in March.[17]

In London, the government came to the conclusion that Sudan must be abandoned to its fate, and the new agent and consul general, Sir Evelyn Baring, was so informed. He transmitted this decision to the Egyptian government.[18] This made sense given the recent loss of Egyptian military manpower (those captured at Shaykan were now part of the Mahdi's army, as usual), the unwillingness of the British government to use British and Indian troops to defeat the Mahdi, and the irruption of repeated uprisings throughout Sudan, as a result of the news of the Mahdi's success against Hicks's army. Colonel Coetlogon, one of Hicks's officers, who had remained in Khartoum, telegraphed to say that he did not believe the city could be held, and in Cairo, military opinion agreed with this. British, Indian and Turkish troops were suggested as relief forces – the British, Indian and Turkish governments all refused. The khedivial government in Cairo was also less than enthusiastic about mounting a relief force. After discussions everywhere and with everyone with an opinion, on 4 January 1884 the British government made it clear that the abandonment of the Sudan was its preferred policy – that is, it was up to Egypt to save the Sudan, if it would, or could. The Egyptian government thereupon, unable to bring itself to make a decision either to reinforce the failure, or abandon the conquest, resigned. Nubar Pasha was appointed Prime Minister with a remit to push through a policy of abandonment.[19]

This all was, however, a failure of Britain's real responsibilities; having taken over Egypt, they were now busy discarding the Egyptian empire that had been constructed with some difficulty and persistence over the previous sixty years. And if anyone had made a study of the development of such Islamic states in the past (no one did, at least no one consulted Ibn Khaldun, who could have pointed out the likely result), it would have been clear that the fervour and excitement that drove the Mahdi and his followers to their initial success would soon die down, and the original quarrelsomeness of the tribes in the Sudan would soon resurface. The Mahdi's state, that is, would fairly soon cease to be aggressive, once it had reached an unwieldy size, and would eventually collapse, or become so weakened that it could be defeated and conquered with relative ease. This would take some time, probably decades, though given the undeveloped nature and political divisions of the Sudan, probably much less, but the human casualties during this abandonment would be large, and it was quite possible that any eventual reconquest attempt would face a determined enemy. In the meantime, even if the British occupiers were not to be used to defend the Egyptian Empire, it was still necessary to build up a new Egyptian army for the defence of Egypt, which would clearly soon be the Mahdi's next target.

For, once the decision to abandon Sudan was reached, the question arose as to the Mahdi's boundaries, and how far he should be allowed to advance. It will have been obvious that the Sudan as a whole was going to be lost, so there was also the question of the fate of the surviving Egyptian garrisons still in the country, and of the outlying fragments of the Egyptian Empire, which would be cut adrift by the Mahdist conquests. It was clear that Sudan was the most necessary part of the Egyptian Empire, not counting Egypt itself, and its loss would entail further losses all around. The policy of abandonment meant a lot more than merely withdrawing Egyptian authority from the Sudan; it had major effects in all the surrounding countries.

The Mahdi's authority was still limited for the moment and his boundaries fluid. (He had not yet reached Khartoum, and was still attempting to bring the Makk Adam in.) There was now a rising in his name in the eastern Sudan, there was fighting to the south in Bahr el-Ghazal province, and the line of the Nile was held by a string of Egyptian garrisons – Hicks's successful preliminary campaign along the White Nile had chased away the encroaching Mahdists, but these retaken posts were certainly vulnerable to attack from the east (the risings there) and the west (Kordofan); Giegler's campaign along the Blue Nile had similarly had no permanent result. The success in the Nuba Hills should have constituted a powerful warning that the Mahdi's army was now a formidable force – no one else had ever conquered those hills. Both sides had now to consider their future options, the British and the Egyptians how to get out of Sudan, the Mahdi how to ensure his control of a much bigger territory, and how to govern his new state, together with securing its expansion – 'Mecca, Medina, Cairo, Jerusalem, Iraq' was his programme, after Egypt. His campaign to gain control of the Nuba Hills during the next six months had shown that internal neutral groups would not be tolerated, any more than hostile groups.

In January 1884 it was agreed in London to send Colonel, now Major General, Charles Gordon to Khartoum to liquidate the Egyptian position.[20] This was not an easy decision. It is doubtful if anyone in authority in London trusted Gordon, who operated along his own track, but he was the man in Britain most experienced in Sudanese affairs, and, after all, his instructions, to withdraw the Egyptian garrisons, were clear. (There were several capable and experienced Egyptian officers who could have done the job, but they were apparently never considered, or perhaps never trusted.)

In February, the Mahdists in the eastern region defeated an Egyptian gendarmerie army under General Valentine Baker (Samuel Baker's brother) at Trinkitat, on the Red Sea coast,[21] and a month later, in March, the Mahdi set up an organisation for his future conquests. Already one commander, Uthman Digna, had been put in command in the Red Sea province, and it was his forces that had defeated Baker. A merchant, Karamallah Kurqusawi, was appointed *amir* in the Bahr el-Ghazal region, and at the end of March, other *amirs* were appointed – Muhammad el-Kheir for the Berber region (along the Nile north of Khartoum), Muhammad Khalid was sent to Darfur (he was already familiar with the region, of course), and Muhammad Uthman Abu Qarja to the Nile, to be in command of the siege of Khartoum, which had begun on 13 March 1884. By then, Gordon was already in the city.[22]

The Mahdi's strategy was clear, and was Islamic-traditional. Each provincial or frontier governor was given a territory with a frontier, and a part of the army, which he was expected to enlarge by local recruitment, and was then expected to enlarge his province – it had been the Prophet's method in his early conquests, and that of his caliphal successors. It had worked in the past, with the original Arab conquests, and with the Turkish conquests. (It had indeed worked with the British Empire in India, and the Spanish conquests in South America, for that matter.) The governors were well motivated, since by success they would become rich and powerful, and their armies would gain access to plenty of loot. It was a generally successful mode of empire building.

Gordon reached Khartoum a month before the siege was begun. He therefore had had sufficient time to evacuate the garrison, and probably any inhabitants who chose to leave, but instead he set about administering his territory – he had, after all, been appointed governor general. It was clear that he intended to stay, and he exchanged letters of defiance with the Mahdi. If evacuation was to take place, therefore, it would have to be accomplished by an expedition mounted from Egypt; Gordon clearly wasn't going to do it.

For the next nine months the war centred on the siege of Khartoum, a matter that has been extensively discussed and described. Briefly, Gordon decided that his mission was really to save the Sudan for Egypt, not just to evacuate the Egyptian soldiers.[23] This elongated the siege, infuriated the British government, but pleased the Egyptian government, which was no doubt also pleased enough to see the British finally becoming seriously involved in Sudanese affairs, and may well have hoped that this was the beginning of the reconquest. Certainly, Gordon eventually decided that this was his purpose. There was the usual British dithering, exhortations to Gordon to obey his original instructions, several attempts to relieve the siege and 'rescue' Gordon, which eventually involved a major expedition under General Wolseley that reached to within two days' travel of Khartoum. Finally, on 26 June 1885, the city fell to the Mahdi's forces and Gordon was shot dead in the process.[24]

During the siege, the Mahdi's forces elsewhere made other conquests. On the Red Sea coast, Uthman Digna's forces followed up their victory over Valentine Baker at Trinkitat by the capture of Tokar and Sinkat; this pushed the British into actually intervening there, as at Khartoum, against their original intentions; a force of 3,000 British soldiers were sent by way of Suakin, commanded by

General Sir Gerald Graham, who had been in command in Alexandria during the Tel el-Kebir campaign. Partly this was in reaction to the uncomfortable victories of the Mahdi and his commanders, since news of British defeats were circulating in Muslim circles throughout the Middle East and India, to considerable glee.[25] A victory was therefore required to demonstrate the continued potency of the British Army. Reinforced by a naval brigade, Graham did the job, inflicting a sound defeat on Uthman Digna's forces at el-Teb, through the use of concentrated British fire, causing 2,000 casualties. Graham also defeated an even larger Mahdist force later (Battle of Tamai). This effectively demonstrated the continued worth of the British colonial tactics of an infantry square and volley fire, as did Wolseley's campaign along the Nile, of course, if anyone cared to look beyond Gordon's fate. Graham was then ordered back to Egypt, leaving two British battalions to increase the garrison at Suakin. He had argued that he could have relieved Khartoum by a march from Suakin to the Nile, but lessons had been learned (Hicks's fate in the desert was relevant), and it would have involved a march not only through the desert but through hostile tribal territory (of the Hadendowa tribe, which had seized the opportunity to assert its independence) as well; this all conjured up visions of a repetition of Hicks's disaster – and anyway, of course, Britain was still not to intervene in the Sudan war.[26]

Elsewhere, the *amir* Muhammad el-Kheir captured Berber on 18 May 1884, which would let the Mahdist block travel along the river. In the south, the *amir* Karamallah made advances in Bahr el-Ghazal, driving the governor, Emin Pasha, in retreat into the southern part of his province. Karamallah had recruited local forces from the Dinka and other tribes, who had originally contacted the Mahdi in Kordofan. The Mahdi's support, as before, was not only religious but also specifically anti-Egyptian as well, but the balance of these emotions in any particular person or group was liable to shift with events and time. It is doubtful that the Dinka had converted to Islam in this process, though perhaps they had promised to;[27] their political stance was thus rather like that which the Makk Adam had attempted to maintain.

By August 1884, the British government had at last decided that, to bring Gordon out, they must send a British force in. It was to be commanded by Sir Garnet Wolseley, as in the war in Egypt. It was not until September, however, utilising the flood of the high Nile to move the boats, that his force began to advance south along the river, and then progress was very slow. He had 10,500 troops, British, Indian, Egyptian, and others, a typically mixed British imperial army. They advanced along the river in a huge flotilla of boats, pulled through the cataracts by conscripted *fellahin*.[28] It took three months to move from Wadi Halfa to Korti (where the course of the river turns from southwards to northeasterly). Here the main force continued along the river, and a 'Desert Column' or 'Camel Column' of 1,500 men mounted on camels was separated off to march across the desert, over the Bayuda to Metemma, opposite Shendi. (Sixty-five years before, the original Egyptian conquering expedition under Prince Ismail had advanced along the same route.) Four steamers had been sent by Gordon to collect them, and had been waiting at Metemma for four months. The aim was mainly to reinforce Gordon – but only temporarily, of course – as he was thought to be in imminent danger, correctly. Muhammad el-Kheir had a major Mahdist force at Berber, and the Desert Column was intercepted at Abu Tulagh (which the British called Abu Klea). The disciplined British square, armed with Martini rifles and firing in volleys, destroyed repeated Mahdist charges, inflicting perhaps 1,000 casualties; the lesson was repeated two days later by the defeat of another force at el-Qubba (Gubat) outside Metemma.[29] But both battles imposed delays on the movements of the relieving forces.

These fights saw the clash of the rival tactical methods: the British force was well supplied, and was able to rest for a while along the way at a convenient well, and then go on to fight in their chosen method, an infantry square, which was the normal British method in colonial warfare at this period – as at el-Teb under Graham. Muhammad el-Kheir, by contrast, used the method of the Mahdi at Shaykan, having waited in relative comfort for the approach of the enemy, this time the presumably weary and thirsty British column, and then charging it, aiming to overwhelm it by sheer numbers and ferocity. It had worked at Shaykan against Hicks's poorly disciplined Egyptian force, which had also been surrounded; it did not work at Abu Klea, where the square was actually briefly broken; at el-Qubba and el-Teb, it did work.

The imperial commander of the Desert Column, General Sir Herbert Stewart, was killed in the second fight, and his successor, Sir Charles Wilson, rested his men for three days at Metemma. In that short period, the Mahdists besieging Khartoum put in their greatest attacks. The defences were overrun, many of the Egyptian soldiers were slaughtered, particularly the Sudanese of the Shaiqiyah tribe, who had been steadily loyal to the Egyptian khedives since Muhammad Ali's time. Others fled, and selected groups and individuals in the population were murdered, Gordon among them, though there was deliberate pressure from the Mahdi to locate and preserve the bureaucrats, since it was intended to set up a proper bureaucratic state, and any Egyptians who could provide the necessary skills and information would be useful, and could be employed – the Mahdi's pragmatism in action once again.

Next day, Wilson and his ships arrived, too late.[30] He had only 260 soldiers on his two steamers, and when he arrived close to the city they were greeted by a great storm of fire from behind the barricades and defences; landing was impossible; it was evident that the city had been taken. Even if he had arrived at the city before it was stormed and he had got into the city, he and his men would probably have perished in the slaughter. His mission was a useless exercise, and did not prove, as some said, that a larger force would have 'saved' Gordon, or relieved Khartoum; it is just as likely that a larger force would have been wiped out. He and the Desert Column were withdrawn to Korti by mid-March. A project to mount an advance from Suakin was mooted, then abandoned; the men at Korti were withdrawn further along the Nile. Finally, the southern boundary of Egypt was established at Wadi Halfa.[31]

It had all been unnecessary, of course. Had the Mahdists let Wilson and his ships through to collect Gordon there would have been no need for a grand assault, the British could have gone away claiming a victory, while the Mahdists could have enjoyed the fruits of their success, and a considerable number of men, including Gordon, would have still been alive. But the Mahdi wanted, even required politically, a spectacular victory that would shout his name throughout the Islamic lands. The junction of Gordon and the relief expedition was also intended, on the other side, to be a political-military disaster for the Mahdi's forces. Both sides, therefore, wanted a battle. The Mahdists did not realise, of course, what the British ships were aiming to do – bring out Gordon and the Egyptian forces, and not to rescue the city – and, of course, Gordon may not have consented to be evacuated, and might well have persuaded Wilson to stay in Khartoum to be defeated alongside him. Gordon thus appears to have had a martyr complex. If he had stayed, the fighting would have been even worse, and quite likely the British casualties even greater, as would the Mahdi's.

The Mahdi had won another war. But he survived his great victory for only five months. He died on 22 June 1885. A brief dispute among the senior followers was quickly resolved when they pledged allegiance to the Khalifa Abdallahi ibn Muhammad as his successor, which it was said Muhammad Ahmad had himself indicated. However, the new man's position had certain elements of difficulty about it, and first of all, he would need to win victories in order to have his authority recognised by all sections. He was of the Ta'aisha tribe from the Kordofan region, and under his rule the Mahdist regime was gradually converted into a normal Muslin monarchy – as, in historical terms, was to be expected.[32]

The death of Muhammad Ahmad the Mahdi was a disaster for his cause. His successors may have mouthed the slogans and accepted the beliefs he propounded, and may have operated in his style, so far as they understood it, but there is no doubt that he was head and shoulders above them all in his political and military abilities. His death removed the engine of Mahdist success and expansionism. The British and the Egyptians, possibly the Ethiopians, and a variety of African states, from the Great Lakes to the Sahara, and west to the Sokoto Caliphate, survived because he did not continue to lead the revolution he had begun. His charisma and inspiration, his ambition, his strategic intelligence, his practicality and pragmatism, were all superior to almost everyone in the contemporary world – Gordon, Baring, the Turks, and the Europeans he encountered. Had he lived longer one may be sure that he would have counted many more successes. His neighbours had a fortunate escape.

Abdallahi, the Khalifa, was perhaps supported in his early struggles to establish authority by the news of the continued retreat of the Egyptian/British expeditionary force. At about the time of his succession, the British-Egyptian rescue expedition was retreating along the Nile as far as Wadi Halfa, having evacuated a series of forts and positions along the river, as originally intended; on the Red Sea coast, the garrison at Suakin was removed. In the next two months the major towns that were already under a desultory siege, Sennar on the Blue Nile and Kassala far in the east, were both taken, so the Mahdist state expanded without serious effort east to the Red Sea and northwards to the Nile's second cataract.

The loss of Sudan was the end of the Egyptian Empire. It had stretched from the Mediterranean to the Equator, along the Red Sea coast and beyond into Somalia, and west almost to the border of Darfur with Wadai. But without Sudan it had lost its essential central element. The Mahdists gradually filled out their conquests in the next years, but soon reached the limits of what they could achieve, which had been set by the British government at Aswan or Wadi Halfa even before Gordon's adventure.[33] Even before the Mahdist state's eventual defeat, its borders had been further retracted, against Ethiopia, against the resistance in the Nuba Hills and western Darfur, and in the far south.

The local Mahdist levies along the Nile allowed the British/Egyptian forces to retire gradually, but when they ventured a more vigorous attack on the retreating forces these turned to fight. This was a force composed of men who had been withdrawn from the posts to the south, perhaps from as far as Khartoum, and who knew by this time what to expect. Most of them were Egyptian, probably in many cases men from the former Egyptian army who had supported Urabi (now in exile). They had competent British generals in command, and won a decisive victory at Qinis (Ginnis), halfway between Dongola and Wadi Halfa. They then retired still further north, unmolested. Wadi Halfa was held from then on by an Egyptian force.[34]

The forcible entry of British military power into the land of Egypt brought a series of changes there, and cut the heart out of the empire established by Muhammad Ali. The British interest was primarily in the financial health of the country, and its ability to repay the international debt; imperial expansion was an expensive business, a fact driven home by the cost of the failed expedition

Muhammad Ahmad el Mahdi; the only portrait of him.

The Suez Canal; a sight to see for Egyptians, who, after all, built it. The ships are depicted as sailing rather too closely together. Much of the canal looks the same today.

Ferdinand de Lesseps, the inspirer of the canal, a true entrepreneur, wheeling and dealing, ignoring debts, and ultimately successful, against heavy odds. He tried the same magic with the Panama Canal, and was defeated.

Sir Evelyn Baring, effective ruler of Egypt for two decades. Later, as Lord Cromer, a high potentate in British politics, especially during the Great War, but always essentially a bureaucrat.

Urabi Pasha, pictured in 1906; the first native Egyptian to have effective rule of Egypt since the pharaohs, but unable to hold on to the power he captured. (*Wikimedia Commons/ CC BY-SA 2.5*)

Alexandria under fire from a British fleet in 1882 – unplanned and unintended, but Admiral Beauchamp Seymour was undeterred by possible criticism.

Brigadier General Sir Garnet Wolseley, conqueror of Egypt (and Ashanti and central Canada earlier). A modern general, as Gilbert and Sullivan pointed out, but a planner rather than an inspiring leader. He failed in Sudan, where he had to improvise. But he got a peerage.

General Charles Gordon, an exciting commander and boss, but generally unable to complete any task he began. He was also disobedient, and over-confident, which brought his death at Khartoum.

Brigadier General Herbert Kitchener, adorned with his medals as *sirdar* of the Egyptian army in Egypt. He was an organiser rather than a fighter, and later organised himself into power in India and as a recruiter for the British Army against Germany. The victor of Omdurman, and Captain Marchand's nemesis.

The Mahdi's tomb, before British shells damaged it, and before General Kitchener rifled it and removed the Mahdi's skull as a souvenir. Queen Victoria was horrified and compelled him to replace it. The tomb is now rebuilt and a Sudanese shrine.

Captain Marchand lands to meet Kitchener at Fashoda. Kitchener was being unusually diplomatic – as per his instructions, of course – and was dressed in his Egyptian uniform and flew the Egyptian flag; no doubt unwilling to play this game, he nevertheless did so, successfully, and may have avoided a war. Marchand's face was thus saved, but he still ended up at the meeting with nothing.

Captain Marchand became, for a time, a French hero, but he had still been humiliated, and France learned a lesson in not challenging a stronger power – until 1914, of course.

Menelik, *negusa nagast* of Ethiopia, was the real winner in the imperial struggle for north-eastern Africa, winning battles, founding cities and unifying his country. Politically, he was head and shoulders above all others involved in the area.

Al-Zubayr Rahma Mansur, slaver and dupe. He was successful as a slaver, and as founder of a principality in the Bahr el-Ghazal area, from which he seized control of Darfur. But he was asked to go to Cairo and there he was held in gilded captivity for the rest of his life – the clever politician outmanoeuvred so easily.

Henry Morton Stanley, reporter and self-proclaimed explorer, but also a brutal killer of Africans. He excelled at newspaper stunts on a large scale, seeking out men – Livingstone, and Emin Pasha, who did not wish to be found. He also excelled in developing distractions to hide his brutality.

The Ripon Falls in Uganda. The river Nile, so long, so essential to life, is also thoroughly awkward fo travellers, with six cataracts in its lower course, and a series of ten waterfalls and cataracts in its uppe course – not to mention the great swamp of the Sudd. (*Andyessex via Wikimedia Commons/CC BY 3.0*)

under Wolseley to bring out Gordon. (Egypt had been supposed to bear the cost, but in the end Britain had to provide a substantial sum, in addition, of course, to the actual soldiers.)[35] The Egyptian government may well have wished to attempt the recovery of Sudan; the British were not interested – at least not yet – so it did not happen; it was a clear demonstration, if anyone needed it, of who was in charge.

The career of the Mahdi was the cause of all this imperial upset. His inspirational work and his political ability was the source of the construction of the new Muslim empire in Sudan, but which ceased to expand with the end of his inspired leadership. None of his successors, not even the Khalifa Abdallahi, had a fraction of his abilities. But his state's failure to expand did not mean peace for its neighbours. He left it presenting an apparent, and at times an actual, threat to all its neighbouring states for the next decade and a half. The fate of his state was a central problem for all those neighbours and far beyond for the rest of the nineteenth century.

The Mahdi was as much an empire builder as Clive of India, or Napoleon, or Julius Caesar. When that coarse soldier Herbert Kitchener dug up his remains, threw the bones into the Nile, and carried off the skull, threatening to present it to the College of Surgeons in London, he was displaying a soldierly contempt for his enemy. Queen Victoria, however, as so often, put her finger on the essential point when she insisted that the skull be properly treated and buried: he was, she pointed out, a head of state, after all.[36]

Chapter 11

The Destruction of the Egyptian Empire: III – The 'Debris'

In the process of their conquests the Mahdists had cut out the most important part of the empire constructed by Muhammad Ali, except for Egypt itself; his empire had been expanded by his khedivian successors, but the excision of Sudan dealt it a mortal blow. The empire had certainly been restricted in its recent expansion in several areas, where it had, at least temporarily, apparently reached its limits; it had been prevented from expanding into the Somali lands in 1876; Kordofan and much of Darfur had been taken at the same time, but they were blocked at the Nuba Hills, and the western part of Darfur, and perhaps by Wadai beyond; Baker and Gordon had marched south to the Great Lakes, also at the same time, but that possible expansion had also been stopped, partly because of local hostility, and the human, political and environmental difficulties, and partly because of the financial meltdown in Egypt itself in the 1870s. The Egyptian Empire had thus become over-extended, but it was not necessarily doomed to retreat or not to expand again; the end of expansion could be regarded as a pause for breath before moving on. Yet it was certainly vulnerable in such a condition to its rivals; it was the Mahdists who dealt the fatal blow.

The Egyptian Empire had been a dominant power in north-east Africa, and even in the Near East, ever since Muhammad Ali's army had conquered Sudan in 1821. In Africa, it was the largest state by far; in the world, it was one of the major imperial powers (not that it is usually counted as such). It threatened, simply by being a neighbour, to take over a long series of other states: the Ottoman provinces in western Arabia, where Muhammad Ali's army had campaigned and had, temporarily, suppressed the Wahhabis; the Ethiopian borderlands (though blocked in a couple of armed attempts); the Somali lands; the countries of the African Great Lakes region; those to the west of these as far as the Congo basin, if not further; the sultanate of Wadai to the west of Darfur and the fragmented polities between Darfur and Wadai, if only control of Darfur could be assured, possibly Cyrenaica. Many of these had looked to be worthwhile prey, until the Mahdi's successes in the heart of the empire destroyed whatever intentions there had been in Egypt to expand into these places.

It was clear that the Mahdists, even after the Mahdi's death, were not going away. It also became clear that Britain was in control in Egypt and unlikely to leave soon, and that the British administration was introspectively determined on no further expansion into Sudan. This would cost money, which the British administration believed it could not afford. With all this, the question arose as to what would happen to the fragments of the Egyptian Empire that littered the surrounding countries – the 'debris' of the empire, as Lord Cromer callously put it.[1]

The Egyptian army had been either disbanded by the British or destroyed by the Mahdists in 1882–5, only for both of these destroyers to actively set about recruiting the dismissed or transferred personnel. The Mahdi, in his normal way, gave the prisoners he captured the choice of being recruited into his army, or death; the British gathered up some of those men they had insisted on dismissing, and sent them into the Sudan as a new defence force. (Some men must have gone through both of these processes when captured in the Sudan, perhaps in Khartoum.) While the British held their financial apron strings, the Egyptians were unable to undertake more conquest expeditions after their forces were withdrawn from the Sudan, or even to send help to those fragments of the empire that survived.

Those outliers therefore quickly fell away into other, equally greedy, imperialist hands. This had already happened in one case. The expansion to Kismayu had been turned back in 1876, when the British backed the Zanzibari claims to that town. The expansion of Egyptian authority along the Red Sea coast, from Suakin to Cape Guardafui, was now also curtailed. This was largely the doing, again, of the British, with the Italians tagging along, and the French watching carefully. The British were seriously determined to eliminate the Egyptian Empire altogether, almost as though they saw it as a rival. In many areas, it was such a rival, in its sheer size, its previous capability for expansion, its control of crucial strategic points, notably the Suez Canal, and its use of slavery, which challenged British anti-slavery policy. The British gave various excuses for the mopping up and dividing up process that followed the Mahdi's victory, citing the need for Egyptian financial retrenchment, which was also their excuse for keeping control of Egypt itself. Of course, it just happened that this retrenchment was designed to enable the Egyptian debt to be paid, of the dividends and the Suez Canal Company to be paid out – and the British government held 40 per cent of its shares, and British firms and banks were holding Egyptian paper. The fact remained that the British participated as enthusiastically in the seizure of the spoils as any other European imperial power.

The evisceration of the empire by the Mahdi's conquests, therefore, attracted attention to these spoils, and to some the possibility of controlling the Red Sea would be a useful prize. The Suez Canal was now operational and successful, and this had transformed the Red Sea into a major international routeway in place of the cul-de-sac it had previously been. The French held Obok in the future Djibouti, taken over in 1862, as soon as the Suez Canal's construction had got under way. Next door was the curious Italian 'commercial' private colony – or forlorn hope – at Assab, made into an official colony in 1882, by agreement with Britain, at the time the latter took over in Egypt. Across the Red Sea was the British possession of Aden, originally seized as a useful coaling station for steamers, but now helpfully placed across from Obok to watch or control the entrance to the Red Sea.

Shortly after the invasion of Egypt, an expedition commanded by General Graham was put in occupation of Suakin, partly as a possible base for a Sudan reconquest and partly to prevent the Mahdists getting easy access to the Red Sea; like Aden, it was usefully placed to dominate the central passage along the Red Sea. Suakin was held, and in British hands, it prevented any Mahdist expansion across the Red Sea, where Mecca and all Arabia would no doubt be vulnerable to the Mahdi's appeal. But it was under perpetual pressure from Uthman Digna's Mahdist forces, and in the next years it was protected by several battles between the garrison and the Digna's forces. It was always necessary to fight in an infantry square, and the small British/Egyptian armies usually won if they were competently commanded. But in 1883, the governor (of the Red Sea Coast province) was Sulayman, the former, and brief, commander-in-chief of Hicks's expedition. After the defeat of a small force he had sent out, he tried with a second, similarly small and unprepared expedition, with the result that it also suffered a similar destruction. (One can see Hicks's point in his complaints about the man, not that he had been any better.) Suakin itself did remain under British/Egyptian control.[2]

In 1884, Bismarck called a conference at Berlin to discuss the increasing interest on all sides in colonising Africa – or rather, in seizing control of sections of Africa from the inhabitants. This had, in part, been provoked by the unilateral British conquest of Egypt, and the Mahdi's success in Sudan. (Probably it was no coincidence that Bismarck intervened in African affairs at the moment when Britain was entangled in Egyptian and Sudanese affairs; his main international aim, after all, was always to keep Britain and France, the two powers involved in Egyptian affairs, at mutual enmity.) The British seizure of power in Egypt had been a clear breach of the general international convention that limited such actions to processes agreed amongst the European Great Powers, and no matter how often the British protested that their presence in Egypt was only temporary, it continued to lengthen, though as it happened, not to expand – at least, not yet. Egypt, even by 1884, looked increasingly like a British quasi-colony.

The main result of Bismarck's conference (called the 'West Africa' Conference, but its geographical remit was much wider than that) was a definition of how to recognise the existence of colonial control. A claim to a territory simply because a lone wandering missionary or explorer had been there, and so had 'discovered' it, was no longer to be sufficient for a valid claim. What was required was actual settlement or possession, but there was no definition of what was permitted, nor any recognition of the existence of African states. There were numerous kingdoms and republics in Africa that were clearly independent entities, even if they were unknown to Europeans. (One accepted method of achieving control was to conclude a treaty with an African state, though this was actually also a recognition that such a state existed, and had the power to make treaties, and so the process created further complications.) The inland areas of West Africa, and the African Great Lakes area, were examples, perhaps above all, Ethiopia. These regions were littered with organised states, some of them of considerable age and competent administration, yet they became victims of this definition of colonial 'ownership'. Only Ethiopia succeeded in blocking conquest, yet why the century-old Sokoto Caliphate, or the four-century-old Sultanates of Wadai or Bornu should become victims of European imperialism was politically irrational, though a mark of their political weakness in the face of European power and weaponry. And resistance to conquest was universal.[3]

So, in the area of the Mahdist state, Assab and Obok could be accepted as legitimate colonies because there were Frenchmen and Italians in occupation and governing these places. Suakin was technically part of Sudan, and had an Egyptian/British garrison, so the British had actual control, at least for the present; it was also possible to regard it as Egyptian. But the rest of the Egyptian territories along the Red Sea coast were being abandoned into the possession of enemies and friends. Sudan could no longer be regarded as an Egyptian province once the Mahdists held it, and the 'debris' of the khedivial empire was available for other imperialists to seize.

The city of Harar, well inland, originally captured for Egypt with some effort, along with Zeila, was ordered to be abandoned. Major Hunter, with two other British officers, was sent to organise the evacuation of the Egyptian officials; an Egyptian official, Radman Pasha, went with them as the Egyptian commissioner – but it was clearly the British officers who were in charge; as elsewhere, the evacuation was on British initiative, not Egyptian. Harar had been a continuous expense to Egypt since it had been annexed. Not that the Egyptian government was happy with abandoning a famous Muslim city of trade, which was then expected to stand by itself, surrounded by active imperialist powers, but it 'reluctantly accepted the inevitable logic of facts', according to

Cromer's comment, which in fact had nothing to do with any 'facts', other than British parsimony.[4]

Hunter had to organise a major evacuation operation. The city had attracted a considerable number of Egyptians during khedivian rule, officials and otherwise, and it contained an Egyptian garrison. There were plenty of Hararis who had accepted their rule without protest and who evidently now felt unsafe at the prospect of the removal of Egyptian authority and protection. Along with the garrison, Hunter had to see to the move of over 8,000 people, both Egyptians and Hararis, to the coast, a distance of 200 miles. It took several months to do this, moving them in sections to the coast at Zeila, and then transporting them by sea to Egypt.

The city was indeed handed back to the previous dynasty, which the Egyptians had displaced. Emir Ahmed, from whom it been taken in 1874, was dead, to the relief of all those whom he had oppressed and corruptly judged. His son, Abdullah, became the new emir when the Egyptians withdrew, but held the post for only two years. In 1887, the *Negus* Menelik of Shoa defeated Abdullah's army and seized the city, and it has remained part of the Ethiopian Empire ever since.[5]

The Bab el-Mandeb, the narrows at the southern entrance to the Red Sea, had attracted a miniature version of the worldwide European struggle for imperial control, with Britain, France, Italy, and now Ethiopia, having posts in or near the strait, not to mention the local Arab powers in the Yemen and the hinterland of Aden. Needless to say, the British regarded themselves as having the most important say in local control, citing their need to have access to a route to India. And it was a British dispensation that rationed out the remnants of the Egyptian Empire.

With the Egyptian collapse all this was available for other powers to seize. The British in Egypt were, as at Harar, insisting on the abandonment of the various Egyptian posts. The crucial ones were Massawa, halfway between Suakin and Assab, Zeila, which had prospered as the port for Harari merchants, Berbera, halfway between Zeila and Cape Guardafui, and between Zeila and Obok was the small port of Tadjoura. Various European powers licked their chops and lunged for these places; Britain stood as umpire in the contest. These places were not just ports of trade, but, seen from India and Aden, and from Egypt, the whole Sudanese and Somali coasts had potential for the establishment of hostile, that is to say, European, naval bases, from which the strait could be dominated or controlled, or the passage interrupted. But for the British to seize all of the Egyptian bases for themselves would surely precipitate a serious clash with the other interested parties; instead, the British managed the division – divide and rule.

In early 1884, a French ship landed a squad of sailors at Tadjoura to inform the inhabitants and the Egyptian authorities that France was taking control of their town – the French, for all their espousal of 'liberty' and 'fraternity' and republican and democratic principles, were always more arrogant than others in seizing a place – someone else's place, to be exact. As an Egyptian town it was technically, through Egypt, part of the Ottoman Empire, and protests were made by the sultan to Britain as Egypt's new co-suzerain of the remains of Egypt's empire, but the British government ignored this, and the French completed their annexation; this extended the French territory of Obok; together they thereby constituted the future French colony of Djibouti.[6]

From the extended French colony of Obok and Tadjoura eastwards along the coast there were just two places of local significance – Zeila and Berbera. The British got themselves into a diplomatic tangle over which power actually had authority at these places, but the Egyptians had seized both of them in 1874 – in Zeila's case, with the permission of the Ottoman sultan – though Berbera's status was unclear to everyone (though it could have been constituted as an independent city-state if anyone had accepted such a thought). As the khedivian regime failed, it fell to the British to sort matters out. They did so by annexing Berbera themselves in 1885; the year after, Major Hunter took control of Zeila before he went on to abandon Harar, evacuating the Egyptians to and through Zeila. He telegraphed, in the condescending and stoic language of British imperialists: 'Force landed at Zeila. Somalis impressed. Governor obliging.' The first part of this message may well have been true; the other two parts seem unlikely to have been so.[7]

The timing of all this imperialist activity in the Bab el-Mandeb is suggestive. The Suez Canal was built in 1859–69, and opened to traffic in the latter year; the British purchase of an effective majority of shares in the canal company was in 1874, and the British conquest of Egypt came in 1882. This is regarded to have been the trigger, partly because it drew attention to the new power of Britain in the Red Sea, but also because it was followed by the collapse of Egypt's ramshackle empire, in many pieces.

The French had moved first, by annexing Tadjoura early in 1884, moving across the bay from Obok, a short journey. By May, the British were actively seeking to establish control of Zeila and Berbera, and by early next year these two places had been seized, and Harar abandoned. A little earlier, in 1882, the Italian private colony at Assab had been taken over by an official government expedition, sent out so secretly that only the captain of the ship doing the deed knew what the mission was.[8]

Two more places along that coast, Suakin and Massawa, remained. Suakin was host to the British/Egyptian garrison, and this put it out of reach of any other European power; in theory it was being held by the British for Egypt, but eventually its geographical location compelled it to become part of Sudan. Repeated attempts by the Mahdist forces were made to take it over, but they all failed; the Anglo-Egyptian defence gradually solidified its possession. Massawa, like the other places along this coast, was technically an Ottoman town, but had been leased from the sultan by the khedive for an annual tribute; it was occupied by an Egyptian garrison. This put it in the vulnerable category, like Harar and Zeila, particularly since the crisis in Egypt had apparently reduced the authority of the local governor. A British officer, Colonel Herbert Chermside, who was based at Suakin as the negotiator with the local tribes, visited Massawa and spoke of 'chaos', and 'indescribable confusion' in the town, and hoped that the 'Massawa question' would soon be settled.[9]

The British government took it upon itself to offer the town to Italy. This 'offer' was denied later by the British, but the message that was delivered to the Italian government was worded in such a way that 'offer' is the only interpretation that fits. The result was that in 1885 an Italian expedition arrived at Massawa to find that the Egyptian garrison in post was being compelled by a British diplomat to yield to the Italian claim, though they had not been told of the change earlier – no doubt a careful omission by the British; an Italian garrison then shared authority for a time with the Egyptian garrison, until the former eventually chased the latter out. This, with Assab, and the coast between, plus an unknown extent of the inland territory, was then constituted into the Italian colony of Eritrea. The Italians were also looking to expand further.[10]

The net result of all this was the partition of the Egyptian Empire of the Red Sea coast between four competing powers, of which Britain took the major part (the ports of Zeila and Berbera, which became British Somaliland, and Suakin); the French a small section that they saw as a possible base for expansion inland; Eritrea (at first just the posts of Assab and Massawa) went to Italy; the Ethiopians took the most immediately valuable part, the city of Harar (but not its usual port at Zeila). This arrangement was obviously designed by the British to take some of the heat out of any possible dispute about their occupation of Egypt by handing out useful posts to possible (European) complainants, and so making them complicit in the original act. It could not be hidden that the three most useful ports along the coast – Suakin, Zeila and Berbera, athwart the route to India – fell to Britain, while the other, minor ports went to the lesser European naval powers. Nor could it be hidden that Harar, in Ethiopian possession, was effectively out of reach of any European state; Ethiopia was, locally, a great power.

This set of operations took place in 1882–5, while the Mahdi conquered the Sudan and Gordon was besieged at Khartoum. Gordon's original task had been, of course, to evacuate the Egyptian garrisons along the river, but there were other Sudanese places that were out of his reach even if he had been able to leave the city. These were well away from the Nile, and most of them were also being attacked.

One group of such bereft places was in the borderlands between Ethiopia and Sudan, half a dozen places from which large numbers of refugees had eventually to be evacuated. The most important of these was Kassala, which was now a large town and had become a major market centre for the Taka region inland from the Red Sea coast. It was besieged from November 1883 by a lieutenant of Uthman Digna. One of the reasons for keeping up the pressure on the British/Egyptian garrison at Suakin, as Uthmam Digna did, was to prevent that garrison from helping out at Kassala. The siege was, however, hindered by the contemporary siege of al-Mager, near to Kassala, by Digna's forces, but when this fell, the Kassala siege was intensified. The city was eventually surrendered in July 1885 to commissioners sent by the Mahdi a month before he died. In addition, two small posts, Amadib and Senhit, were evacuated in the spring of 1885, their garrisons being moved to Massawa and then evacuated to Egypt.[11]

The location of the westernmost posts along the Ethiopian borderlands put them between the area controlled by the Mahdi, and that under the government of the Emperor Yohannes of Tigray. Their only way to safety, assuming the posts could not be expected to survive for very long, was through Ethiopian territory. In early 1884, Admiral Sir William Hewett, who had landed the Indian troops at Suez in 1881, and was commander-in-chief of the Royal Navy's Indian Ocean fleet, travelled into northern Ethiopia to negotiate a safe passage for the isolated men. He met Ras Alula, who was governor of the northernmost province, Hamasien, with his governor's seat at Asmara. They negotiated a treaty that permitted the garrisons and the civilians who wished to evacuate to do so across Ethiopian territory. In return, Massawa – still under Egyptian control at that point – would be open to Ethiopian trade, including the reception of firearms and ammunition. The region to the north of Alula's territory, Bogos, would be transferred to Ethiopia. The terms were very much in Ethiopia's favour, but it would be up them to secure their gains. The treaty was signed at Adowa in June, and ratified quickly by the Emperor Yohannes.[12]

The result, however, was also very satisfactory from the Egyptian viewpoint. Early in 1885, the two small posts, Amadib and Senhit, in what is now Eritrea, were successfully evacuated; the emperor provided Ethiopian troops as escorts for the journey across his country. An Egyptian officer, Sa'd Rif'at, efficiently reached al-Qallabat (Gallabat) and brought out a convoy of soldiers and civilians, and in the process conducted a successful interview with the emperor, persuading him to provide an escort, and negotiating all sorts of difficulties, physical and diplomatic; he also negotiated the evacuation of al-Jira (Gera). Only one of the besieged garrisons – at al-Qadarif (Gedaref) was actually captured by the Mahdists. The basic reason for the Ethiopian attitude was, of course, a certain degree of apprehension as to the future intentions of the Mahdists; the persistence of Egyptian garrisons in these places might well be used as a Mahdist excuse to attack.

In the process, something like 10,000 soldiers and civilians were successfully escorted to Massawa for onward passage to Egypt.[13] This was a considerable total, more than had been removed from Harar, indicating that there had been a serious colonising effort by Egyptians in the area, especially at Harar. By the end of 1885 there were no more of these isolated posts left, which was satisfactory, but it also meant that the Mahdists, under their new *khalifa*, would be able to concentrate on expanding their new state, without having to deal with the these isolated posts first. In the midst of all this activity, the Khalifa sent a message to the Emperor Yohannes, requiring his conversion to Islam and his submission. He cannot have expected compliance, and in that, at least he was not disappointed. In the process of rescuing the fugitives, the Mahdists and the Ethiopians had several times clashed in war (see chapter 12).

The most curious remnant of the Egyptian Empire was Equatoria, and this was the most difficult to deal with. The Mahdist offensive southwards from Darfur, after the destruction of Hicks's army, had conquered the Bahr el-Ghazal province, and in 1884 the *amir* Karamallah had taken prisoner the governor there; this was Frank Lupton Bey, a former sailor who had been promoted to governor by Gordon. (He was held at Khartoum, and died in 1888.)[14] The Mahdists had been helped by a considerable sentiment in favour of the Mahdi among the Dinka tribes, though this, as in Darfur and Kordofan, was more the result of a detestation for Egyptian rule than for any religious or political allegiance. The Dinka had been subjected to extensive slave raiding, and when that became less onerous – the Mahdists were much less addicted to slave hunting than the Egyptians, and were hostile to the slave raiders in their fortified *zeribas* – this was succeeded by cattle raids that were conducted by the Egyptian garrisons to feed themselves.[15]

South of the Bahr el-Ghazal, which was within relatively easy reach of Darfur, particularly now that the Taqali kingdom in the Nuba Hills had been suppressed, was the province of Equatoria. This had been organised as a province originally in a perfunctory way by Sir Samuel Baker, and had then been put on a rather more secure foundation by Gordon after Gessi's successful campaigns. Even so, it was a less than securely held region. It was partly protected from attack from the north by the Sudd and the rivers and forests of the Bahr el-Ghazal region, and it was certainly at a considerable distance from the centres of Mahdist power. Karamallah, based in the Bahr el-Ghazal province, made attempts to invade this farthest south territory, but he did not get far. This would have been a valuable conquest, for beyond the Sudd the country was a productive region, producing quantities of food and plenty of animals, which would have been a useful foundation for securing supplies for further conquests. Both Bahr el-Ghazal and Equatoria were particularly rich in cattle; for a couple of generations, ivory had been one of its major products, being especially prized for its quality.

The governor, since shortly after Gordon left in 1876, was Emin Pasha, who had been Edward Schnitzler at home in Austria and Germany; in Sudan he converted to Islam, though not too seriously. He headed off Karamallah's first approach by offering him a rather distant submission, which had much the same sincerity as that made by the Dinka. Most of his troops, particularly the Egyptians and the Sudanese soldiers, had no wish to be the Mahdi's subjects, but there was a minority to whom his doctrines and purposes did appeal. Cunningly, Emin sent these Mahdist sympathisers to Karamallah with his message of submission; they all stayed with the Mahdists, as he had expected, so that Emin was then left with his loyal troops alone. These had earlier persuaded him not to surrender, as he had probably originally intended. Karamallah made several further attempts to enforce Emin's submission, which must be regarded as theoretical only, but the environment – that is, the Sudd and the forest – defeated Karamallah's expansion efforts even more decisively than the opposition of Emin's soldiers.[16] After 1885, Emin was more or less freed of the Mahdist threat for some time.

Emin, along with his soldiers, remained in effective control of Equatoria, and in practical independence. He was told, in a message replying to an appeal for assistance that he had sent by way of Zanzibar to the khedivial government, that the government was no longer interested in holding Equatoria.[17] He could not therefore expect to receive any help or supplies from Egyptian sources. He had had no supplies from the north for more than two years before Karamallah's tentative advances, and he was not going to receive any more in view of the severing of communications between Egypt and Equatoria by the Mahdist War and conquests. Hence the cattle raids by his garrisons, which annoyed the neighbouring villagers almost as much as the earlier slave raiding.

Emin was able to hold on for a time, but his outlying posts were slowly being lost to attacks by the local tribes, who, like the Dinka, had been subjected to slave and cattle raiding by the Egyptian and Sudanese garrisons, and were keen to remove any likely bases for their resumption. His territory gradually shrank to a line of posts along the Nile from Lado southwards. These final posts continued to be subject to raids by the local people. They had learned the practice from their victims, and clearly understood Emin's isolation. He was able to communicate with Egypt by way of Zanzibar, explaining his isolation, but did not ask to be pulled out; the message from the government in Cairo effectively left him to act as he chose, and so in independence. Nevertheless, the news of his isolation provoked another British frenzy of guilt-and-rescue when his 'plight' became known. Projects to 'rescue' him — not his choice of words — were constructed, and Henry Morton Stanley was hired to make another of his violent and disastrous journeys by way of the Congo to bring him out. Emin was reluctant to leave, but he seems to have been persuaded at last when a new Mahdist attack on his position approached.[18]

When Stanley and Emin met in mid-1888 at Lake Albert, there were three disputants angling for control of Equatoria. Those in actual occupation of the region were Emin's soldiers, who were mainly southern Sudanese. They had no wish to leave. There was also a contingent of Egyptians who had been exiled by Khedive Taufiq because they were adherents of Urabi, and they also intended to stay. Stanley and Emin discussed the matter at Lake Albert in April, but the former had been unable to persuade Emin or his soldiers to leave.[19] (This response, of course, destroyed the entire basis of Stanley's expedition.)

From the north, a Mahdist force under Umar Salih, 1,500 soldiers carried in 3 steamers and 9 sailing ships, had left Omdurman in June 1888. This force reached Lado, Emin's northernmost post on the Nile, in October. Meanwhile, Emin's soldiers had mutinied in August, mainly against Stanley and his plans to evacuate them. Emin and one of Stanley's lieutenants, Jephson, were jailed by the mutineers at Dufile, one of Emin's main posts halfway between Lado and Lake Albert.[20]

Umar Salih sent messages demanding Emin's surrender. The mutineers, led by Fadl al-Maula Muhammad, a Sudanese officer, killed Umar's envoys, which in effect was a declaration of war — not that Umar Salih had been intending anything less. Fadl's deed was designed to send a defiant message, and at the same time was guaranteed to infuriate the enemy and to make it impossible for Emin's mutineers to surrender without facing death. (It is unlikely that they would have survived in any event; it was routine for defeated but defiant enemies of the Mahdists to be killed.) Umar advanced as far as Dufile, whence Emin and Jephson were released by their captors to avoid their capture. At this point Emin was finally alone, many of his soldiers having abandoned him, and now he had the support only of Stanley, whose purpose was, of course, to take him away. Stanley took him (and Jephson) and some of his followers off to Zanzibar and Europe. Emin finally left his little empire with Stanley on 10 April 1889.[21]

Emin had been a governor appointed by the khedivial government in Cairo, and it had attempted to cast him adrift back in 1885. This decision was only indirectly reported to him, but his continued occupation of the area meant that Egypt could still be said to have retained a distant claim to the Equatoria province while he was there. His removal ended the viability of that claim. The Equatoria province was now really independent, under the governorship of Fadl al-Maula Muhammad, the chief of the mutineers, supported by those of Emin's former soldiers who remained. But it was now also the centre of a series of claims, or rather arbitrary grabs, by all its neighbours, rather like the more decorous process that had divided up the Egyptian remnants along the Red Sea.

By 1889, the contenders for this region were: the British, approaching from the East African coast, and primarily interested in contacting the kingdoms in the Great Lakes region; possibly the Germans, who were moving into the future Tanganyika from the Indian Ocean coast in parallel with the British in Kenya; certainly the Belgians from the Congo were interested; and, as always, the Mahdists, who had managed to reach as far south as Dufile, travelling and campaigning along the White Nile. In addition, there was Fadl and the mutineers, who were in actual occupation, and owed allegiance by this time only to themselves: they must be counted as an independent state for this brief time. And this was the region in which the newly recorded (to Europeans) states of Buganda, Bunyoro and Toro, and the rest, also existed; in a sense, Fadl and his men were an addition to this Central African state system. This was another fragment of the destroyed Egyptian Empire for others to quarrel over, but it also, of course, involved the Great Lakes kingdoms. With Emin's departure, this was no longer to be considered part of Egypt's empire, any more than the posts on the Red Sea taken by the European powers, or Darfur, which was mainly now part of the Mahdist state.

The Egyptian Empire had thus been dismantled, and its parts seized by predators, African and European. The only real victors in the process were the Mahdists, who the gained control of Sudan, Darfur, Kordofan, much of the Red Sea coast region, and an indeterminate area of the southern provinces; in this the Mahdists had been doing the work for the various other powers that were interested in seizing control of other fragments, by cutting out the last of the empire in Sudan. The most sinister activity was by the British, who had been involved in the transfer of all the Red Sea territories to Italy (Massawa), France (Tadjoura), and the Ethiopians (Harar and the evacuated posts along the border, and some of the evacuated posts along the border), all against the wishes of the khedivial government. They had even double-crossed the Ethiopians, for part of the Treaty of Adowa with Ras Alula had permitted Ethiopian trade to pass through Massawa, but less than a year later, that port was delivered, through British diplomacy, to the Italians, who had no real interest in that treaty or in assisting the Ethiopians, upon whose empire they had already laid a beady, greedy eye. The Adowa treaty was thus discarded, from the British point of view, once the Egyptian garrisons at al-Qallabat and the rest had been brought out, and once Massawa was taken by the Italians. This British treachery may be added to the deliberate British policy of destroying Egypt's empire in the name of financial retrenchment, to the ultimate benefit in the end mainly of themselves.

The Egyptian Empire had therefore been destroyed in the short time between the Mahdist victories in Kordofan in 1883 and the evacuation of Emin Pasha from the Great Lakes region in 1888. It had taken fifty years or so to acquire, and a tenth of that to be destroyed. The way in which its parts had been taken over, under British supervision and participation, made it clear to Egyptians that they would not be able to recover any of it in the future. This did not mean that the issue was finished with, however. The surrounding predators, European and African, were not yet satisfied, and the repercussions of the empire's destruction would resonate for a long time yet.

Chapter 12

The Wars of the Mahdists

The Mahdist state, under both the Mahdi and his successor the Khalifa Abdallahi, was an aggressive polity. It was also somewhat unstable in political terms, and suffered disputes between the constituent tribes, and civil wars.[1] In economic terms it was a state of a fairly primitive type, its population mainly depending on subsistence agriculture and some trade, most of it in portable goods; landed wealth was in only a few hands, particularly the rulers'. The aggressive impulses of the state – built-in by its very nature, as a *jihad* state – directed it to attack all its neighbours, the Christian lands to bring them into Islam, the Islamic lands to cleanse them of heresy and infidel practices, pagan lands to convert their populations; a civil war in Darfur grew out of a quarrel between the Mahdists and the Sanusi in the region.[2]

No doubt, if the Khalifa had sufficient resources, armies would have moved out in all directions. In fact, there were four enemies that had existed from the start of the Mahdi's work, and which, if further progress was to be made, it was necessary to defeat – Egypt to the north (Muslim), Ethiopia to the east (mainly Christian), the lands in the Upper Nile to the south (pagan), and the Taqali hillmen in the south-west (partly pagan, partly Muslim). The western frontier, which may have looked more enticing from an expansionist point of view, with its soft and porous borders and its weak neighbouring states, never became a true field of conquest, because of the western territories that were already part of the state – Darfur and Kordofan – which were even more unstable than the rest, and were often the scenes of internal fighting, as well as a continuous active frontier, altogether not a good basis for imperialist campaigns.[3] The possibilities in the southern and western direction were shown by the later career of Rabeh.[4]

The possibility of expanding at Egyptian expense was also to be closed off. The conquests in Sudan had been relatively easy, in part because the khedivial forces were scattered, corrupt, outnumbered and unequal to the task – though those who were captured and incorporated into the Mahdi's army proved to be notably competent, at least in comparison with their fellow warriors who were recruited from the tribal forces. (The fact that the Egyptian forces were fighting against a charismatic Islamic leader may have had a good deal to do with their poor performance in opposing him; they must have had doubts that they should actually be opposing him.) The Mahdi's pragmatic attitude to warfare had allowed the adoption of more effective weaponry and tactics, which also had their effect, and the enforcement of greater discipline on his tribal forces. The fact that Egypt itself was undergoing a revolution and conquest by the British, and its army was being defeated, while the Mahdi was simultaneously fighting in Sudan, had also obviously distracted its government, and undermined the resistance of the Egyptian occupation forces in Sudan.

These advantages, however, had been overcome by 1885 when the Mahdist armies suffered their defeats at Suakin (more than once) and on the Nile at Qinis. If progress towards the conquest of Egypt by the Khalifa was to be made – it was an obvious aim – some way of defeating the British infantry tactics of fighting in squares, with artillery, rifles and volley fire, had to be found. This would actually require a much greater degree of discipline in the Mahdist forces than the tribal levies would probably tolerate. So further progress in combating the British tactics never really occurred, despite the inclusion of the trained men who had enlisted as prisoners after the various battles. A moment's consideration will also have made it clear that, if and when the British decided to take their revenge for their expulsion from Sudan, the Mahdists' military problem would become insoluble, and they would face defeat. It must have been realised by men on both sides that the death of the Mahdi had removed the real engine of power for the Mahdist cause; the Khalifa Abdallahi was certainly a competent ruler, but not in the same league as the inspiring and clever Muhammad Ahmad, and he could not command the same loyalty from his followers; a certain relaxation of tension in Egypt could be allowed.

The obvious route to success against Egypt would have been to stimulate disaffection and rebellion among the Muslims in Egypt, but this does not seem to have been seriously attempted; instead, there was a widespread assumption amongst the existing Mahdists that a favourable attitude already existed among many Egyptians. This was a result of their success so far, and of the feeling of self-confidence and holy justification. In the absence of providing strict military discipline, both the Mahdi and the Khalifa were putting their faith in conquests by crowds of amateur soldiers who had to be inspired to fight. Their battle tactics were, and remained, an overwhelming charge by spearmen, though with increasing numbers of modern weapons many also became competent rifleman, if often rash and inaccurate.

The man put in command of the invasion of Egypt was Abd al-Rahman al-Nujumi, a cunning and intelligent commander who had the devotion of his troops, qualities that led to him being regarded with suspicion by the Khalifa. This attitude to his subordinate commanders distinguished Abdullahi from the Mahdi, who was less angry and more confident – and a more competent ruler.

Al-Nujumi was put in charge of the northern expedition in 1886, but a series of crises inside the Mahdist state prevented him from moving until 1889. By then the new Egyptian army had been fully recruited, had become trained, was commanded by British officers well accustomed to commanding 'natives' – most were seconded from the Indian Army – and the troops themselves had been well trained in British tactics. They therefore posed a severe problem for the section of the Ansar that were with al-Nujumi. One of the crises that delayed al-Nujumi was a famine, which affected both Sudan and Egypt. In the absence of any allocated or provided supplies, the army had to scavenge for food among the inhabitants on its march northwards; but these were already suffering from the same famine and the requisitions met with little success.

These military afflictions – hunger, thirst, desertion, and a watchful and competent enemy – delayed the Ansar's advance for three years. Above all, the expectation that the Egyptian villagers would welcome the soldiers and feed them was disappointed from the very start. Al-Nujumi was soon compelled to report to the Khalifa that the earlier assumption that the Egyptians were really Mahdist in sentiment and would welcome the Ansar was wrong. That is, the conclusion had to be that the movement rested on the disposition and attitudes of the Sudanese tribes only, and was possibly not applicable to other Muslim states; no doubt, this was a great disappointment to the Khalifa. He will have understood, and will not have underestimated, the effects of the death of the Mahdi himself.

The end of the northern expedition came at the village of Tushki, 50 miles north of Wadi Halfa, but still south of Aswan. The Egyptian garrison at Wadi Halfa had watched as the Ansar passed by in the desert, well clear of them – an encouraging sign for the Egyptian soldiers, since it presumed the Ansar's fear of them. Al-Nujumi believed he could get support further north, so he chose to ignore the garrisons along the river – probably a mistake since victories at the start would have convinced both his own soldiers and the enemy that his invasion was much more formidable than it turned out to be. In accordance with Mahdist practice and victories, he would have increased his rather small force by recruiting any surviving prisoners. By the time the army reached Tushki, however, the 5,000 troops with which he had started out (accompanied by 8,000 followers – no wonder they all went hungry) had been reduced by death and desertion to about 3,000 warriors. They faced an army mainly composed of Egyptian soldiers (with a British contingent approaching, but which arrived too late for the battle) under a skilled tactician, General Sir Francis Grenfell, the *sirdar* (commander-in-chief) of the Egyptian army who was well experienced at facing Mahdist armies. A personal reconnaissance by Grenfell chose the place where his men would fight, and the accompanying British cavalry force, commanded by Colonel H.H. Kitchener, blocked al-Nujumi's attempt to bypass Grenfell's force and attack from the flank and rear. Al-Nujumi had decided again to avoid combat, hoping to bypass the Egyptian force, and so reach the settled and populated and productive lands; by now he knew he would find little or no support in Egypt, and that his invasion tactics were not working.

The Ansar expedition, already severely reduced, was thus compelled to fight in adverse conditions, and was comprehensively defeated. About 1,200 of the Mahdist troops died in the battle, compared with 70 of the Egyptian troops killed or wounded, and a vigorous pursuit over the next three days killed or collected most of the rest as prisoners; 5,000 'refugees', mainly followers, slaves and servants of the Ansar, took shelter with the victors (who had sufficient food, of course). Al-Nujumi was wounded three times in the battle, and died soon afterwards; his body was defended to the death by a small loyal force.[5]

Consul General Baring claimed that 'the aggressive power of Mahdiism collapsed' as a result of that defeat at Tushki,[6] but this only applies in relation to the single attack on Egypt. The high rate of desertions from al-Nujumi's army does argue a failure of resolution amongst the supposed fanatics, but hunger and thirst are the more likely causes. There were other targets than Egypt for the Khalifa's hopes of expansion, and he was able to muster major forces for other wars. In fact, an examination of his wars suggests strongly that the main enemy he thought he faced was Ethiopia, not Egypt, and that the attack on Egypt was as much al-Nujumi's personal project as a collective Mahdist enterprise, which would be an explanation for the Khalifa's suspicions (and for its failure). The numbers involved suggest this – whereas al-Nujumi had an army never more than 5,000 strong in his doomed invasion of Egypt, in the wars with Ethiopia armies of up to 60,000 and more were sent to invade that country, or mustered in defence.

The conclusions to be drawn from the result of the battle at Tushki were applicable to both sides. The destruction of al-Nujumi's army, by starvation, desertion and defeat, demonstrated that untrained enthusiasm was not good enough, even under a skilled commander; how widely this was appreciated in the rest of the Ansar, or among the commanders, is not clear, but the communications within Mahdiism were relatively good, so some realisation of the truth will have percolated. One conclusion reached may have been that long-distance desert expeditions were best avoided, and it was better for the enemy to approach, so suffering the debilitation of a long approach march before battle. On the Egyptian side, the victory, against a fairly small Mahdist army, but under a well-known commander, was clearly heartening. It showed that Egyptian soldiers, under competent command and trained in British tactics, were fully capable of defeating a larger army of fanatics. This understanding will have spread through the new army, with a concomitant increase in confidence.

It may be pointed out also, however, that the eventual Mahdist state occupied a distinct geographical region, and that its borders, through which it would need to penetrate in order to expand further, were distant from the centre of government and difficult to maintain and control. Al-Nujumi's expedition had to march through a desert land for several hundred miles before reaching a worthwhile area to attempt to conquer; the Ethiopian border was the line between the lower land, which rose to about 2,000 feet above sea level, and the Ethiopian highlands, which were 6,000 feet higher; in the south were the swamps of the Sudd and the difficulties of the Upper Nile region; on the west was endless savannah and hills where progress was blocked by a series of well-established states, which could only be reached, like Egypt, by a long journey that would take the necessarily large Mahdist expeditionary force a long way from Khartoum, which thus could be vulnerable in the Ansar's absence. That these obstacles were actually overcome in all directions in the next ten years is a tribute to the strength of belief of many of the Mahdist troops, but a condemnation of their commanders, who failed in every case to capitalise on their soldiers' endurance.

Further expansion of the Mahdist state could therefore only take place by dispatching small expeditions, such as that of Karamallah to the Bahr el-Ghazal area or al-Nujumi to Egypt, or Uthman Digna against Suakin – as in Ireland or Spain, small armies would be beaten and large armies would starve. (Al-Nujumi's army suffered both.) The Khalifa was, geographically, in a bind, and his natural suspiciousness prevented any real attempt to cut through the dilemma. Above all, the enmity of the large state of Ethiopia effectively prevented the mounting of a major attack westwards for fear of an Ethiopian expedition from the east in the Ansar's absence.

The Nuba Hills had been the object of a serious effort of conquest even in the lifetime of the Mahdi, and the Makk Adam had been deported, and had died a prisoner. The commander of the Ansar in the area, Hamdan Abu Anja, set about the difficult task of the conquest of the hills. The Nuba area had been attacked several times in the past, but had never been conquered. Hamdan succeeded. He established a succession of camps, in the north-west, in the south-west and in the south-east, and campaigned in each area, targeting chiefs and kings, killing resisters, and eventually accepting the successive surrenders of various groups. To add to Taqali misery, an outbreak of smallpox raged through the area. Those who surrendered after resistance were deported to the Nile Valley, and were used in later Mahdist campaigns; others fled from the fighting into Darfur and Kordofan. One of the Makk Adam's sons, Ali wad

Adam, held out in the hills, but was hunted by the Ansar and forced to move repeatedly. By 1887, it could be claimed that the Taqali kingdom had been conquered.[7] It was a major achievement, indicating the strength of will of the Mahdist forces. (Hamdan's strategy, it may be noted, was essentially that which the British under Roberts and Kitchener instituted in South Africa between 1900 and 1902, minus the concentration camps – unless the deportations to the Nile Valley counted as such.)

The irruption of Mahdist power into Sudan in 1883–5 had a major effect on Ethiopia, which was perceived by the Mahdists as an immediate threat, and this presumption produced an immediate change in Ethiopian policy. This is shown by the cooperative attitude of the Emperor Yohannes to the British request for assistance in evacuating the Egyptian garrisons (see chapter 11). Previously one of the major enemies of Ethiopia had been the vanished Egyptian Empire, as shown by several minor wars since the 1830s, the British invasion of 1868, which killed the Emperor Tewodros, and then by the failed Egyptian invasions of the north in the 1870s. In one sense the conquest by the Mahdists in the Sudan did not alter the geopolitical situation, since for the Ethiopians they simply took the place of the old Egyptian enemy on the northern and western borders, though their new enemy was rather more powerfully organised, more numerous and fanatically dangerous. For an empire ruled by a Christian aristocracy, but where a large proportion of its population were Muslims, a Mahdist attack could be much more difficult to face than one by the Egyptians – the khedives had never been the vigorous proselytisers of Islam that the Mahdists were.

To the Mahdists, however, Ethiopia, a large, populous, and vigorous imperial state, was an obvious and dangerous enemy, and as a Christian power, it was a place to be attacked. At the same time, it would no doubt be able to call on other Christian powers in Europe for support. It had defeated the Egyptian attack in 1875 without difficulty, but not the British invasion of 1868. It seized control of Muslim Harar, and even worse from the Mahdist viewpoint, this annexation had been welcomed by the Muslims of that city, whose possibilities of profitable trade were thereby increased. Egyptian rule was not popular anywhere, and the Ethiopians, old and well-known neighbours and customers, were at least familiar. The Ethiopians had cooperated with the British/Egyptians in removing the borderland garrisons that were under Mahdist siege or threat, so depriving them of the booty and the prisoners the besiegers anticipated, though the places themselves thereupon fell to the Mahdists. In the process, the Ethiopian forces had fought Mahdist forces in more than one place, though admittedly on a small scale. The treaty agreed between Admiral Hewett and Ras Alula had led to the cession of the Bogos territory in the north to the Ethiopians, the very area that the Egyptians had invaded in the past, and an obvious place from which to invade the empire. The whole process could have looked to the Mahdists very like the early stages of a military alliance between Ethiopia and Britain.

Furthermore, the condition of Ethiopia had changed markedly since Yohannes's accession to the imperial throne in 1871, not just diplomatically, but politically and militarily as well. The aftermath of the fall of the Emperor Tewodros, brought about by the successful foreign invasion by the British Indian Army under Napier, then the British withdrawal, which was followed by the subsequent civil warfare, had stimulated a consolidation of the major Ethiopian states into just two, both of considerable power. The Emperor Yohannes had established a stable regime in the north, based on his own kingdom of Tigray, from which he also dominated the whole of the north of the country; after a fractious few years he had then made an alliance with the other major Ethiopian ruler, Negus Menelik of Shoa, who dominated the south in the same way, and they contrived a durable division of the country between them. Both men were alert to threats, and were anxious to arm themselves with the most available military technology – part of Yohannes's price for permitting the Egyptian garrisons to be withdrawn through his territory was access to the port of Massawa to import guns; he had assisted Napier's invasion earlier, and in exchange had received surplus British weaponry. He, as his relatively good relations with Menelik suggests, was a man able to construct trustworthy political friendships, so that he could employ able people in sensitive situations. One of these was Ras Alula in Hamasien, the region north of the Mareb River, and in Bogos, which Alula negotiated to acquire as part of his price for evacuating the garrisons. He remained in post for about thirty years, always trusted.

In addition, Yohannes promoted the marriage of Menelik with an aristocratic northern lady, Taitu. Both had been married before – and indeed, Menelik's daughter Zauditu had recently married Yohannes's son Araya – but Taitu was to be a major asset to Menelik in his ambitions. She was intelligent, well educated, a devout Christian, and fully capable of taking independent political initiatives. The marriage in 1883 was followed in the next years by the tentative beginnings of Menelik's new residence, first by the discovery of old ruined churches in Entoto, a favourite camping place for kings on their rounds of inspection; both Menelik and Taitu – the latter first – founded new churches in the area. A palace followed, and the place swiftly developed into the new capital city, as others arrived to populate a place evidently favoured by the *negus*. It was given the name Addis Ababa, 'New Flower'. When Yohannes died in 1889, Menelik was the obvious imperial successor, and his new city became the new imperial capital.[8]

Menelik of Shoa also used the security of his northern border while Yohannes was his ally to campaign vigorously to extend his territories southwards. In a sense, Addis Ababa was on his southern frontier, and was the armed camp from which these conquests were launched. A series of small Galla kingdoms were conquered, or voluntarily submitted to avoid conquest, and this pushed the Shoan frontier up to 300 miles southwards, and probably doubled the kingdom's population. This in turn made Menelik's kingdom the largest of the Ethiopian states, brought him considerable wealth, and opened up the south to more vigorous trade. Meanwhile, he and Taitu – she was clearly an equal partner – also made efforts to convert the conquered people to Christianity; Taitu was particularly fond of founding new churches. Both were intrigued to find ruined or unfinished churches in the conquered lands, which suggested to them that they were actively reclaiming lost Christian lands rather than conquering new ones. And in 1887, Menelik defeated the recently restored *amir* Muhammad of Harar, incorporating that city into his kingdom, and gaining a wealthy city and an easier route to the sea by way of Zeila.[9]

A further change had also taken place in the north. The British had permitted Italian forces to occupy Massawa, and had then withdrawn the Egyptian garrison from the town and the guard posts nearby.[10] For the present, there were few Italians there, and those who had arrived were badly equipped and without instructions – wearing winter uniforms more suitable for Europe, for example – and any Italian officer who looked around could only be apprehensive. Ras Alula was established in Asmara on the plateau above the coastal lowland in which Massawa was, frowning down on the port, and he also controlled the territory to the north (Bogos) and south (part of Tigray) and down to the very border of Massawa. Alula was not pleased to find Italians in occupation of the town, which had been the main trading port for the northern regions of Ethiopia. In addition, by helping to bring the Egyptian garrisons out of the borderland forts, he had earned the enmity of the Mahdists. But the Italians were alone; the British were thought to have been gained as friends in taking over Massawa, but they soon vanished along with their Egyptian garrisons. Similarly, if the Ethiopians thought they had gained the friendship of the British, by cooperating in the evacuations, this did not translate into any practical or political help. Such was the normal behaviour of great powers towards the lesser powers; the British were particularly liable to make and then break promises.

There were thus now three competing powers in this small region – Italians, Tigrayans, and Mahdists – and for the next years, they fought each other. The existence of an independent Shoa under Menelik may be counted as a fourth land power, while in the background, hovering like a threatening spectre, was Britain, not to be trusted, having betrayed the Ethiopians over Massawa, and then abandoned the Italians in that place. The Italians had suggested they might assist in the wars in Sudan, offering to help in rescuing Gordon, trusting to earn future help from Britain if needed, but they found, first, that their efforts were unwelcome, and, second, that their offers – to assist Gordon at Khartoum, and to intervene at the siege of Kassala – were far beyond their capabilities (which the British would have realised). The initial Italian garrison in Massawa was of no more than a few hundred men; it was quite inadequate, even to hold the town, and would have been expelled had anyone felt it worth attempting. Their estimate of the Mahdist strength was obviously as awry as their exaggerated ambition. They then found that their local aims, to emerge from Massawa and move their forces onto the higher ground and healthier territory of the high Ethiopian plateau, were blocked by Ras Alula and the Emperor Yohannes, while they also suffered a heavy death rate from disease and from the heat.[11]

The Ethiopians were also concerned at Mahdist activities. In extracting the Egyptian garrisons their forces had clashed with the Ansar more than once. At al-Qallabat the Mahdist siege had been broken by an Ethiopian attack, in support of Sa'd Rif'at's mission to bring out the garrisons, but the subsequent evacuation of that post allowed the Mahdists to capture it afterwards without violence, and perhaps to claim a victory. At al-Jira, the same process took place: the Mahdist siege had been broken by an Ethiopian attack, followed by an evacuation. These Ethiopian successes, and earlier fights with Egyptian forces, may have given the Ethiopians the impression that the Mahdists' fighting ability had been exaggerated. They will certainly have annoyed the Mahdists.

Uthman Digna had finally oversaw the surrender of Kassala in June 1885. Ras Alula had moved to relieve the siege, but had arrived too late, and when he met Digna's forces at Kufit he was at first defeated; however, he returned to the attack the next day (23 September) and won a sanguinary victory. His purpose had been to bring out the garrison, but this was now impossible, so he returned to Asmara. The Mahdists could have interpreted this as a retreat, and Alula had certainly suffered serious casualties. But Uthman Digna had declared war on him, and the Khalifa was also incensed, particularly since the Ethiopians had given refuge to some Sudanese dissidents with whom he had quarrelled.[12] There was plenty here to build up Mahdist–Ethiopian enmity, quite apart from their religious differences, which included Yohannes's summary rejection of the Khalifa's summons to convert and submit.

For a year and more after the surrender of Kassala, the Khalifa was preoccupied with putting down rebellions and establishing his authority over the state he had inherited. In January 1888, however, he ordered the gathering of a great army in the region of al-Qallabat, with the intention of taking on the Ethiopians. Since the capture of Kassala, the Mahdists at al-Qallabat had been sending raids into Ethiopian territory, so keeping the war alive, and, of course, increasingly annoying the Ethiopians.[13] This operation was one of the reasons al-Nujumi was unable to pursue his northern campaign; Karamallah in Bahr el-Ghazal was operating at this time as well.

The Ethiopians were themselves distracted during that period. In 1887, Italian activities out of Massawa became as annoying to Ras Alula as the Mahdist raids were annoying to the Emperor Yohannes. As their neighbour, Ras Alula had been suspicious of Italian intentions towards Massawa from the start, and with good cause. Their tentative moves out of Massawa were aimed at occupying the abandoned Egyptian posts that lay around the town as a defence, and this had confirmed him in his enmity. Alula certainly saw this as the first steps in Italian expansion efforts. One of the Italians' tactics, which Italy had already used in the Danakil Desert out of Assab, was to send out 'scientific missions', such as surveyors with an escort of soldiers, which could easily be converted into something more political and territorial, while any survey could be used to claim the surveyed territory. Their purpose, according to the decisions of the Berlin West Africa Conference, was that they could then claim to have occupied the places their expedition had reached, though this was stretching that provision well beyond its original meaning. Whether Ras Alula knew of these self-regarding European conditions or not, he clearly understood what was happening. The latest of these 'missions' consisted of one engineer and a military escort, which was scarcely larger than the traditional adventurous missionary so strongly criticised at the conference. Ras Alula arrested them and jailed them at Asmara, accusing them either of invasion or trespassing. He also protested at the Italian occupation of each of the abandoned Egyptian posts, in terms of increasing exasperation, as his protests were always ignored.[14]

The Italian garrison at Massawa had grown to almost 3,000 troops, many of them locally recruited Eritreans. The Egyptians had evacuated only their own regular soldiers when they left the town, and had left behind the irregular soldiers they had recruited locally to supplement their garrison. These were referred to as *bashi bazouks* by the Egyptians; the Italians took them over on the same terms as the Egyptians had used, and called them *ascari*; the Italians were quite pleased to discover that they were a lot cheaper than their own regular soldiers, and were to a degree already trained; being local, they had some knowledge of the territory. There is no evidence they were yet loyal in any way – except for their pay – to the Italians, though as natives of the region they had plenty of information, if the Italians had only asked.[15]

Ras Alula, angered to action at last by the Italians' disdainful attitude, laid siege to one of the old Egyptian posts, Sahati, in 1887. The siege was not pressed very strongly, and the defence was effective, but a lot of noise was made, and messages at last went to Massawa reporting a severe shortage of supplies in the post. As Ras Alula had expected, a column of Italian troops came out to the post's relief. It consisted of an undisciplined crowd of very recently arrived Italian soldiers, who behaved as though they were on a joyful country walk, while the attendant *ascaris* steadily faded away from the march – they had evidently anticipated what was going to happen.

The column was ambushed by a force of 20,000 Ethiopian soldiers, and totally destroyed; 430 out of the 540 Italians were killed. This was the 'battle' of Dogali. The Italian press had a field day inventing gruesome details, such as Ethiopians killing the wounded, castrating them, and their women dancing on the dead, none of which happened. But in north-east Africa it was a turning point.[16]

In Egypt, Consul General Baring took note of the problem caused by the Italian aggression, and still more by its defeat. The massacre at Dogali caused a great fuss in Italy, and the Italian government solved the internal problem this caused for them by sending out an expeditionary force of 20,000 men to reinforce the garrison at Massawa, and possibly to gain revenge by invading the country of Ras Alula. (European powers, having been defeated by 'native' forces, always felt that they had 'lost face', and had to regain it.)

Baring feared the development of a larger war in Eritrea, which was certainly likely, and sent one of his consuls, Gerald Portal, to assuage wounded egos and calm uncertain tempers. The British having friendship, so they believed, with both parties might consider themselves to be arbiters, but the British in Europe were also anxious to keep Italy onside in an informal alliance to maintain the geopolitical European balance. Portal, therefore, presumably on Baring's instructions, expended his efforts mainly on dissuading the Ethiopians, so that, by doing so, he was taking the Italian side in the dispute. Ras Alula, when interviewed, felt he could push the Italians out of Massawa and into the sea whenever he chose, but he was given no encouragement at all.

Indeed, Portal was very concerned that Alula intended open war with the Italians. He went on to see Yohannes (who had earlier privately scolded Alula for his belligerence) only to find that Yohannes supported his governor in everything. He made the unanswerable point to Portal that the British had brought the Italians to Massawa, and so the quarrel was Britain's fault in large part, and pointed out that if England had been invaded by Ethiopians, they would have fought in its defence, just as Ras Alula fought the invading Italians. Portal scuttled out, diplomatically inept.[17]

The Italians, having landed their large expeditionary force, started to march inland, but then decided that their main purpose had to be to defend Massawa – perhaps they had heard of Ras Alula's threat to push them into the sea – and resorted to constructing fortifications, and to diplomacy. They made further contact with Menelik of Shoa, assuming that as the king of half of the country he would be vulnerable to an intrigue against Yohannes. At the same time, the

Egyptian guard posts outside Massawa were reoccupied and refortified, in effect building an impregnable wall to defend the colony.[18]

Meanwhile, in the al-Qallabat region, the Khalifa had collected a new force, bringing in extra warriors in from Darfur and Kordofan. Commanded by Hamdan Abu Anja, the victor of the Nuba Hills campaign, this army was sent to invade the neighbouring Ethiopian provinces of Gondar and Gojjam in June 1888. The invasion was pushed on much more determinedly than that of the Italians, or, earlier, than that of the Egyptians; it was also very much larger than either of these invasions. Anja reached and sacked the old Ethiopian capital at Gondar.[19] It was no coincidence this was a region that was under a local king who owned no clear allegiance to either Yohannes or Menelik; the Khalifa had clearly been doing his research on the political condition of Ethiopia. At this time, also, in Eritrea, Ras Alula watched as the Italian expeditionary force inched its way forward for 19 miles and then fortified the line of ex-Egyptian forts around Massawa, but then went no further. He no doubt felt he had made his point.

The Italians had been cultivating Menelik of Shoa since the 1870s through Pietro Antonelli, who had arrived in the country as a private traveller and had struck up a friendship with Menelik. He then became an amateur diplomat, and set himself up as a European adviser to the *negus*. The Italians were apparently interested in detaching Menelik from Yohannes, while Menelik, very wary, and fully alert to Antonelli's own purposes, was reluctant to be drawn into anything definitive. This hard-to-get attitude resulted in the Italians making increasingly generous offers, seeking to buy an alliance. In 1881, they promised to provide 2,000 Remington rifles for Menelik's army. When the rifles were delivered, two years later, a new treaty was negotiated covering several areas, commercial and judicial, and a most-favoured nation status for Italy.

The installation of the Italians at Massawa in 1885, however, brought Menelik back to wariness. In the later 1880s, Antonelli was able to supply more guns, and in 1887, the year of the Battle of Dogali, he agreed to provide another 5,000 rifles, but could not persuade Menelik to like Italy's work in the developing problem in the north. Then the further Italian courtship of Menelik by Antonelli was hindered by the parallel activity of Italy in landing the much larger expeditionary force at Massawa to avenge the defeat of Dogali.[20] The Italians should by this time have realised that what they were doing in the north had as great an effect on Menelik as it did on Yohannes and Alula; Menelik was not to be separated from the other two by an amateur diplomat and a few guns.

The event that, however, altered the whole situation came in early 1889. The attack on Gondar by the Mahdists had damaged Yohannes's standing with his people. Menelik seemed superficially to be taking the Italian part in the northern problem by his relationship with Antonelli, and he allied with Ras Adal, the ruler of Gojjam, who had been the commander against the Mahdists at al-Qallabat. This alliance appeared to Yohannes to be a threat. His only legitimate son died of smallpox at about this time, jeopardising the succession. The partition agreement of 1882 between Yohannes and Menelik had included a provision that the latter would be the emperor's successor, but Yohannes now put forward another of his sons, Ras Mangasha, the son of a concubine, as his choice. Menelik, father-in-law of another Yohannes's sons, was annoyed, of course, but did not actually move against the emperor right away.

Yohannes thus faced a series of problems, north, south, and west, internal and external, all coming to the boil at the same time: the problem of the succession, the quarrel with Menelik, the threat of an Italian attack out of Massawa, and the probability of another Mahdist invasion. He could put aside the succession problem for the moment, and the Mahdists were taking their time getting organised, so he decided to deal with Menelik first, intending to prevent any attack by him while the external enemies were still not ready. He made a move southwards in June 1888, ravaging Gojjam, the province of Ras Adal, who had been promoted to *negus* (king), taking the name Tekle Haymanot; the province was thoroughly sacked. This attack was evidently indirectly aimed at Menelik, Tekle Haymanot's ally, and it appeared that Yohannes was about to go on to attack Shoa itself. In reply, Menelik moved to support the Gojjamis, and mustered his Shoan army. Yohannes quickly overran Gojjam and forced Tekle Haymanot to submit,[21] but did not go on to invade Shoa, as had been expected, and he and Menelik successfully negotiated a peace, Menelik offering an acceptable apology. Yohannes's internal problem had been solved, and the lesson delivered, at least with temporary effect.[22]

It was another Mahdist threat that had stayed Yohannes's further advance southwards. In January 1889, he had sent a message to the Khalifa, asking for peace, clearly another response to the surrounding problems that he was facing, an attempt to pick off his enemies singly; his approach was unlikely to mark his intention to conclude a definitive and longlasting peace with the Khalifa, which would necessarily involve his conversion to Islam, but such talks might delay any Mahdist attacks. If one of the international issues he confronted could be dealt with diplomatically, the overall problem would be considerably eased. In fact, in the result, he had been able to make his peace with Menelik, while the Italians at Massawa came out of the town and then sat down and built their fortifications, and showed no signs of intending anything more. So when the Khalifa replied with an adamant refusal of talks and the suggestion, once again, that Yohannes convert to Islam, the answer was that Yohannes would go first to al-Qallabat to gain revenge, and then he would attack Khartoum.

And so there took place one of the greatest battles of the nineteenth century, with 100,000 Ethiopians facing 70,000 Mahdists. And just to prove that numbers are not always decisive, it was the lesser force that won, though only just. Yohannes had Ras Alula with him, also his son Ras Mangasha, and his nephew Haile Mariam. The battle, at Metemma, with such large forces involved, both using the same simple and direct tactics, was hardly scientific, but the Mahdists had fortified themselves inside a large *zeriba* behind a newly dug deep ditch, possibly a Sudanese attempt at a British square, but more likely a larger version of the slave traders' forts that had dotted the Bahr el-Ghazal. The sheer numbers involved on both sides militated against any serious effort at command and control, and against any clever manoeuvres, though Yohannes had a force in reserve and was able to intervene when Ras Mangasha needed help after Haile Mariam was killed. Until then the Ethiopian assault had been pushing the Mahdists back.

The death of a commander was always a crucial moment in such a battle, and Yohannes's arrival in the midst of the fighting was such a moment. His measures steadied the forces under Ras Mangasha, but then Yohannes was wounded. He was hit three times by Mahdist bullets, no doubt targeted specifically by snipers. He was carried out of the fight. The death of Haile Mariam had already caused confusion amongst his part of the army, and now the wounding and removal of Yohannes brought the whole Ethiopian army to a collapse. The Ethiopian soldiers fled the field, and the Mahdists were able to make a successful attack and mount a pursuit.

Yohannes died next day, having named Ras Mangasha as his chosen successor. Mangasha and Ras Alula, the latter wounded, got away, but the party carrying Yohannes's body back for burial was caught by the pursuing Mahdists, and his attendants were killed; the emperor's body was beheaded, and the head sent to the Khalifa to be displayed in Khartoum.[23]

The unexpected death of Yohannes naturally caused confusion in Ethiopia, but did not produce a dispute over the succession, which was perhaps unexpected. Yohannes had named Mangasha as his successor before he died, but Mangasha refused to claim that inheritance, though he established himself as *negus* in Tigray; other claimants also failed to act. Menelik therefore succeeded as *negusa nagast* (emperor), the first effectively undisputed accession for centuries.[24]

At the time, the country was suffering a major series of natural disasters. There was a plague of rinderpest, which killed 90 per cent of the cattle in the country – the disease first appeared in Eritrea, brought by the Italians, and then spread south; the monsoon rains failed, bringing famine; perhaps a third of the Ethiopian population died. (This famine also affected Sudan and Egypt – and damaged the Mahdist campaign against Egypt, which ended at al-Nujumi's defeat and death at Tushki.) In the circumstances, it was surely a relief that any crisis over the imperial succession was brief.

Menelik had the draft of the treaty with Italy awaiting his signature, which would provide him with 5,000 more rifles. Antonelli had included in the treaty provisions that Menelik would accept the Italian ambition to rule in Eritrea. This only meant that he would stand aside from the approaching conflict between the Italians and Ras Alula. It would allow the Italians to move out of Massawa and onto the upper plateau, effectively ceding to them the region called Bogos. Ras Alula had secured this territory from Egypt only ten years before, but during the crisis with the Mahdists, of the recent past, he had abandoned Asmara. In the awkward position of facing plague, famine, a Mahdist victory, and the death of the emperor, Menelik decided to sign the treaty, essentially adopting Yohannes's diplomatic tactics of dealing with one threat at a time. He was enlisting Italy as an ally to ensure his own eventual imperial succession. The Italians then moved at once, clearly believing the treaty gave them the right to invade the north. At last, they were making use of their large expeditionary force. The key to the region was Keren, a difficult and defendable pass, control of which would block any Mahdist adventure from the west. This was occupied early in June, and then Asmara was taken in August.[25]

This was all in accordance with the provisions of the Treaty of Wichali ('Ucciali' to the Italians), between the Italians and Menelik. But there had been cheating by the Italians, both in this treaty and in a subsequent supplementary agreement negotiated in Rome later in 1889 by Menelik's nephew, Ras Makonnen. Crucial words in the two agreements differed between the Italian and the Amharic versions. In the Wichali treaty, the Amharic version gave Menelik an *option* to employ Italian good offices in his contacts with other European states, but the Italian version had it that he was *obligated* to do so – hence the Italian assumption that they had taken over Ethiopia as a protectorate; in the later convention agreed by Ras Makonnen in Rome, in which the borders of the Italian sphere were discussed, the Italian version used the term from the Treaty of Berlin of 1884, that the boundary would be drawn in accordance with 'effective possession'; in the Amharic version, the phrase 'as of today' replaced it. There can be no doubt that these differences were deliberately included by the Italians, with a view to justifying their later claims to authority over Ethiopia as against the other European powers; they would, of course, only show the Italian version to the Europeans.[26]

The Italians triumphantly informed the other European powers that Ethiopia had become an Italian 'protectorate' as a result of the two agreements, and in the north they steadily expanded their occupation – thereby instituting 'effective possession', but only after it had been claimed, which was the wrong way round, in the terms of the Berlin treaty. On 1 January 1890, the bounds of the colony were published in the announcement of the establishment of 'Colonia Eritrea'. Even before that happened, however, Menelik had made it clear, by writing directly to the European powers (which, of course, the Italians claimed he could not do), that he rejected the Italian version of the agreements. One of his clerks had already detected the changed wording in the Treaty of Wichali, and this led to an examination of Ras Makonnen's agreement as well. The Italians had been extremely clumsy in their cheating; their deception had, as it happens, stored up a great deal of future trouble for themselves. An additional Italian blunder, possibly by sheer carelessness, was that the version of the treaty in Italian had not been signed, though the Amharic version had; only the Amharic version was therefore a legal treaty, and the wording here was the foundation for Menelik's later complaints. It is therefore ironic that King Umberto presented Ras Makonnen with an unusually extravagant gift – 28 cannon and 26,000 rifles, plus ammunition. Makonnen also used an Italian loan to buy millions of cartridges. Menelik had suddenly become very much better armed, but was also fully equipped with a serious grievance.[27]

The Mahdist wars between 1885, when they captured Khartoum, and 1889, the year of the battles of Tushki and Metemma, had seen a vigorous effort to extend their territory, but none of those efforts had been successful. The battle in which Yohannes was mortally wounded, Metemma, took place on 9 March 1889; six months later, on 3 August, the Mahdist expedition against Egypt was defeated and annihilated at the battle at Tushki. This second battle was a disaster, with the (relatively small) Mahdist force totally destroyed; the first was almost as bad, a victory that had been bought at great cost. Over against Egypt the advanced posts along the Nile south of Wadi Halfa were withdrawn, with Dongola becoming the Mahdist headquarters in that area, leaving a neutral zone of 200 desert miles between these places. A number of the local chiefs made contact with Egyptian authorities, offering a sort of conditional submission.[28] On the Ethiopian frontier, no attempt was made to exploit the problems of the cattle plague in Ethiopia, or the accession of a new emperor. In the Suakin area, a bickering war continued in which unfortunate villages changed hands more than once, but no serious changes were discernible, resulting in a similarly inconclusive situation. Even in the Taqali kingdom in the Nuba Hills, the resistance continued, and the conquest had only been achieved by massacre, massive depopulation, and much of the population fleeing; no objective observer would accept that the region had been permanently subdued. In the south, a Mahdist force had advanced to deal with the defiance of Emin Pasha, but he vanished to Europe with Stanley, and the Mahdists only moved as far along the White Nile as Dufile. It could be called a victory but was hardly one to set against the defeat and a drawn battle.

It was not that the Mahdists had run out of aggressive steam, but that Sudan was suffering from the same famine that afflicted Ethiopia (and Egypt), brought on by the low Nile, which was a result of the failure of the monsoon rains in Ethiopia, and which had so crippled the Egyptian expedition. The Khalifa was also beset by plenty of other problems within his own territories. But it is worth noting that the year 1889 in north-east Africa was a major turning point.

The enmity between Ethiopia and the Mahdist state had followed on from that between Ethiopia and Egypt as controller of Sudan; no matter how the Mahdists believed that a new era had come with their victories, the continuing conflict with Ethiopia was actually an old feature of the geographical and historical situation, one that had existed for centuries. In the more recent past, the fighting between the mountains and the lower land – the Nile Valley, in effect – had happened regularly from the 1830s to 1889, involving gradually increasing forces on both sides and increasingly lethal weapons at each stage. The effects on the two states, however, had been different. The repeated failures of the Mahdists to secure a victory, despite reaching into Ethiopia to sack the old capital at Gondar, were similar to its failure to expand elsewhere after the capture of Khartoum and the death of the Mahdi. The attacks on Egypt had failed, and next year, 1890, the son of Makk Adam would return to Taqali to head the resistance there. The Khalifa Abdallahi might have been a competent ruler, but he did not exude the same charismatic inspiration that had driven the conquests achieved in the years of the Mahdi's leadership, and his suspicion of successful generals such as al-Nujumi could be paralysing. The Egyptian forces were now clearly able to defeat the Mahdists, who had not succeeded even at Suakin, and soon the Italians, the weakest and least competent of the European powers, would show that they could do the same.

For Ethiopia, on the other hand, it seems clear that the presence of an antagonistic power such as the Mahdist state as a neighbour had inspired the country to revive the old unity that had saved it from conquest in the past. Emperor Tewodros, though his rule was ultimately a failure, had shown what was required, though his methods had been brutal. He had been succeeded by a series of rulers, culminating in Yohannes and Menelik, whose aims were to expand and to unify their country. The most telling moment came just before Yohannes was killed in that Metemma battle, when he and Menelik were armed for war against each other, but instead they gritted their teeth and made a peace agreement, Menelik apologising – which must have been hard for him to do. Then, when Yohannes was killed, his son Ras Mangasha chose not to challenge Menelik for the succession, thereby avoiding a probable civil war. From 1889 onwards, Ethiopia was a united, expanding, comparatively well-armed power, the greatest power in North Africa, a condition in large part brought about by its reaction to the Mahdist threat – and to that of the Italians as well – and the Italians, having cheated in the treaty, had then been conned into supplying modern arms while aiming to attack the colony of the country that was supplying them.

The Mahdists, therefore, had ceased to expand, at least against the enemies to west, north and east. It might have seemed that their new realm was merely a temporary phenomenon, though as yet none of its neighbours was prepared to put that to the test. In fact, it was a state that was fully capable of expansion still, in the same way that Egypt had expanded, by moving into the south against the factional and disorganised victims in the Upper Nile region.

Chapter 13

The Upper Nile Problem

The year 1889, one that was significant for Ethiopia and for the Mahdist state, was also the year when Emin Pasha left his province of Equatoria, reluctantly and after long delays. He succumbed at last to Stanley's importuning; Stanley, of course, needed to bring Emin out to justify the enormous expense of his 'expedition'. This marked the definitive end of any Egyptian responsibility for the southern province, not that any such responsibility had been displayed now for several years. As a result, the area became a free-for-all for a whole set of greedy and impatient imperialist states, just as had the more accessible 'debris' of the destroyed empire of Muhammad Ali. There were still those in the area west of Lake Albert who might proclaim loyalty to the khedive, but the khedive knew nothing of them, and probably did not care if he never learned of them. His empire had, after all, been dismantled and the parts widely distributed, lost for ever.

The region, which may conveniently be called the 'Upper Nile', was thus a vortex in which many actors were interested in what happened, in gaining access, and, if possible, seizing control. It is difficult to account for the eager attention that the area attracted. Certainly, it is partly swamp, often flooded, and its condition is exceedingly hot and humid, with a monstrous number of insects with a ferocious taste for human blood. It did not in itself justify such anxious attention. We may therefore reasonably assume that it was not for its physical or botanical attractions, but for its geographical position, and its access to other regions, that it was so desired. That interest and attention was due to the actions of the Mahdists, and to their opponents. The conflict between the aggressive Mahdists and their enemies had spilled over into a new country.

In that year, Emin finally left his province. He was the only authority who could claim any sort of legitimacy in Equatoria, and his departure meant that he was succeeded by the group of soldiers he had commanded. They had mutinied and imprisoned him under their leader, Fadl al-Mula Muhammad. Fadl's group was mainly composed of Sudanese soldiers, most of whom objected to being taken away from the area, and they soon split into two groups, one group who stayed with Fadl, and a dissident group of about 200 soldiers, clerks and servants who were professedly loyal to Egypt. These broke away from the rest, led by

Salim Bey. Salim had been loyal to Emin until he left. Emin had appealed to Stanley to wait for them, aiming to return with them to Egypt, as they appeared to wish, but Stanley replied he could not delay – so continuing his self-centred brusqueness, indeed cruelty, towards everyone. Salim and his dwindling party remained in the area until 1894.[1]

So the only group that could possibly claim some sort of legitimacy in ruling the Upper Nile area, if not actually the Equatoria province, were the mutineers under Fadl who had remained there after the group divided. They were by this time hardly numerous or strong enough to exercise real control over very much territory. On any objective view, they had neither power nor any claim in political right, other than their tenuous occupation, and only if they held on against all challenges would they become firmly established, and so legitimised. But there were plenty of pretenders anxious to succeed them and Emin Pasha.

Predators were approaching the region from all sides – British and Germans from the Indian Ocean to the east, Belgians from the Atlantic through the Congo from the west, Mahdists from the north, French more distantly from the west, plus, of course, increasingly angered tribal groups all around from much closer. The region in question was in fact greater than the area occupied by Fadl's group, and indeed greater than the old province of Equatoria. It included the Bahr el-Ghazal province, which had been largely evacuated by the Mahdists after a rising by the native tribes of the Great Lakes area, together with the kingdoms west of Lake Victoria, Buganda, Bunyoro, Toro, Acholi and the others southwards from there. The prize was considerable, both in itself, and in the potential for the control of a strategic region.

When Stanley finally extracted Emin Pasha in April 1889, he had left Fadl al-Mula more or less in control of part of this area, governing from his main centre at Wadelai on the north shore of Lake Albert. The country and its people had by this time become reasonably well known, in a superficial away, to the European powers – 'by far the best explored and best-known section of the African continent',[2] not that that was much of a recommendation. In 1888, Sir William MacKinnon, an experienced entrepreneur in Africa, had set up the British Imperial East Africa Company, as a means of channelling investment capital into the exploration and exploitation of the future Kenya, Uganda and the Kilimanjaro area (this last known to be fertile and populous).[3] Uganda, the modern name for the northern region of the organised kingdoms, had become a target for missionaries, so much so that Catholics, Protestants, Muslims and pagans all jostled for influence and for converts. It was because of the authority of the kings that the missionaries flooded into the region, assuming that by persuading the kings to convert they would bring their subjects with them, and then boast of their success. The kings, of course, were more interested in using the missions to increase their own authority. This religious contest soon became violent; religious civil war was thus another European export.[4]

South of the future Kenya, exploration by German explorers and missionaries had examined the country that became Tanganyika (now the mainland part of Tanzania), and they were also interested in the Kilimanjaro area. In 1886, they and the British had agreed a line of division from the coast to Lake Victoria, leaving the Kilimanjaro area on the German side, and in 1890 this line was extended due west across the lake to the border of the Congo Free State, putting most of the Great Lakes kingdoms firmly in the British 'sphere of influence'.[5] The German area, south of the line, was the region that had been exploited in the past generation and more by Arab slave traders out of Zanzibar and the coastal towns that were under the sultan of Zanzibar's control. German penetration followed the Arab slave route along which captured slaves from the Congo area were brought to Zanzibar for export. The claims by European states to the inland areas largely respected the sultan's territory along the coast, defined as stretching 10 miles inland from the coast and from Kismayu in Somalia to the Rovuma River, which was the northern border of Portuguese Mozambique. That initial respect did not last long. Zanzibar Island itself was regarded, perhaps informally for a time, as under British protection, not that the sultan was too keen on the idea. Such protection was eventually seen to have put his mainland territory at British disposal.[6]

The second of the Anglo-German agreements, in 1890, was the product of overt competition. The kingdoms west of the Great Lakes were all outside the area demarcated in the first agreement of 1886, whose line ended at the eastern shore of Lake Victoria. The Germans now employed Emin Pasha, who had returned to Africa, and who was, of course, familiar with much of the area. They organised an expedition to go to Uganda, with Emin as the expert. He had enlisted with the German service in the region, and was the ideal person to lead such an expedition.[7] The British East Africa Company was persuaded by the Foreign Office to engage one of their colonial officers to do the same. Within a couple of weeks this was arranged – notably fast work for the Foreign Office – and a party of around fifty, under Frederick Lugard as agent for the company, would go with the object of planting British power in Buganda.[8] In London, the Foreign Secretary and Prime Minister, Lord Salisbury, organised the new treaty, swapping various mainly notional claims to barely known African territories for British pre-eminence in Uganda and – the item which particularly attracted the Germans – ceding the island of Heligoland in the North Sea in exchange for a clear title to Zanzibar. Heligoland was the last European remnant of the old Electorate of Hanover; situated in the estuary of the Elbe, as a British island it had long been an eyesore to the Germans, or perhaps a bone in the German throat, not least since German unification in 1871. With the development of more powerful naval and land artillery, however, it had become very vulnerable. The treaty settled several other issues, and resulted in the solution of several disputed items in East Africa.[9]

The two Anglo-German agreements on the division of East Africa, of 1886 and 1890, effectively deterred any German interference in most of the Great Lakes kingdoms – though two of them, Rwanda and Burundi, fell into the German sphere of influence. (The earlier German interest in the Witu area from Lamu to Kismayu, the northernmost stretch of the sultan of Zanzibar's coast, was among the items that were extinguished by the new treaty.)

In Uganda, Frederick Lugard found himself leading one side in a civil war in 1892, but the net result was the establishment of British influence in the country.[10] Henry Morton Stanley stoked up British fears when he returned to Britain in 1890. He was celebrated for his 'rescue' of Emin, and in interviews with the press he suggested that it would be possible to divert the waters of the White Nile, and so starve both Sudan and Egypt, at least during the period when those countries relied on that river's water (December to July), if not when the flood came along the Blue Nile. He did not go into detail, hardly surprisingly, since he was probably mainly concerned to divert attention from his own appalling conduct during the 'rescue' of Emin Pasha's expedition. Despite the huge impracticality of the idea, the fears in Britain over foreign control of the Upper Nile, already present, intensified.[11] The low Nile of 1888–9, and the accompanying famine in Egypt, Sudan and Ethiopia, provided a reminder of what could result.

The Uganda expedition under Lugard, however, had been costly, and the expense had fallen on the East Africa Company. The British government had funded a survey to discover the best route for a railway from the coast to Lake Victoria, but would not provide funds for building the railway itself. There was a fear that the activities of Catholic missionaries in Uganda might prompt a French intervention in support of them (despite the strongly secular trend of French policy at the time). The company, having pointed out this Catholic threat in a public campaign, succeeded in getting enough subscriptions from British Protestants to continue its occupation of Uganda for another couple of years from 1892.[12] When Lugard returned to Britain late in that year, he campaigned for the occupation to be continued, and in the end, the British government agreed to fund this for a time.[13]

The consul in Zanzibar was Gerald Portal, the hapless diplomat of the former Mission to Abyssinia. He was a keen imperialist, and he was dispatched to Uganda with a rather vague set of instructions, appointed as 'Commissioner' to Uganda by Lord Rosebery, the foreign secretary at the time. His task was to deal with several problems, some of which had been left festering by Lugard when he was withdrawn. It was made clear to Portal by Rosebery that he was expected to act for, and report in favour of, a continuation of the occupation.[14] When the East Africa Company's remit ran out on 1 April 1893, Portal seized the moment and hoisted the Union flag in place of the Company's own flag, making the British government now responsible. He then died, in January 1894, rather confirming his general haplessness. His posthumously compiled report, based on his surviving notes and documents, was published in April after some delay, and, to no surprise, recommended that the country be made a formal protectorate.[15]

In 1884, the West Africa Conference in Berlin had recognised the existence of the Belgian exploration or settlement in, and elements of control of, the basin of the Congo River as a personal project of King Leopold II of the Belgians. This was the Congo Free State, a badly misnamed territory of very great extent – 'free' was an insult to the enslaved, mutilated, and murdered people of the region who were unfortunate enough to come into contact with Leopold's men. The treatment of Africans at the hands of Leopold's employees became a byword for cruelty and murder.[16] By 1890, the Belgian penetration through the Congo region was approaching the Great Lakes, and MacKinnon, whose East Africa Company was close to failing even then, made an agreement with the Free State which effectively set the Nile as the boundary between their areas of operation.

This was no more than an informal agreement, but it was enough to allow Leopold to push his exploring parties further forward into the region that was under the influence and control of Fadl al-Mula. Fadl's group, only a few hundred strong by this time, was clearly also failing, and the Congolese approach was a rescue. The Belgian head of an expedition, Jules Milz,[17] contacted Fadl and persuaded him and his men to take service with the Belgians; once this was accepted, Milz appointed Fadl as governor of 'Equatoria' and gave him a set of Belgian flags to fly.[18]

This comfortable development brought the Belgian authority as far east as Wadelai on the Nile to the north of Lake Albert (recognised as one of the sources of the Nile). According to Fadl's new appointment, his authority extended into the land to the north – for 'Equatoria' (in Arabic '*Khatt el-Istiwa*') could only refer to the former Egyptian and Mahdist province of that name, along the Upper Nile from Lake Albert to Fashoda. It was a Belgian claim to both the area west of Lake Albert and to the Nile north for an indefinite distance; the use of the term Equatoria was a deliberate obfuscation, since few in Europe had any idea of the position or extent of this area. And it was other Europeans who were the audience to which the Belgian claimants were playing in this matter.

But there was a spoiler on its way – a new Mahdist force. After failing to expand north and east after the battles in 1889, the Khalifa had urged his men to expand southwards. Late in 1893, a year after Fadl and Milz had joined forces, Muhammad Uthman Abu Qarja was dispatched south along the Nile to make an inspection of the situation in Equatoria; Abu Qarja had been used often, ever since the Hicks expedition, by both the Mahdi and the Khalifa as a diplomat and a troubleshooter. He took up his command at al-Rajjaf, a little south of Lado and Gondokoro. It seems he had no new troops with him, and cannot have been expected to do more than accomplish some administrative tasks and report on conditions.

Al-Rajjaf was a post on the Nile, one of Gordon's old foundations, and Abu Qarja arrived there at about the same time that the Belgians were linking up with Fadl al-Mula further south. Abu Qarja appears to have stabilised the situation along the Nile, and was then superseded by Urabi Daft'allah, who, with a force of 300 men carried in two steamers, arrived at al-Rajjaf in October 1893. In the normal mode of any newly appointed Mahdist governor, Urabi at once reported on how badly Abu Qarja had conducted his administration, then set about raiding the local tribes for slaves to be sent off to Khartoum, and finally turned to act against Fadl.[19]

In January 1894, Urabi took his forces south from al-Rajjaf in search of Fadl and his force, who was presumably regarded as a Mahdist renegade or perhaps as a rebel – he was certainly seen as an enemy. Urabi first went into the Azande country, but then heard that his prey was actually at Wadelai on Lake Albert. The two forces met at Wadelai, which was one of those places that appears repeatedly as a rendezvous at this time and area. Fadl and his men were defeated in the battle that followed, and Fadl was killed; his papers, including the record of the agreement with Milz and the Belgians, were captured and sent to the Khalifa. The Belgian flags of the Congo Free State, which Milz had given Fadl, were also captured and sent to Khartoum as trophies.[20]

This was the end of Fadl and his force and whatever pretensions he had entertained. Urabi made a sweep in search of other Belgian posts in the region over the next ten months, finding and driving out, or destroying, eight stations planted in the area by the Belgians; this also persuaded the people at other posts to evacuate, but then one defeat by a small Belgian force was enough to put an end to this minor Mahdist campaign, and Urabi turned to report his successes to the Khalifa. When he returned to al-Rajjaf, however, he found that communications northwards were blocked. The Sudd had thickened and the floating rafts of plants had coalesced, so that all available passages were closed up. An attempt to send his messages by land failed. Urabi was then out of touch with Khartoum for the next two years, a crucial period.[21]

The next Belgian expedition, led now by Commandant F. Delanghe, made a new attempt to reach the Nile, and succeeded in planting a couple of posts beside the river. But his campaign was as destructive as most Belgian explorations, and infuriated the local peoples. With the Mahdists approaching, he had to pull out, going west as far as Mundu on the Uele River. He had enlisted an Azande chieftain called Renzi and his men, but, as the Belgians were steadily driven back and reduced in numbers by guerrilla attacks, Renzi turned against them. Fadl's men – those who remained alive – had been left in their original region close to Lake Albert, effectively abandoned. Renzi and the Azande then struck at Belgian and Mahdist posts indiscriminately from late 1893 and into 1894. The area between Lado and Lake Albert was ravaged and reduced to ruin and chaos; in effect, Delanghe's campaign had been defeated, and this Belgian claim to Equatoria had clearly failed.[22]

The Upper Nile region had therefore become a region of active Great Power contest, if, at least in this context, Belgium can be called a great power. By 1894, it seemed that the Mahdists were winning, at least with respect to their contest with the Belgians, who had lunged east as far as Lake Albert, but had then been driven away. Fadl al-Mula, the power in place in the area west of the lake, had been eliminated, his area taken over by the Belgians who recruited him, and then, along with the Belgians, he and his men were defeated by the Mahdists, who killed more of them. (A few men survived, to be recruited, or perhaps rescued, by the East Africa Company.)

On the other side of Lake Albert, in the kingdoms, the British were winning. They had cut out the Germans by the simple expedient of offering them the small island in the North Sea that was no longer of any use to the Royal Navy. The speed with which the Germans had been dismissed was a clear indication that they were not serious about colonising Africa, only in using Africa as a lever in support of their policies in Europe. (But once having acquired colonies, they had to exploit them, which they did in a particularly brutal fashion, in this behaving worse even than the Belgians.) The British had secured Uganda by supporting one party in Buganda in the religious civil war – Lugard's doing – and then seizing the moment of the expiry of the East Africa Company's authority to raise the Union flag – Portal's doing. Several Ugandan kingdoms thus had become a British protectorate; other European states were thus warned off; this was the result, though no one could claim it had been planned or intended. It might have been one of those developments that the British had secured 'in an absence of mind', but it was more a matter of muddle, confusion and improvisation.

But the Belgians were still not very far away, and the Mahdists had shown they had a surprisingly long reach from Khartoum, and an ability to win the small battles that were all that could be mounted by anyone at such a distance from all their bases. Even more distantly, there were the French, brooding over perceived wrongs they had suffered at British hands in Egypt, and preparing new expeditions into Central Africa, one of which, the Mission Monteil, had been planned in 1893, and had almost got going in 1894, but had eventually failed to start.

The prospect of the Monteil mission, planned to be exceptionally well armed, and aiming to seize the length of the White Nile between Lado and Fashoda, had alarmed both King Leopold and the British. Lugard had been sent to Paris to investigate and had reported on its danger. Rennell Rodd was sent to Brussels to see King Leopold, and in only a fortnight an agreement was reached whereby the west bank of the White Nile from Fashoda south to Lake Albert was to be leased to Leopold's Congo Free State. But the agreement also included a British project to connect Lake Albert and Lake Tanganyika by a narrow leased land corridor, as a route for a potential Cape to Cairo railway. This lay through territory allocated by treaty to the Germans, and when the agreement was published, both the French and the Germans were infuriated. Thus, the agreement fell apart almost at once. It had not helped that none of the allocated territories were occupied by any of the powers involved, as they had all agreed was necessary at the West Africa Conference ten years before. Rosebery attempted to recover by a direct agreement with the French, but failed. Monteil's mission had now also failed – Monteil himself was not keen on it – but yet another expedition was being organised. (This eventually, after some problems, became the Marchand Mission.)[23]

The Italians were also involved in all this kerfuffle, but not quite so closely. Their colonial performance was erratic, operatic, and oftentimes farcical, the commanders prone to extravagant gestures and claims; they were in thrall to a hysterical press in Italy, and were greedy to display Italy's ability to act as a Great Power, even if no one took them seriously as one. Their claim to a protectorate over Ethiopia, though publicly and convincingly denied by Emperor Menelik, seems to have been largely accepted in Europe, where no one wanted to get into an argument with the Italians, for fear of upsetting the European power balance.

One element of Italian intentions was to extend Ethiopia's border as far as the Nile. In this, they were encouraged by a couple of agreements reached with Britain. The disagreement between Italy and Ethiopia on the interpretation of the Treaty of Wichali did not prevent European states (including Britain) from accepting that Italy had established a protectorate of sorts over Ethiopia; this at least marked out Ethiopia as a strong Italian interest, and meant that other European colonial powers tended to stay away. Britain in particular was keen to keep Italy onside in the naval balance in the Mediterranean, and made a pair of treaties by which Italy purported to allocate sections of Ethiopia to Britain. In a treaty in 1891, a slice of western Ethiopia, including a part of the country extending towards the White Nile, and a section along the southern border adjacent to the East African Company's area were marked out for Britain (later Kenya). The second area might have been useful, though the Company was hardly in a position to take it over, but the fact alone was a recognition of Britain's right to act as the Mahdists' heir to adjacent parts of the Nile. Three years later, in 1894, another agreement purported to allocate a strip of land bordering on British Somaliland – scarcely occupied as yet – to that colony.[24]

These agreements were never implemented, and in fact they were in violation, once again, of the procedure laid down by the West Africa Conference in 1884, which had insisted on actual occupation before a claim could be accepted, still less handed on to someone else. After 1896, Italy could no longer even pretend to any authority in Ethiopia, not even by forgery or subterfuge (see chapters 12 and 14). There is little or no sign that the British ever intended to take over their supposedly allocated Ethiopian territories. The purpose of the agreements was purely diplomatic, gestures to indicate British support for Italian aspirations, in the same way that the Mediterranean Fleet was a passive supporter of Italy by deterring other intrusions in Europe. The crucial relationship in all this was French enmity towards Italy, rival Mediterranean powers; and in East Africa the presence of the French colony of Djibouti, planted strategically on the doorstep of Ethiopia, gave the French colonial lobby a sense of their having a chance at dishing Italy there.

None of the actors in this contest were serious about taking control of Uganda except Britain. The British had the same concerns as France, for both thought of the Upper Nile as an area that they felt it necessary by then to control as an adjunct to Egypt, or to assist in the realisation of nebulous fantasies in Africa, like the Cape to Cairo railway or control of the flow of the Nile. The fantasies of controlling the waters of the White Nile near its source were not actually seen as fantasies, but as distinct possibilities, or fears, by such a serious and sceptical statesman as Lord Salisbury, at least to the extent of preventing any other country being able to institute such a scheme.

Salisbury had actually been one of the first in the field. As far back as 1890, he had been promoting British actions in East Africa. He confirmed Zanzibar as a British protectorate, encouraged the formation of the East Africa Company as a surrogate imperial agent, and persuaded the Chancellor of the Exchequer to fund the survey for the proposed Uganda railway.[25] It has been theorised that these items can be brought together into a cohesive policy, by which Salisbury articulated the British advance from the coast to Uganda and the Upper Nile as a means of undermining the Mahdist regime from the south, and providing

Britain with a base in East and Central Africa. The idea was that a British advance along the White Nile out of Uganda would threaten the Mahdists so seriously that a (subsidiary) blow from the north out of Egypt would destroy that regime easily.[26]

This had been the background to the Anglo-German treaties, to the Anglo-Italian agreement which left the Sudan clearly as an Egyptian – that is, British – responsibility, and to the promotion of Lugard into Uganda, and so to the Anglo-Congolese agreement, which so quickly failed. But Salisbury lost office in 1892, and Lord Rosebery, Foreign Secretary in Gladstone's fourth administration (1892–4), and himself Prime Minister for a year after Gladstone resigned, did not share this set of ideas; when he sent Portal into Uganda it was with the explicit aim of securing that country against advances by Belgium and the Mahdists, not as a move in a game of greater imperial strategy. And when Salisbury came back into power in 1895, he did so with a much clearer idea of the difficulties that would be involved in any advance from Uganda towards Khartoum than he had appreciated earlier. In effect, he had abandoned the anti-Mahdist intention of using the Upper Nile as a base against the Khalifa, but by then it was clear that the route through the Sudd in particular was extremely difficult, and that several other powers were keen to secure control of the Nile in this area, and so other methods had to be used; in essence, he had adopted Rosebery's policy.

The issue, that is, turned out to be wider than simply the problem of the Upper Nile. This was certainly a central element, but events elsewhere also had their effects. The first was, inevitably, the condition of the Mahdist state by 1893–4; second was the issue of the relations of Italy and Ethiopia in that time and the following two years. Third was the problem of the activity of Rabeh, the predator soldier who was rampaging and devastating in the region between the Congo and Darfur. In the background also were French intentions, the fourth element, while Belgian intentions were a fifth. At the centre was the line of the White Nile, repeatedly cited in agreements – Anglo-Congolese, Anglo-Italian – as a boundary, while the French had their eyes on it as well.

Lord Salisbury in London, one of the main players in African matters in these next years, returned to office as Prime Minister and Foreign Secretary in 1895. He had been closely involved on the Upper Nile issue when in office until 1892, but he had modified his views by the time he returned. In particular, so fraught had the issue become that he now saw it as a particular aspect of his policy towards Europe, rather than simply an African issue, which he had considered it to be earlier.

Salisbury was concerned to keep Italy on its feet and as part of the European concert, which meant encouraging it to remain part of the Triple Alliance along with Germany and Austria-Hungary. If Italy lost British support, it became vulnerable, particularly to the French, and a Franco-Italian entente, perhaps achieved by French pressure, would then dominate the Mediterranean. It was the Royal Navy's Mediterranean Fleet that kept the French Navy away from Italy's many vulnerable ports and coasts. Italy's colonial ambitions must therefore be indulged, so long as they steered clear of the Nile headwaters. And yet the Italians found themselves at war with the Mahdists, and also quarrelled repeatedly with Ethiopia. This was a partly enclosed set of problems: Salisbury needed to keep Italy away from the Upper Nile (which would be accessible to them if they could control Ethiopia), but without annoying that country so much that the Italians realised that he was blocking their way. It was a tricky issue, but one decidedly playing to Salisbury's abilities, a triangle of Italy-Ethiopia-the Mahdists, with Salisbury watching carefully, and intervening reluctantly when he felt it necessary.

It was becoming steadily clearer that the central issue was not so much the Nile, or Uganda, or even Ethiopia, but the Mahdist state. By the 1890s, this was perceptibly in decline, though still militarily powerful in its primitive way. It had suffered more than one defeat in the years since 1889, yet it was still aggressive. It faced the now united Ethiopians, and was blocked out of expanding into Egypt, but then Mahdist raids began to be made against the Italians who had occupied Eritrea, and the expedition southwards made progress again the Belgians. Possibly, it was thought that the Italian forces in that colony were an easy target. The *ascari* whom the Italians had recruited had, after all, failed to participate in the fighting at Dogali – though several hundred Italian soldiers against 20,000 Ethiopians would have brought disaster to the *ascari* as well, if they had remained with the Italians. It may have been assumed that this was their normal attitude of disloyalty instead of a reaction to accompanying a clearly incompetent Italian force. If that was the calculation, it was wrong. In December 1893, the Mahdist commander at al-Qallabat, Ahmad Ali, having received permission from the Khalifa to mount raids against the Italians, took a force on a raid and attacked the fort at Agordat in Eritrea. The raiders were completely defeated by an Italian force consisting of 2,000 *ascari* commanded by 75 Italians. Ahmad Ali himself was amongst those killed.[27]

This success was followed by an Italian offensive. Kassala was a major Mahdist garrison fort in a key strategic position facing both the Italians and the Ethiopians. In 1891, Italians had agreed with the British that Sudan and the Mahdists was an Egyptian problem (that is, British), but that the Italians could take over Kassala in an emergency. This made them keep a clear eye on the condition of the garrison in the town; in May 1894, it became clear that the garrison had been much reduced – many of the soldiers had been transferred to al-Qadarif when supplies ran short at Kassala. The Italians decided, rather stretching the agreement further than the British had expected, and buoyed up by their victory at Agordat, to attack the town. The British were informed what the Italians were intending, and on 17 July the attack was put in and swiftly captured the town; the conquest was solemnly renamed Forte Baratieri, after the Italian commander in Eritrea.[28] The renaming rather implied that the Italians thought they would be able to keep the town.

These victories, exaggerated in the Italian reports, certainly encouraged them to move against Ethiopia. The result of these fights will also have convinced them and others that the Mahdist state was weakening. It had failed in most of its enterprises in the past few years, except in the small expedition against Fadl and the Belgians, neither to be seen as a serious force, and these were perhaps not even well known outside the contested area. Now the Mahdists had been defeated by the Italians, who were generally despised as soldiers. The Italian forces were commanded by men who owed their military reputations to participating in Garibaldi's campaign in 1860, in which there had been little serious fighting, but plenty of collapsing enemies when these were threatened. If they could be beaten by the Italians, so the reasoning would go, the Mahdists must be failing.

At this time also, various Italians were exploring, hunting and wandering about Somalia, the stretch of coast backed by desert stretching from Kismayu to the north-east as far as Cape Guardafui. It was fairly unprepossessing in many parts, but there were a couple of rivers leading north into what was to become southern Ethiopia as Emperor Menelik extended his range and conquests, and at least one Italian saw that, with Eritrea and Somalia in Italian hands, Ethiopia could be said to be surrounded. But for the moment this was only a tentative colonial adventure into a desert land.[29]

The Italians were meanwhile also encroaching on Ethiopian territory from the north. They had cultivated Ras Mangasha, the son of Emperor Yohannes, who was ruling in Tigray, and the Italians supposed him to be seeking revenge for having lost out to Menelik in the imperial succession. But in 1894 he was judged to have 'betrayed' the Italians, who had been deceiving themselves about his attitude all along. He had accepted their presents, including firearms, and this to the Italians seem to imply dependence, and that Mangasha was under their 'protection'. The two sides fell into a fight at Coatit (or Senafe) in Tigray. The Italians were just about victorious; they followed the retreating Tigrayans, and in a surprise night attack succeeded in dispersing Mangasha's forces. Mangasha's forces were not seriously damaged in these encounters, but he now quite deliberately and openly shifted his support to Menelik.[30]

The expansionist and predatory policies of the Mahdist state naturally set up resistant forces who were designed to stop their attacks. In Egypt, it was in large part the threat of a Mahdist invasion that had compelled the British to reconstitute the disbanded Egyptian army. In Ethiopia there is little doubt that one of the factors involved in the reunification of the empire in the 1870s and 1880s was the threat from the huge Mahdist armies, such as that which reached and sacked Gondar, and that whose attack resulted in the death of the Emperor Yohannes. Only a united Ethiopia could field armies large enough to confront them; in 1889, when Yohannes was defeated and killed in battle, one of the elements in both Mahdist and Italian calculations had been the possibility of separating Yohannes from Menelik.

There were also other factors, including personal ambitions and threats from Egypt and from Europe, but one of the earliest and most powerful was that from the Mahdi and then the Khalifa. The intermittent and difficult Mahdist expansion southwards towards the Great Lakes region was at last working out for the Mahdists in the 1890s, and if the Mahdist state had lasted longer, it would no doubt have continued – it had been blocked in every other direction. The successful resistance by Egypt and Ethiopia, and later by the Italians, was therefore instrumental in directing the Mahdist expansionist impulse southwards, seeking out, as it did, easy conquests. It is no accident that the battles and defeats of 1889 and the defeats at Agordat and Kassala were followed by Mahdist campaigns against Fadl al-Mula and the Belgians.

There was another aspect to this process. In the Bahr al-Ghazal region, the slaving activities that Gordon and Gessi and others tried to suppress was the result of the demand for slaves, particularly in Sudan and Egypt, but the Mahdists were less interested in the trade – though they certainly purchased enslaved victims sent from that area. The slavers with their *zeribas* were, of course, their predecessors in the region, and their activities had so damaged the area that it should have been an easy conquest. The Mahdist success in conquering Sudan tended to suppress the export trade in slaves, particularly once the market in Egypt failed when the British took control. But the absence of the slave trade in one direction did not suppress the traders, nor indeed slavery. Their capability had been dominated in the 1870s by the success of al-Zubayr, who, by getting many of the traders into a quasi-unified group – by force – he had created a strong mobile military unit; his conquest of Darfur was an indication of the strength of that organisation. He was, however, up against a more cunning rival in Darfur and lost out to Egyptian intrigue, though his organisation survived his subsequent imprisonment in Egypt; even the killing of his son Sulayman, who had tried to continue his work, did not destroy it; he had clearly constructed a competent organisation.

Sulayman was succeeded in the Bahr el-Ghazal by one of al-Zubayr's slaves, or possibly his son by one of his slaves, Rabeh al-Zubayr (or perhaps ibn al-Zubayr), who took over command of Sulayman's army after its defeat. He had a relatively small force at first, which was put at 1,200 men, but they were well equipped with firearms, making it, as with the slavers before him, a more formidable force than anyone else in the region commanded. The Egyptian commander Romolo Gessi, who had defeated Sulayman, had failed to capture Rabeh, but Gessi's enmity, ability and armed strength were too great a threat, so Rabeh took his army away westwards. This was in effect a mobile state, rather like that of Fadl al-Mula in the Great Lakes area, complete with families, slaves, servants and hangers-on; the latter would include merchants eager to buy the captured slaves and send them on to the major markets.[31]

Rabeh's was the archetypal predatory state, not one desirous of territory, at least at first, but one for whom the existing population was there to be enslaved and sold, or killed. He camped at first in the area west of the Bahr el-Ghazal province and beyond the Bahr al-Arab River. This was south-west of Darfur, south-east of Wadai and north of the Ubangui River, a major tributary of the Congo. This territory, comprising two regions called Dar Runga and Dar al-Kuti, was astride the watershed territory between the streams flowing west to Lake Chad, those south to the Congo and those east to the Nile. This gave Rabeh a number of neighbours whom he could raid when he had sufficiently devastated his own chosen base. One of his victim communities, to the south, was the Azande, already battered by the slave owners; the tribal units eventually united to resist him; the Belgians and the Mahdists also came under attack.

Rabeh's exploits were a result, in part, of the successes of the Mahdi, and he had attempted to join with him after the capture of Khartoum in 1885. He set out on the journey in person, but along the way, he apprehended a plot to assassinate him and turned back – or it may be that he had news of the Mahdi's death and that this deterred him; maybe it was a decision of the Khalifa, who could scent a political rival at a long distance.

The Mahdi had been corresponding with other Muslim powers in the months after his success at Khartoum and before his death. He was contacted by some Moroccans who were living in Egypt and who invited him to make an attempt on Morocco; he summoned the Emperor Yohannes in Ethiopia, but his suggestion that he convert to Islam was ignored; he corresponded with Hayatu al-Said, a discontented member of the Sokotan royal family. He diplomatically negotiated with the various sultans and tribes west of Darfur, and with the sultan of Wadai, and he was in contact with Rabeh. He asked for and accepted gestures of submission from all these rulers. Sultan Yusuf bin Muhammad al-Sharif of Wadai, for example, wrote a diplomatically ambiguous reply to the Mahdi's call in August 1885, in which he proclaimed that 'the time is the time of Mahdia, and not of worldly kingdoms' and 'the Mahdi is the Sultan of his time, and all the other governors are his followers', thus implying submission without performing it.[32] Emperor Yohannes, of course, did not make such a gesture.

These contacts are evidence of the Mahdi's ambition, rather than his achievement, but they fit in with the vision he reported in which he had listed Arabia, Iraq and Jerusalem as preliminary conquests before taking Egypt. Now he was envisaging Ethiopia, Wadai, West Africa and Morocco as subjects for his attention also. The success he had achieved in the Nile Valley was greeted with a mixture of cheer, apprehension and caution, but only the head of the Sanusi in Libya was profoundly and vocally hostile, as, of course, were Yohannes and the Egyptians, under British control.[33] Considering that he had been successful in gaining control of Sudan in only two years, starting with a few hundred badly armed and wholly untrained followers, one must suppose that, had he lived on, he would have had further successes, if not perhaps all those that he aimed for. The Islamic states he had his eye on were all in one way or another ripe for the jihadic cleansing he was performing in his conquered lands. He was undoubtedly one of the most remarkable men of the nineteenth century.

It is clear that Rabeh, whether hostile to the Khalifa Abdallahi or not, deliberately turned away from Sudan after the Mahdi's death. This was in part because of Romolo Gessi's military ability and pressure, though he had left the area by then, and partly because the decline in the market for the slaves he had been collecting and also because he was apparently rebuffed by the Khalifa. He was independent in his own devastated region whereas in Sudan he would be a subordinate. Had he joined the Mahdists when Abdallahi was in power, they would undoubtedly have come to blows. By 1887, Rabeh was hostile to the Mahdist state and was raiding into its province of Darfur. But an attack he made on Wadai was defeated, and this deflected him even further westwards. His ally and son-in-law Muhammad al-Sanusi became established in a region of Ubangui-Chari and defeated a small French expedition, sent under Paul Crampel to examine the area east of Lake Chad. The French group was 'almost annihilated', and Rabeh collected their weapons.[34] Together Rabeh and al-Sanusi then attacked the kingdom of Bagirmi, between Wadai and Lake Chad, a country already much damaged by civil wars and invasions during the previous century; the king was killed and his capital devastated. Rabeh was now within reach of the complex of kingdoms in West Africa. He then first collided with the Bornu kingdom, which collapsed when he defeated it. (Bornu had been a jihadic state after the accession of Muhammad al-Amin al-Kanemi in 1808; next was the jihadic Sokoto Caliphate, now well gone into decadence and division, and ripe for a new dose of reform. By 1893, Rabeh had made himself king of the large ancient state of Bornu, which meant that he was now the immediate neighbour of the Sokoto Caliphate.)

This was yet another extraordinary career, almost as impressive as the Mahdi's. Rabeh operated with only a small army; he still had only about 2,000 men when he defeated the Bornu king's 15,000. His westward move had therefore brought a scion of the Mahdist state into contact with the successors of the jihadist Sokoto Caliphate founded eighty years earlier by Usuman dan Fodio, and one of the inspirations for Muhammad Ahmad's own *jihad*. In Bornu, Rabeh settled for some years, building a new capital, though his old habits and his raids and slave taking conducted at his neighbours' expense were undiminished. As a promoter of Islam, however, he is hardly convincing. It must have looked as though he had achieved his aim of gaining a kingdom, but he was still dangerous. He had already clashed with the French – Crampel's hapless expedition – and was soon to do so again. And the British were seeking to expand north along the Niger River into Sokoto, which was Rabeh's new neighbour. The future was ominous for all these states and their invaders.

This discussion of Rabeh has pulled the story well away from the Upper Nile and the Great Lakes, even further from Khartoum. Yet his adventures, like the unification of Ethiopia, and the British seizure of Uganda, were all in some degree the result of the Mahdi's career in Sudan, as were the coming intrusion of Italian, French and Belgian forces into the area – and, of course, the British, whose intrusion was to be the most devastating of all. Rabeh's violent career had weakened his victims, and had led to some of them looking to Europeans for help, so his career was also encouraging the intrusion of European imperialists. Rabeh was killed in fighting the French in 1900, and his son died fighting the British in 1901; Bornu was then divided between the British, the French and the Germans.

In the same period as Rabeh was active, in Kenya the new railway was surveyed, intending to connect Lake Victoria (and its ferry boats) with the Indian Ocean ports; in 1895, the building of the 'Uganda Railway' was begun. And another railway was being planned to reach the Nile from the Atlantic through the Congo Free State, though it was never built. The Kenya–Uganda railway reached Kisumu on Lake Victoria in 1902, but the extension to Entebbe in Uganda was not built until 1928, the same year a branch from the German railway from Dar es-Salaam to Lake Tanganyika was connected with Lake Victoria at Mwanza. The defeat of the Mahdists in 1898 had evidently reduced the urgency for such railways, but their construction was another effect of the Mahdist adventure, first in provoking railway building, then in cramping it.

In Sudan, by 1896 the British/Egyptian campaign of conquest was also being conducted in part by building railways; and again railway construction ended with the completion of the conquest, not to be resumed until the 1920s. These railways, if built and linked together, would have brought Uganda and the Upper Nile into easier contact with the Indian Ocean ports, with the Atlantic, and with the Mediterranean. They were not necessarily going to pay their way, still less pay the costs of their construction, but they must be seen in the same light as providing soldiers with the latest weapons – Gatling guns, Maxim machine guns, and artillery. That is, the railway in Africa was a military weapon, capable of penetrating to the very centre of the continent. Without a war to fight, notably the finally perceived need to eliminate the Mahdist state, there was no incentive to build more lines. And once that had been destroyed, the railway construction halted.

In north-east Africa, the stimulus to attack the Mahdist regime came when it had been weakened sufficiently to become an easy target, but also when it became clear to the British government that there was a competition in play whereby another European power might seize the Upper Nile region (see chapter 15). And yet, in 1894, when Fadl al-Mula was killed in battle, when Rabeh was settling in to rule as king of Bornu, when the Union flag was raised in Uganda to connect Uganda with the Indian Ocean ports, and a formal protectorate was instituted, the Upper Nile was still untaken, except tentatively along the line of the river by the Mahdists. If it was the case that this was the key to imperial power in Central Africa, as numerous imperialists at the time seemed to believe, and as Stanley and Lugard had already proposed in 1892, it was still available, so long as the Mahdists could be beaten. Such a task had been beyond most imperialists so far.

Chapter 14

The Contenders: Italians and Ethiopians

It would have become clear that the Egyptian invasion of Sudan in the 1820s and the subsequent Mahdist Sudanese rebellion in the 1880s had much wider repercussions than merely changes of authority in the Nile Valley. The effects were felt at first by the Sudanese kingdoms that were conquered, and then by the Egyptian Empire, which was destroyed by the rebellion. With the Mahdists in control of the country now called Sudan, the effects had been felt in Egypt, in Ethiopia, in Darfur, in the Upper Nile region, along the Red Sea coast, and in Somalia; the first effects came with the Egyptian imperial expansion, and then more so with the Mahdist conquests. The effects extended into Wadai, the Great Lakes region, and towards West Africa with the conquests of Rabeh, who had built a new kingdom close to the vulnerable Sokoto Caliphate. Less direct effects were felt in other Islamic countries, notably by expressions of sympathy in Morocco, the Sokoto Caliphate, and Egypt, and of enmity in Egypt (again), Libya, and the borderlands of Darfur. The Mahdi's career and success could well be an inspiration to other Islamic holy men, as did the career of the Prophet and those of Usuman dan Fodio and al-Hajj Umar were to Muhammad Ahmad. The career of Rabeh was a direct effect of Mahdist success, and though brutal, it showed what could be achieved by a small well-armed force in African conditions, as did the early successes of the Mahdi's small army. All the new jihadist states in the Sahel region had begun with small forces and had faced little resistance from their enemies and victims, at least at first.

Hostile reaction to the Mahdists came from Ethiopia, the Great Lakes kingdoms, Wadai, Egypt, France, Italy and Britain, and these varied states were stimulated to mount hostile moves to either suppress the Mahdist power, or to profit from its weakening and its eventual collapse. This Mahdist 'event' between 1880 and 1900 was a dominant problem for all its neighbours, an inspiration for all its sympathisers, and an opportunity for its enemies for a generation. It had drawn Belgians westwards to the Nile, British officials and forces from the Indian Ocean to Lake Victoria, Germans through Tanganyika, and French expeditions from the Atlantic coast of Africa right across to East Africa. The last chapter indicated the eventual failure of Mahdist expansion; this chapter will consider who were contemplating, or actively aiming, to seize the Mahdist state, or part or parts of it.

Inevitably the most active and powerful enemy was the British administration that had been installed in Egypt, using mainly Egyptian and Indian troops for its wars. For some time no direct attempt at conquest of the Sudan was made, since it had been deemed unnecessary once the Mahdist threat to Egypt had been blocked with the failure of al-Nujumi's invasion. But then, suddenly, this condition changed.

The decision to begin to retake Sudan on behalf of Egypt was made at a Cabinet meeting in London on 12 March 1896, and telegraphed next day to Kitchener and Cromer by the Prime Minister, Lord Salisbury.[1] This permission came suddenly and without notice, though it was not wholly unexpected. The first intention was to march as far as Dongola, but no further. This was to appear to be either a preliminary to a full-scale invasion of Sudan, or a statement of later intent. Holding Dongola would secure control over the neutral region between Wadi Halfa and Dongola, which had existed since al-Nujumi's attack in 1889 had been defeated. Alternatively, it was an operation aimed at distracting the Mahdists from some of their other enterprises, in particular to take the Mahdists' attention away from attempting a serious attack on the Italians in Eritrea in the wake of their devastating defeat by the Ethiopians at Adowa, which had taken place at the beginning of the month (and which will be discussed later in this chapter). Or, of course, it would leave the enemy (as well as the British) in some doubt of British-Egyptian future intentions.

However, another reason is that the Khalifa Abdallahi had ordered a mobilisation even before the news of the Italian defeat at Adowa became known in Khartoum. The mobilisation had been decided on at a meeting in January 1896 of the Khalifa with several of his chiefs, and was to be aimed at retaking Kassala, with a secondary force directed to the north to distract the British and Egyptians and prevent them from interfering – it was clear that the Khalifa was well informed of the diplomatic interaction between the Europeans. The threat to Kassala was clearly an attempt to take advantage of Italian and Ethiopian preoccupations with their mutual war; in the north, the Mahdists and the British/Egyptians were thus aiming to distract each other from that opportunity.[2] It is curious that both sides were employing the same methods of decision – cabinets, chiefs – and the same distraction techniques, more or less simultaneously; it is also clear that the British move along the Nile to Dongola was in part an anticipation of the Mahdist move against Wadi Halfa; both sides knew well what the other was doing and planning.

It therefore appears probable that it was mainly for the purpose of distracting the Mahdists from their attacks on Kassala that Lord Salisbury ordered the

Egyptian army to march, and so aid the Italians in their difficulties. This operation was thus an outcome of the international politics of Europe. The threat of an increased Mahdist force on the Nile front facing Egypt was not to be welcomed, nor was the probability of a Mahdist defeat of a European power, but there were plenty of other reasons that were involved in the decision. All the powers who had been active in the past decades in north-eastern and East Africa were involved, as were those further afield, in Nigeria, French West Africa, and the Belgian Congo, for example. Their mutual target was now the swamplands of the Upper Nile and the Bahr el-Ghazal; for the British this also meant undertaking the conquest of Sudan, since that was their only way of reaching that targetted area; it was also something many had expected to be started for several years.

The Mahdist state was thus one of the lesser targets in the war in which it was eventually to be crushed and eliminated. Its record of government in the past few years had been poor to abysmal, and many of its constituent tribes had begun to develop an obvious hostility to the Khalifa's rule. The state's expansion – one of the main reasons for its existence – had clearly ceased several years before. It had failed to reach into Egypt, Eritrea, Ethiopia, Uganda, or into the territories westwards, despite attempts made in all these directions. It was thus failing in its main purpose as laid out for it by the Mahdi, its founder, which was to bring infidels into Islam, and ensure that Muslims followed the correct Islamic path. Once the state had ceased to expand, it had become just another Muslim country devoted to its own continuance. The loosening of the allegiance of some of the Sudan tribes was evidently an opportunity for the Mahdists' enemies to take advantage of the state's weakness; the enemies, therefore, were gathering.

The state's continuance was threatened by all those powers that had been victims of a Mahdist attack in the past fifteen years, and, since they were also still potential victims, they were now very much on their guard. No neighbour could relax, for a new attack might emerge from Sudan without warning, or without any immediately obvious reason; such an attack was especially likely if the victim was momentarily weakened by some disaster or defeat. In the period 1894–6, that state in a weakened condition was the Italian colony of Eritrea.

There were, however, other dangers and contradictions. First was the appreciation in Britain and in Egypt that a hostile power might gain control of the Upper Nile region, now understood to consist of the course of the Nile from the location of Fashoda south to the Great Lakes and west along the Bahr el-Ghazal and its tributaries, a region up to 1,000 miles from north to south, and as much from east to west. At the lakes, the ultimate source of the river, Britain had gone to some trouble to secure access to, and some control in, Uganda. It had developed access to the lakes and to the first section of the White Nile from the lakes northwards, though that control was precarious and disputed by the local kingdoms, and by other Europeans in the area. From there north to Fashoda, there were swamps and rivers feeding into the White Nile, and the appalling Sudd. The combined waters of this area coalesced into a single stream just south of Fashoda, where rivers from west (the Bahr al Ghazal), south (the Nile), and east (the Sobat, out of Ethiopia) joined into one stream. Fashoda itself was a fort on a small area of land rising above the waters, and was now seen to be a crucial place for local control over a large area; there was a fort on the island occupied by a small Mahdist contingent.

The Mahdists were in control of the line of the Nile for some distance south of Fashoda, but the area they held was limited, and was the target for all surrounding powers – British, Belgians, Ethiopians, and French, even Italians if their 'protectorate' of Ethiopia was accepted. It was surely curious, and a commentary on imperial ambitions, that all these outsiders were anxious to gain sovereignty over an area of swamp and the occasional island.

King Leopold's Congo Free State had attempted to gain control of the river from Lake Albert northwards, but had been driven out by the last Mahdist offensive in the area, which had also removed Fadl al-Mula and his small band of Sudanese soldiers; Fadl died, but some of his soldiers were collected and employed by the British. Leopold, however, had come away from this attempt with the promise of the lease of part of the west bank of the White Nile north of the Great Lakes, based on the town of Lado, an area that became known as the Lado Enclave.[3] It included Lado itself, and several places that had featured as bases for various forces in the recent past – al-Rajjaf, Gondokoro, Dufile, and Wadelai, as far south as Lake Albert, which was the border of the kingdom of Bunyoro. Control of this area brought the Congo State as far as the White Nile along a lengthy stretch.

This was a crucial part of this southern area from which to control the surrounding territory, and potentially the Nile itself. Yet it was only to be a lease for Leopold's lifetime; until then the eastern border of the territory was more or less internationally recognised.[4] The exact extent of the lease was never agreed, and there were discussions about this for several years. Both sides were perhaps aiming to spin the talks out until Leopold died, when the question would become moot.

One of the aims of the Belgians, coming from the Congo, was therefore to occupy this area as a means of enforcing their successive agreements with Britain, and yet part of it was already under Mahdist control. The actual boundary between the Congo Free State and the territory that the British claimed (which was actually the whole of the Mahdist state) was agreed to be the Congo–Nile watershed, whose actual location had never been discovered, but was clearly somewhere to the west of the Nile.

The Belgians had moved tentatively into the Bahr el-Ghazal province in the early 1890s, but the Mahdists' campaign in the area had forced them to retreat, even when agreement with Britain technically brought them the Lado Enclave. This had left the Bahr el-Ghazal region open to other contenders. The Mahdists had withdrawn, the Belgians pulled out by agreement with the French, and it seemed to be available for whoever could occupy the area – none of the contenders had 'effective occupation' in accordance with the West African Conference requirement ten years before, though this was a condition more honoured in being ignored than in being applied. In fact, the Mahdists had sent a force to investigate what the Belgians were doing, and it was only the Belgians' withdrawal that preserved them from being attacked. But even as the Belgians were pulling out, the French were preparing yet another expedition, also aimed at the Bahr el-Ghazal and the Upper Nile. The variety of agreements (based on no actual occupation, nor even on any detailed knowledge) indicates that at last the European states had developed a determination to seize the swamps. This was partly greed for African territory, but in the background was the hope that it might lead to war in the Nile Valley, and hence the chance to blackmail the British in Egypt.

King Leopold made an agreement to cooperate with the French and both countries would send expeditions; the French one was commanded by Captain Jean-Baptiste Marchand; along with that agreement, Leopold conned the Belgian government into taking over the debt of the Congo State. He then, freed of the burden of the debt, and presumably confident that if he got into debt again the Belgian state would once more bail him out, developed great ambitions, dreaming of taking over Eritrea from the wounded Italians, leasing Kassala and more from the Egyptians, and campaigning out of the Lado Enclave as far north as Khartoum.[5] What he actually did was, eventually, to send two expeditions to secure the Lado Enclave.

Unlike the Congo State's expeditions, the French move in the same direction was to be accomplished quietly. The British, who were no nearer the area in question than Uganda or Egypt, and in neither area capable of greatly extending their power, would therefore be presented with Belgian possession of the Lado Enclave, and a French presence in the Bahr el-Ghazal area, a pair of *faits accomplis*. The French and Belgians aimed at the same region, theoretically in concert, though they were actually, of course, in competition, and if they jointly succeeded, they would no doubt soon intrigue against each other, and one partner would be betrayed.

Just as keen to reach the Upper Nile as Leopold, the French had already attempted on two occasions to send expeditions from western Africa towards the Nile. These were partly seen as ways of persuading the British to end their occupation of Egypt (as they had repeatedly promised), but linked with them in some French minds was their equivalent of the 'Cape to Cairo' ambition, which floated in British minds, but swung round through ninety degrees – a continuous French-controlled territory from Senegal to Djibouti, both already under French occupation. Recent military successes in West Africa had brought French power eastwards along the upper Niger to and beyond Timbuktu, and they were treating with the British about further advances. They had Rabeh in particular in their sight, but also Samori. There was, when Marchand's mission was planned in November 1895, much still to do if this trans-Africa idea was to be seriously contemplated, but Marchand was part of it, and the governor of Djibouti was gaining influence in Ethiopia at the other, eastern, end of the ambition. French 'missions' succeeded one another, and the plans had a tendency to change; eventually, the notion of a great French Dominion encompassed all North and East Africa – Algeria to the Gulf of Guinea and Dakar to Djibouti. The original idea had been to gain a foothold in the Upper Nile region as a means of persuading the British to leave Egypt – in effect, a threat to interfere in some way with the flow of the Nile waters. Second thoughts, however, showed that the removal of the British from Egypt would be a most unlikely outcome – a British attack on the perpetrators of the threat would be much more likely, and would be produced more quickly. The eventual intention behind the Marchand expedition was to extend French colonial territory into the Upper Nile region and to link up with the French presence in Ethiopia. That is, French intentions tended to vary with the person voicing them.

The first of the French expeditions had been the Mission Monteil, which had failed in 1894 when diplomatic complications in Europe, together with Monteil's own lackadaisical approach, killed the project.[6] The intention to move onto the Upper Nile was then entrusted to Victor Liotard, the governor of the Upper Ubangui province, the French territory located south of the Bahr el-Ghazal (and south of Rabeh's predatory conquests in Bornu), but north of the Congo Free State. Liotard had experience of the conditions and was knowledgeable of the peoples of the region, and so had the advantage that he was already close to the object of any expedition in the Upper Nile; on the other hand, he was responsible for administering a region that had been badly damaged by the slavers from the north, by the raids by Rabeh, and was being encroached on by the Belgians. He had been working hard to calm the people down and organise the area's recovery, and so, reasonably enough, he put his governor's responsibilities before a hare-brained scheme delivered to him by politicians and bureaucrats out of Paris who knew nothing of the region or its people. He did move the Mission Liotard forward after some time into the Bahr el-Ghazal province, news of which advances reached Europe in fragments. But it took him two years to reach two places, Deir Zubayr and Tampura. These were in the old Mahdist Bahr el-Ghazal province but neither of them were very far across the vague boundary of his own province.[7]

The rumours of these two expeditions – that of Liotard did actually accomplish something, if not very much – filtered back to Europe. In March 1895, the British Undersecretary at the Foreign Office, Sir Edward Grey – Rosebery's colleague and the Foreign Office's spokesman in the House of Commons – declared that the British/Egyptian 'sphere' covered the whole Nile Valley. This would be interpreted as including the area of the Bahr el-Ghazal, which was a Nile tributary. The French took no heed of what might also be interpreted as a British threat to block their expedition. But the government of which Grey was a member resigned in June, and Salisbury took office as Prime Minister and Foreign Secretary. By then, the French had concocted yet another plan, larger, wider, and more ambitious, which became the Mission Marchand. By then also, however, the British had made their decisive move.

The events that eventually brought the British to make their move took place in Ethiopia, where Italy had moved forward its forces into Ras Mangasha's Tigray kingdom, marginally defeating his forces. They, of course, claimed a protectorate over Mangasha's territory, or perhaps an alliance with him. But Mangasha had broken with the Italians, the two had fought at Coatit, and so now these Italian forces were seen not as Mangasha's allies but as foreign invaders of Ethiopia. In September 1895, the Emperor Menelik published a warning throughout the Ethiopian Empire that the country was in danger.[8] He struck a welcome chord; no doubt it was widely understood that Italy was the active enemy, but it was only the latest of such enemies – the Egyptians, the British and the Mahdists had all attacked in the recent past, and all from the same northern area, where the Italians had their Eritrean colony. There was a surge of support for the emperor and his administration, and he had a very large potential source thereby for a great army. Italy was the obvious enemy, but the Mahdists had also still to be reckoned with.

The Italians also had to watch out for the Mahdists. Their occupation of Kassala had eventually brought a Mahdist response and the town was blockaded by a Mahdist force.[9] If it was taken, there was little doubt that the Mahdists would move on to invade Eritrea again, and this time in full force. The Italians had succeeded in arousing the enmity of the two most formidably armed forces in Africa at the same time, though it was extremely unlikely that the two would cooperate, even against their common enemy.

The immediate cause of the fighting in Ethiopia was the actions of Ras Mangasha. After breaking with the Italians and being driven southwards – and making an alliance with the Emperor Menelik – he gathered his forces once more and advanced with the intention of capturing Adigrat. He was campaigning, of course, within his own kingdom of Tigray, which the Italians claimed to have taken for themselves. The Italian commander, General Oreste Baratieri (the captor of Kassala), had got to the town first, but then found himself short of resources to face the new attack. He made a quick visit to Rome to secure more. When he returned to Eritrea, Mangasha was once again attacking Adigrat, and had to be driven off again. It was at this point that Menelik issued his proclamation that the country was in danger. If Mangasha was driven southwards and out of his kingdom, the Italians would be able to penetrate into central Ethiopia, and with some skilful diplomacy they might be able to find Ethiopian allies. One reason for Menelik's proclamation of national danger was to pre-empt such an Italian move, and bring the men of central Ethiopia decisively onto his own side.

Menelik was using diplomacy himself as well as gathering his armed forces. He had earlier begun talks with the Khalifa, tactfully sending Muhammad al-Tayyib, an Ethiopian Muslim, to open peace talks. The Khalifa rejected the early suggestion of a treaty (August 1895), but Menelik repeatedly sent his envoy to Khartoum as a way of keeping the talks going. There was no result, the Khalifa being unwilling to make any concessions or agreement with the Christian infidels, but it clearly suited both rulers that the talks should go on.[10] The Khalifa could be in no doubt that a great battle was approaching; he was not displeased that his two Christian neighbours were fighting each other; he may well have been contemplating an attack on the loser. The talks also had the advantage of unsettling the Italians, who thought the two African powers might be discussing an alliance; the British also imagined the same. Menelik's move was a classic piece of diplomatic deception.

Menelik also tried diplomacy with the Italians. His governor at Harar, Ras Makonnen, had experience with negotiating with the Italians. He went down to Zeila, Harar's normal port, which was part of the British protectorate of Somaliland, to suggest peace negotiations. The Italians were not interested, being convinced that Ethiopia was a weak and divided country. Earlier, the Italians had proposed to launch a flank attack, through Zeila and Harar, which would presumably pin down Ras Makonnen's forces, but the British, holding Zeila, refused their permission.[11] The British were attempting to maintain a diplomatic balance, in both North Africa and Europe.

Menelik gathered an army of about 100,000 men, who were often accompanied by wives, children and slaves, greatly increasing the size of the moving host. The regional tribal contingents were commanded by their own chiefs or governors. It was so great a number that he had to spread them out for ease of logistics. He sent Ras Makonnen forward with the Harari contingent (his mission to Zeila had made it clear that there was no danger of an Italian force coming from that direction). Makonnen could thus move north, and there he was joined by the forces of Ras Mangasha and Ras Wole Betul, who was the brother of Empress Taitu. They all gathered at Amba Alagi, a fortified hill where the Italian advance force had been placed.

General Baratieri had a force of about 8,000 men, partly Italian regular soldiers and partly *ascaris*. He divided them between the force at Amba Alagi, under Major Pietro Toselli, a second force at Makalle commanded by General Giuseppe Arimondi, and a third force, which he kept under his own hand. All three divisions were well separated, and, of course, were therefore also weak and could only support each other with difficulty. The nearest force to Toselli was Arimondi's at Makalle, but that was 34 miles away. Arimondi was supposed to march to join Toselli, but equally, Toselli was supposed to retire from his advanced position so that the two forces could join together. Ras Mangasha and his colleagues had 30,000 men facing Toselli's 2,000. Even with Arimondi's joining Toselli's, the Italians would be greatly outnumbered. Toselli was actually reinforced by 2,000 to 3,000 Tigrayans who had chosen the Italian side, but he was still heavily outnumbered, by at least six to one.

The Ethiopian attack on Toselli's force came on 6 December 1895. The advance came in columns, one pressing against the Italian left, which was driven back on the Italian centre; the second column came in on the right, and with similar results. The Italian force was thus forced back and was concentrated in a much smaller area. Then, at about 11 am (the fighting had begun about dawn), a huge Ethiopian column about 15,000 strong drove straight at the Italian centre (along the 'English road', which the British had built twenty years before for their attack on the Emperor Tewodros). The Italian infantry was now concentrated around the four guns the Italians had; as the Ethiopian column approached, the gunners were able to fire over open sights, scarcely needing to aim. Their shots could be seen landing within the column and exploding; a hole was made in the column, but then the gaps quickly closed up and the column came on, apparently hardly damaged.

Toselli had perforce brought all his men together, and made preparations to retire, but rather late in the encounter; the great central column was perhaps unexpected. As soon as his guns ceased firing in their preparation to leave, the Ethiopian mass charged, and drove the whole Italian force into retreat. The retreat was as unpleasant as such things always are. A group of about 300 held together for several miles under Lieutenant Bodrero, and got away; others, often wounded, got to Makalle independently during the next days, but the total actually lost on the Italian side was about 1,500 – in effect, a quarter of Baratieri's army had been obliterated; their Tigrayan allies suffered similarly, but at least the survivors could go home. The Ethiopian casualties were reckoned – by the Italians – at double that number, no doubt an exaggeration. Toselli was killed, supposedly heroically.[12]

The main surviving group, the 300 under Lieutenant Bodrero, met up with Arimondi's force, which was about 1,500 strong, several miles from the battlefield, and the whole force came under attack almost at once. Arimondi decided to retire to his base at Makalle. A long march brought them to the town, but with only 2,000 men or less, Arimondi decided that retirement even further north was required. He left a garrison of half his force at Makalle under Captain Giuseppe Galliano. He was harassed on the march, and burdened with wives and civilians, but most of them reached Adagamus – one of the many defendable mountain positions in Ethiopia – and safety; it was a notably successful march, repeatedly under attack, covering over 100 miles in a little over three days.[13]

The garrison at Makalle held out for about a fortnight. Captain Galliano had gathered supplies from the countryside and had repaired the defences, but the only water source was outside the walls. Empress Taitu, who was present with her husband and his army, commanding her own forces, was apparently the first to point out the advantage of cutting off that supply.[14] Hence, the brevity of the siege, whose length was exaggerated by Italian journalists in search of a heroic story, quadrupled to forty-five days. The lack of water meant that the whole garrison was reduced to the need to surrender quickly, without having put up much of a fight. Menelik accepted the surrender and allowed them all to march out, complete with their guns.[15] This evidence of Ethiopian self-confidence did not register with General Baratieri when he heard of it, fixated as he was in his attitude of superiority and contempt.

The reaction in Italy to these defeats was similar to that in Ethiopia when the Italian threat became all too clear. After the news of Amba Alagi arrived, thousands of men volunteered to go to serve in the army in Eritrea in a sort of ecstasy of patriotism. Most of them were untrained, but went anyway. General Baratieri consequently found himself with a new army of 40,000 men, which was concentrated mainly in the port of Massawa. This was eight days' march from the likely scene of the fighting – a march that went from a port at sea level on the Red Sea to 8,000 feet above sea level, over unmaintained tracks. Baratieri also received thousands of mules and horses, but amidst all this he did not have enough provisions for either his men or his animals.¹⁶ Compare the Italian muddle and inefficiency with the success of the Ethiopians in providing for an army more the twice the size of the Italian.

Menelik had brought his army forward as far as the neighbourhood of Adowa. For a month, the opposing forces marched and manoeuvred in the hills and ravines south of the town, while the two sides gathered their strengths and organised their forces.¹⁷ Menelik was in command on the Ethiopian side, apparently calm and confident. Baratieri on the Italian side was overstressed, probably ill, and under pressure both from his subordinate generals, who shared his contempt for the enemy and hungered for a victory, and from the Italian government, which wanted an 'authentic victory', a phrase implying that earlier 'victories' had been puffed-up press releases and little more. He was also, on the very eve of battle, about to be dismissed, though he did not yet know it. These generals were all either veterans of the Garibaldian war over thirty years before, or had absorbed its methods and ethos – one aspect of which was a propensity for intrigue, which was shared by the politicians. An intrigue had been mounted to replace Baratieri with General Antonio Baldissera, who was already secretly on his way to take over; it was his good fortune that he did not arrive in time.¹⁸

The Italian force in Eritrea was reckoned at about 35,000 men by February 1896, already reduced somewhat by desertion and sickness, but only half of the total manpower was actually available at the battle site, 17,700 men, Italians and *ascari*. The Ethiopian army it was facing was reckoned by an Italian to have had 80,000 infantry, armed with rifles, and about 9,000 cavalry, so outnumbering the Italians five to one (figures for once more or less accurate). In artillery, the two sides were of almost equal strength, forty-two guns with the Ethiopians, fifty-six with the Italians. The infantry on both sides was reasonably well armed – the Ethiopians with the Italian-supplied muskets and rifles bought through Antonelli or acquired by Ras Makonnen.¹⁹ In military skills, the two were different but still roughly equal; in generalship, the Italians were as badly outclassed as they were outnumbered.

Baratieri, as before, divided his army into three columns, who were to approach the enemy position along different routes, and were intended to join together at the decisive moment to launch an overwhelming joint attack. He had evidently learned nothing from the previous defeat. This was, of course, a Napoleonic battle concept, the three columns supposedly intended to converge on the enemy position simultaneously, but it was not carried out with Napoleonic speed or precision. It is of interest that the Ethiopians had used a version of this attacking process at Amba Alagi, but the actual attack there was somewhat differently planned (and was well conducted and more successful). Whereas the Ethiopians had a good knowledge of the country they were fighting in, the Italian forces had only inaccurate maps, and had apparently done no proper reconnaissance; and once again, their three columns remained too far separated to provide any joint support.

The result, in a fairly confused and disjointed battle, was that each Italian column, fighting separately for the most part, suffered about the same number of killed – 7,000 in total – but the Italians also lost about 3,000 prisoners and up to 2,000 wounded. In essence, up to two-thirds of the Italian army in the field became casualties, killed, wounded or prisoners. The Ethiopian army had perhaps 10,000 killed and wounded; the high number of wounded was due to the fact that in contrast to the Italian plan it was the Ethiopians who took the offensive in the fighting. In percentage terms, the Italians had 66 per cent of their forces as casualties, while the Ethiopians lost about 20 per cent, perhaps less; the Italian army in Eritrea was effectively destroyed, while the Ethiopian army was still complete with their guns.[20] It was very much a functioning force, and clearly capable, if Menelik chose to march down to the coast at Massawa, of challenging the remaining Italian forces, though the coastal climate would clearly hamper the Ethiopians even more than the same land had damaged the Italians.

After that defeat, the newly arrived Italian commander General Baldissera held to the common Italian attitude of superiority, and still tried to impose onerous conditions on Menelik in the subsequent peace talks. Menelik, in effect, simply wanted the Italians either to go home or to stay behind the boundary of Eritrea that had already been agreed. There was a widespread rising of Tigrayans against the Italian occupiers and their collaborators. When Baldissera attempted to negotiate and to impose his conditions, Menelik broke off the talks, and went back to Addis Ababa to a great welcome; the Italians eventually made peace in October on Menelik's (very moderate) terms.[21] By this time, of course, the Italian government had fallen as a result of the defeat – which could not this time be hidden behind false stories of heroics and press lies – and there was a new Italian administration in office, one that had perhaps a more objective view of what had happened, as it had not been responsible for the disaster.[22]

This massive Italian defeat had effects much wider than those between the two antagonists. The Mahdist attack on Italian-held Kassala, which had been announced in January 1896, was certainly encouraged. The French plans for an expedition under Captain Marchand were pushed forward, though they still did not get started until later in 1896; French relations with Menelik were developed and encouraged, with the aim of linking the two movements by French explorations and intrigues from the Atlantic and from the Red Sea, with Fashoda on the Nile to be the junction point. The Mahdist forces under Urabi Daft'allah at al-Rajjaf on the Upper Nile finally received the news from Khartoum by a small steamer in July. The British attempt to distract the Mahdists from any attempt to interfere, by their forward movement along the Nile to Dongola, failed, but it quickly morphed into a new operation.

Chapter 15

Advances to Contact

In London, Lord Salisbury had reacted to the news that fighting had begun in northern Ethiopia by authorising the advance along the Nile from Wadi Halfa to Dongola, an authorisation that came with some surprise to the military authorities in Cairo. It looked like an unusual intervention in African affairs by the Prime Minister, but in fact, apart from giving some support to the Italians in Africa, he was also supporting them against French enmity in the European power game. The possibility of the Royal Navy's Mediterranean Fleet intervening in a Franco-Italian dispute would prevent the French Navy from threatening the vulnerable Italian coastal cities. Acting in support of Italy in its African crisis was a useful means of providing support without exacerbating the situation between Italy and France, who, in Europe, constantly fought a war of words.

In Africa, Salisbury saw that the crucial point was Kassala. If the Italians were defeated there, their colony of Eritrea would be wide open to a Mahdist invasion, particularly in the obviously demoralised condition of the colony and its partly disarmed condition after the defeat at Adowa. He appears to have been clear that the result of the battle would not be an Ethiopian invasion of Eritrea, for that would destroy the Italian position there, and leave the colony open to a Mahdist invasion when the Ethiopians withdrew. The Emperor Menelik had all along shown a careful restraint, and would be careful in victory to avoid the Mahdists reaping an easy victory of their own. Neither Menelik nor Salisbury wanted the Mahdists to become a more formidable enemy than they already were.

Sure enough, the first item that General Baldissera attended to was the relief of the siege at Kassala.[1] This was successfully accomplished by 5 May, though by this time the British/Egyptian campaign along the Nile had begun, which proved to be the decisive move in the campaign of conquest. An Italian garrison remained in Kassala, and came under renewed Mahdist attack early in 1897, at which point the Italian decision was taken to hand the town back to the British, a benefit that Salisbury probably did not expect.[2]

Little more than ten days after the news of the Battle of Adowa arrived, Salisbury telegraphed to General Kitchener, the *sirdar* (commander-in-chief) of the Egyptian army, giving him the authority for the Egyptian army to advance along the Nile from Wadi Halfa as far as Dongola. It will not have escaped Salisbury's political mind that a campaign against the Mahdists would be a popular move in Britain, as well as providing support to the Italians, helping them to recover from their defeat. As a clever politician, Salisbury was striking at several useful targets all at once. It would also be a public gesture of support for Italy in the European political situation, while not too obviously antagonising France, which was not involved in the issue of Kassala.

The brief Sudanese campaign that followed, along the Nile, was self-contained. It was aimed to capture Dongola, which was the key to any further advance along the Nile, since beyond the town, the countryside was flat and moderately productive, so it was no longer the terrible desert of the 400 miles from Wadi Halfa. And yet it was a campaign intended to stop at Dongola, for exploitation beyond that point was not the aim. Accordingly, only that stretch north of Dongola would have to be fought for, and it had been an empty no man's land since al-Nujumi's defeat. The greatest difficulties were logistic, and the greatest number of casualties were caused by disease, when a cholera outbreak in Egypt reached as far as the army.

That is to say, this was a campaign in which engineering skills were at a premium, and General Kitchener was by training an engineer. (He also had earlier experience in the Sudan, having taken part in the Wolseley campaign in 1884–5.) The advance to Dongola was achieved by stages, with an armed camp established at the end of each stage. Behind the front, a railway was built along the land recently travelled, as a means of bringing forward supplies. (This part of the campaign is reminiscent of a Roman imperial campaign, with roads behind the front and daily advances and camps, as no doubt the classically educated officers who had read Caesar and Tacitus fully appreciated.) There was a railway route already in existence from the 1885 campaign, but much of it had been abandoned, and its equipment, and anything of use, had been appropriated by the local people and used for their own purposes. But the route had been engineered and it could be reused after repairs and any necessary reconstruction, and then extended. This would solve the logistics problem, above all providing supplies to the soldiers, adequately and quickly.

The Mahdists knew what was coming, and when the Egyptian army advance force approached, they moved their troops forward to Akasha, 80 miles south of Wadi Halfa, where a Mahdist reconnaissance patrol turned up; it was chased away by an Egyptian cavalry unit.[3] Beyond that, the Mahdists were distinctly unenterprising; they made no attempt to attack the supply line behind the Egyptian camps, or to damage the sections of the railway as they were built, or to interfere with the construction parties building the extension. The original

Mahdist commander, Hammuda Idris, was replaced by Uthman Isa al-Azraq, who was a Dongolan, but the Mahdist passivity continued.[4] It is possible that the Mahdists knew that the British/Egyptian advance was only intended to go as far as Dongola, and so did not see any need to indulge in any fighting. However, Kitchener, who was familiar with the region from the earlier campaign against al-Nujumi's army, and was knowledgeable about the communities his forces were advancing against, was suitably alert.

The first advance, as far as Akasha, took place on 20 March 1896 (only a week after Salisbury's telegram of permission to advance). The Egyptian army staff under Kitchener had clearly planned out the campaign well in advance – they had had ten years to think about it, after all. There was, of course, the problem of money, and an argument between Cairo and London as to who should pay, but this was eventually sorted out, as were Cromer's hurt feelings at the decision to advance being made without consulting him, even though he was technically Kitchener's superior.[5] On the other hand, Baring had only reached the rank of major in the army and it is unlikely that Kitchener would let him forget it.

There was another problem, that of manpower, and it was necessary to concentrate all forces at the active front, and not spread them too widely or thinly – this had been the Italian fault at Amba Alagi, after all. The base at Suakin on the Red Sea coast had been intermittently active since the original Mahdist conquests; the appointment of Uthman Digna to be the Mahdist commander in the area had been the real engine of warfare there. The garrison of Egyptian and British troops was often involved in local fights all through the Mahdist occupation of the interior and was well experienced in fighting them. The Egyptian garrison at Suakin was therefore now moved to the Nile, and replaced by 4,000 Indian troops, who found their new situation boring, but this did concentrate the most experienced forces on the active front along the Nile.[6]

The greatest expense was, of course, on materials, which had to be manufactured or purchased from a variety of sources. A new set of steamers were ordered from Britain, based on a design suggested by Kitchener. The railway was supervised by a French Canadian engineer, Lieutenant Percy Girouard, who had worked on the Canadian Pacific line. It required sleepers to be obtained from Turkish forests, and artisans to be recruited in Egypt to build the railway, who had to be trained for the task on the job. This was in addition to the reinforcements acquired from India.[7]

By 21 May 1896, the railhead was only 22 miles from Akasha. The Mahdist army in the lower Nile region was concentrated at Ferkeh (or Firket), a dozen miles south of Akasha. Kitchener advanced his force quietly to a position a little north of Akasha, out of sight and knowledge of the Mahdists, who apparently did not send out reconnaissance patrols, and prepared to attack from there. His plan was to detach a 'desert column' of 2,000 men, cavalry, cameleers, and horse artillery, which would move quickly and quietly to a position beyond the Mahdist camp. The remainder of the army, 7,000 infantry, the artillery, and a Maxim gun battery, advanced along the river road at night. After a rest, the last march brought the army just before dawn to an open space in front of the Mahdist camp, which remained unaware of the imminent attack, though the infantry advance cannot have marched silently, even if it was relatively quiet. The sound of firing from beyond the Mahdists was the signal that the desert column was in its intended position, and the battle was won at that moment. The Mahdists, taken thus by surprise, as usual fought desperately; the Egyptian army, reinforced by the 1st North Staffordshires, and using British infantry tactics, destroyed them with disciplined fire – and, of course, artillery and Maxim guns. The desert column moved to the river road behind the Mahdist position, and when the Mahdists retired, or fled, from the battlefield they were intercepted. Of the 3,000 or so in the Mahdist camp, 1,000 were killed, 600 were captured, and the rest scattered. The Egyptians had twenty-two killed and ninety-one wounded.[8]

The victory demonstrated the efficiency and resolve of the new Egyptian army. It also opened up the river for the gunboats, at least when the level of the river rose, which this year was a little late. The water level was sufficient for the gunboats to pass the cataracts only in August, a month later than usual. (The immobilised army suffered almost 1,000 dead at this point from the cholera epidemic.)

The next stage in the advance began on 12 September 1896, but three days later at al-Hafir the enemy, using, for once, sensible tactics, held up the march. The Mahdists occupied the west bank of the river, and had entrenched their positions; the Egyptian army marched along the east bank, and needed to cross over, both to get at the enemy army and to attack Dongola. The Mahdists had some artillery with which they threatened the steamers and any men crossing in small boats. They prevented, in that position, the steamboats from getting past, and were in a good position to prevent any of the soldiers crossing the river, which they had to do to attack Dongola.

After a cross-river bombardment, which did little damage, Kitchener had a rumour planted that he would march upriver anyway, and would be able to capture Dongola and the families of the Mahdist soldiers at a crossing further south. It is a mark of the declining morale and fanaticism of the Mahdist troops that this rumour persuaded many of them to move away from their entrenched position at al-Hafir.[9] The Egyptian army was then able to cross the river and approached the remaining Mahdists in battle array. Some of the chiefs of the Mahdist army wished to stand and fight, but the sight of the Egyptian army steadily approaching in its inexorable marching order persuaded them not to do so. The relentless nature of a disciplined army's approach march was always intimidating. The steamers then passed al-Hafir without damage. The Mahdist commander, Muhammad Bishara, aimed to make a stand at al-Urdi just north of Dongola, but by that point he had lost too many men from his forces to be able to fight a much larger army, and when he rode out to reconnoitre as the Egyptian army approached in its steady and relentless way, he understood that further fighting was pointless. Dongola was taken on 23 September without much of a fight.[10]

This was supposed to be the end of this campaign, Dongola being the original stated target, but Kitchener was convinced that it would be possible for his army to go further, and that in terms of morale it would be a good move if they could achieve something beyond the army's original aim. He made a visit to London, carrying an intelligence report, compiled by Colonel Francis Wingate, to the effect that the French were moving in from the Congo (this was Marchand's expedition, which had hardly got started as yet) and that the Mahdists and the Ethiopians were aiming to make a joint campaign against the British. This last was clearly based on reports of Menelik's negotiations with the Khalifa, which in fact had gone nowhere – Wingate was evidently exercising his busy imagination in this case. His report was not an intelligence summary, but a scare tactic, and Kitchener must have known it. It took some doing to imagine that the Khalifa and the Emperor Menelik would cooperate in anything, but perhaps it suited Salisbury and Kitchener, and even Cromer, to accept Wingate's 'interpretation'. Salisbury allowed himself to be persuaded by Kitchener to permit a further advance, at least to Abu Hamed, at the northern point of the great Bend in the river, possession of which place was needed if the planned trans-desert railway was to reach a useful terminal.[11]

The steamers were now able to sail further up the river without hindrance. The Mahdist army at Dongola dispersed, and the river, now having risen sufficiently, was open for the next 200 miles. The army followed on and established a series of garrisoned posts as far as Merowe, just short of the Fourth Cataract, about 150 miles short of Abu Hamed.

Any further offensive had to wait for the railway to catch up once more, and for supplies to be accumulated. Kitchener, like others before him who had travelled this way on camels, had chosen the route across the Nubian Desert from Wadi Halfa to Abu Hamed for the railway, rather than following the twisting river route. This reduced the length of track to be laid by at least half. The next move forward would therefore take place when the rail track reached fairly close to the Nile again at Abu Hamed. That moment came in late July 1897. Lieutenant Girouard, the engineer, scouted for railway equipment and for locomotives (some were lent to him by Cecil Rhodes, arranged during a visit Girouard made to Britain for other supplies), after which the work could proceed once more.

Boats suitable for use on the river were also brought out from Britain, mostly in sections, to be put together at a new engineering workshop established at Koshi. Kitchener's favourite was the *Zafir*, built to his own design – though its boiler burst at its first try-out.[12] But repairs and improvements were carried out, reinforcements came, and the river rose. These ungainly but shallow draught ships were well armed and capable of bombarding any fort close to the riverside or any visible Mahdist force onshore. They could also carry troops forward, and carry casualties swiftly back to the hospitals.

This pause in operations lasted from September 1896, when Dongola was taken, until early August 1897, when a detachment of 2,700 men under Major General Archibald Hunter marched at night from Merowe across the Bayuda (as Ismail's army had done in 1821). They attacked the Mahdist garrison at Abu Hamed, capturing the place by a surprise attack.[13] Once the town was taken, the railway would be able to reach Abu Hamed, then the army could advance further along the river towards the centres of Mahdist power.

Abu Hamed was supposed to be the end of the advance (just as Dongola and Merowe had been), but a local nomad group reported that the next place along the river, the important town of Berber, was not garrisoned by 6,000 Mahdists as had been reported, but was more or less clear of the enemy. A force of Sudanese troops reconnoitred the town, found it really was not being held by any Mahdist troops, and moved in to occupy it.[14] Berber was another crucial capture, for it was the route centre for several cross-desert tracks including the shortest route to Suakin on the Red Sea. It had no garrison because the Mahdists in the town had mutinied and moved away southwards, not wishing to be attacked while on strike. From Berber, two of the gunboats went on to ad-Damar, at the junction of the Nile and the Atbara River, and drove the Mahdist force (who were the mutineers) even further away. A new fortified dockyard was soon developed there ('Fort Atbara') – another example of the engineering capabilities of the Royal Engineers. Exploitation of the capture of Dongola had therefore brought control of another 400 miles of the river, and Khartoum was now only 200 or so miles ahead of the advanced posts of the invading army. Another pause to allow the more distant forces to catch up was called for now, and a new plan would have to be made for a further advance, while proper reconnaissance was needed, and supplies and forces collected.

During that year, the existence of the international competitors became clear, partly as a response to the British/Egyptian advance. In the Congo, Baron Dhanis attempted to move his large force of 3,000 Congolese troops and porters into the Lado area. Such a major effort was clearly both an occupation force for the Lado Enclave and a force intended for further aggression beyond. King Leopold still seriously dreamed of a campaign as far north as Khartoum. By agreement with Leopold, the French expedition under Marchand began its tedious and difficult journey towards Fashoda, at first along the Congo River. Fashoda was not necessarily the target Marchand's expedition was aiming at originally, though it was where they did expect to meet a French expedition coming from Ethiopia.

The Emperor Menelik, now free of the Italian threat, sent out expeditions to the west in an attempt to establish his authority at some point on the Nile. And from Djibouti (now becoming called French Somaliland), Governor Léonce Lagarde journeyed up to Addis Ababa to establish closer diplomatic relations with the emperor on behalf of France. Marchand knew of these diplomatic moves, and his real target was Addis Ababa, not merely the lump of mud and a decrepit fort on the Upper Nile that was Fashoda. His aim was to link up with Lagarde in Addis, and presumably then establish strong relations with the Ethiopian emperor.

From Uganda, there came rumours of British progress northwards, and news of actual British campaigns against refractory local tribes. This all kept the Belgians and the French and the Ethiopians nervous.[15] It was in 1898 that all these crosscurrents of ambition finally reached the Upper Nile, as did, decisively, the British campaign of conquest southwards along the Nile from Egypt. For, no matter what the aims were of the various competitors, the real prize of this competition was not Fashoda, nor a diplomatic agreement with the Ethiopian emperor, nor the establishment of a small army at the Lado Enclave, which could not be more than a temporary post, since the enclave was to be handed back on King Leopold's death. No, the only prize worth reaching for was the entirety of the Mahdist state, and only the British had a sufficiency of armed force in the region, together with the means to support it, to make that aim credible.

It will be sensible to deal with each of these competitors one at a time, pretenders as they all were to the Mahdist inheritance. The British advance has already been described, and the next chapter will deal with the subsequent events by that army. The Belgian expedition of Baron Dhanis was a major effort to bring a serious Belgian power to the Nile, and was paralleled by a much smaller Belgian expedition under Captain Louis-Napoléon Chaltin. Dhanis drove his command into mutiny, partly through his harshness, and partly because he chose to go through the tropical forest along the Aruwimi River, rather than by an easier route to the north. This alternative route, besides being less onerous had he managed to follow it to the source, would have brought him through the mountains west of, but close to, Lake Albert; however, mutiny and disease ended his progress well before that point. His advanced troops, cutting their way through dense forest, eventually refused to go any further, and this mutiny rippled back through to the rearward troops. Dhanis escaped alive, but his expedition was over.[16]

The Belgians were not yet counted out, despite Dhanis's failure. Captain Chaltin used the Uele River route to the north of Dhanis's route, marched through less dense country than Dhanis was tackling, and reached the Nile on 17 February 1897 (three days after Dhanis's force, still well short of Lake Albert, began breaking up). Chaltin met and defeated a Mahdist force under Urabi Daft'allah at al-Rajjaf. The Mahdists were driven out, and retreated northwards downriver to Bor. Chaltin occupied the post at al-Rajjaf, which was just south of Lado and within the Lado Enclave. His small force also defeated a counter-attack by Urabi Daft'allah's troops, but the Belgians were unable to go any further. Leaving a force in al-Rajjaf as its garrison, Chaltin took leave to return to Belgium, but then shortly afterwards he was sent back again, with instructions to move north along the river, this time with Fashoda in his sights. And yet, without reinforcements, he still could not advance, though by holding al-Rajjaf he had staked Leopold's clear claim to the Lado area.[17]

In Djibouti, Léonce Lagarde, governor of Obok and Tadjoura, had been informed of the various French 'missions' that had set out from the west to attempt to reach the Upper Nile – both Monteil's, and then Liotard's – and had seen both of them fail. The third attempt, Marchand's expedition, set out in early 1897, after a year of preparation. By agreement with the Congo State, they began from Brazzaville and followed the Congo River. They were to be met by a French expedition from Djibouti when they reached the Nile, thus jointly establishing a 'French route' across Africa, though who would follow it was a puzzle, and how they expected to persuade Menelik to permit them to travel through his dominion regularly, presumably armed and disciplined, is not known.[18]

Menelik and Lagarde got on very well – Lagarde was created 'Duke of Entoto' (a title he took seriously) – and the emperor encouraged a French expedition under Captain Clochette to travel from Addis Ababa westwards, aiming for Fashoda and the Nile. But Lagarde, having gained his favoured position at the Ethiopian court, hindered later French attempts, fearing to lose his influence to another Frenchman.[19] Nevertheless, Menelik did provide a large escort for the onward French expedition – he was even more anxious to establish his political position on the Nile than were the French; in other words, Menelik was using the French explorers, just as Lagarde and the other French were trying to use Menelik. Given that Menelik had the vastly greater local power, there could be no doubt who would come out the winner of this part of the international competition to reach the Nile.

As usual with these expeditions, the first attempts failed. The French were not accustomed to the hazards at first, but a later attempt, headed by the Marquis de Bonchamps, who took over from the dying Clochette, did almost reach the Nile. It was more an Ethiopian expedition, however, than French, for the French were accompanied – escorted? supervised? watched? – by five companies of Ethiopian infantry as well as having a retinue of Ethiopian porters. They left Addis Ababa in the late summer of 1897, about the same time that the British forces were establishing themselves at Fort Atbara, and several months after Marchand left Brazzaville. The French had been successfully delayed by skilful Ethiopian bureaucratic 'difficulties', as well as by Lagarde's unwillingness to help, but once they had begun, de Bonchamps' party made progress. They had instructions from Menelik to plant both Ethiopian and French flags on the left and right banks of the Nile when they got there. Captain Chaltin had already reached al-Rajjaf in February, but his force was too small to affect matters seriously and he had been unable to move on.

De Bonchamps travelled along the route of the Sobat River, which flows due west out of the Ethiopian Highlands to join the Nile about 50 miles south of Fashoda. But the route along the river took them out of the cool healthy Ethiopian highlands down into the low-level, fever-infested swamplands. The Ethiopians, even more vulnerable to the climate and the diseases than the Europeans, died in their tens and hundreds, and all the Europeans became sick. The expedition came to a halt about 100 miles short of the Nile, at the confluence of the Sobat and the Ajjubbi (or Pibor) River, and was unable to advance further. One man, Charles Michel, found a leaky pirogue in the river and paddled it down the Sobat to the junction with the Nile, but he could not get across the latter river, blocked by the Sudd vegetation, and had no idea where he really was, whether he was in the Nile or the Sobat or a lake, nor could he see the farther shore, though he later claimed that he had come close to Fashoda. He returned to the base camp, and the whole party turned back towards Addis Ababa.[20]

A second Ethiopian expedition commanded by Dejazmatch Tessama came down from the highlands by the same route; some of the surviving Europeans joined it. French pressure had induced Menelik to instruct Tessama to assist the French, though it was clear that Tessama was in command, and the French believed that this meant that the Ethiopians were doing this to assist their own, French, ambitions. Again, like the Italians the year before, they were assuming that the Ethiopians, being African, were of an inferior species, and a large army of Ethiopians could be dominated and instructed by a small European group by a display of arrogance and orders. But Menelik had told Tessama to plant the Ethiopian flag at the Nile, not that of the French; if the French wanted to plant their own flag there, that was their business. He clearly did not accept that such an action had any real significance; the French, however, would have understood what it meant, or perhaps it would be best to say they thought they understood.

Tessama's expedition did reach the Nile, though of the 10,000 men who had started on the expedition, only 800 were left at that point, after disease, accident, detachments and desertion had taken their toll. (These expeditions are sometimes described as 'French', but they were certainly, in numbers of participants, commanders and origin, overwhelmingly Ethiopian.) Ethiopian and French flags were planted on an island in the river (the French flag was taken there by a Russian who was accompanying the expedition; all the French who were still present were too weak to risk swimming to the island); then the expedition withdrew back along the Sobat.[21] No one ever saw the flags again; no doubt, the local inhabitants took them away to make use of their materials. Ethiopian territory today extends along the Sobat to within 100 miles of the Nile, that is, as far as the point at which the first 'French' expedition effectively stopped.

Other expeditions were sent out by Menelik, along part of the Blue Nile that flows in a 2,000-foot-deep valley on its way from the highlands to the White Nile; another went south to Lake Rudolf, in the desert inland of Somalia. These were all in the name of marking out territory for future Ethiopian conquest and annexation. The geographical conditions in the lowlands were inimical to occupation by Ethiopians from the highlands, as the deaths of the expedition members demonstrated, but the existing populations would be required to give submission.

While the Anglo-Egyptian expeditionary force during 1896 and 1897 defeated the Mahdists at Dongola and occupied the Nile as far as Merowe and then advanced to Abu Hamed, Berber and Fort Atbara, the other contenders all advanced towards Fashoda, in the midst of the Sudd. Only the Mahdists reached it by the time Kitchener's forces advanced to Khartoum. The Belgian garrison around al-Rajjaf could not move further along the river in either direction, blocked by the Mahdists at Bor, and deterred by the British in Uganda; Bunyoro was now part of the British protectorate, so the British border lay along the shore of Lake Albert. The whole crisis was to be over by the time they could be helped. The Ethiopians had reached the east bank of the Nile but had failed to stay there, and their casualties were disabling. The French who travelled through Ethiopia had managed the same, though they were few in number, and were completely dependent on Ethiopian guidance and supplies and assistance. They had also retired without establishing a permanent presence. The British in Uganda had failed to make any advance, being similarly weak in numbers and thoroughly tangled up with local politics and warfare. Only the British expedition into the Sudan, still stuck at Berber and Fort Atbara, and the French of Marchand's expedition making their painful way from the Atlantic coast, were still contenders.

The overall conclusion to be drawn for these expeditions is that they were all lucky that the British were advancing south at the same time. If any state had established its legal claim to the Upper Nile region, north of Uganda, it was the Mahdists. They were present along the river in several posts and forts, and they were able to advance into the Bahr el-Ghazal in greater numbers than any European state. And apart from the British advancing from Egypt, none of the European competitors was present in the region in sufficient strength to prevail if the Mahdists decided to remove them. In other words, the expeditions of the Belgians to the Lado Enclave, of the French to Fashoda, of the Ethiopians and French to the Nile from the east, were only able to achieve their limited and temporary successes because the British were occupying the Mahdists' attention elsewhere. The European competitors were all operating under the distant protection of the British/Egyptian army.

Chapter 16

The Invasion of Sudan

The Belgian expeditions towards the Upper Nile, aimed at the Lado Enclave, had mixed fortunes; one, that of Baron Dhanis, failed completely, the other, under Captain Chaltin, reached the Lado Enclave, but was unable to make any further progress in the face of much hostility in the area. At roughly the same time, the Italians, after their crushing defeat at Adowa, retired into Eritrea and Somalia; they were similarly quite unable to make any further progress, partly due to their overall military incompetence (though they had successfully fought the Mahdists at Kassala) and partly through the powerful Ethiopian opposition.

The British had two irons in this complex competitive fire, in Uganda and on the Nile in Sudan, approaching the Upper Nile area, which was everyone's target, from north and south, but they made as little progress as any other European expedition during 1896 and 1897. The possibility of an advance from Uganda was thwarted by repeated problems within Uganda itself; from the north, the slow progress of the railway across the desert south from Wadi Halfa held up any further advances. At last, the capture of Abu Hamed in August 1897 opened up the possibility of advance along the next section of the river, and the Mahdist mutiny at Berber opened the Nile route as far as the River Atbara. But it was only a start; the British forces had not yet come into serious contact with a true Mahdist army.

The Franco-Ethiopian expeditions towards the Nile just about reached the river at the last gasp of their efforts, and at once withdrew, and constituted clear warnings to the Ethiopians of the dangers of such lowland ventures; the French effort in Ethiopia was partly thwarted by the unwillingness of Governor Lagarde to assist any expedition not run by himself, for fear that it might persuade Emperor Menelik to withdraw his favour from him; and the new expedition from the west, under Captain Marchand, was making only slow progress, taking eighteen months to reach Fashoda from Brazzaville.

Just three of these expeditions, then, were thus still alive in the second half of 1897, the British invasion from Egypt, Marchand's group travelling from Brazzaville on the Atlantic coast, and the British in Uganda. In this last matter, however, the British faced continuing difficulties in Uganda itself, together with opposition from tribes outside the area of the kingdoms beside the Great Lakes. The British presence in the area was clearly one of the most disturbing elements, upsetting both to the Ugandans and to the neighbouring tribes, so by intervening the British had brought the trouble down upon themselves.

During 1897, opposition came from the Nandi tribe east of Lake Victoria. This tribe had been making progress against its neighbours for some time, while one of those neighbours, the pastoralist cattle-herding Masai, had been struck simultaneously by a smallpox epidemic, and by rinderpest in their cattle, which were their meat and drink, literally.[1] The Nandi, in their confidence and expansionism, inevitably resisted the British advances and they continued fighting until 1899.[2] Within Uganda itself the problem was at least temporarily dealt with in the usual imperial way, first by the application of violence, and then by the application of technology – the Uganda Railway reached as far as the site of Nairobi (not yet founded) during that year, and was to reach Lake Victoria at Kisumu by the end of the century. This, with steamships on the lake, rendered all Uganda within reach of British forces where necessary, while the railway opened up Kenya ('British East Africa') in the same way.

But these countries, and indeed the whole region, were apparently very disturbed. The British intervention added a new level of conflict on top of the intra-kingdom conflict in Uganda, and the Nandi–Masai disputes in Kenya; the various disputes made the situation very difficult. As a result of all this, the region was unlikely to calm down soon; it would take all the energy of the exiguous British forces present and available, over several years, to establish a tenuous control and to organise a sort of peace in the area.

So the prospect of any advance northwards along the White Nile from Uganda towards the Sudan was now out of the question for the foreseeable future; the outbreak of the South African ('Boer') War in 1899 meant there was little in the way of British armed forces available for use elsewhere. The British in Uganda were as unable to advance as the Belgians in the Lado area just to the north of them; and in 1897, the Mahdists at Bor could not advance either – the whole region from Fashoda to Lake Albert was thus in a state of political paralysis. But if one of these blockages could be broken – the British in Uganda, the Belgians in Lado, the French in the Congo and Ethiopia, the British again on the Nile – probably the whole region would be transformed by European advances. It remained to see which attempt would succeed. If the Mahdists succeeded in defeating the British/Egyptian invasion, at that point the other expeditions would be in dire danger, and would no doubt retreat at speed. The future of the whole area depended on the result of the war in Sudan.

The French expedition of Captain Marchand from the Congo, heading for Ethiopia, and the British invasion of Sudan from Egypt, and heading south, were the only ones still in active movement. The British had a clear advantage in all this. They were operating with a major army, which none of the competitors could match locally; second, they claimed Mahdist territory on behalf of Egypt as a territory in rebellion, which had never been legally or formally relinquished by the Egyptian khedives, and which they were clearly entitled to recover – and they were using an army largely made up of Egyptian soldiers to do it. Further, they were advancing over much friendlier territory, which may have been desert, but it was much easier to traverse than the waters and vegetation rafts of the Sudd.

On the other hand, the British had gambled all on victory in war, whose outcome was uncertain. The Mahdist forces were numerous and formidable, and all the artillery and Maxim guns might not prevail against overwhelming forces.

Any competitors who intruded into the Sudan were there either by invitation or by permission of Britain or Egypt, or they were invaders, possibly allied with the rebel state (as was rumoured about Emperor Menelik) and could be expelled by force – or their home country could be attacked in Europe. The problem of foreseeing a British advance and success was that, despite having the preponderance of European armed force in the contest, they had yet to meet the main Mahdist army, and that had fielded armies of more than 50,000 men in the recent past, and had defeated even the Ethiopians in open battle.

The diplomatic position had been made clear to the European competitors: to the Italians by Kitchener in person at Massawa when he visited the port to arrange the process of taking over from them at Kassala,[3] to the Belgians at Lado (which they were permitted to occupy by a treaty agreement, which therefore implied their acceptance of the British case),[4] and to the French, though it had not been explicitly accepted by the French, either in France or in Africa. However, the fact that the French had been sending expeditions towards the Upper Nile in near secret testified to their understanding of the British and Egyptian position – but also to their disagreement with it, and their ambition to gain territory there. They regarded the Upper Nile region as available to other imperialists, that is, themselves, and could point out that the Egyptians and the Mahdists had never occupied it in detail or as a whole, and any occupation had been abandoned, while several places in the Bahr el-Ghazal were already in French occupation thanks to Liotard's actions.

When the British/Egyptian forces captured Abu Hamed, which, when the railway was constructed that far would be the key to the advance against the Mahdists, Marchand's expedition had struggled through the Congo as far as the Nile swamps. Both expeditions faced serious obstacles, but of different sorts – the French had to get through the Sudd, an extremely difficult journey that took them nearly another year;[5] the British had to fight several difficult battles on the way to Khartoum, and there would be still more fighting to be done even after the city was taken; it took them a year to fight through to Khartoum, and another year to ensure full control of the remains of the Mahdist state. In the end, the two competitors, with all the obstacles that each faced, reached Fashoda on the Upper Nile within two weeks of each other.

The size of Marchand's expedition was half a dozen Frenchmen and a varying number of Africans, some from Senegal, others from the Congo area. They carried arms, and the Senegalese at least were trained and effective soldiers. In the Upper Nile, such a force might be potentially decisive, for all other armed groups who had reached the area were small, rarely more than a few hundred, often considerably less, and usually much less well armed than the French. So the small French party that reached Fashoda was immediately in control of the region around the fort. The men were able to fight off a Mahdist attack by ship, and built up their defences by reconstructing the old fort, though the Mahdists, as they did when blocked by the Belgians, only retreated a fairly short way, and so did not surrender much territory; what the French party acquired was theirs only until the Mahdist party they had encountered could be reinforced and came to retake Fashoda; the Mahdists' main attention was inevitably devoted to the British advance, so the French actually remained undisturbed in Fashoda because of the British invasion. This French occupation could well have been the basis for a claim for sovereignty in European terms – an acquisition by conquest – except that Egypt and the Mahdists both had prior claims.

The French may have been strong enough to see off a Mahdist force of two rickety ships that could be badly damaged by fire from the shore, but they still had a Mahdist force to the north of them at Renkh and another to their south at Bor. Beyond that, they were nowhere near strong enough to defy either a larger Mahdist attack or the British force that was on its way.

The British were in no hurry. Abu Hamed and Berber were taken by General Hunter's forces in August 1897, and soon the new foundation of Fort Atbara established British/Egyptian control of another vital point, at the confluence of the Atbara with the Nile. This advance – at least 800 miles from Wadi Halfa – now necessitated a pause, to receive reinforcements, to gather supplies, bring up ships, complete the railway, and organise the new dockyard. The Khalifa was gathering his main force at Omdurman, on the west bank of the Nile opposite Khartoum, and it proved to be a most formidable force, several tens of thousands of warriors. A pause in the British/Egyptian advance was clearly called for, to bring up a sufficient force to be able to meet the Khalifa's challenge. Fort Atbara had to be built to block any advance from further up the Nile by the Mahdist forces, and supplies had to be accumulated, as had sufficient men – and the more reinforcements arrived, the more supplies were needed. And Kitchener needed to consider just how he was to cope with the huge forces of the enemy.

The advance to Fort Atbara had changed the geographical potential for campaigning. Instead of being limited to the river as the route of advance, with occasional desert crossings, there were now huge areas of open country available. For a start, from Fort Atbara there were now two southern routes, along the two rivers, the Nile and the Atbara, each lined with villages and towns, and therefore with the possibility of acquiring local supplies. To the east was the territory as far as the Red Sea, including the port of Suakin, connected by the caravan route to Berber. This route was reopened as soon as Berber was captured; there was also another route, from Suakin to Kassala, the mushroom-grown town taken by the Italians from the Mahdists, and soon an object of the Egyptians for recovery. And along the Ethiopian frontier from Kassala to the Blue Nile there were a series of towns – al-Qadarif, al-Qallabat, and so on – and forts, originally occupied to defend the Mahdist territories against Ethiopian attack, and all still held by Mahdist forces.

There was, in other words, plenty here for the invaders to deal with before they began an advance against Omdurman and that huge army. The Mahdist cavalry could scatter and indulge in guerrilla warfare, which would certainly delay any Egyptian advance, so desert wells needed to be seized. Any number of tasks had to be undertaken, areas cleared of the enemy, diplomatic contacts made with the various tribes, supplies assured. Many of these tasks could be accomplished with the men at hand, especially once the railway reached Abu Hamed – Kitchener at once ordered that it be extended to Berber from there – but any serious opposition would render the invading army extremely vulnerable. Kitchener needed more troops, and needed to ensure that his single supply line was secure.

The Khalifa Abdallahi had called in military contingents from the wider provinces, particularly from Kordofan, his homeland. He expected an imminent assault on his capital, and he needed to keep his troops close in case more rebellions took place. This had the obvious effect of leaving the more distant Mahdist provinces available for the Egyptian forces to take over to recover their control – if they could spare the forces. The Nile provided a highway for the British ships, who sailed to bombard Metemma, 100 miles south of Fort Atbara, the place where the Emperor Yohannes had been defeated and killed eight years before. They dispersed the Mahdist forces there, though only temporarily; Uthman Digna, who had been withdrawn from the Red Sea area with his experienced forces, was at Adarama, 90 miles up the Atbara. When it became clear that he was to be the target for an expedition by General Hunter from Fort Atbara – though Hunter's planned attack was delayed by the need to wait for supplies to reach him – Digna moved across the river, camping 100 miles away. His transfer was slow and laborious, for it took a month to move his forces and camp followers across the Blue Nile using the few canoes he had. So when Hunter's force arrived at Adarama, the place was empty; he burned it and retired.

When Digna's force moved to the western side of the Atbara, therefore, much of the east of the country had effectively been abandoned by the Mahdists, though there were isolated groups still active, and the frontier forts facing Ethiopia were still occupied. The route to Suakin from Berber was now clear and available, and it became possible to relieve the Italian garrison at Kassala; Kitchener went to Massawa to arrange matters with the Italian command, and the relief was finally carried out in December. An Egyptian force under Colonel Parsons was landed at Massawa and marched through Eritrea; the handover was completed by the end of the year,[6] and Parsons inherited, along with the town and its fortifications, a battalion of local levies recruited by the Italians (just as the Italians had inherited an Egyptian-recruited force of *ascaris* when they took over at Massawa). He took them out to capture two villages nearby, partly as a test to see if they were loyal to their new commanders, and willing to fight against the Mahdists. Parsons was so pleased at the levies' conduct that he retained them; he had doubled his force as a result, and had expanded the territory he controlled, particularly in the direction of al-Qadarif, held by a Mahdist force. No doubt during his visit Kitchener took due note of the demoralisation of the Italian forces as a result of their defeat at Adowa, and they readily agreed to hand over Kassala, which originally they had hoped to hold on to.

The east was now mainly clear, and the western provinces had sent their forces to Omdurman, which was convenient for Kitchener. He could ignore both eastern and western regions and concentrate on the Khalifa's main army. The prospect of fighting a wide-ranging war in the open country now no longer existed, so he could plan his next advance in the knowledge of the location and strength of his precise target. The size of the force he commanded was about 10,000 men, and included just one British infantry battalion. This was certainly not enough to tackle the Khalifa's army, which was estimated to be about 40,000 strong, possibly more; it would probably be even larger than this when the battle came. Uthman Digna also had 5,000, and the force at Metemma, commanded by Mahmud Ahmed, was about 10,000 strong; it could be assumed that these would go to Omdurman, where the main army was concentrated, when the attack came. Any British/Egyptian advance along the Nile would clearly force all three of the Mahdist forces to unite, and no doubt, others would arrive in the emergency.

Contemplating this, Kitchener decided he needed reinforcements, and specifically more British troops. He could hardly get more Egyptian troops, since he had almost the whole Egyptian army under his command in the Sudan already. The Egyptian army had done well so far, and in particular the Sudanese battalions had fought enthusiastically. (These were recruited in southern Egypt, from Nubians, and from prisoners captured in fighting the Mahdist forces, who were pleased to be part of an army they reckoned was likely to win.) But there were no more than a few more Egyptian soldiers now available in Egypt. Furthermore, the Egyptian troops were Muslims, commanded by Christians, and were being asked to fight a Muslim army, a particularly fanatical one – not a comfortable situation. Kitchener therefore asked for a brigade from the British occupation forces stationed in Egypt. This was provided – three battalions from the Egyptian occupation force, and one from Malta, put under the command of Major General William Gatacre.[7]

Kitchener's request had stimulated a great deal of jealousy amongst his rivals among the British commanders. General Sir Francis Grenfell, his predecessor as *sirdar*, was suddenly appointed as commander-in-chief in Egypt by the War Office, which was a nest of Kitchener's opponents. This was clearly seen as a threat to his position and Grenfell was carefully positioned as a successor should Kitchener make an obvious mistake. However, Kitchener had the explicit support of Cromer and Salisbury, two heavyweight politicians quite sufficient to overwhelm even the intriguing officers in the War Office. On the other hand, Kitchener himself was left without any personal assurances from his superiors and became very nervous; eventually he threatened to resign, apparently as a move to compel a declaration of open support.[8] The reinforcements out of the British occupation force were eventually authorised at the beginning of January 1898.[9]

The Khalifa was having comparable, if different, difficulties. Probably, in part, because he had kept his army concentrated at Omdurman for a likely attack, they were suffering from a shortage of supplies of food. (This was an advantage Kitchener owed to his slow and deliberate advance – he had accumulated sufficient supplies, but the Khalifa's forces were busy consuming theirs.) The food shortage did not affect the great concentration at Omdurman, which could draw on the stores in the city, which were replenished from the lands to the south, but the smaller armies, such as those under Mahmud Ahmed and Uthman Digna, were supposed to be supplied also from the great central store. They found their supplies tended to be interrupted by British/Egyptian patrolling activities, particularly by the steamers, which blocked or captured the Mahdist supply boats. (And, of course, the army in Omdurman would always be the first to be supplied.)

The long supply line from Egypt to Fort Atbara was, for any strategist, an obvious target, and it is surprising that the Mahdists did not take advantage of its vulnerability. The Mahdists had plenty of cavalry, at least of an undisciplined sort, and every post along the railway was held only by a small force. But the Khalifa did not organise attacks on them or the railway. This may have been a failure of imagination on the Mahdists' part, or an ignorance of the importance of the railway to Kitchener's army, but the Mahdists themselves suffered from enemy forces interrupting their supply lines; a similar retaliation would normally be the obvious retort. But the Mahdists did not make any real attempts to do this. Perhaps they were fixated on the size of their great army and its use as a single force in a single great battle. But Kitchener must have been relieved that they did not launch such raids; possibly also Kitchener was equally relieved that it was the Khalifa who was in command of the Mahdist forces, and not the more imaginative and adaptable Mahdi, who had clearly been a clever strategist.

The Khalifa did have some useful strategic ideas, but found it difficult to implement them. He kept urging Mahmud Ahmad to attack the Egyptians at Berber or Fort Atbara, but that commander dithered over plans, complained of lack of supplies, and suffered a mutiny, which he had to put down before he could move. It had been a mutiny that had opened Berber to Kitchener's forces; apparently, discipline and loyalty were not always present in the Khalifa's army; calling in loyal forces from his Kordovan homeland was undoubtedly a sensible move. Eventually, Mahmud Ahmad and Uthman Digna were ordered to combine their forces, and Digna produced a plan of attack that the Khalifa accepted. The joint force moved across the Blue Nile, which had become too dangerous to camp close to due to the threats from the British steamers, and marched to the Atbara River; from there the aim was to attack either Fort Atbara or Berber.[10]

Kitchener by this time had received the brigade of four battalions he had requested – the Royal Warwickshires, the Lincolnshires, the Cameron Highlanders and the Seaforth Highlanders, something less than 4,000 men – and he had brought forward many of the troops who had been left on guard and in administration along his line of communication. The delay in the expected Mahdist forward movement had thus wasted the opportunity of attacking the smaller Egyptian force, and when Mahmud Ahmad finally got under way, early in February 1898, the British brigade had arrived, travelling along the extended Sudan Military Railway. The delay was increased by the slow progress in moving the Mahdist forces across the Nile, which took two weeks to accomplish. By then the British forces had joined together at Fort Atbara.

Kitchener understood that the Mahdist attack planned by Uthman Digna would be directed at the main allied base at Berber, which was certainly one of the possible targets. To reach it, the Mahdist army must cross the Atbara River, and then march through the desert to avoid Fort Atbara, before attacking Berber. Berber was an attractive target, being lightly defended by only a small garrison. But on bypassing Fort Atbara the Mahdists' force would be exposed to an attack from the fort's garrison. If Berber held out for more than a couple of days, the attackers could be besieged from two directions, taken between the relief force and the garrison. The choice of Berber as a target was thus the choice of the easier target without considering the likely consequences. One must assume that this was due to a decision by the inexperienced Mahmud Ahmad, or by the Khalifa; Uthman Digna was too wily a commander to be caught in such a trap.

But Kitchener voided all such speculation by marching to the attack before the Mahdists had begun their move. He advanced his main force along the Atbara River route, first to secure the crossing point at al-Hudi, 10 miles upstream from Fort Atbara. The Mahdists had aimed to cross there, but detected his move and concentrated towards an alternative crossing point further upstream at Nakheila. This would compel them to make a much longer desert march, if they set off towards Berber, and would leave them even more exposed to attack on the longer march; it would also compel the allied army to make a considerable desert march of its own. Kitchener had formed an entrenched camp at al-Hudi on 20 March 1898, then next day moved on to Ras al-Hudi, a few miles further on, making another entrenched camp there. Mahmud Ahmad's army did the same at Nakheila, though their camp was called a *zeriba* by the British; the rival camps cannot have looked very different from one another, though perhaps the British one was the cleaner and tidier. The Mahdist camp was found by the Egyptian cavalry reconnaissance teams, on 30 March, after several days of searching. Four days later, a second reconnaissance found that the Mahdists had not moved. The assumption was that they were waiting to be attacked, the usual Mahdist tactic. Kitchener had hoped they could be tempted to attack him, but he would now need to be the attacker.[11]

The British/Egyptian army now consisted of the four battalions of Gatacre's newly arrived British brigade, three brigades of Egyptian/Sudanese infantry under Generals Hector MacDonald, Archibald Hunter and John Maxwell, and a fourth brigade in reserve under Colonel David Lewis. It also had four field batteries and ten Maxim guns. The cavalry was about 900 strong, considerably outnumbered by the Mahdist horsemen, but better mounted and disciplined, and better armed.

The Mahdist camp was roughly circular, and was positioned beside the river, which was largely dry this season. It was defended by the thorn hedge of the *zeriba*, which was backed by a stockade, and then by a newly dug trench. The trench covered only about half the circle, and there was a gap in the circuit close to the river, so there was provision for retirement, or escape, or most likely to ensure easy access to water.[12] (The fact that the gap was the way the Mahdists escaped made the British assume that that was its purpose; but the camp had existed for at least a fortnight, and supplies of water were probably more on the minds of the soldiers than possible escape in a battle – water could be found by digging into the river bed, even if the flow of water had apparently ceased.)

The interior of the camp was pitted with holes and short trenches, in which the Mahdists sheltered when under attack. The Mahdist anticipation was that their thorn-hedge fortifications would hold up the British/Egyptian assault, and they would suffer casualties from Mahdist fire when they stopped to break through the hedge, but that the fight would continue as a melee in the interior of the camp. The Mahdist cavalry was outside, possibly aiming to charge in when the attackers were stuck on the *zeriba* thorns.

This was a formidable position and Kitchener approached slowly and cautiously, constructing a defensive camp each night. He sent an Egyptian battalion in three gunboats to Hosn bin Naya, a village on the White Nile where Mahmud Ahmad had his supply depot. Only lightly defended, this was captured quickly, depriving the Mahdists of these supplies, and intelligence was found that the force that was in the *zeriba*/camp had been 19,000 strong when it set out, but had shed deserters on the way. The Egyptian battalion moved on to Shendi, which was captured and burned, then returned to Fort Atbara.[13] There were also some clashes between reconnaissance patrols from both sides between the rival camps; these were by no means as easy fights as the capture of the supplies.

The British/Egyptian army marched to the attack on the night of 7/8 April 1898, halting three times on the way to rest the men and orient themselves. In the morning, they were disappointed to see that the Ansar had been fully aware of their approach and that surprise had not been achieved, though the slow advance had surely warned the Mahdists of an impending attack for the last several days, even if they had not put out scouts to watch the enemy's progress; the Mahdist soldiers were largely out of sight in their camp, hidden behind the surrounding barriers and in the foxholes and trenches within their *zeriba*.

It is customary to detail the British/Egyptian force in its battalions, while counting the total of Mahdist force as a round number. The imputation is that the Mahdists had a much larger force than the allies. This was certainly the case in the Omdurman battle later, but at the Atbara, the 15 Allied infantry batallions and 4 cavalry units numbered very close to the Mahdists' 15,000. The battle was thus between roughly equal numbers, a factor that perhaps explains Kitchener's greater caution in his approach march than in the later encounter;

it was also the case that he was attacking an entrenched camp, never an easy proposition, whereas at Omdurman he was defending his own chosen position.

An hour was required for deploying the soldiers, then the artillery spent an hour and a half bombarding the thorn barrier in front of the stockade and formed the first line of the defence. Even so, the thorn obstacle remained largely in position when the infantry attacks were ordered, about 11 am. (Just so were the bombardments of enemy trenches in the Great War similarly often failures; the Mahdists' thorn hedges may seem primitive, but they were as effective as barbed wire entanglements.)

The allies attacked all along the line; most is known about the British contingent's work, since this was where the aspirant soldier authors were.[14] The plan was that the Cameron Highlanders, deployed in line in front of the other battalions, would break into the *zeriba* by destroying the thorn barrier, and then the other three battalions, deployed in column, would march through to attack the Mahdists in the interior; nothing so elaborate, however, was planned for the Egyptian/Sudanese battalions.

The plan did not work, though it must have looked good on paper. The Cameron Highlanders were slow at breaking through the hedge – the task was certainly difficult. The Egyptian brigade of General Hunter was actually the first into the enemy camp. On the British front the attacks in column resulted in the four battalions becoming all mixed together, and then together they attacked the very resistant thorn *zeriba*; then all of them, more or less mixed together, poured into the interior.

Inside the camp, the fighting was fierce and close – so the Mahdist plan did work. The Mahdists fired at close range from their holes and trenches, but not very effectively – they had a tendency to fire too high – and many of them then resorted to spears; similarly, the British used their bayonets when at close quarters. The fiercest action was within the centre of the camp where Mahmud Ahmad's bodyguard defended a sort of inner citadel. The 11th Egyptian Battalion, composed of Sudanese, suffered very heavy casualties in this fight, and only succeeded in taking the position with the help of other battalions. Mahmud Ahmad was taken alive inside the building, sitting on a carpet preparing for death. The Sudanese who captured him did not oblige him, and he was made prisoner. His colleague Uthman Digma escaped, as he usually did. Kitchener personally interviewed Mahmud Ahmad, who had retained enough *savoir-faire* to point out that he was Kitchener's 'equal in rank' – commander of an army under more senior commanders. (The British/Egyptian attack had been very similar to that normally carried out by the Mahdists – an undisciplined charge by everyone in a mass – and in the camp, the fighting was mostly hand-to-hand;

no doubt, when he saw what had become of his careful planning, Kitchener was relieved he had approached the enemy camp with caution.)

For all the apparent intensity of the fighting, it was over fairly quickly – some accounts claim it lasted only five minutes, though this seems distinctly unlikely. The British suffered only 25 killed, and the Egyptians 57, though there were about 450 wounded. It is estimated that 3,000 of the Mahdists were killed, and about the same number wounded – but this is the usual vague number produced by the attackers. As it became clear that the fight was over, most of the Mahdist soldiers escaped through the gap left in the *zeriba* close to the river. They fled southwards along the dry bed of the river, though some were killed along the way by pursuers. As many or more were taken prisoner. These figures, estimates all, mean that well over half of the 15,000 Mahdists had survived, though many of them must have been wounded; such a defeat would have convinced many simply to go home, but they were resilient and an army could be reconstituted from them, simply by sending out a summons for a new gathering, and for reinforcements. The experience of this battle made the prospect of having to fight an army of Mahdists three or four times the size of the army at the Atbara battle daunting, to say the least.

The victory at Nakheila (called the Battle of the Atbara by the British) destroyed the last major Mahdist army outside Omdurman, though it could be reconstituted; even so, it was still only a subsidiary force. Victory over the Khalifa's main force was by no means guaranteed. Kitchener knew that he faced an army at least three times the size of that which he had just beaten, and his conclusion was that, once again, he did not have enough troops or supplies to complete the conquest. Another quick visit to Britain netted Kitchener another brigade of British troops, mainly those already in the Mediterranean area – Egypt, Malta, Gibraltar – but others had to be sent out from Britain. These were organised, along with those already present, as the British Division, under Gatacre's command, organised in two brigades under Generals Andrew Wauchope and Neville Lyttelton. A fourth Egyptian brigade was also added to the original three, and they were all organised as the Egyptian Division of four brigades under General Hunter. The Egyptian cavalry contingent was increased, and the British 21st Lancers were added; plus an increased Camel Corps and another horse artillery battery. (Of the Egyptian battalions, eight were composed of Egyptians, and eight of Sudanese/Nubians.) Two British and four Egyptian field batteries, and an Egyptian horse battery were included. On the river, Commander Colin Keppel commanded a squadron composed of a variety of armed ships, ten in all. Altogether, the Egyptian/Sudanese forces were twice the size of the British in all arms.[15]

The total allied force was now a little over 25,000 men, and to support them on the campaign sufficient rations for three months, above what they consumed on a daily basis, had to be accumulated. The main supply base was moved from Berber to Fort Atbara, and a new workshop was established at Abatieh, north of Berber, partly to service Commander Keppel's gunboats.

These forces arrived at and beyond Fort Atbara during late July and August, mostly travelling by train along the new railway, but then marching on foot in the hottest part of the year; some were fortunate enough to be able to travel by ship. This mechanical transport system was, of course, a major constraint as well as an essential ingredient, and is the explanation for the relatively slow process of the arrival of these reinforcements. The rails were only single track, using the narrow gauge of 3' 6", the same gauge as the planned Cape to Cairo railway, by Kitchener's decision, though by 'borrowing' Cecil Rhodes's locomotives this gauge was made necessary in any case. There was only a limited amount of rolling stock and locomotives, which had to be worked hard, and the gunboats had to wait until the high Nile before being risked in passing the cataracts.

The Khalifa was also making his military preparations, gathering supplies from the fertile lands in the Gezira (the land between the White and Blue Niles) and the south. He sent steamers south to collect food supplies from the Shilluk of the Upper Nile – it was two of these ships that clashed with the French at Fashoda, and so revealed for the Khalifa that he had yet another enemy. But supplies were a major difficulty, since he had gathered an army of over 50,000 men at Omdurman, all of whom had to be fed, as had the sizeable civilian population of the city. The domination of the river as far as Omdurman by the British gunboats made it difficult to send supplies to the forward positions, so, despite having fortified and garrisoned the gorge at al-Sabaluqa, 40 miles downriver from Omdurman, where a resolute defence would have been possible, the Khalifa was compelled to withdraw his men from there because he could not supply them.[16] Nevertheless, the logistical task was accomplished.

When Kitchener moved his forces forward, therefore, he was able to send them along the Nile route, unhindered, and to establish a new camp at Wad Hamed, about 10 miles north of the abandoned gorge. Without a fight, or rather as a result of the victory at Nakheila, the allies had thus secured control of 150 miles of the river. At Wad Hamed, Kitchener's army was only 60 miles from Omdurman, and the al-Sabaluqa gorge, the best place for the Mahdists to block his advance, had been ceded to his forces by the enemy without a fight.

The final advance along the river began on 3 August, led by the Sudanese battalions, marching, and the Egyptian battalions on steamers. A further base was established at Jebel Royan, the southern height of the Sabaluqa gorge hills, and the whole gorge had thus been taken. The gorge was part of the sixth cataract restraining traffic along the river, and the gunboats were now able to reach and cruise the last stretch of the river before Omdurman. On 31 August 1898, the infantry reached as far as the village of al-Iqayqa, called al-Engeige by the British, only about 6 miles short of Omdurman. The cavalry, sent on a reconnaissance patrol, discovered that the Ansar were camped behind the Jebel Surgham, just south of al-Iqayqa.[17] Kitchener's careful advance, as before the Atbara battle, had secured control of the river as far as the very threshold of the enemy capital, but at the expense of a very long and potentially vulnerable supply line.

At first, it was supposed that the Ansar intended an immediate attack on the invaders, but then they were seen to be setting up camp, and it seemed that the Khalifa had thought that the allies themselves were intending a night attack; they had, after all, made their final approach at Firket and at Nakheila during darkness. Gradually it became clear to both sides that neither would attack that day, 1 September, or the next night. But that meant that a battle next day was certain. Whatever conclusions each commander came to, it was an uneasy night for both sides, for the suggestion of a night attack kept many awake. Kitchener ordered his forces to sleep in their uniforms with arms close by; inevitably, there were enough false alarms to disturb those who had actually gone to sleep. The allied army was enclosed in a *zeriba*, but the Mahdists disdained such protection.[18] These details made it clear that the battle would be a Mahdist attack on the allied fortified camp – the opposite of the Atbara battle, but a reversion to the original Mahdist tactics.

All these forces were on the left, or west, bank of the Nile. On the opposing bank a party of warriors from the Ja'aliyin tribe, which had suffered severely from Mahdist punishments, and had welcomed and joined the Anglo-Egyptian invasion with some enthusiasm, combined with a gunboat-and-barges force on the river to clear away the Mahdist forces along that bank. Commander Keppel, the latest representative of an old naval family, took the ships south along the river, while the Ja'aliyin warriors scampered along the shore, eagerly removing any Mahdists they found from the villages, and reconnoitring for any larger groups. At Halfiyeh, Keppel bombarded the three forts in the village, and then the Ja'aliyin moved in to clear out any survivors. The same combined process took place at Tuti Island, at the confluence of the White and Blue Niles, and so located between Omdurman and Khartoum. Occupation of that island would threaten both places. Again, the forts were bombarded and taken. Then Keppel set up the guns of the 37th Field Battery on shore and bombarded Omdurman, across the White Nile, taking the all too visible tomb of the Mahdi, a conspicuous large white-domed building, as their main target, which was damaged.

The allies' defensive position put their backs to the river, with their protective *zeriba* describing a semi-circle behind which their forces lay; at either flank, in the river, were the gunboats, so extending the defensive position, as far as the two lines of hills standing on either side of the plain. That position included the village of al-Iqayqa, which was built on a slight rise on the riverbank, and faced the open plain bounded to the right and left by hills, the Jebel Surgham on the left (the south) the Kerreri Hills to the right (the north), so the field of battle was a rectangle between two lines of hills and with the river to the east, but open to the west, whence the attack must therefore come. The ships flanked the army position and were able to fire on the enemy as it approached without hitting their own forces.

The Mahdists' camp was 'behind' (that is, south of) the Jebel Surgham. They launched their attack about 6.30 am on 2 September, though Kitchener had expected it earlier, at dawn, and his men had been lying at arms and awake since 4.30 am. The main force came round the western end of the Jebel Surgham into the plain. Kitchener had sent out the Camel Corps and the Egyptian cavalry into the Kerreri Hills on his right, together with his Egyptian horse artillery battery and four Maxim guns, with the intention of harassing the flank of the Mahdists as they approached the allies' *zeriba*, and so extending the flanking position of the ships. They were also to assist the 3rd Egyptian Battalion, standing on the right flank, of whose steadiness he was not sure. The *zeriba* contained a considerable force of artillery – more than thirty guns, and more Maxims; each Egyptian battery had six guns and two Maxims – while the ships in the river, ten gunboats, were also armed with as many guns and even more Maxims. If the Mahdist army attacked, as was to be expected, there was quite enough firepower ranged against it to destroy a large part of their army at a considerable distance, before they ever reached the *zeriba*.

The Ansar surged round the western end of the Jebel Surgham, and at once a detachment turned off to deal with the cavalry and Camel Corps on the Kerreri Hills, which were an obvious and substantial danger to the Mahdist advance, and must have seemed an easy target. The Mahdist detachment moved to attack this flanking threat, while the main force of the Mahdists turned eastwards to charge the allied *zeriba*. This would suggest that, unusually, a fairly careful reconnaissance had been conducted by the Mahdists, possibly from the hills of the Jebel Surgham as soon as it was light, which would explain the unexpected delay in the attack. The movement of the Egyptian cavalry into the hills would have been all too obvious, visible from the dust they threw up, if not in detail. It is generally assumed by modern historians that the Mahdists did not patrol or reconnoitre, but simply charged blindly at their enemy, but this is so unlikely as to be laughable – reconnaissance had clearly taken place at Nakheila and at the fights before Dongola. Coming round the Jebel Surgham, the Mahdist forces knew in advance about the Egyptian cavalry and the associated guns on the hills, and exactly where the *zeriba* was.

The attack on the Kerreri Hills' detachment began the battle, and successfully preoccupied the Egyptian cavalry there; certainly, their presence did not interfere with the initial main attack, nor did their Maxims. The Mahdist main force came forward dragging some guns of their own in their midst, and these opened the main attack – possibly the whole army halted before this in order to form up after their lengthy approach march. The Mahdist artillery's shots did not reach as far as the *zeriba*, but this was the signal for the allied artillery to open fire in turn, and their guns had a greater range while their aim was much better. The guns on the gunboats could also fire, and the Mahdist charge was hit repeatedly, though it did not stop. (One is reminded of the failure of the Italian guns to affect the Ethiopian charge at Adowa – such a charge carried the men forward automatically; and, of course, if others were hit, that meant that the survivors had not been hit and could continue to advance.)

The allied infantry began firing when the enemy came to within about 1,500 yards, using the Maxim guns; the infantry had more modern and much more accurate rifles than the Mahdists had, and they fired, at least at first, in disciplined volleys. (The British had Lee-Metford rifles, whereas the Mahdists used a wide variety of rifles that had been collected from defeated enemies over the last fifteen years; the most modern ones they had were apparently some Remingtons.) The Mahdists' charge therefore failed. None of the Ansar came within 800 yards of the British forces, though they got a little closer to the Egyptians, whose older Martini-Henry rifles had less range; even there, the charge was stopped at 500 yards.

The detachment in the Kerreri Hills meanwhile came under attack from an estimated 10,000 warriors, outnumbering them perhaps ten to one. They were forced into a withdrawal, aiming to make a stand on one of the hills; two of the guns of the horse artillery were abandoned during this retreat. Eventually they were driven back until they were close to the river, but from there one of the gunboats could shell the Mahdists. The Camel Corps escaped under cover of the gunboat's bombardment to take refuge with the main army behind its *zeriba*; the Egyptian cavalry, on the other hand, retreated northwards, deliberately enticing the Mahdists into a chase. After 3 or 4 miles, the Mahdists seem to have realised that they were being distracted, and they broke off the chase and turned back. The Egyptian cavalry then followed them as they retired, and went on to join the main allied forces once more.

The whole Mahdist force, unable to get to grips with the allied forces, retired about 7.30 am, reforming behind the Jebel Surgham. Kitchener sent out patrols to these hills, which were found to be unoccupied. The 21st Lancers went beyond them to locate the main enemy forces. Kitchener then sent the several infantry brigades out from the *zeriba*, forward into the 'rectangle', which was partly covered by the Mahdist dead. One brigade, under Lieutenant Colonel John Collinson, remained at the village inside the *zeriba* to guard the transport and the wounded. The rest fanned out in a wide array from the river end of the Jebel Surgham and across the open plain; in this move, gaps developed between the several brigades. Clearly it was assumed that the fight was over, an assumption based on experience, since the defeat of a Mahdist attack was usually followed by its retreat, as at the Atbara battle – and what was going on behind the Jabal Surgham was not known, for no reports came from any reconnaissance forces sent out.

The fight was not in fact over, only temporarily halted. The main Mahdist force, under the Khalifa's personal command, reassembled west of the Jabal. It had by this time been seriously reduced by casualties and by desertion. The detachment that had chased the Egyptian cavalry returned to occupy the Kerreri Hills, a movement apparently not noticed by the allied forces. Several separate engagements followed. The 21st Lancers, including the attached Lieutenant Winston Churchill, charged an enemy force occupying a *khor* (a dry stream bed) south of the Jebel, with little effect on the main action, though it suffered notable casualties – it was a pointless charge, brought on by the colonel's wish to do something, anything, a throwback to the old attitude of a less than properly disciplined unit, and a cavalry force that became uncontrollable once involved in a charge, long a major fault of British cavalry.[19]

The Khalifa's main force returned to the fight, and charged two of the brigades, Lewis's and MacDonald's, which were somewhat advanced in front of, and separated from, the rest of the allied force and separated from each other. This was very careless of Kitchener, and especially of the brigade commanders. The renewed Mahdist attack induced the other brigades to form up alongside them and extend the line, so that the line later spread right across the open plain. The Mahdist main force made their second charge and were again rebuffed.

The Mahdists made a third charge, supported this time by the detachment that had chased the Egyptian cavalry and had now returned to threaten the right flank of the allied army. The target was the two brigades that still seemed to be partly isolated, Lewis's and MacDonald's. These were now supported by detachments from Wauchope's brigade, which were sent forward, while Collinson brought his own brigade out of the *zeriba*, and the returned Egyptian cavalry extended the line still further. The British/Egyptian army had ended up in the traditional posture of battle, with the infantry line of regiments and brigades flanked by cavalry to the left (the 21st Lancers – though it had been badly damaged by that senseless charge) and the right by the Egyptian cavalry, which was more competently led and commanded.

The repeated attacks by the Mahdists were unexpected. Presumably, it was the Khalifa's presence and command that brought the later attacks to be mounted. He had sensibly taken advantage of Kitchener's decision to come out of the *zeriba* without having investigated the condition and position of the enemy forces, either the main force or the detachment to the north, and the allied forces had thereby been taken by surprise. Kitchener was rescued, as so many British commanders have been, by the fighting qualities of his men, particularly those in MacDonald's brigade, composed of three Sudanese and one Egyptian battalion, who weathered the attacks by the full force of the combined Mahdists.

The Mahdist casualties had by this time included many of their commanders, their positions in the attack having been in the forefront of the charges. The Khalifa, however, had survived. His conduct of the battle had been more dexterous than those of most of his commanders, but, of course, it was just as disastrous for his forces, or, given that they had made three charges, even more so. (His conduct of the campaign, however, had been lamentable – that long, single allied supply line should have been severed, repeatedly, during the British/Egyptian advance, and had been ignored; mounted guerrilla raids should have cut the railway, and isolated units and camps should have been harassed; but none of this was even attempted; these omissions allowed the allies a clear uncomplicated approach.)

The Khalifa retired to Omdurman and aimed to re-collect and revive his army, but the defeat was too shattering, at least for the moment. The city came under almost immediate threat from Kitchener's own forces, and Commander Keppel's ships continued their own bombardment. It is reckoned that the Mahdists suffered 30,000 casualties, in killed, wounded and captured (of which 10,000 were killed). This is, for once, a British calculation partly based on a body count after the battle, so it can be taken as approximately correct; the allies suffered about 450 dead. This was a little less than those taken at the Nakheila battle; of the allied casualties, one sixth were suffered by the 21st Lancers, a single regiment (seventy-one killed and wounded), the price of that pointless charge.[20]

The allied pursuit of the retreating Mahdists was hampered by isolated acts of resistance by survivors, wounded or separated, in which the Mahdists, experts at close fighting, often had the best of it. The chase by individual battalions and even smaller units was soon therefore abandoned. The cavalry, re-formed, both British and Egyptian, were sent to encircle the city to prevent any Mahdists from leaving, though it was considerably too late by then. An infantry force, consisting of three Sudanese battalions, one Egyptian battalion, plus a field battery, under General Maxwell, marched in formation against the city, led by Kitchener and his staff. There was some resistance from behind an interior wall in the city, which was quickly removed. Individual warriors in the city fought on, and when Kitchener's party reached the Khalifa's residence, it was soon found that he had left, with his treasures and his favourite wife, and his servants with him.

The conquerors explored the city, the Khalifa's house (not a palace, but comfortable), the prison, where a variety of prisoners, several of them Europeans, were released, the streets – a 'rabbit warren' was the usual derisive comment, but that only showed that it was a typical Near Eastern and African city. This was all done cautiously since there was still resistance from survivors of the battle, not helped by the occasional shell sent from one of the ships whose gunners had spotted an apparent concentration of the enemy.[21]

The difficulty of securing control of Omdurman against that intermittent resistance, and the slow investigation of conditions in the city, enabled the Khalifa to get well away. After a few miles, he caught up with the survivors of the defeated army, who were still operating as an army, and was greeted with enthusiasm. The defeat had evidently not damaged their spirits or their loyalty. The pursuit by the Egyptian cavalry failed catch up with him, and was abandoned after two days. Meanwhile, the occupation of Omdurman, against sporadic resistance, slowly succeeded; if this had been intended as a delaying tactic, it clearly worked, occupying the allies and permitting the Khalifa to escape.[22]

On 7 September, four days after the capture of the city, but while firing was still taking place there, the steamer *Tewfikieh* arrived, with its Mahdist crew. The ship had been one of those sent by the Khalifa to gather supplies in the south, and had been driven away from Fashoda. Its crew, unaware when they arrived of the defeat of the Khalifa's army, reported, apparently quite loquaciously, that they had clashed with a French party at Fashoda a fortnight before.[23]

This was hardly a surprise to Kitchener, who knew of the French expedition under Marchand, and had heard rumours of French attempts to instigate the Ethiopian emperor to move against the British – though these reports came from Wingate, which by now, given his mistakes and exaggerations, must have been regarded as a tainted source, so the reports were probably either inaccurate or exaggerated, or even invented. Whatever their source, it was yet another issue for Kitchener to deal with.

It cannot be said that Kitchener and his commanders had displayed skilful generalship in this battle. Kitchener had certainly chosen a sensible position, bearing in mind the normal tactics of a mass charge of the Mahdists, but he had effectively lost control when the Mahdists retired after their first great charge failed. His brigade and division commanders had permitted the several units to separate, and were almost caught by the Mahdists' second charge. He had attempted to station a small unit to threaten the Mahdists' flank but when it was driven away, he did not consider that the enemy would adopt the same procedure, so that the army was threatened from both flanks and the front in the second charge. The tactics used in the pursuit were akin to those of a blunderbuss, simply a single march, with no thought that the Mahdists could and would move faster than he could. Then there was the pointless and wasteful charge by the Lancers.

Altogether not the brightest jewel in the British Army's reputation. The only saving grace was that the enemy was even worse.

Chapter 17

Fashoda and Other Places

Kitchener had been promoted to the rank of major general in the British Army during his Sudan war, but when he went to Fashoda, he was in his uniform as *sirdar* of the Egyptian army. He had with him two Sudanese battalions and one Egyptian field battery, with its six guns and two Maxims, carried in five steamers. All this was to emphasise that the conquest of Sudan was an Egyptian venture, done on behalf of the khedive, and so the recovery of a province that had been in rebellion. He was already, therefore, in advance of the meeting, defusing the crisis, which he was insisting was not a quarrel between Britain and France, no matter how the French, and indeed the rest of the world, saw it. Just to be sure he was not misunderstood, Kitchener also had a company of the Cameron Highlanders on board, a sign of the British backing for the khedive, and, of course, his officers were mainly British.[1] As a message it was to a degree ambiguous, but perhaps he hoped his own uniform would convey the decisive point; on the other hand, a degree of ambiguity would do no harm if it confused the French party.

The expedition encountered a Mahdist force of about 500 soldiers at Renkh, about 150 miles north of Fashoda; this was the force driven off by the French earlier, and the existence of the Mahdist post had been revealed by the crew of the *Tewfikieh* when it returned to Omdurman. Similarly, the Mahdists had clearly heard news of the war and of the Mahdist defeats, for they fired on the steamers as soon they came within range. (Alternatively, the white faces of the officers made it clear that here were more Europeans, automatically enemies, like the French they had already fought at Fashoda.) Their steamer, the *Safieh*, was quickly damaged by a shell, and, given the forces and weaponry at Kitchener's disposal, the Mahdists soon lost the fight. The 11th Sudanese Battalion was landed and captured a few prisoners, but most of the Mahdists escaped. It only needed the interrogation of a few prisoners to provide information about the local situation.[2]

Kitchener's expedition, pleased no doubt with another victory, however small, sailed on. Ten miles short of Fashoda, Kitchener halted his ships and sent on a letter to the 'Commander of the European Expedition at Fashoda', announcing his intention to visit next day, 19 September 1898.[3] The French, like the Mahdists earlier, already knew of the British victory, and Kitchener's letter confirmed both that he commanded an Egyptian expedition, and that the victory over the Mahdists had taken place. He did not reveal that the Khalifa was still in the field, nor that large areas of the Sudan were still in rebellion. (Given that Marchand already had a good deal of information about events to the north, he probably understood that the war was still going on.) For an apparently almost uninhabited land, news certainly travelled well and quickly in the southern Sudan.

Kitchener had received clear instructions as to his behaviour and conduct from Lord Salisbury;[4] Marchand – who was seriously outnumbered and outgunned in the confrontation – was at pains to be as polite and conciliatory as it was possible to be in the circumstances. Neither commanders could hope to solve the geopolitical problem they faced by meeting in an African swamp. That was an issue for the politicians and foreign offices in Europe (and Egypt) to deal with. As the man with the power on the spot, Kitchener was generous, handing out stores of food, and yet also intimidating, for he insisted on leaving a garrison of a whole battalion of Sudanese in the Fashoda fort, a few hundred yards from the French camp, and on hoisting an Egyptian flag as a symbol of his claim (he had been dissuaded from placing a Union flag as well, as being too provocative to the French).[5] This reinforced the message of his uniform and his soldiers. The flag confirmed his message that he was reclaiming a rebel land for the khedive. Neither man receded in any way from their claims of possession, nor was expected to.[6]

Kitchener sailed on, further up the Nile, and landed his second Sudanese Battalion at the mouth of the Sobat River, where the French and Ethiopians had earlier planted a flag, which was no longer present. This action at this particular place implies that he was fully aware of the Ethiopian/French journeys from Addis Ababa to that point on the Nile earlier in the year, and that he was making it clear that the Sobat area was also part of that area of Sudan that was in rebellion, and which he was reclaiming for the khedive. Salisbury had commented that there was also the danger of a confrontation with the Ethiopians.[7] In fact, the defeats of the Khalifa's forces had already caused Emperor Menelik to become distinctly less keen on the French friendship with Governor Lagarde; the disastrous Ethiopian casualties in their expeditions to the lowlands must have also convinced him that his people had no future on the Upper Nile. Once again, it was clear that the news moved quickly; it is worth noting that Menelik's political relationships were carefully calculated, and that his reactions to events were designed to align his empire with the most powerful of his European neighbours, who, gorged with conquests, might well be the least greedy. After Omdurman, paradoxically, this meant the conquerors, Britain and Egypt, who were old enemies.

Kitchener left his soldiers in post and sailed back to Omdurman. He reported to the government in London, where the news emerged with a British slant. Marchand was left without any means of communicating his own version of the events for some time, so it was the British interpretation that was the only one that was known to Egypt and Europe at first for some time. This was officially published on 26 September, and, of course, set off a famous diplomatic crisis.[8] The French government reacted to the public outrage at the supposed derogatory treatment of Marchand and his people by ostentatiously moving some of their warships from the Mediterranean to the Atlantic, sailing past Gibraltar and docking at the French naval base at Cherbourg. This was a naval port originally developed to be a direct naval threat to Britain; the message could hardly have been clearer. Diplomatic notes and accusations accompanied this supposedly warlike preparation.[9]

Cool appraisals in both London and Paris, even while this move was taking place, showed that there was little likelihood that war would come. France was not equipped to attack Britain, certainly not over control of an African swamp, and, even more certainly, not by sea. Internationally, the French still saw Germany as their prime enemy; internally, the country was seriously distracted by the frequent fall of governments – that which had to respond to the Fashoda matter had been in office only days when the crisis emerged – and by the vicious internal crisis of the Dreyfus affair, which was boiling up nicely at this point, and in which the reputation of the French army had been badly damaged. So the Fashoda 'incident' had to compete with much more absorbing and difficult problems, and anyway, Fashoda was a far distant place and of little value in itself.

Diplomatically, the French were largely isolated. Locked into permanent hostility to Germany since the Franco-Prussian War, and equally hostile to Italy, they had made an alliance with Russia, but Russia was not interested in helping out in a colonial dispute, especially with France in such a mess internally. The German kaiser pointedly sent his congratulations on the British victory to Queen Victoria. Italy was as weak and as divided internally as France, and sided with Britain – again, as a protection against French hostility. And in Lord Salisbury, the French faced as cunning a politician and diplomatic player as any in Europe at the time. By simply waiting until the French calmed down, not making any threats, but resting his case on actual possession of Sudan by military victory and its occupation by the conquering forces, and counting on the impossibility of the French succeeding in any hostile enterprise, Salisbury gradually wore away French indignation. Finally, the French government ordered Marchand and his team to withdraw; Marchand and one of his officers had already left by British steamer through Egypt to present their reports; the rest left Fashoda in December by the Sobat route through Addis Ababa and Djibouti, as the expedition had originally intended.[10]

The resolution of the crisis was thus never so difficult as the press (and British historians) would claim; in Europe, it only lasted a few weeks, but it did solve all sorts of African problems. Of course, the real solution had been achieved in advance by the British conquest of the Mahdist state. The British – that is, Egyptian – control of the Upper Nile was vindicated, and the boundaries of the Sudan could be marked out, though their actual determination had to wait for arbitration and decisions by a European authority. King Leopold's ambitions for expanding the Congo State were decisively blocked, though he held the Lado Enclave for a while, and continued to be a general nuisance,[11] and the extent of the enclave remained in dispute for another decade. Leopold died in 1909, which was some sort of a resolution of that issue. Ethiopia was free of the Italians, and was able to develop its own power and in its own way. The British conquest of Sudan and the consequent evacuation of the French expedition removed an awkward problem and settled for the next sixty years the conditions of power in north-east Africa, with the exception of the temporary Italian conquest of Ethiopia in 1935–41, whose independence was recovered with relative ease by Ethiopian partisans and a British invasion.

The British control of Uganda was confirmed by the application of protectorate status, and by the imposition of another protectorate, later a colony, on Kenya. Above all, however, it was the construction of the railway from Mombasa to Lake Victoria that, as with the Sudan Military Railway, was the real confirmation of this. It had been begun in 1896, subsidised by the British government, and by 1899 it had reached what soon became the site of the city of Nairobi; its continuation as far as Lake Victoria by 1901 – 400 miles – was the decisive geopolitical achievement, and it is clearly significant for the situation in the Upper Nile that the railway was being built even as the Sudan expedition was conquering the land to the north. Like the Sudan Military Railway, which carried British and Egyptian soldiers to war over a track almost 2,000 miles long, the Uganda Railway could do the same over a shorter distance, from the Indian Ocean to close to the Upper Nile. Indeed, in a conflict in the Kenyan coastlands in 1895–6, a regiment of Indian soldiers had been transported from India to Kenya in a fortnight, and campaigned there successfully.[12] (This was simultaneous with another Indian force that took control of Suakin during the Anglo-Egyptian conquest.) Using the Uganda Railway, the Indian army was able to reach into Central Africa within a couple of weeks of sailing from India. No surrounding power could do the same, at least not until the Germans built their own main line through German East Africa (Tanganyika), and that did not reach Lake Tanganyika until 1914, while the forces had to come a far greater distance.

The diplomatic effects of the conquest of Sudan travelled even wider, but it is first necessary to complete the story of the events in the country itself. The conquerors of Omdurman had still to complete their work in that city, while Kitchener was attending to the French at Fashoda. There were at least two Mahdist armies still in the field while Kitchener and Marchand were discussing the fates of their empires. The Khalifa had moved to Kordofan, and had gathered the survivors of his army there. His succeeding campaigns quite deliberately used the memory of the Mahdi's presence and early career to inspire his people. He first went to Kordofan, where the Mahdi had originally gathered a considerable force, and had won his first great victory over General Hicks, and he was able to revive the old enthusiasm. The Khalifa's first aim was to congregate his force at Jabal Qadir, the old Mahdist base, and then to go on to retake Omdurman, where he calculated he still had considerable appeal and support. In this, he was probably correct, going by the continuing resistance to the conquering force in the city after it was taken.[13] To get from Jabal Qadir to Omdurman he would march past Aba Island, the Mahdi's original base, and the site of his first victory. No doubt, he planned an evocative visit to the island on his way.

The second still-existing Mahdist force had been stationed at al-Qadarif on the Ethiopian border, under the command of Ahmad Fadil. It was on guard against any intervention from Colonel Parsons' force at Kassala. Fadil had been summoned, rather late in the campaign, to reinforce the Khalifa's army at Omdurman, but the battle was fought while he was still on the way. He turned back, only to find that Parsons had marched to take the opportunity of his absence to attack the apparently abandoned el-Qadarif. They fought near the town, and as usual the more disciplined and better equipped allied force – an Egyptian infantry battalion and the locally recruited Arab levies Parsons had enlisted from former Italian service – was victorious. Ahmad Fadil's army suffered serious casualties.[14] He retreated, and then decided to march to join the Khalifa in Kordofan. This in fact meant he had to fight several times along the way, and his force steadily lost men, partly by desertion, partly by casualties, and partly by the difficulty of crossing the Blue Nile at Roseires, where he was attacked by Colonel Lewis, who had been stationed nearby specifically to protect the crossing. He had two Sudanese battalions, two Maxim guns, and a unit of Arab irregulars, and they suffered 200 casualties in the fight; Ahmad Fadil's force suffered over 2,000, of which, three-quarters were made prisoners. The fight at Roseires virtually destroyed Fadil's force, and it took even more damage in the difficulties encountered in crossing the White Nile.[15] Ahmad Fadil did eventually deliver his remaining force to the Khalifa in Kordofan, but it was only a small contingent by then.

The combined and reinforced *khalifan* army had marched from Jabal Qadir and headed for Omdurman. It was intercepted by a small force under Colonel Walter Kitchener, the *sirdar*'s brother, who, with only two Sudanese battalions, sensibly preferred to avoid a fight against the Khalifa's relatively well-armed 7,000 men. A new allied force under Colonel Sir Francis Wingate, of almost 4,000 men, then set out to intercept the Khalifa's army.

It was, of course, vital that the army did not reach Omdurman, where a recent incident had reminded all there of the precarious situation in the city. Muhammad al-Sharif, the Mahdi's son-in-law, who had been one of the Khalifa's commanders, had been imprisoned there, and then moved into house arrest, and on 27 August 1899, he and two of the Mahdi's sons were re-arrested on suspicion of planning a rising, possibly to be coordinated with the arrival of the Khalifa's army. If so, the timing suggested that the Khalifa's purpose and approach was well known in the city. The plotters were then tried by a court martial after an attempt had been made to rescue them – which to the British simply confirmed their intentions. They were then shot. The whole matter produced much ill feeling in the town. Had the Khalifa reached it with his army while such feeling existed it is clear he would probably have received much support.[16]

Hence also Wingate's considerable interception force. The two armies met at Umm Diwaykarat, only a few miles south of the Mahdi's Aba Island, where Muhammad al-Sharif had lived when he was under house arrest. The battle took place on 25 November 1899, well over a year after Kitchener's capture of Omdurman. The Khalifa's force was still 5,000 strong, but this time the opposing forces were almost equal in size. Once again, as at all these battles, it was Wingate's Maxim guns that were the most effective weapon in the defeat of the Mahdist army. The most notable casualties were the Khalifa himself and Ahmad Fadil, both killed; the Khalifa's son, Uthman Shaykh el-Din, was wounded and captured; he died the next year, still a prisoner.[17]

The deaths of these men, and of Muhammad al-Sharif and the Mahdi's son, all within two months, can be said to have brought an end to the Mahdi's work. As always, the Mahdi's political scheme had been to build a dynastic state as much as a religious one. The religious motive appears to have faded somewhat towards the end, but the wider Sudanese support for the Khalifa was obvious. More than one author dealing with the subject has remarked that it was the end of the Mahdist adventure, or words to that effect. And yet its ramifications continued to affect large areas of Africa outside the Sudan, and to a degree they still do. In the immediate neighbourhood of the Sudan, it meant that the Italian colony in Eritrea was now safe, especially since its commanders and governors refrained from challenging Ethiopia again; it was also clear that Britain was being protective towards the Italian colony. Ethiopia, similarly, refrained from adventuring against either the Italians in Eritrea or the British/Egyptians in the Sudan, though both Italians and Ethiopians cautiously expanded their authority into Somalia. To the Ethiopians this was not a particularly attractive country, dry and dusty, but it was possible in the next years to agree boundary lines between Ethiopians and Italians and the British colonies in Somaliland and Kenya to the south; by 1908, Ethiopia's borders with all its neighbours were clearly marked out.

The British colonies of Kenya and Uganda were no longer essential as anti-Mahdist bases, not even potentially so. The defeat of the Mahdists and the rebuff of the French at Fashoda had almost cleared the way for a connection to be developed between the Sudan and Uganda, through the intervening Upper Nile route and region. The fact that Britain controlled both sides of the Sudan and Uganda border reduced the area's geopolitical importance to nil. The route between the two lands was scarcely used except by small parties and explorers. This was partly because of the well-known difficulty of traversing the Sudd, but also from the fact that the White Nile beyond the Great Lakes tumbles over a long series of rapids and waterfalls; the water route was thus far more difficult and slower – indeed impossible – than that by land, and there was no intention to develop it. Travellers were reduced, as elsewhere, to walking.

The British never did build a railway to connect their East African track with that in the Sudan, though plans do exist for doing so now, under African auspices, particularly now that the Upper Nile region has made itself independent as the Republic of South Sudan, which has oil resources, and wishes to have access to Kenyan ports without having to go through the remnant of Sudan, from which it has seceded. The independence of this new state has therefore revived the region's geopolitical importance to some extent, with several civil wars providing opportunities for neighbours and others to interfere.

In the aftermath of the Sudan conquest, the need for the British to be careful and delicate in handling the conquered Sudan prevented them from handing it over to Egyptian rule once more – that had been the basic cause of the Mahdi's rising and his success, after all – but at the same time its Egyptian connection prevented Sudan from being finally annexed as a British colony. Hence the creation of the 'Anglo-Egyptian' Sudan. This was actually ruled by a handful of British colonial bureaucrats, with only the name preserving the decreasing Egyptian interest. The denouement came in the 1950s, when Britain progressively pulled its forces out of Egypt, and then suffered a defeat at Egyptian hands in the 'Suez Crisis' in 1956. As a result of this, the condominium in Sudan unravelled and the Sudan became an independent state, and was left to sort out its own problems.

The establishment of British authority in the Upper Nile region, therefore, not only cut out its competitors from the region – Belgian, French, Ethiopian, Italian, Egyptian and Mahdist – it also settled the various disputes that had gathered round the area and who should solve them, and had permitted settled borders to be negotiated, laid out, and agreed in a leisurely way. There remained disputes over these borders, revived since the end of the colonial administration, in which claims are made that, since they were decided by colonialists – by definition, evil and illegitimate authorities – they were themselves illegitimate; this is notable in the borders around Ethiopia, but British power in the Upper Nile prevented any continuing disputes during the colonial period.[18]

There were other items that had to be attended to if the map was to be tidied up – an imperialist's notion, of course – though there was little urgency about any of them. The defeat of the Khalifa's last army allowed Kordofan to be reoccupied, and the Nuba Hills to the south of that territory returned to its habitual condition of near-independence, with the restoration of the former dynasty. They could have been briefly subdued by a British or Egyptian expedition, but this was never going to be a permanent condition, and it was never much of a priority for the colonial governments. Further west, the kingdom of Darfur had been conquered only superficially and briefly, first by the Egyptians, then by the Mahdists, like the Nuba Hills, and the Mahdists' authority had already evaporated while the Khalifa ruled. Whereas the Kordofan area had to be repossessed by the Egyptian regime because of its strong support for the Mahdi and his successor and its constantly disturbed condition, Darfur was less important, as well as more distant. The British found a nephew of the last pre-Mahdist king, a man called Ali Dinar ibn Zakariyya, and put him on the restored Darfurian throne; in the same way, the Taqali kingdom had freed itself, and was reclaimed by the previous dynasty.[19]

The Azande people, living to the south of these regions, beyond the Bahr el-Ghazal, had survived the slave raids by men such as al-Zubayr and Rabeh. They had become the object of the several attacks over the twenty years after the Mahdist conquest of Bahr el-Ghazal. Their capable king, Yambio (Gbudwe, to Africans), gained several victories that ensured his people a decade of peace, but then he was killed by a British expedition; the land was then divided between the Sudan and the Congo State, the almost invisible Congo–Nile watershed being the agreed boundary, supposedly determined by a contracted missionary who could only determine which side of the watershed he was on by pouring water on the ground and noting which way it drained. In the process, British/Egyptian control of the Bahr el-Ghazal region was asserted.[20]

It is to be expected that there were consequences in the neighbouring countries as a result of the conquest of Sudan, since most of them had been affected by the Mahdist episode, but it is also the case that it had some even wider results. To the west, in the Lake Chad area, the kingdom set up by Rabeh, the former slave of al-Zubayr, was separated from the Anglo-Egyptian Sudan by the newly re-independent Darfur, and by Wadai, which had fended off the Mahdists, and then had defeated Rabeh's attack a few years before. Rabeh's kingdom, however, survived for only a couple of years after the suppression of the Mahdists in the Sudan. Rabeh claimed to be loyal to the Mahdi and the Khalifa, or at least to have been inspired by them, but this had no political effect on either of them. His career was, of course, a consequence of the Mahdi's work, even if Rabeh was hardly a missionary of Islam. To him, however, his connection back to the Mahdi was some justification, and the British in Nigeria, the French in West Africa, and the Germans in Cameroon all acted to suppress him. His territory became divided between these three European imperialists, and in the process of the European conquests, the land was devastated yet again. The British, as they had done in Darfur and Taqali, found a surviving member of the old Bornu dynasty and set him up as an emir in part of Northern Nigeria. To the east of Rabeh's brief kingdom, the Wadai Sultanate fell to the French finally in 1912 after a decade of intermittent conflict. It held out rather longer than any other of these states, partly as a result of its remoteness. Only four years later, in Darfur, the last of these old kingdoms, Sultan Ali Dinar decided that the Ottoman Empire and its allies were most likely to be the winners in the Great War, and was thereupon conquered by a British expedition and incorporated into the Anglo-Egyptian Sudan.[21] The Taqali king, Jayli wad Adam, who took up the kingship in 1898, adopted the traditional neutrality of his dynasty, and his kingdom survived in complete obscurity until the Sudanese Republic gradually suppressed it and other semi-independent fragments, a process completed by about 1970.[22] It will be noted that it is not only Europeans who are imperially minded.

The British advance against Rabeh's kingdom was a consequence of the expedition into the area that they renamed as Northern Nigeria. This was essentially the former Sokoto Caliphate of Usuman dan Fodio rounded out to include a few other areas to give it a neat geographical boundary. The caliphate had existed for ninety years by the time the British forces reached it. Usuman dan Fodio's example of a Muslim revival had been followed by al-Hajj Umar, who was only finally suppressed two years before the Mahdists; the non-Islamic Samori was also suppressed by French conquest about 1900. The British seized the Sokoto Caliphate a few years later, conquering the several emirates in sequence; the French followed on by conquering Wadai. The emirates of

Northern Nigeria generally survived under a fairly benevolent British colonial rule; in the lands taken by the French such authorities were suppressed in the name of republicanism.

The connection between Usuman dan Fodio's successful career of revolution and conquest and the other jihadists in Africa was tenuous but clear. The first of these jihadists to be inspired was Muhammad al-Kanemi, who gained power in Bornu, and emerged as an enemy of the Sokoto Caliphate, even though both were Muslim revivalists; he therefore emerged as a rival to Usuman, but was clearly inspired by him. Al-Hajj Umar travelled back from his Mecca pilgrimage and stayed in Sokoto long enough to marry the daughter of Muhammad Belo, Usuman's son and successor. Umar developed a *jihad* campaign that extended from the Atlantic coast to Timbuktu, in the process conquering several ancient kingdoms. He died in battle in 1864, and his empire did not survive, in the first place because his subjects detested him, second because his successors fought amongst themselves, and third, because eventually the French drove them all out.

Another military resister in the region was Samori, who operated in the lands south of those seized by Umar, a little later than him, dying as a prisoner of the French in 1900 after a series of campaigns over the previous quarter-century. Again, it was a brief and unstable empire, though of some size at its height, but not a *jihad* state – nationalist is perhaps a better description. These, and others, were inspired by the Sokoto Caliphate's success, and by the threat posed by French advances inland from the coastal posts. Samori's rule lasted until 1896, when he was finally defeated by the French; Umar's main successor, Ahmadu Seko, finally died after taking refuge in Sokoto in 1898. Wadai may well have resisted the French in Islam's name; Ali Dinar of Darfur was eventually suppressed by the British when he came out in support of the Ottoman Empire in the Great War; these two final European conquests were at least inspired by the memory of Usuman dan Fodio and the Mahdi. That is, Muhammad Ahmad the Mahdi was not alone in his jihadist inspiration. These West African jihadists were his contemporaries. They responded to the disturbed conditions in West Africa in the same way that one of the main causes of the Mahdi's uprising was the misery produced by the Egyptian Empire.[23]

Turning the issue about, it may be noted that one of the inspirations behind Muhammad Ahmad the Mahdi had been the success of the Sokoto Caliphate, just as it had been for the jihadists in West Africa. And just as the Mahdist state was perceived as a danger to all its neighbours and was therefore suppressed, so a series of British campaigns against the dozen or so Sokotan emirates, into which the caliphate had been divided, was organised. Frederick Lugard (fresh from Uganda) operated from a political base at Lokota at the confluence of the Benue and Niger rivers, on the southern boundary of the caliphate. These were conducted with minimal forces – never more than 1,000 men per expedition – and were able to tackle the emirates one at a time, resulting in the conquest or submission of all of them between 1900 and 1903. (This was reminiscent of the original conquest by Usuman, who tackled the emirates one at a time.) The emirs were left in place, as was the caliphate's religious authority – which, of course, was one of the reasons for their relatively easy conquest. This inaugurated a process that Lugard described as 'indirect rule', an adaptation of a similar condition in India.

The French to the north were a potent source in bringing the emirs into submission – the French were a good deal more ruthless in their conquests and routinely eliminated monarchies – both Umar and Samori had vanished and their kingdoms with them. The extinction of Rabeh's kingdom by the French, with British and German assistance, had been total and much more brutal than anything the British did in Nigeria; in fact, the British revived part of that destroyed kingdom of Bornu. The French also suppressed the ancient Wadai dynasty, which after a long resistance of at least a decade was clearly far too well entrenched and too dangerous to be allowed to continue.[24] It is notable that Lugard had been instrumental in the imposition of protectorate status – a version of indirect rule – on Uganda, and that Lieutenant Seymour Vandeleur, who had also campaigned in East Africa, was one of the British conquerors in Nigeria.[25]

Just as the establishment of the Sokoto Caliphate had been the apparent end point of a whole series of earlier Muslim *jihads* in West Africa going back to eleventh-century Morocco, and the inspiration for a new set of *jihads* in the same region, though much more violent, so Usuman dan Fodio's own *jihad* had been one of the inspirations for Muhammad Ahmad's *jihad* in the Nile Valley. Then his example was also one of the inspirations to resistance to European conquest in other parts of northern Africa, whether Muslim or not, as it was in the defeat of a series of Egyptian armies, and the hard fight made by the Khalifa's men against the joint British/Egyptian forces. Certainly, it was one of the causes of Rabeh's activities as he moved west from the Bahr el-Ghazal to Lake Chad and beyond.

But in reverse, it was also one of the main inspirations for the European advances in West Africa that were contemporary with Kitchener's campaigns – if a *jihad* state on the Nile was so hard to defeat, the *jihad* emirates in the Niger region constituted a clear threat as well. The French had fought for several decades to defeat Umar and Samori. The man in charge of the effort in Nigeria, Lugard, had been one of those who had clamped British control on Uganda, when it seemed to be threatened by Mahdist conquest. There seems no doubt that the prospect of the continued existence of independent African states, as in

Uganda and Nigeria, was one of the matters that persuaded Lugard to institute his conquests. That is, these independent states were seen as threats just as much as the Mahdists in Sudan, because their independence would be inspirational to those taken over by the imperial powers. And resistance to imperial conquest was widespread throughout the continent. By exploiting the dissensions between the several emirates into which the Sokoto Caliphate had become separated, Lugard was able to secure control very cheaply, as far as Lake Chad. An Anglo-French convention signed in 1898 (the year of Fashoda) included provisions for dividing Rabeh's kingdom between those two and Germany, which was done during 1900–1, when the French attacked and defeated Rabeh and then his son and successor. The British set up a survivor of the former Bornuan dynasty as emir in part of his family's former kingdom. The French took over most of that kingdom, in their usual ruthless republican fashion. It is instructive that Britain and France could conclude such an agreement in West Africa even as they argued fiercely about their mutual ambitions in East Africa; it puts the importance of the Fashoda 'crisis' in its place.

The direct and indirect effects of the Mahdi's brief but successful career of only a few years were therefore spread from Zanzibar to Cairo, and from the Red Sea to the Niger River and the Atlantic Ocean. The results, however, were not only geographical, but chronological as well. European conquests in North and East Africa were resisted everywhere. The conquest of the Sudan was perhaps the most spectacular example, both of successful resistance, and then of powerful defeat, but fighting took place throughout the northern half of the continent – Egypt, Libya, Algeria, Morocco, West Africa, Wadai, Darfur, as well as the Congo, Sudan, and East Africa. The leaders of the African resistance in many cases were Muslims, but their resistance inspired, and was copied by, non-Muslims, including Christians (as in Ethiopia). The successes of the European conquerors came in a rush in the generation after 1885, coincidentally with the equipment of European armies by a variety of machine guns, which were a major step up from even riflemen's volley fire. Earlier attempts had been defeated by African resistance, African diseases, and the African environment, but from the 1880s on, European weaponry – 'we have got the Maxim gun, and they have not' – military skills, and anti-bacterial medicines prevailed. But the European conquests also came after the success of the Mahdi in his brief five-year career. His success, combined with the continuing existence of the Sokoto Caliphate, and the campaigns of Samori and the successors of al-Hajj Umar made it clear that the European conquerors had a difficult job on, and so they were compelled to make their final efforts, in the knowledge that they now had the lethal weapons.

The motivation of the Muslims was, of course, that they objected most strongly to being defeated and ruled by Christian infidels. The non-Muslims, however, were just as resistant, if not quite so strongly motivated by religious impulses. And all of these had the same motivations to continue resistance under subsequent colonial rule. The clamping down of colonial rule after the initial conquest, usually an unpleasant process and often violent, was followed by arrogant rulers extracting African wealth for European use. But resistance continued in various other ways, some of which were at times violent, such as a revolt at Bussa in Nigeria in 1915,[26] and in the decision by Ali Dinar of Darfur to take the Turkish side in 1916; in Ethiopia, the brief Emperor Lij Iasu converted to Islam from Ethiopian Christianity and seemed about to ally with the Ottoman Empire in the same year, before he was overthrown in an internal coup. One result, once physical resistance seemed impossible, as it was seen to be in most places, was a continual increase in the appeal of Islam for many Africans, simply because of the identity of interest between Muslims and Africans in opposing the colonial rulers.[27] This continues in most West African states, both in conversions to Islam and in violent uprisings, such as the Boko Haram rebellion in Nigeria, and the Islamic insurrections elsewhere. These may be considered to be continuations of such resistance, since those states that emerged from the colonial system into independence were mainly versions of the colonial regime in a new guise. The fragility of the European authority in West Africa is clear: once one colony – Gold Coast – acquired its independence, as Ghana, then the whole colonial system vanished within three years.

The administration of the reconquered 'Anglo-Egyptian' Sudan was technically Egyptian, but in fact was conducted by British officials. The model was perhaps British rule in India, with a thin layer of powerful officials ruling over a reluctant but generally quiet native population. That population was actually kept quiet by the memory of, and continuing threat of, military force; it was recovering from the violence and destruction of the previous twenty years. This British tactic of making a country a 'protectorate' was applied in various ways to several East African states – Egypt, occupied but a monarchy (seceding from the Ottoman Empire at last in 1914); the Sudan became the 'Anglo-Egyptian Sudan', an imitation of the Indian situation but invented by the colonial officials, and with an emphasis on the 'Anglo'; Uganda remained a protectorate until its formal independence, with the kings kept in office, but these were dismissed with independence as collaborators with the conquerors, willing or not. Kenya began as a protectorate and became a directly ruled colony, which produced a major rebellion, the Mau Mau, suppressed as brutally in the 1950s as in every earlier colonial rebellion. Each could be said to have been given an administration suited to its needs, except that their administrations were now centred more on the needs of the colonial rulers than of the previous African and Muslim rulers. The succeeding African rulers were as avid for tax revenues as their predecessors, African or European.

So the peace brought about by colonial conquest became a condition in which Islam could spread further amongst the African population, and this was a clear declaration of opposition to colonial rule. It is hardly surprising that such colonial rule lasted only a little over half a century in most of Africa. It is also altogether fitting that the country that first emerged into independence from the colonialists was the Sudan, where the resistance, inspired by the Mahdi's example, was more effective than most.

The crisis over the rule of Sudan was thus not merely a case of British campaigns against 'dervishes' or 'fuzzy-wuzzies' – terms that appear designed to bypass the Islamic nature of the enemy – and was not only a matter of battles at Khartoum and Omdurman, as so many books have it, and still less a matter of the relationship between General Gordon and Prime Minister Gladstone. It was part of a much wider and more significant African movement, the clash between European aggression, temporarily superior in weaponry, and the slow African political development of local monarchies and religious changes, a development that was interrupted by the brief European domination. As the most spectacular military event in Africa in the nineteenth century, it was an inspiration to African resistance elsewhere – the first war in the Sudan, it should be recalled, in 1882–5, was a comprehensive European defeat, and was followed by the Ethiopian defeat of its Italian enemy. The fact that the Sudanese resistance was inspired by a Muslim *jihad* campaign was only one aspect of such situations in the northern half of Africa, and the fact that the fight to reconquer the land was very different led directly to Sudanese independence in 1956, which again was the obvious inspiration for the swift emancipation of the rest of Africa in the next twenty years.

Finally, it may be pointed out that the European moment in Africa was only brief. Taking the two centuries and a half since the 1770s (when Usuman dan Fodio began his preaching mission), the European intrusion simply stopped African developments and historical movements for a couple of generations: they have revived since 2000.

Notes

Chapter 1
1. A.J. Butler, *The Arab Conquest of Egypt*, 2nd ed., revised by P.M. Fraser, Oxford, 1998.
2. Walter E. Kaegi, *Muslim Expansion and Byzantine Collapse in North Africa*, Cambridge, 2010.
3. E.A. Thompson, *The Goths in Spain*, Oxford, 1969, reprinted 2000; W. Montgomery Watt, *A History of Islamic* Spain (Islamic Surveys 4), Edinburgh, 1967, chapters 1–3; Roger Collins, *Early Mediaeval Spain, Unity in Diversity, 400–1000*, London, 1983, chapter 5; selection of original sources for the invasion are in Kenneth Baxter Wolf (ed.), *Conquerors and Chroniclers of Early Medieval Spain*, Liverpool, 1999, and Colin Smith (ed.), *Christians and Moors in Spain*, Warminster, 1993.
4. For the process and its chronology in the Near East, Richard W. Bulliet, *Conversion to Islam in the Mediaeval Period, an Essay in Quantitative History*, Cambridge, MA, 1970; however, his thesis does not seem to fit well with West Africa; of course, for many communities, rule by Muslim rulers did not become extensive for many centuries.
5. This is the thesis of Ibn Khaldun, a widely travelled philosopher, but originally from North Africa: *The Muqaddimah, An Introduction to History*, Franz Rosenthal (trans. and ed.), London, 1967.
6. Amira K. Bennison, *The Almoravid and Almohad Empires*, Edinburgh, 2016.
7. Ibn Khaldun, *Muqaddimah*, chapter 3, 'the dynasties'.
8. Roderick J. McIntosh, 'Clustered Cities of the Middle Niger', in David M. Anderson and Richard Rathbone (eds.), *Africa's Urban Past*, Oxford, 2000, pp. 19–35; Graham Connah, *African Civilisations, Precolonial States in Tropical Africa, an Archaeological Perspective*, Cambridge, 1987, chapters 5 and 6.
9. E.W. Bovill, *The Golden Trade of the Moors*, 2nd ed., revised by Richard Hallett, Oxford, 1968.
10. An outline history of these centuries (tenth to eighteenth) is in J.D. Fage, *An Introduction to the History of West Africa*, 2nd ed., Cambridge, 1964, which has a useful bibliography, though the text is rather Europe-centred.
11. John W. Blake, *European Beginnings in West Africa, 1454–1578*, London, 1932.
12. Useful collections of essays on internal African slavery and slave trade are: Paul E. Lovejoy (ed.), *Slavery on the Frontiers of Islam*, Princeton, NJ, 2004, and Elizabeth Savage (ed.), *The Human Commodity: Perspectives on the Trans-Saharan Slave Trade*, London, 1992.
13. Much of my account of Islam in West Africa is based inevitably on J. Spencer Trimingham, *A History of Islam in West Africa*, Glasgow, 1962; detailed footnotes will not therefore be needed.
14. For example, the expedition of five Nasamones from Tripolitania to the Niger in Hellenistic times: John Ferguson, 'Classical Contacts with West Africa', in L.A. Thompson and J. Ferguson (eds.), *Africa in Classical Antiquity*, Ibadan, 1969, pp. 1–25, at p. 10, referring to Herodotos IV, 172.

15. B.O. Oloruntimehin, *The Segu Tukulor Empire*, London, 1972, pp. 14–17; this is the prime source for the information in this section.
16. Basil Davidson, *The Growth of African Civilisation: History of West Africa, 1000–1800*, London, 1965, pp. 244–50; Trimingham, *A History of Islam in West Africa*, chapter 5.
17. Fage, *Introduction*, chapters 5 and 6.

Chapter 2

1. Muhammad al-Tūnisī, *In Darfur*, Humphrey Davies (trans.), New York, 2020.
2. Trimingham, *A History of Islam in West Africa*, p. 159; John Wright, 'The Wadai–Benghazi Slave Route', in Elizabeth Savage (ed.), *The Human Commodity*, pp. 175–9.
3. Gobir is perhaps the least well known of the Hausa kingdoms; even the names of the kings are uncertain or unknown before the mid-eighteenth century. The genealogy of the last pagan dynasty is in S.J. Hogben and A.H.M. Kirk-Greene, *The Emirates of Northern Nigeria*, London, 1966, p. 417; ibn Umar's expulsion is noted in Trimingham, *A History of Islam in West Africa*, p. 195.
4. Ibraheem Sulaiman, *The African Caliphate: The Life, Works and Teaching of Shaykh Usman dan Fodio (1754–1817)*, Bradford, 2009; Mervyn Hiskett, *The Sword of Truth: The Life and Times of Shehu Usuman dan Fodio*, Oxford, 1973.
5. Trimingham, *A History of Islam in West Africa*, pp. 126–36, for a summary of Hausa history, though, there is more detail in Hogben and Kirk-Greene, *Emirates*.
6. M.G. Smith, *Government in Zazzau: A Study of Government in the Hausa Chiefdom of Zaria in Northern Nigeria from 1800 to 1950*, Oxford, 1960.
7. Joseph P. Smaldone, *Warfare in the Sokoto Caliphate: Historical and Sociological Perspectives*, Cambridge, 1977; Hogben and Kirk-Greene, *Emirates*, pp. 116–30, is a survey of the conquest; part II of the book contains a description of the several emirates.
8. Ahmad Attahiru Sifawa, *Colonial State and Urbanisation in Sokoto Metropolis, Northern Nigeria, c. AD 1903–1960*, Beau Bassin, Mauritius, 2011.
9. Hogben and Kirk-Greene, *Emirates*, for individual emirates, Smith, *Zazzau*, and *The Affairs of Dawra*, Berkeley and Los Angeles, 1978.
10. Map in Smaldone, *Warfare*, p. 55, where the 'hostile enclaves' are the resistant unconquered pagan societies.
11. Trimingham, *A History of Islam in West Africa*, 200.
12. al-Tūnisī, *In Darfur*; Wright, 'Wadai-Benghazi Slave Route', note 15.
13. B.O. Oloruntimehin, *The Segu Tukulor Empire*, London, 1972, for a detailed account of Umar's early career.
14. A.S. Kanya-Forstner, 'Mali-Tukolor', in M. Crowder (ed.) *West African Resistance: The Military Response to Colonial Occupation*, London, 1971, pp. 53–79.
15. Yves Person, 'Guinea-Samori', in Crowder (ed.), *West African Resistance*, pp. 111–43.
16. B. Olatunji Olonumtimehin, 'Senegambia-Mahmadou Lamine', in Crowder (ed.), *West African Resistance*, pp. 80–110.
17. al-Tūnisī, *In Darfur*.

Chapter 3

1. P.M. Holt, *Egypt and the Fertile Crescent 1516–1922*, London, 1966, chapter 11.
2. Al-Jabarti, *History of Egypt*, Jane Hathaway (ed.), Princeton, NJ, 2006; J. Christopher Herold, *Bonaparte in Egypt*, London, 1962.
3. Coincidentally, it was the defeat of the German Nazi army at Alam Halfa and el-Alamein in Egypt in summer 1942 that revealed the hollowness of German militarism in Hitler's war.

4. Brian Lavery, *Nelson and the Nile: The Naval War against Napoleon Bonaparte 1798*, London, 1998; Sam Willis, *In the Hour of Victory: The Royal Navy at War in the Age of Nelson*, London, 2013, chapter 4.
5. Nathan Schur, *Napoleon in the Holy Land*, London, 1999.
6. Piers Mackesy, *British Victory in Egypt, 1801: The End of Napoleon's Conquest*, London, 1995.
7. David Chandler, *The Campaigns of Napoleon*, London, 1966, part 4; John D. Grainger, *Lieutenant General Sir Samuel Auchmuty*, Barnsley, 2018, chapter 4; Auchmuty was a colonel in the Indian contingent, and in the end he was the senior British officer as the occupation force diminished; *Al-Jabarti's History of Egypt*, Jane Hathaway (ed.), Princeton, NJ, 2009, pp. 173–216; al-Jabarti was a local historian contemporary with the events he recorded; he is eloquent on the French, but he ascribes their defeat to the Ottomans; the 'English' are barely mentioned.
8. Al-Jabarti, pp. 213–20.
9. Ibid., pp. 225–7.
10. Ibid., pp. 285–9.
11. Afaf Lutfi al-Sayyid Marsot, *Egypt in the reign of Muhammad Ali*, Cambridge, 1984, pp. 36–74.
12. For these, see Marsot, *Muhammad Ali*, chapters 6, 7 and 8.
13. Robert G. Ridley, *Napoleon's Proconsul in Egypt: The Life and Times of Bernardino Drovetti*, London (n.d.), p. 308.
14. The machine manufacture of textiles is a low-skilled, labour-intensive activity, but one that weans the workers away from domestic industry and subjects them to a regular schedule of work; it had been the pattern of industrial development in Britain, the United States, Japan and elsewhere – first textiles, then other industries.
15. These innovations are still going on; on a visit to Egypt a quarter of a century ago, my driver excitedly pointed out the latest innovation, a plantation of banana plants.
16. Al-Jabarti, pp. 326–30, reports briefly on the early measures.
17. For a description of the effects of a low Nile, see Abd al-Latif al-Baghdadi, *A Physician on the Nile*, Tim Mackintosh-Smith (trans.), New York, 2022; it refers to the years 1200 and 1201, but the effect had not changed in the interval.
18. Marsot, *Muhammad Ali*, 200, quoting a British Foreign Office document of 1811.
19. Ibid., pp. 200–206; al-Hajj Umar was in Arabia at this time, and was strongly influenced by the Wahhabi teaching.
20. Marsot, *Muhammad Ali*, 204; Henry Dodwell, *The Founder of Modern Egypt: A Study of Muhammad 'Ali*, Cambridge, 1931, p. 61; Abd al-Hamid Batnik, 'Egyptian–Yemeni Relations (1819–1840) and their Implications for British Policy in the Red Sea', in P.M. Holt (ed.), *Political and Social Change in Modern Egypt*, London, 1968, pp. 281–90.
21. Marsot, *Muhammad Ali*, pp. 214–17.
22. Afaf Lutfi al-Sayyid Marsot, 'Muhammad Ali and Palmerston', in D. Hopwood (ed.), *Studies in Arab History*, Oxford, 1990, pp. 61–75.
23. Grainger, *Auchmuty*, pp. 96–7.
24. Brian Fagan, *The Rape of the Nile: Tomb Robbers, Tourists, and Archaeologists in Egypt*, New York, 1975.
25. Ridley, *Napoleon's Proconsul*.
26. Patricia Usick, *Adventures in Egypt and Nubia: The Travels of William John Bankes (1817–1855)*, London, 2002.
27. Bibliographies listing most of these accounts are in, for example, Daniele Salvoldi (trans. and ed.), *From Siena to Nubia: Alessandro Ricci in Egypt and Sudan 1817–22*, Cairo

and New York, 2018, Fagan, *Rape of the Nile*, Ridley, *Napoleon's Proconsul*, and Usick, *Adventures*, p. 32. Of these, Ricci (in Salvoldi) and Bankes (in Usick) did travel south beyond Aswan.
28. Al-Jabarti, pp. 324–5.
29. Salvoldi, *From Siena to Nubia*, 177.
30. Richard Hill, *Egypt in the Sudan, 1820–1881*, Oxford, 1959, pp. 7–8.
31. Ibid., p. 4, note, on the general ignorance of the Sudan in other lands; one must presume, however, that the government in Cairo had more information than most.
32. Note 26.
33. Hill, *Egypt in the Sudan*, pp. 7–8; Salvoldi (ed.), *Siena to Nubia*, pp. 278–80.
34. An elaborate, though barely comprehensible, account of the inhabitants of Sudan before the invasion is in *A History of the Arabs in the Sudan and Some Account of the People Who Preceded Them and of the Tribes Inhabiting Dárfūr*, by H.A. MacMichael, 2 vols., Cambridge, 1922.
35. Salvoldi (ed.), *Siena to Nubia*, p. 272.
36. Al-Jabarti, p. 343.
37. Hill, *Egypt in the Sudan*, p. 9; this is the best account of the campaign.
38. Salfoldi (ed.), *Siena to Nubia*, pp. 277–9.
39. George B. English, *A Narrative of the Expedition to Dongola and Sennar...*, Boston, 1873 (republished at Collingwood, Victoria, Australia, 2017); English enumerates the force on pp. 1–2.
40. Hill, *Egypt in the Sudan*, pp. 12–13.
41. Salvoldi (ed.), *Siena to Nubia*.
42. Ibid., pp. 313–16.
43. For details of the former and new methods of taxation, see Hill, *Egypt in the Sudan*, pp. 13–15.
44. Ibid., p. 23.
45. Ibid., pp. 15–16; Alan Moorehead, *The Blue Nile*, London, 1962, pp. 191–2; Salvoldi (ed.), *Siena to Nubia*, p. 39.
46. Hill, *Egypt in the Sudan*, p. 15.
47. Ibid., pp. 16–17.
48. Hill, *Egypt in the Sudan*, pp. 17–18.

Chapter 4

1. Janet J. Ewald, *Soldiers, Traders, and Slaves: State Formation and Economic Transformation in the Greater Nile Valley, 1700–1885*, Madison, WI, 1900, pp. 53–6.
2. Gerard Prunier, 'Military Slavery in the Sudan during the Turkiyya (1820–1885)', in Elizabeth Savage (ed.), *The Human Commodity*, pp. 129–39, at p. 130.
3. Ewald, *Soldiers, Traders, and Slaves*, chapter 3.
4. Hill, *Egypt in the Sudan*, pp. 46–8.
5. Paul Santi and Richard Hill (trans. and eds.), *The Europeans in the Sudan, 1834–1878*, Oxford, 1980, with two translated accounts of Muhammad Ali's search for gold, pp. 52–73; Hill, *Egypt in the Sudan*, pp. 66–8.
6. A British naval expedition helped drive the Egyptian forces from Syria in 1840, and menaced Alexandria until Muhammad Ali agreed to a peace, and a definitive withdrawal into Egypt.
7. Hill, *Egypt in the Sudan*, pp. 10–11.
8. Ibid., pp. 17–19.

9. I. Pallme, *Travels in Kordofan*, London, 1841, p. 192; Hill, *Egypt in the Sudan*, pp. 57–8.
10. The main local source for the conquest and early part of Egyptian rule is 'Tarikh muluk al-Sudan', translated in H.A. MacMichael's *A History of the Arabs in the Sudan*, vol. 2, Cambridge, 1922, pp. 354–430.
11. Ewald, *Soldiers, Traders, and Slaves*, p. 55.
12. Hill, *Egypt in the Sudan*, p. 100; Santi and Hill, *Europeans*, p. 203, a letter from an Italian on a campaign for slaves as far as Gondokoro in the 1860s.
13. Hill, *Egypt in the Sudan*, p. 67.
14. Ibid., pp. 67, 100, 133–5.
15. James Bruce, *Travels to Discover the Source of the Nile, In the Years 1768–1773*, London, 1804; Alan Moorehead, *The Blue Nile*, London, 1962, part 1.
16. Ibid., pp. 31–3.
17. Robert O. Collins, 'The Nilotic Slave Trade: Past and Present', in Elizabeth Savage (ed.), *The Human Commodity*, pp. 140–61.
18. G. Thibault, 'Expeditions egyptiennes du Nil Bleu', *Bulletin de la Societe geographique de Paris*, 1841. A translation into French of Salim's official report is in the same journal for 1842.
19. Hill, *Egypt in the Sudan*, pp. 68–70; this exploratory work is ignored by Alan Moorehead, *The White Nile*, London, 1960, and by most European authors, fixated as they are on European explorers.
20. Ibid., p. 20.
21. Collins, 'Nilotic Slave Trade', pp. 141–3; Hill, *Egypt in the Sudan*, chapter 6, largely ignores this operation.
22. Hill, *Egypt in the Sudan*, pp. 97–9.
23. Ibid., pp. 143–4.
24. Paul B. Henze, *Layers of Time: A History of Ethiopia*, London, 2000, pp. 119–25.
25. Hill, *Egypt in the Sudan*, pp. 33–4.
26. Ibid., pp. 70–4.
27. Ibid., p. 83; Henze, *Layers of Time*, p. 134.
28. Hill, *Egypt in the Sudan*, p. 89; Ewald, *Soldiers, Traders, and Slaves*, chapter 4.
29. Hill, *Egypt in the Sudan*, pp. 135–6; D.A. Low, 'The Northern Interior, 1840–84', in Roland Oliver and Gervase Matthew (eds.), *History of East Africa*, vol. 1, Oxford, 1963, pp. 337–40.
30. Hill, *Egypt in the Sudan*, p. 135; Collins, 'Nilotic Slave Trade', p. 149.
31. Hill, *Egypt in the Sudan*, pp. 136–8.
32. Ludwien Kapteijns, *Mahdist Faith and Sudanic Tradition: The History of the Masalit Sultanate, 1870–1930*, London, 1985, pp. 62–3.
33. Collins, 'Nilotic Slave Trade', pp. 149–50.

Chapter 5

1. Marsot, *Muhammad Ali*, pp. 198–203.
2. Hill, *Egypt and the Sudan*, pp. 74, 87.
3. Favoured by Adolphe Linant de Bellefonds, an engineer who was in control of public works for Muhammad Ali: Hill, *Egypt in the Sudan*, p. 67.
4. Ibid., p. 99.
5. Halford L. Hoskins, *British Routes to India*, London 1928, chapter 9; Sarah Searight, *Steaming East: The Hundred-Year Saga of the Struggle to Forge Rail and Steamship Links between Europe and India*, London, 1991, chapter 3.

6. Accounts of the planning and construction of the canal are in John Marlowe, *The Making of the Suez Canal*, London, 1964, and Lord Kinross, *Between Two Seas: The Creation of the Suez Canal*, London, 1968; a shorter account is in Hoskins, *British Routes*, chapter 14.
7. Darrell Bates, *The Abyssinian Difficulty*, London, 1979, and Percy Arnold, *Prelude to Magdala: Emperor Theodore of Ethiopia and British Diplomacy*, Richard Pankhurst (ed.), London, 1992, are comprehensive accounts; see also Moorehead, *Blue Nile*, part 4.
8. A near contemporary account is by William McEntyre Dye, *Moslem Egypt and Christian Abyssinia; or, military service under the Khedive, in his provinces and beyond their borders, as experienced by the American Staff*, New York, 1880 (reprinted recently n.d.); chapters 17 and 18 deal with Arendrup's expedition.
9. Hill, *Egypt in the Sudan*, pp. 120–1; Dye, *Moslem Egypt*, gives an elaborate and diffuse account.
10. Hill, *Egypt in the Sudan*, pp. 109, 140–1.
11. Ibid., pp. 141–142; Dye, *Moslem Egypt*, notes this Egyptian expedition at several places in his account. It may be noted that Zeila has become a place where Ethiopia hopes to establish a free port, in what is the former British Somaliland, which has been effectively independent for several decades.
12. Giuseppe Finaldi, *A History of Italian Colonialism, 1860–1907: Europe's Last Empire*, London, 2017, pp. 19–25.
13. Hill, *Egypt in the Sudan*, p. 142.

Chapter 6

1. The people of the country call it Ethiopia. Foreigners, notably Arabs and other Muslims, and hence Europeans, call it 'Abyssinia', which is regarded as an insulting term by the inhabitants; here the more polite term, Ethiopia, will be used.
2. This period is highly confusing. Henze, *Layers of Time*, makes a valiant attempt to provide a coherent account, but even he gives up at times – pp. 119–25 for this period; also, A.H.M. Jones and Elizabeth Monroe, *A History of Ethiopia*, Oxford, 1935 and 1955, pp. 127–33. The relative shortness of these citations indicates the problem and the lack of sources.
3. Bates, *The Abyssinian Difficulty*; Arnold, *Prelude to Magdala*; Moorehead, *Blue Nile*, part 4; Henze, *Layers of Time*, pp. 132–43; all Ethiopian histories describe these events, but these books have more detail and better bibliographies than most.
4. Its latest attempt has been in the 2020s.
5. Henze, *Layers of Time*, pp. 145–6.
6. Ibid., p. 146.
7. The best account of the kingship's rise is by R.H. Kofi Darkwah, *Shewa, Menilek and the Ethiopian Empire, 1813–1889*, London, 1975, chapters 1 and 2 on the early history of the dynasty; also, Henze, *Layers of Time*, pp. 127–32.
8. Darkwah, *Shewa*, pp. 22–34, for Sahle Selassie's reign.
9. The Ethiopian royal titles are *ras* (equivalent to duke or prince), *negus* (king), and *negusa nagast* (king of kings, that is, emperor).
10. Darkwah, *Shewa*, pp. 34–6; Henze, *Layers of Time*, pp. 131–2.
11. Darkwah, *Shewa*, pp. 46–8.
12. Darkwah, *Shewa*, pp. 52–5; Henze, *Layers of Time*, p. 144.
13. Henze, *Layers of Time*, pp. 147–8; Darkwah, *Shewa*, pp. 75–6; Dye, *Moslem Egypt*, gives enormous and diffuse detail on this conflict.

Chapter 7

1. Salim merits a single sentence in the Wikipedia article on the 'Sources of the Nile'.
2. Hill, *Egypt and the Sudan*, pp. 68–9.
3. Arnold J. Toynbee, *Between Niger and Nile*, Oxford, 1966, pp. 28–33.
4. The idea is not dead – the Blue Nile is being dammed in Ethiopia, a project that has excited complaints and protests downriver; note also the effect of the construction of many dams along the course of the Mekong in Southeast Asia.
5. Tim Jeal, *Explorers of the Nile: The Triumph and Tragedy of a Great Victorian Adventure*, London, 2011.
6. Hill, *Egypt in the Sudan*, pp. 135–6.
7. Ibid., p. 139; useful biographies of Gordon, which include sections on his work in the south Sudan in the 1870s, include Archibald Forbes, *Chinese Gordon*, London, 1886, Lord Elton, *General Gordon*, London, 1954, and Anthony Nutting, *Gordon: Martyr & Misfit*, London, 1966; for Baker and Gordon in the region, see D.A. Low, 'The Northern Interior, 1840–1884', in Roland Oliver and Gervase Mathew (eds.), *History of East Africa*, vol. 1, Oxford, 1965, pp. 339–43; also, Jeal, *Explorers*.
8. It is also clear that well into the period of British rule in the 'Anglo-Egyptian Sudan', slavery continued, the British administrators fearing the effects of wholesale emancipation, or any attempt towards it; Robert O. Collins, 'The Nilotic Slave Trade, Past and Present', in Elizabeth Savage (ed.), *The Human Commodity*, pp. 140–61.
9. Olivia Manning, *The Remarkable Expedition: The Story of Stanley's Rescue of Emin Pasha from Equatorial Africa*, London, 1947, p. 33.
10. Hill, *Egypt in the Sudan*, pp. 144–8, a helpful and balanced account, unhampered by being linked with Gordon's later disaster at Khartoum.
11. The memoirs of C.C. Geitler (*The Sudan Memoirs of Carl Christian Geitler Pasha, 1873–1883*, Thirza Kupper (trans.), Richard Hill (ed.), Oxford, 1984) give a good deal of information about the telegraph system and its development; he was a telegraph engineer who rose quickly to be director general, and eventually, because Gordon liked him, to be his deputy governor general. He also made enough in his service to retire to Germany after escaping from Khartoum in 1882. There is a map of the telegraph network as at 1880, map 3 in the plate section of the book; see also Hill, *Egypt in the Sudan*, pp. 130–1, 157–8.
12. Hill, *Egypt in the Sudan*, pp. 158–60.
13. Ibid., p. 151; this scheme is not mentioned in any of the biographies of Gordon I have consulted, a factor that rather militates against their reliability; omitting madcap schemes might suggest other omissions.
14. For a helpful discussion on this, see the introduction in Santi and Hill, *Europeans in the Sudan*, pp. 1–33.
15. David S. Landes, *Bankers and Pashas, International Finance and Economic Imperialism in Egypt*, 2nd ed., New York, 1969.
16. John Marlowe, *Anglo-Egyptian Relations, 1800–1953*, London, 1954.
17. Landes, *Bankers and Pashas*, and more succinctly, Marlowe, *Anglo-Egyptian Relations*, chapter 4, for this extended crisis.
18. John Marlowe, *Spoiling the Egyptians*, London, 1974, pp. 242–4.
19. Ibid., pp. 247–8; Lord Cromer, *Modern Egypt*, London, 1911, chapter 7; Cromer was part of the administration at the time, and resigned.
20. Marlowe, *Spoiling the Egyptians*, pp. 249–50.
21. Ibid., p. 251.

22. Ibid., pp. 248–9.
23. Cromer, *Modern Egypt*, p. 109, claims it would be raised to 150,000 men.
24. Cromer, *Modern Egypt*; part I of this book is an extended decision of this crisis.
25. Marlowe, *Anglo-Egyptian Relations*, pp. 102–104.
26. Cromer, *Modern Egypt*, chapter 10.

Chapter 8
1. Marlowe, *Anglo-Egyptian Relations*, p. 115.
2. Forbes, *Chinese Gordon*, pp. 197–8; Nutting, *Gordon*, p. 165, cites his dislike of Taufiq and Baring (who was actually in Egypt at the time he resigned); Elton, *General Gordon*, pp. 260–3; there are other biographies but these three provide a good range of opinions on the matter.
3. Hill, *Egypt in the Sudan*, pp. 148–51.
4. Ibid., p. 149.
5. Ibid.
6. Afaf Lutfi al-Sayyid Marsot, *Egypt and Cromer: A Study in Anglo-Egyptian Relations*, London, 1968, pp. 8–9.
7. Ibid.; Marlowe, *Anglo-Egyptian Relations*, pp. 115–16.
8. Cromer, *Modern Egypt*, pp. 148–51.
9. Hill, *Egypt in the Sudan*, p. 149.
10. P.M. Holt, *The Mahdist State in the Sudan, 1881–1898: A Study of its Origins, Development and Overthrow*, 2nd edn., Oxford, 1970, p. 40; Holt gives a breakdown of the army into provincial garrisons; his total of '40,000' is not matched by the detailed figures, which amount to 32,000.
11. The Mahdi's early life is detailed, with variations, in Trimingham, *Islam in the Sudan*, Oxford, 1949, pp. 93–4; Holt, *The Mahdist State*, pp. 45–9; Theobald, *Mahdiya*, pp. 27–32; Fergus Nichol, *The Mahdi of Sudan and the Death of General Gordon*, Stroud, 2004, reprinted as *The Sword of the Prophet* (with the former title as a subtitle and with a different pagination), Stroud (n.d.); I have used the first edition.
12. Holt, *The Mahdist State*, pp. 49–50.
13. Ibid., p. 54.
14. Ibid., pp. 52–3.
15. Ibid., pp. 53–4; Ewald, *Soldiers, Traders, and Slaves*, pp. 120–1.
16. Ibid., pp. 54–5; Nicoll, *Mahdi*, pp. 77–8.
17. Holt, *The Mahdist State*, p. 55.
18. Ibid.
19. It is worth noting that Muhammad Ahmad at Aba and Colonel Urabi in Cairo had been able, almost at the same time, to judge accurately the likely responses of their putative enemies, and had prepared themselves and their followers.
20. Ibid., pp. 55–6; Theobald, *Mahdiya*, pp. 34–5, using a good deal of conjecture.
21. Holt, *The Mahdist State*, p. 56; Nichol, *Mahdi*, pp. 85–6 (unfairly critical of Muhammad Rauf); Theobald, *Mahdiya*, p. 35.
22. Nichol, *Mahdi*, pp. 90–2; Holt, *The Mahdist State*, 56–57; Theobald, *Mahdiya* 35–36.
23. Nichol, *Mahdi*, p. 91, shows a map of the suggested route.
24. Holt, *The Mahdist State*, pp. 56–7; Theobald, *Mahdiya*, p. 36.
25. Holt, *The Mahdist State*, p. 57.
26. Trimingham, *Islam in the Sudan*, p. 154; Nichol, *The Mahdi of Sudan*, pp. 78–9.
27. al-Sayyid Marsot, *Egypt and Cromer*, pp. 10–12; Marlowe, *Anglo-Egyptian Relations*, p. 115.

28. Marlowe, *Anglo-Egyptian Relations*, pp. 116–17.
29. Ibid., pp. 117–19; al-Sayyid Marsot, *Egypt and Cromer*, pp. 14–15.
30. al-Sayyid Marsot, *Egypt and Cromer*, pp. 17–18; Marlowe, *Anglo-Egyptian Relations*, pp. 60–1.
31. Marlowe, *Anglo-Egyptian Relations*, p. 120; ignored by al-Sayyid Marsot.
32. Holt, *The Mahdist State*, p. 57; Nichol, *Mahdi*, pp. 105–106.
33. Giegler, *Memoirs*, pp. 188–92.
34. Holt, *The Mahdist State*, pp. 68–9.
35. Giegler, *Memoirs*, pp. 205–206, lists the regular units in al-Shallali's force, in such a way as to imply he was quoting an official document; the force totalled 2,050 men, but he ignores the irregulars, who appear to have at least doubled that total; Holt, *The Mahdist State*, p. 58, for an estimate of the Mahdi's numbers
36. Marlowe, *Anglo-Egyptian Relations*, p. 121.

Chapter 9

1. al-Sayyid Marsot, *Egypt and Cromer*, p. 21.
2. Philip Mansel, *Levant: Splendour and Catastrophe on the Mediterranean*, London, 2010; along with Alexandria, he discusses Smyrna and Beirut; Alexandria receives as much attention as the other two put together.
3. Ibid., chapter 4.
4. Details in al-Sayyid Marsot, *Egypt and Cromer*, pp. 17–21; Marlowe, *Anglo-Egyptian Relations*, pp. 113–23.
5. Cromer, *Modern Egypt*, p. 225, mentions one instance.
6. al-Sayyid Marsot, *Egypt and Cromer*, pp. 20–2; Mansel, *Levant*, pp. 118–20; Marlowe, *Anglo-Egyptian Relations*, p. 122.
7. al-Sayyid Marsot, *Egypt and Cromer*, pp. 20–1; Cromer, *Modern Egypt*, pp. 224–5.
8. al-Sayyid Marsot, *Egypt and Cromer*, pp. 24–5.
9. Laird Clowes, *The Royal Navy: A History From the Earliest Times to 1900*, London, 1903, p. 327, for Seymour's orders, and a plan of the bombardment itself; a second version is in Donald Featherstone, *Tel El-Kebir 1882: Wolseley's Conquest of Egypt*, London, 1993, pp. 14–15; William Wright, *A Tidy Little War*, Cheltenham, 2009, chapter 3.
10. Clowes, *Royal Navy*, vol. 7, pp. 331–6, quotes several accounts and reports.
11. Colonel J.F. Maurice, *The Campaign of 1882 in Egypt*, London, 1887 (reprinted Uckbridge n.d.), pp. 11–12; Clowes, *Royal Navy*, vol. 7, pp. 336–9.
12. Marlowe, *Anglo-Egyptian Relations*, pp. 123–4: al-Sayyid Marsot, *Egypt and Cromer*, p. 26.
13. Cromer, *Modern Egypt*, p. 25 note.
14. Maurice, *Campaign of 1882*, p. 16, calls this a 'useful effect' understanding that it benefited the British invasion, though it was supposed to reassure Urabi.
15. Maurice, *Campaign of 1882*, pp. 21, 29–32; Clowes, *Royal Navy*, vol. 7, p. 339.
16. Marlowe, *Anglo-Egyptian Relations*, p. 125.
17. al-Sayyid Marsot, *Egypt and Cromer*, p. 26; Maurice, *Campaign of 1882*, quotes the khedive's written authority for the landing.
18. Maurice, *Campaign*, pp. 4–6.
19. Ibid., p. 7.
20. There are four useful accounts of the campaign and battle: Maurice, *Campaign*, is the Official History: Richard Simkin, *The War in Egypt* (an illustrated account), London, 1883 (reprinted Uckbridge n.d.); Featherstone, *Tel El-Kebir*; Wright, *A Tidy Little War*, is a rather bloated account; Maurice's is the preferred version.

21. Maurice, *Campaign*, chapter 4.
22. Ibid., p. 41.
23. Ibid., gives the figures as understood later by the British.
24. Ibid., pp. 38–40.
25. Featherstone, *Tel El-Kebir*, reproduces an apparently contemporary picture of this (a drawing), though this is hardly evidence; it is, however, exactly the sort of rumour that will be spread in the circumstances of this type of warfare.
26. Featherstone, *Tel El-Kebir*, pp. 38–42, with illustrations.
27. Ibid., p. 49; Maurice, *Campaign of 1882*, pp. 49–50.
28. Maurice, *Campaign of 1882*, pp. 63–4.
29. Details of the British units used are in appendices II and III of Maurice, *Campaign of 1882*, pp. 112–13.
30. Maurice, *Campaign of 1882*, pp. 71–106; Featherstone, *Tel El-Kebir*, pp. 68–8.
31. Marlowe, *Anglo-Egyptian Relations*, pp. 127–32; al-Sayyid Marsot, *Egypt and Cromer*, pp. 26–9.
32. Lord Cromer, *Modern Egypt*, London, 1911, chapter 11; Marlowe, *Anglo-Egyptian Relations*, pp. 127–35.
33. John Marlowe, *Cromer in Egypt*, London, 1970, pp. 70–80; al-Sayyid, *Egypt and Cromer*, pp. 38–56; Roger Owen, *Lord Cromer: Victorian Imperialist, Edwardian Proconsul*, Oxford, 2004, chapter 10; the title of consul general instead of ambassador was due to the fact that Egypt was still technically part of the Ottoman Empire.
34. Owen, *Cromer*, p. 184.
35. It is worth noting that Ismail, when he went into exile, was accompanied by boxes full of treasure; no attempt appears to have been made to recover this wealth for the benefit of the country from which he had extracted it.
36. Afaf Lutfi al-Sayyid Marsot, 'The British occupation of Egypt from 1882', in Andrew Porter (ed.), *The Oxford History of the British Empire, The Nineteenth Century* (vol. 3), Oxford, 1999, pp. 651–64.

Chapter 10

1. Holt, *The Mahdist State*, pp. 74–6; Rudolph Slatin, *Fire and Sword in the Sudan: A Personal Narrative of Fighting and Serving the Dervishes, 1879–1985*, F.R. Wingate (ed.), London, 1896, p. 270.
2. Holt, *The Mahdist State*, pp. 74–5.
3. Ibid., p. 62, based on Mahdist manuscripts.
4. Ewald, *Soldiers, Traders, and Slaves*, pp. 121–2; Theobald, *Mahdiya*, p. 39.
5. Joseph Ohrwalder, *Ten Years' Captivity in the Mahdi's Camp*, F.R. Wingate (trans.), London, 1892; Wingate did the same with Slatin's memoirs.
6. Theobald, *Mahdiya*, p. 40; Holt, *The Mahdist State*, p. 63.
7. Ohrwalder, *Ten Years' Captivity*; Ohrwalder was a witness from his captive status.
8. Bara and al-Ubaiyid: Holt, *The Mahdist State*, pp. 60–5.
9. Ibid., pp. 74–6.
10. Rudolph Slatin, *Fire and Sword in the Sudan*.
11. Theobald, *Mahdiya*, pp. 52–4.
12. Cromer, *Modern Egypt*, pp. 279–80.
13. Ewald, *Soldiers, Traders, and Slaves*, pp. 121–2.
14. Cromer, *Modern Egypt*, p. 278, note, quoting the British consul Power at Khartoum.
15. Holt, *The Mahdist State*, pp. 71–3; Theobald, *Mahdiya*, pp. 60–2.

16. Quoted in Nicoll, *The Mahdi of Sudan*, p. 146.
17. Ewald, *Soldiers, Traders, and Slaves*, pp. 122–4.
18. Owen, *Cromer*, pp. 188–9.
19. Cromer, *Modern Egypt*, pp. 289–97.
20. Ibid., p. 189; Holt, *The Mahdist State*, pp. 87–8; Fergus Nicoll, *Gladstone, Gordon and the Sudan Wars: The Battle over Imperial Intervention in the Victorian Age*, Barnsley, 2013, pp. 38–60.
21. Holt, *The Mahdist State*, pp. 84–5; Baker's forces were basically untrained in military work.
22. Ibid., pp. 116–22.
23. The literature on Gordon is extensive and repetitive, and too often fixated on reactions in Britain. I have used: Cromer, *Modern Egypt*, Holt, *The Mahdist State*, Theobald, *Mahdiya*, Nicoll, *The Mahdi of Sudan*, and Michael Asher, *Khartoum: The Ultimate Imperial Adventure*, London, 2009. For specific accounts of 1884–5, there are John Marlowe, *Mission to Khartoum*, London, 1969, Adrian Preston (ed.), *In Relief of Gordon: Lord Wolseley's Campaign Journal of the Khartoum Relief Expedition, 1884–1885*, London, 1967; there are no doubt other accounts, but these should suffice. A recent discussion of the British end is Nicoll, *Gladstone, Gordon and the Sudan Wars*; Gordon's own journal and a quantity of associated letters and accounts were published as early as June 1885: A. Egmont Hake (ed.), *The Journal of Major-Gen. C.G. Gordon, CB, at Khartoum*, London, 1885.
24. 'Shot' is correct, though the popular version, based on an inaccurate painting, is that he was speared; Nicoll, *The Mahdi of Sudan*, p. 260, quoting a Mahdist source.
25. Nicoll, *The Mahdi of Sudan*, p. 247, quoting E. Sanderson, *The British Empire in the XIX Century*, vol. 2, London, 1897, p. 256.
26. Cromer, *Modern Egypt*, pp. 417–19; Holt, *The Mahdist State*, p. 86; Cromer, *Modern Egypt*, chapter 21; Nicoll, *The Mahdi of Sudan*, pp. 247–48; Clowes, *Royal Navy*, vol. 7, pp. 350–5.
27. Nicoll, *The Mahdi of Sudan*, pp. 202–204; Iain R. Smith, *The Emin Pasha Relief Expedition, 1886–1890*, Oxford, 1972, pp. 18–21.
28. Clowes, *Royal Navy*, vol. 7, pp. 357–9.
29. Ibid., pp. 360–5; Holt, *The Mahdist State*, p. 102; Nicoll, *The Mahdi of Sudan*, pp. 251–3.
30. Holt, *The Mahdist State*, pp. 100–103; Nicoll, *The Mahdi of Sudan*, pp. 263–4; Wilson was widely blamed for this apparent lapse.
31. Charles Royle, *The Egyptian Campaign 1882–1885*, London, 1885 (reprinted London, 2013), pp. 406–29.
32. Holt, *The Mahdist State*, pp. 202–22 – 'the Ta'aisha autocracy'.
33. Cromer, *Modern Egypt*, pp. 379–80.
34. Holt, *The Mahdist State*, p. 142; Theobald, *Mahdiya*, p. 132.
35. Cromer, *Modern Egypt*, p. 451.
36. Philip Magnus, *Kitchener: Portrait of an Imperialist*, London, 1958, pp. 135–6.

Chapter 11
1. Cromer, *Modern Egypt*, heads his chapter on this subject, 'The Debris of the Sudan', chapter 30.
2. Ibid., pp. 308–309, 424, 519–20.
3. For West Africa, for instance, see the essays in Michael Crowder (ed.), *West African Resistance*.

4. Ibid., p. 501.
5. Henze, *Layers of Time*, p. 152; Cromer, *Modern Egypt*, p. 501; Dankwah, *Shewa*, pp. 104–108.
6. Cromer, *Modern Egypt*, p. 503.
7. Ibid., pp. 499–500, 502.
8. Giuseppe Finaldi, *A History of Italian Colonisation, 1860–1907: Europe's last Empire*, London, 2017, p. 24.
9. Quoted in Cromer, *Modern Egypt*, p. 503.
10. Cromer, *Modern Egypt*, pp. 503–506; Finaldi, *History of Italian Colonisation*, pp. 49–51.
11. Cromer, *Modern Egypt*, p. 497; Holt, *The Mahdist State*, p. 166.
12. Cromer, *Modern Egypt*, p. 498; Henze, *Layers of Time*, pp. 155–6.
13. Cromer, *Modern Egypt*, pp. 497–9; Holt, *The Mahdist State*, pp. 168–9.
14. 'Frank Lupton', Wikipedia.
15. Smith, *Emin Pasha*, p. 20.
16. Ibid., pp. 21–2.
17. In fact, he heard of this indirectly, from sources in Egypt who had heard of the Egyptian decision: Smith, *Emin Pasha*, pp. 29–30, quotes W. Junker, *Travels in Africa 1882–1896*, A.H. Keane (trans.), London, 1892, vol. 3, p. 532; Junker had been with Emin in Equatoria before leaving for the coast.
18. Emin's situation has produced several detailed (and repetitive) accounts. Smith, *Emin Pasha*, is perhaps the most coherent and informative; also Olivia Manning, *The Remarkable Expedition*, London, 1949, A.J.M. Jephson, *Emin Pasha and the Rebellion at the Equator*, London, 1890 (reprinted New York, 1969), was by a member of Stanley's expedition. There are also: Roger Jones, *The Rescue of Emin Pasha: The Story of Henry M. Stanley and the Emin Pasha Relief Expedition, 1887–1889*, London, 1972; and Henry M. Stanley, *In Darkest Africa; Or, the Quest, Rescue and Retreat of Emin, Governor of Equatoria*, London, 1890; these two last titles indicate clearly that it has been Stanley's journey that has interested later authors, not Emin's 'plight' – though Smith does pay some attention to the situation in Equatoria. For this, see Richard Gray, *A History of the Southern Sudan, 1839–1889*, Oxford, 1961.
19. Smith, *Emin Pasha*, pp. 157–66; Jones, *Rescue*, chapter 6; Jephson, *Emin Pasha*, p. 16.
20. Holt, *The Mahdist State*, p. 217.
21. G.N. Sanderson, *England, Europe, and the Upper Nile, 1882–1899*, Edinburgh, 1965, p. 40; Gray, *Southern Sudan*, pp. 162–4.

Chapter 12
1. The early problems the *khalifa* faced are detailed in Holt, *The Mahdist State*, pp. 141–6.
2. Ibid., p. 158.
3. Ibid., pp. 147–65.
4. The complicated history of the southern area, the Upper Nile and the Great Lakes area, together with the adventures of Rabeh, will be discussed in chapter 13.
5. Holt, *The Mahdist State*, pp. 176–82; Cromer, *Modern Egypt*, pp. 509–16.
6. Cromer, *Modern Egypt*, p. 516.
7. Ewald, *Soldiers, Traders, and Slaves*, pp. 123–6.
8. Henze, *Layers of Time*, pp. 151–2.
9. Darkwah, *Shewa*, pp. 97–110.
10. Fidaldi, *Italian Colonialism*, pp. 49–52.
11. Ibid., pp. 49–51.

12. Holt, *The Mahdist State*, p. 169; Henze, *Layers of Time*, p. 156.
13. Holt, *The Mahdist State*, p. 170.
14. Finaldi, *Italian Colonialism*, pp. 52–5.
15. Ibid., p. 52.
16. Ibid., pp. 51–62; Jones and Monroe, *History of Ethiopia*, pp. 137–8; Henze, *Layers of Time*, p. 157.
17. Henze, *Layers of Time*, pp. 156–8; Finaldi, *Italian Colonialism*, p. 67; Portal later published his own account of *My Mission to Abyssinia*, London, 1892; he clearly believed he had been successful.
18. Finaldi, *Italian Colonialism*, p. 68, emphasising that this restriction was on instructions from Rome.
19. Holt, *The Mahdist State*, pp. 170–2; Henze, *Layers of Time*, p. 158.
20. Henze, *Layers of Time*, p. 161; Darkwah, *Shewa*, pp. 67–8; Finaldi, *Italian Colonialism*, pp. 92–3.
21. Henze, *Layers of Time*, pp. 159–60; Darkwah, *Shewa*, pp. 81–2.
22. Henze, *Layers of Time*, p. 159; Darkwah, *Shewa*, pp. 98–9.
23. Henze, *Layers of Time*, pp. 159–60; Holt, *The Mahdist State*, pp. 172–3.
24. Henze, *Layers of Time*, p. 160.
25. Dankwah, *Shewa*, pp. 73–4; Henze, *Layers of Time*, pp. 160–1; Finaldi, *History*, p. 94.
26. Henze, *Layers of Time*, pp. 161–2; Finaldi, *History*, pp. 94–6.
27. Jones and Monroe, *History of Ethiopia*, p. 139.
28. Holt, *The Mahdist State*, pp. 184–5.

Chapter 13

1. Smith, *Emin Pasha*, pp. 256–61.
2. Sanderson, *England, Europe*, p. 9.
3. Ibid., pp. 43–4.
4. Smith, *Emin Pasha*, p. 269; Oliver and Mathew, *A History of East Africa*, vol. 1, pp. 402–407.
5. Sanderson, *England, Europe*, pp. 44–6; Robert O. Collins, *King Leopold, England, and the Upper Nile, 1899–1909*, New Haven, 1968, pp. 21–4.
6. Oliver and Mathew, *East Africa*, pp. 420–5; Sanderson, *England, Europe*, pp. 100–103, for the British government's discussions on this.
7. Smith, *Emin Pasha*, pp. 288–9.
8. Oliver and Mathew, *East Africa*, pp. 383–4; Sanderson, *England, Europe*, pp. 58–66.
9. A clear survey is in Colin Newbury, 'The Partition of Africa', in *The Oxford History of the British Empire, the Nineteenth Century*, Oxford, 1999, pp. 639–40.
10. Emin, employed on the German expedition, hoped to extend German influence into Uganda at this time, but then moved into the Congo, where, in October 1892, he was murdered: Oliver and Matthew, *East Africa*, p. 444.
11. Smith, *Emin Pasha*, pp. 294–5; Sanderson, *England, Europe*, chapter 1, on the White Nile regime; he suggests that a barrage aimed at interrupting the White Nile in the low water season could successfully starve Egypt (p. 10).
12. Oliver and Mathew, *East Africa*, p. 388.
13. Sanderson, *England, Europe*, p. 102.
14. Ibid.
15. Gerald H. Portal, *The British Mission to Uganda in 1883*, London, 1894; this was compiled by Rennell Rodd from notes and diaries left by Portal and his brother after their deaths;

it is not clear how much is by Portal or his brother and how much by Rodd; pp. 179–267 concern Uganda.
16. Fictionalised by Joseph Conrad in *Heart of Darkness*, 1899; for an interesting discussion, see Maya Jasanoff, *The Dawn Watch: Joseph Conrad in a Global World*, London, 2017, part III.
17. The expedition is usually entitled from the name of the original leader, G.F. van Kerkhoven, but he died on the journey; Wilz had been his second-in-command.
18. Sanderson, *England, Europe*, pp. 95–6.
19. Holt, *The Mahdist State*, pp. 219–20.
20. Ibid.; Sanderson, *England, Europe*, attributes this campaign to Umar Salih, but he did not get through to Fashoda until 1896.
21. Holt, *The Mahdist State*, pp. 220–1; see Sanderson, *England, Europe*, pp. 3–4, on this Sudd episode.
22. Sanderson, *England, Europe*, pp. 95–6.
23. Collins, *King Leopold, England*, pp. 38–43; Sanderson, *England, Europe*, pp. 140–4.
24. Noted in Alberto Sbacchi, *Legacy of Bitterness: Ethiopia and Fascist Italy, 1935–1941*, in chapter 10, 'Anglo-Italian Relations and Ethiopia', pp. 269–315, at p. 274, referring to Wondinmeh Tilahun, *Egypt's Imperial Aspirations*, Addis Ababa, 1979.
25. Sanderson, *England, Europe*, pp. 33–4, 43–5.
26. J.A.S. Grenville, *Lord Salisbury and Foreign Policy: The Close of the Nineteenth Century*, London, 1970, pp. 114–15.
27. Finaldi, *Italian Colonialism*, pp. 103–104; Holt, *The Mahdist State*, p. 214.
28. Holt, *The Mahdist State*, pp. 214–15; Finaldi, *Italian Colonialism*, pp. 105–106.
29. Finaldi, *Italian Colonialism*, chapter 9.
30. G.F-H. Berkeley, *The Campaign of Adowa and the Rise of Menelik*, London, 1896 (reprinted n.d.), pp. 58–82; Henze, *Layers of Time*, p. 167.
31. The Wikipedia article 'Rabih az-Zubayr' is a useful summary of Rabeh's career; Trimingham, *A History of Islam in West Africa*, pp. 218–19, has another brief summary.
32. Quoted from a translated copy in the Cairo archives in Kapteijns, *Mahdist Faith*, p. 75.
33. Holt, *The Mahdist State*, pp. 113–15.
34. Sanderson, *England, Europe*, pp. 119, 121.

Chapter 14
1. Philip Magnus, *Kitchener*, London, 1958, p. 96, quotes from Salisbury's message.
2. Holt, *The Mahdist State*, pp. 227, 230.
3. Negotiated between Britain, France and Leopold: Sanderson, *England, Europe*, pp. 185, 305; Robert O. Collins, *King Leopold, England, and the Upper Nile, 1899–1909*, New Haven, CT, 1968.
4. Collins, *King Leopold, England*, indicates the various proposals in a series of maps.
5. Sanderson, *England, Europe*, p. 306.
6. Ibid., pp. 140–5.
7. Ibid., pp. 125–7.
8. Henze, *Layers of Time*, p. 166; Finaldi, *Italian Colonialism*, pp. 116–17.
9. Holt, *The Mahdist State*, p. 227, an announcement from the Khalifa that the town was to be retaken.
10. Holt, *The Mahdist State*, pp. 215–16, 227–8.
11. Henze, *Layers of Time*, pp. 167–8.

12. Berkeley, *Campaign of Adowa*, pp. 128–43; Finaldi, *Italian Colonialism*, pp. 119–21; Henze, *Layers of Time*, p. 167; Italian sources, based on reports of the battle, are thoroughly unreliable.
13. Berkeley, *Campaign of Adowa*, pp. 145–53.
14. Finaldi, *Italian Colonialism*, p. 123.
15. Berkeley, *Campaign of Adowa*, pp. 128–43; Finaldi, *Italian Colonialism*, pp. 119–21; Henze, *Layers of Time*, p. 167.
16. Finaldi, *Italian Colonialism*, pp. 120–1, 126.
17. Berkeley, *Campaign of Adowa*, pp. 238–59, on Italian preparations.
18. Ibid., pp. 127–8.
19. Berkeley, *Campaign of Adowa*, pp. 267–8, tabulates the rival strengths, but he relies on Italian statistics.
20. Berkeley, *Campaign of Adowa*, pp. 178–216; Finaldi, *Italian Colonialism*, pp. 122–4; Henze, *Layers of Time*, p. 168.
21. Henze, *Layers of Time*, p. 171, on the explanation of the Ethiopian point of view; Berkeley, *Campaign of Adowa*, pp. 355–7, comments for the Italian.
22. Finaldi, *Italian Colonialism*, pp. 132–9, ignores the peace agreement, in favour of Italian reactions.

Chapter 15

1. Berkeley, *Campaign of Adowa*, pp. 357–62.
2. Ibid., pp. 365–6; it was not an Italian 'issue', as Berkeley says, since the Italian occupation was only with British permission.
3. Holt, *The Mahdist State*, p. 230.
4. Ibid.
5. Owen, *Lord Cromer*, p. 287; Cromer, *Modern Egypt*, pp. 524–6.
6. Cromer, *Modern Egypt*, p. 528.
7. 'An Officer' (Lieutenant H.L. Prichard), *The Sudan Campaign, 1896–1899*, London, 1899, pp. 16–19.
8. H.S.L. Alford, *Egyptian Soudan, Iits Loss and Recovery*, London, 1898, pp. 89–95; Charles Royle, *The Mahdist Campaign, Sudan 1884–98* (reprinted 2013), pp. 535–7; 'Officer', *Sudan Campaign*, pp. 28–32; Holt, *The Mahdist State*, p. 230.
9. Royle, *Mahdist Campaign*, pp. 540–1; Michael Asher, *Khartoum, the Ultimate Imperial Adventure*, London, 2005, pp. 315–18.
10. Holt, *The Mahdist State*, p. 231.
11. Mark Simner, *The Sirdar and the Khalifa: Kitchener's Reconquest of Sudan, 1896–98*, London, 2017, pp. 109–10.
12. Philip Ziegler, *Omdurman*, London, 1973; this incident is noted in most accounts, sometimes gleefully.
13. Holt, *The Mahdist State*, p. 234; Ziegler, *Omdurman*, pp. 28–9; 'Officer', *Sudan Campaign*, pp. 103–11, noting that it was not so easy a capture as most accounts suggest; Alford, *Egyptian Soudan*, pp. 164–9.
14. Holt, *The Mahdist State*, p. 235; 'Officer', *Sudan Campaign*, pp. 115–20.
15. Sanderson, *England, Europe*, pp. 272–6, 293, 305–306.
16. Ibid., pp. 304–306; the mutineers escaped to the south of Dhanis's route and held out for several years.
17. Ibid., p. 307.

18. One of the best accounts of the Marchand expedition is by Patricia Wright, *Conflict on the Nile: The Fashoda Incident of 1898*, London, 1972, pp. 128–72.
19. Sanderson, *England, Europe*, p. 294.
20. Wright, *Conflict*, pp. 192–3.
21. Sanderson, *England, Europe*, pp. 294–6; Wright, *Conflict*, pp. 192–4.

Chapter 16
1. D.A. Low, 'British East Africa: The Development of British Rule 1894–1912', in Vincent Harlow *et al.*, *History of East Africa*, vol. 2, Oxford, 1965, pp. 1–56, at pp. 3–4.
2. Ibid., pp. 4–5, 17–18; a less formal account is in Seymour Vandeleur, *Campaigning in the Upper Nile and Niger*, London, 1898 (reprinted 2005), pp. 107–48.
3. Magnus, *Kitchener*, p. 118.
4. Sanderson, *England, Europe*, p. 185.
5. Wright, *Conflict*, pp. 139–63.
6. 'An Officer', *Sudan Campaign*, pp. 132–3; Simner, *Sirdar*, pp. 116–17; Royle, *Sudan*, pp. 552–4.
7. Simner, *Sirdar*, pp. 117–18.
8. Magnus, *Kitchener*, pp. 110–16.
9. Simner, *Sirdar*, pp. 117–18.
10. Holt, *The Mahdist State*, discusses in detail the Khalifa's difficulties in 1897 (pp. 232–6); and the Atbara plan (pp. 237–8).
11. Simner, *Sirdar*, pp. 119–21; 'An Officer', *Sudan Campaign*, chapter 10; Royle, *Sudan*, pp. 555–64.
12. A plan of the camp is in Royle, *Sudan*, p. 566, and a larger copy in Simner, *Sirdar*, p. 7.
13. 'An Officer', *Sudan Campaign*, p. 149.
14. For accounts of the battle, see: Royle, *Sudan*, pp. 565–74; Alford, *Egyptian Soudan*, pp. 214–24; 'An Officer', *Sudan Campaign*, pp. 151–8; Simner, *Sirdar*, pp. 123–32; G.W. Steevens, *With Kitchener to Khartoum*, Edinburgh, 1896, pp. 140–60; Asher, *Khartoum*, pp. 341–58; Holt, *The Mahdist State*, p. 238.
15. Simner, *Sirdar*, pp. 133–4; 'An officer', *Sudan Campaign*, pp. 179–80.
16. Holt, *The Mahdist State*, pp. 236, 240.
17. The approach march: Simner, *Sirdar*, chapter 9; Asher, *Khartoum*, pp. 365–7; Alford, *Egyptian Soudan*, pp. 236–56; 'An Officer', *Sudan Campaign*, pp. 173–84; Steevens, *With Kitchener*, pp. 218–48.
18. Simner, *Sirdar*, p. 137.
19. This is described in Winston Churchill, *The River War: The Reconquest of the Sudan*, London, 1899, revised 1902, pp. 272–80, and reprinted several times since.
20. Simner, *Sirdar*, pp. 228–31, tabulating the casualties in all the fights of the campaign.
21. Simner, *Sirdar*, pp. 178–81; 'An Officer', *Sudan Campaign*, pp. 216–22; 'rabbit warren' is Steevens, *With Kitchener*, a typically lazy journalistic comment.
22. Simner, *Sirdar*, p. 186.
23. Ibid., p. 193; 'An Officer', *Sudan Campaign*, p. 229.

Chapter 17
1. Royle, *Sudan*, pp. 608–11; Sanderson, *England, Europe*, pp. 332–4.
2. Wright, *Conflict*, p. 174.
3. Magnus, *Kitchener*, p. 141; Sanderson, *England, Europe*, pp. 334–6; Wright, *Conflict*, pp. 176–9.
4. Sanderson, *England, Europe*, p. 332; Cromer's instructions were similar.

5. Sanderson, *England, Europe*, pp. 333–4.
6. Wright, *Conflict*, pp. 177–9.
7. Sanderson, *England, Europe*, pp. 335–6.
8. Ibid., pp. 339–62, for a detailed account.
9. Wright, *Conflict*, p. 189.
10. Ibid., pp. 197–206.
11. Collins, *King Leopold*, passim.
12. Harlow et al., *History of East Africa*, vol. 2, pp. 7–8.
13. Holt, *The Mahdist State*, pp. 241–2, quotes a vision experienced by one of the Khalifa's followers to this effect.
14. Ibid., p. 242; 'An Officer', *Sudan Campaign*, p. 234.
15. 'An Officer', *Sudan Campaign*, pp. 235–56, quoting from a 'Royal Engineer's Journal'; this is the only detailed account of these events.
16. Holt, *The Mahdist State*, p. 242; this incident is rarely noted in British accounts, though the execution does look rather hasty.
17. Ibid., pp. 242–3; 'An Officer', *Sudan Campaign*, pp. 257–9; Simner, *Sirdar*, pp. 208–12.
18. J.R.V. Prescott, *Political Frontiers and Boundaries*, London, 1987, detected a dispute or an unsurveyed border on almost every boundary; see his map 10.3, p. 256.
19. Simner, *Sirdar*, p. 216.
20. Collins, *King Leopold*, pp. 206–12.
21. Simner, *Sirdar*, pp. 216–18.
22. Ewald, *Soldiers, Traders, and Slaves*, pp. 130–5.
23. J.A. Fage, *An Introduction to the History of West Africa*, Cambridge, 1964; Martin A. Klein, *Islam and Imperialism in Senegal*, Edinburgh, 1968; J. Spencer Trimingham, *A History of Islam in West Africa*, Oxford, 1962, are rather old texts, but useful; see also the references to the Sokoto Caliphate in chapter 1.
24. The French routinely disestablished the dynasties of the countries they conquered; those dynasties that survived the colonial governments tended to be suppressed by their republican-minded independent successors. The Nigerian emirates did not outlast British protection, but the dynasties continue, though without power.
25. Seymour Vandeleur, *Campaigning on the Upper Nile and Niger*, London, 1898 (reprinted 2005), chapters 12 to 22.
26. Michael Crowder, *Revolt in Bussa: A Study of British 'Native Administration' in Nigerian Borgu, 1902–1935*, London, 1973.
27. Trimingham, *A History of Islam in West Africa*, pp. 224–31.

Bibliography

Alford, H.S.L., *Egyptian Soudan, Its Loss and Its Recovery*, London, 1898.
Arnold, Percy, *Prelude to Magdala: Emperor Theodore of Ethiopia and British Diplomacy*, Richard Pankhurst (ed.), London, 1992.
Asher, Michael, *Khartoum: The Ultimate Imperial Adventure*, London, 2005.
Bates, Darrell, *The Abyssinian Difficulty*, London, 1979.
Batnik, Abd al-Hamid, 'Egyptian–Yemeni Relations (1819–1840) and their Implications for British Policy in the Red Sea', in P.M. Holt (ed.), *Political and Social Change in Modern Egypt*, London, 1968.
Bennison, Amira K., *The Almoravid and Almohad Empires*, Edinburgh, 2016.
Berkeley, G.F-H., *The Campaign of Adowa and the Rise of Menelik*, London, 1896 (reprinted n.d.).
Blake, John W., *European Beginnings in West Africa, 1454–1578*, London, 1932.
Bovill, E.W., *The Golden Trade of the Moors*, 2nd edn., revised by Richard Hallett, Oxford, 1968.
Bulliet, Richard W., *Conversion to Islam in the Mediaeval Period: An Essay in Quantitative History*, Cambridge, MA, 1970.
Butler, A.J., *The Arab Conquest of Egypt*, 2nd edn., revised by P.M. Fraser, Oxford, 1998.
Cailliaud, Frederic, *Voyage a Méroé ... au-delà de Fàzoql .... 1821 et 1822*, 4 vols. of text and 3 vols. of plates, Paris, 1823–7.
Chandler, David, *The Campaigns of Napoleon*, London, 1966.
Churchill, Winston S., *The River War: An Account of the Reconquest of the Sudan*, London, 1902.
Clowes, Laird, *The Royal Navy: A History From the Earliest Times to 1900*, vol. 7, London, 1903.
Collins, Robert O., 'The Nilotic Slave Trade: Past and Present', in Elizabeth Savage (ed.), *The Human Commodity: Perspectives on the Trans-Saharan Slave Trade*, 1992, London.
Collins, Robert O., *King Leopold, England, and the Upper Nile, 1899–1909*, New Haven, 1968.
Connah, Graham, *African Civilizations: Precolonial cities and states in tropical Africa: an archaeological perspective*, Cambridge, 1987.
Conrad, Joseph, *Heart of Darkness*, London, 1899.
Cromer, Earl of (Evelyn Baring), *Modern Egypt*, London, 1911.
Crowder, Michael (ed.), *West African Resistance: The Military Response to Colonial Occupation*, London, 1971.
Crowder, Michael, *Revolt in Bussa: A Study of British 'Native Administration' in Nigerian Borgu, 1902–1935*, London, 1973.
Darkwah, R.H. Kofi, *Shewa, Menilek and the Ethiopian Empire, 1813–1889*, London, 1975.
Davidson, Basil, *The Growth of African Civilisation: History of West Africa, 1000–1800*, London, 1965.
Dodwell, Henry, *The Founder of Modern Egypt: A Study of Muhammad 'Ali*, Cambridge, 1931.
Dye, William McEntyre., *Moslem Egypt and Christian Abyssinia; or, military service under the Khedive, in his provinces and beyond their borders, as experienced by the American Staff*, New York, 1880 (reprinted n.d.).

Egmont Hake, A. (ed.), *The Journals of Major-Gen. C.G. Gordon, CB, at Kartoum*, London, 1885.

Elton, Lord, *General Gordon*, London, 1954.

English, George B., *A Narrative of the Expedition to Dongola and Sennaar* ..., Boston, 1873 (republished Collingwood, Victoria, Australia, 2017).

Ewald, Janet J., *Soldiers, Traders, and Slaves: State Formation and Economic Transformation in the Greater Nile Valley, 1700–1885*, Madison, WI, 1990.

Fagan, Brian, *The Rape of the Nile: Tomb Robbers, Tourists, and Archaeologists in Egypt*, New York, 1975.

Fage, J.D., *An Introduction to the History of West Africa*, Cambridge, 1964.

Featherstone, Donald, *Tel El-Kebir 1882: Wolseley's Conquest of Egypt*, London, 1993.

Ferguson, John, 'Classical Contacts with West Africa', in L.A. Thompson and J. Ferguson, *Africa in Classical Antiquity*, Ibadan, 1969.

Finaldi, Giuseppe, *A History of Italian Colonialism, 1860–1907: Europe's Last Empire*, London, 2017.

Forbes, Archibald, *Chinese Gordon*, London, 1886.

Geitler, C.C., *The Sudan Memoirs of Carl Christian Geitler Pasha, 1873–1883*, Thirza Kupper (trans.), Richard Hill (ed.), Oxford, 1984.

Grainger, John D., *Lieutenant General Sir Samuel Auchmuty, 1756–1822*, Barnsley, 2018.

Gray, Richard, *A History of the Southern Sudan, 1839–1889*, Oxford, 1961.

Grenville, J.A.S., *Lord Salisbury and Foreign Policy: The Close of the Nineteenth Century*, London 1970.

Harlow, Vincent, Chilver, E.M. and Smith, Alison (eds.), *History of East Africa*, vol. 2, Oxford, 1965.

Hathaway, Jane (ed.), *Al-Jabarti's History of Egypt*, Princeton, NJ, 2009.

Henze, Paul B., *Layers of Time: A History of Ethiopia*, London, 2000.

Hill, Richard, *Egypt in the Sudan, 1820–1881*, Oxford, 1959.

Hiskett, Mervyn, *The Sword of Truth: The Life and Times of Shehu Usuman dan Fodio*, Oxford, 1973.

Hogben, S.J. and Kirk-Greene, A.H.M., *The Emirates of Northern Nigeria*, London, 1966.

Holt, P.M., *The Mahdist State in the Sudan, 1881–1898: A Study of its Origins, Development and Overthrow*, 2nd edn., Oxford, 1970.

Hoskins, Halford L., *British Routes to India*, London, 1928.

Jasanoff, Maya, *The Dawn Watch: Joseph Conrad in a Global World*, London, 2017.

Jeal, Tim, *Explorers of the Nile: The Triumph and Tragedy of a Great Victorian Adventure*, London 2011.

Jephson, A.J.M., *Emin Pasha and the Rebellion at the Equator*, London, 1890 (reprinted New York, 1969).

Jones, A.H.M. and Monroe, Elizabeth, *A History of Ethiopia*, Oxford, 1935 and 1955.

Jones, Roger, *The Rescue of Emin Pasha: The Story of Henry M. Stanley and the Emin Pasha Relief Expedition, 1887–1889*, London, 1972.

Junker, William, *Travels in Africa 1882–1896*, A.H. Keane (trans.), London, 1892.

Kaegi, Walter E., *Muslim Expansion and Byzantine Collapse in North Africa*, Cambridge, 2010.

Kapteijns, Ludwien, *Mahdist Faith and Sudanic Tradition: The History of the Masālīt Sultanate, 1870–1930*, London, 1985.

Khaldûn, Ibn, *The Muqaddimah: An Introduction to History*, Franz Rosenthal (trans. and ed.), London, 1967.

Kinross, Lord, *Between Two Seas: The Creation of the Suez Canal*, London, 1968.

Klein, Martin A., *Islam and Imperialism in Senegal*, Edinburgh, 1968.
Landes, David S., *Bankers and Pashas: International Finance and Economic Imperialism in Egypt*, 2nd edn., New York, 1969.
Lavery, Brian, *Nelson and the Nile: The Naval War against Napoleon Bonaparte 1798*, London, 1998.
Lovejoy, Paul E. (ed.), *Slavery on the Frontiers of Islam*, Princeton, NJ, 2004.
Low, D.A., 'The Northern Interior, 1840–84', in Oliver, Roland and Mathew, Gervase (eds.), *History of East Africa*, vol. 1, Oxford, 1963.
Low, D.A., 'British East Africa: The Development of British Rule 1894–1912', in Vincent Harlow et al., *History of East Africa*, vol. 2, Oxford, 1965.
McIntosh, Roderick J., 'Clustered Cities of the Middle Niger', in David M. Anderson and Richard Rathbone (eds.), *Africa's Urban Past*, Oxford, 2000.
Mackesy, Piers, *British Victory in Egypt, 1801: The End of Napoleon's Conquest*, London, 1995.
MacMichael, H.A., *A History of the Arabs in the Sudan: And Some Account of the People Who Preceded Them and of the Tribes Inhabiting Dárfūr*, 2 vols., Cambridge, 1922.
Magnus, Philip, *Kitchener: Portrait of an Imperialist*, London, 1958.
Manning, Olivia, *The Remarkable Expedition: The Story of Stanley's Rescue of Emin Pasha from Equatorial Africa*, London, 1947.
Mansel, Philip, *Levant: Splendour and Catastrophe on the Mediterranean*, London, 2010.
Marlowe, John, *Anglo-Egyptian Relations, 1800–1953*, London, 1954.
Marlowe, John, *The Making of the Suez Canal*, London, 1964.
Marlowe, John, *Mission to Khartoum: The Apotheosis of General Gordon*, London, 1969.
Marlowe, John, *Cromer in Egypt*, London, 1970.
Marlowe, John, *Spoiling the Egyptians*, London, 1974.
Marsot, Afaf Lutfi al-Sayyid, *Egypt in the reign of Muhammad Ali*, Cambridge, 1984.
Marsot, Afaf Lutfi al-Sayyid, 'The British occupation of Egypt from 1882', in Andrew Porter (ed.), *The Oxford History of the British Empire, The Nineteenth Century* (vol. 3), Oxford, 1999.
Marsot, Afaf Lutfi al-Sayyid, 'Muhammad Ali and Palmerston', in D. Hopwood (ed.), *Studies in Arab History*, Oxford, 1990.
Marsot, Afaf Lutfi al-Sayyid, *Egypt and Cromer: A Study in Anglo-Egyptian Relations*, London, 1968.
Maurice, Colonel J.F., *The Campaign of 1882 in Egypt*, London, 1887 (reprinted Uckbridge, n.d.).
Moorehead, Alan, *The White Nile*, London, 1960.
Moorehead, Alan, *The Blue Nile*, London, 1962.
Newbury, Colin, 'The Partition of Africa', in Andrew Porter (ed.), *The Oxford History of the British Empire, The Nineteenth Century* (vol. 3), Oxford, 1999.
Nicoll, Fergus, *The Mahdi of Sudan and the Death of General Gordon*, Stroud, 2004 (reprinted as *The Sword of the Prophet*, Stroud, 2004).
Nicoll, Fergus, *Gladstone, Gordon and the Sudan Wars: The Battle over Imperial Intervention in the Victorian Age*, Barnsley, 2013.
Nutting, Anthony, *Gordon: Martyr & Misfit*, London, 1966.
(Prichard, Lieutenant H.L.), 'An Officer', *The Sudan Campaign, 1896–1899*, London, 1899.
Ohrwalder, Joseph, *Ten Years' Captivity in the Mahdi's Camp*, F.R. Wingate (trans.), London, 1892.
Owen, Roger, *Lord Cromer: Victorian Imperialist, Edwardian Proconsul*, Oxford, 2004.
Pallme, Ignatius, *Travels in Kordofan*, London 1841.

Portal, Sir Gerald H., *My Mission to Abyssinia*, London, 1892.
Portal, Sir Gerald H., *The British Mission to Uganda in 1883*, London, 1894, compiled by Rennell Rodd.
Prescott, J.R.V., *Political Frontiers and Boundaries*, London, 1987.
Preston, Adrian (ed.), *In Relief of Gordon: Lord Wolseley's Campaign Journal of the Khartoum Relief Expedition, 1884–1885*, London, 1967.
Prunier, Gerard, 'Military Slavery in the Sudan during the Turkiyya (1820–1885)', in Elizabeth Savage, *The Human Commodity*.
Ridley, Robert G., *Napoleon's Proconsul in Egypt: The Life and Times of Bernardino Drovetti*, London, (n.d.).
Royle, Charles, *The Egyptian Campaigns, 1882 to 1885*, London, 1885 (reprinted London, 2013).
Salvoldi, Daniele (trans. and ed.), *From Siena to Nubia: Alessandro Ricci in Egypt and Sudan 1817–22*, Cairo and New York, 2018.
Sanderson, Edgar, *The British Empire in the Nineteenth Century*, vol., 2, London, 1897.
Sanderson, G.N., *England, Europe, and the Upper Nile, 1882–1899*, Edinburgh, 1965.
Santi, Paul and Hill, Richard (trans. and eds.), *The Europeans in The Sudan, 1834–1878*, Oxford, 1980.
Savage, Elizabeth (ed.), *The Human Commodity: Perspectives on the Trans-Saharan Slave Trade*, London, 1992.
Sbacchi, Alberto, *Legacy of Bitterness: Ethiopia and Fascist Italy, 1935–1941*, Lawrenceville, NJ and Asmara, Eritrea, 1997.
Schur, Nathan, *Napoleon in the Holy Land*, London, 1999.
Searight, Sarah, *Steaming East: The Hundred-Year Saga of the Struggle to Forge Rail and Steamship Links between Europe and India*, London, 1991.
Sifawa, Ahmad Attahiru, *Colonial State and Urbanization in Sokoto Metropolis, Northern Nigeria, c.AD 1903–1960*, Beau Bassin, Mauritius, 2011.
Simkin, Richard, *The War in Egypt* (an illustrated account), London, 1883 (reprinted Uckbridge, n.d.).
Slatin, Rudolph C., *Fire and Sword in the Sudan: A Personal Narrative of Fighting and Serving the Dervishes, 1879–1895*, F.R. Wingate (ed.), London, 1896.
Smaldone, Joseph P., *Warfare in the Sokoto Caliphate: Historical and Sociological Perspectives*, Cambridge, 1977.
Smith, Iain R., *The Emin Pasha Relief Expedition, 1886–1890*, Oxford, 1972.
Smith, M.G., *Government in Zazzau: A Study of Government in the Hausa Chiefdom of Zaria in Northern Nigeria from 1800 to 1950*, Oxford, 1960.
Smith, M.G., *The Affairs of Daura*, Berkeley and Los Angeles, 1978.
Stanley, Henry M., *In Darkest Africa; Or, the Quest, Rescue and Retreat of Emin, Governor of Equatoria*, London, 1890.
Steevens, G.W., *With Kitchener to Khartum*, Edinburgh, 1896.
Sulaiman, Ibraheem, *The African Caliphate: The Life, Works and Teaching of Shaykh Usman dan Fodio (1754–1817)*, Bradford, 2009.
Theobald, A.B., *The Mahdiya: A History of the Anglo-Egyptian Sudan, 1881–1899*, London, 1951.
Thibault, G., 'Expeditions egyptiennes du Nil Bleu', in *Bulletin de la Societe geographique de Paris*, 1841.
Tilahun, Wondinmeh, *Egypt's Imperial Aspirations over Lake Tana and the Blue Nile*, Addis Ababa, 1979.

Toynbee, Arnold J., *Between Niger and Nile*, Oxford, 1966.
Trimingham, J. Spencer, *Islam in the Sudan*, Oxford, 1949.
Trimingham, J. Spencer, *A History of Islam in West Africa*, Glasgow, 1962.
al-Tūnisī, Muhammad, *In Darfur*, Humphrey Davies (trans.), New York, 2020.
Usick, Patricia, *Adventures in Egypt and Nubia: The Travels of William John Bankes (1786–1855)*, London, 2002.
Vandeleur, Seymour, *Campaigning in the Upper Nile and Niger*, London, 1898 (reprinted 2005).
Wikipedia, 'Frank Lupton'.
Wikipedia, 'Rabih az-Zubayr'.
Willis, Sam, *In the Hour of Victory: The Royal Navy at War in the Age of Nelson*, London, 2013.
Wright, John, 'The Wadai-Benghazi Slave Route', in Elizabeth Savage (ed.), *The Human Commodity: Perspectives on the Trans-Saharan Slave Trade*, London, 1992.
Wright, Patricia, *Conflict on the Nile: The Fashoda Incident of 1898*, London, 1972.
Wright, William, *A Tidy Little War: The British Invasion of Egypt 1882*, Cheltenham, 2009.

Index

Aba Island, 51, 104–10, 242–3
Ababda, tribe, 35–7, 40
Abatieh, 230
Abbas I, khedive of Egypt, 55, 60
Abd al-Qadir Pasha Hilmi, 113, 132
Abd el-Rahman, 36, 160
Abdullab tribe, 41
Abdullah, emir of Harar, 150
Abdullah ibn Mahmud, Khalifa, 111, 133, 143–5, 159–62, 167, 170–1, 175, 186–7, 189–91, 195, 211, 221, 223–4, 230, 234
   escaped from Omdurman, 236, 242–3
Abdullahi, king of Gwandu, 16
Abercrombie, General, 26–7
Abidin Bey al-Arnaut, 39–40
Aboya, 80
Abu Hamed, 39, 211, 212, 216, 218, 220, 222
Abu Haraz, 114
Abuja, 15
Abukir, 26, 123, 125
Abu Klea, 142
Abu Tulogh, 142
Abu Zaid, ford, 51
Abyssinia, 180
   see also Ethiopia
Acholi, 178
Adal, 79
Adal, Ras (Tekle Haymanot), 171
Adamawa, 16
Adam wad Umar, Makk of Taqali, 106, 109, 133, 134, 136–8, 141, 163, 175, 181
Addis Ababa, xi, 65, 165, 205, 213–15, 239, 241
Aden, 61–2, 64, 68, 70, 148, 150
Adowa, 77, 153, 157, 195, 207, 223
Afar, tribe, 69
Afqara, 81

Africa,
   Central, 34, 71, 82–3, 89, 94, 184
   East, xv, 34, 88, 180, 196
   North, xv
   West, xiv–xv, 2–6, 9–11, 17, 19, 23–5, 49–50, 89, 149, 199, 246–50
Agordat, 187, 189
Ahmad, emir of Harar, 150
Ahmad Ali, 187
Ahmed al-Tijani, 2
Ahmad Fadil, 242
Ahmad Pasha abu Widam, 52, 54, 74
Ahmad Taha, sharif, 114
Ahmadu ibn Mahmud Lobo Cissé, 18–20, 22, 24
Ahmadu Seko, 23–4, 247
Aissa, wife of Umar, 20
Ajjubbi (or Pibor) River, 215
Akasha, 208–10
Albanians, 28
Albert, Lake, 34, 56, 88, 136–7, 177–8, 181, 183–4, 197, 213, 216, 219
Alexandria, 30, 61–2, 86, 95, 128, 132, 140
   bombardment, 119–20, 122–3
   riots, 115–80
Algeria, xiv, 6, 249
Ali Dinar Abu Zakkariyeh, Sultan, 245–7, 250
Alison, Major General Sir Archibald, 120–1
Ali wad Adam, 160–4
Ali wad Helu, Khalifa, 111
Almohads, 3–4, 104–105
Almoravids, 3–4, 104–105
Alula, Ras, 153, 157, 164–70, 172–3
Amba Alagi, 209
America, 5
Amiens, Treaty of, 27
Anatolia, 53

Anglo-Congolese agreement, 186
Anglo-German agreement, 179–80, 186
Anglo-Italian agreement, 126
Ankober, 78, 80–1
Annesley Bay, 66, 76
Antonelli, Pietro, 170–1, 173
Arabia, xiv, 4–5, 11, 20, 30, 36, 38, 42, 50, 53, 60, 86, 146, 148
Araya, son of Yohannes IV, 165
Ardagatchew, 79
Arendrup Bey, 66, 83
Arikel Bey Nubar, 66
Arkiko, 61
Aruwimi River, 213
Ashanti, 4
Asmara, 153, 166–8, 173
Assab, 68–9, 80, 82, 149, 151
Aswan, xii, 2, 32, 34, 37, 43, 48, 50, 85, 88, 161
Atbara River and Fort, 34, 41, 212, 214, 216, 218, 221–2, 225–6, 230
  battle, 227–9
Atlantic Ocean, xii, xv, 5, 178, 190, 249
Atnatewos, Ethiopian *abuna*, 78
Axum, 78
Azande, tribe, 58–9, 71, 91, 182–3, 190, 245

Bab el-Mandeb, 64, 67–8, 150–1
Badis VI, Sultan of Sennar, 37
Baggara tribe, 111
Bagirmi, 191
Bahr al-Arab River, 190
Bahr el-Ghazal, 34, 53, 56, 58–9, 66–7, 71, 73, 83, 87, 91, 93, 113, 139, 141, 154–5, 163, 168, 172, 178, 189, 196, 198–200, 220, 245
Baird, General Sir David, 27
Baker, Sir Samuel, 56–7, 71, 87–90, 93, 106, 146
Baker, General Valentine, 139–40
Baldissera, General Antonio, 205
Banks, William, 38
Bara, 37–8, 134
Baring, Evelyn, 128, 138, 162, 169
  see also Lord Cromer
Basrah, 68
Bawa Jan Gworzo, emir of Gobir, 11

Bayuda, 37, 142, 212
Bedouin, 30, 37
Begemdar, 83
Beja, nomads, 92
Belbeis, 126
Belgium, Belgians, xiv, xvi, 157, 177, 183, 186, 190, 197–8, 213–14, 217, 219–20
Benin, 5
Benue River, 247
Berber (city), 34–5, 37, 39–41, 49, 51, 92, 140–1, 212, 216–17, 221–3, 225–6, 230
Berber (nomad tribe), 5
Berbera, 68, 71, 85, 93, 150–1
Berlin, 148, 168
  treaty of, 173–4, 181
Bezabeh, 80–1
Bismarck, Otto von, 96–8, 126, 148
de Blignières, Ernest, 95
Bogos, 153, 164–6, 173
Boko Haram, xiv, 17, 250
Bonchamps, Marquis de, 215
Bor, 51, 214, 216, 219, 221
Bornu, 14–16, 18, 20, 22, 24
Brazzaville, 214, 215, 218
Britain, British, xii–xiv, 1, 54, 97, 116–19, 157, 249
  and Arabia, 61
  and East Africa, 178, 179, 217
  and Egypt, 25, 27, 48, 62, 116–26, 135, 147
  and Ethiopia, 63, 67, 69, 76–7, 166, 185
  and Mahdists, 194–5, 206, 217, 220
  see also Royal Navy
British Army units:
  Brigade of Guards, 125
  Camel Corps, 229, 232–3
  Cameron Highlanders, 225, 228, 238
  Highland Brigade, 125
  Household Cavalry, 125
  King's Royal Rifles, 120
  Lincolnshires, 225
  Royal Engineers, 120
  Royal Staffordshires, 120, 210
  Royal Worcestershires, 225
  Seaforth Highlanders, 225
  19 Dragoon Guards, 125
  21 Lancers, 229, 234, 237
  37th Field Battery, 231

Bruce, James, explorer, 50–1, 86
Brun-Rollet, A., 52
Brussels, 184
Buganda, 7, 89, 93–5, 157, 178–9, 183
Bunyoro, 57–8, 89, 94, 157, 178, 197, 216
Burundi, 89, 180
Bussa, 250
Byzantine Empire, 1

Cailliaud, Lieutenant Frédéric, 46
Cairo, 27, 29–30, 32, 49–50, 58, 61, 92, 99, 111–12, 116, 121, 126, 137–8, 207, 209, 249
Cameroon, 246
Cape of Good Hope, xiv, 62
Caucasus, 25, 31
Cavour, Count, 69
Chad, Lake, 10–11, 17–18, 190–1, 246, 248–9
Chaltin, Louis-Napoléon, 213–15, 218
Cherbourg, 240
China, 3, 12, 29
Churchill, Lieutenant Winston, 234
Clochette, Captain, 214–15
Coatit, 188, 200
  see also Senafe
Coetlogon, Colonel, 138
Collinson, Lieutenant Colonel John, 234
Colvin, Sir Archibald, 128
Congo, colony, xiii, xvi, 1, 5, 59, 87–8, 146, 156–7, 178, 181, 196, 211, 219
  'Free State', 179, 181, 184, 192, 197–8, 214, 241, 245
Congo River, 213–14
Conrad, Admiral, 116, 119, 122
Constantinople, 27, 54, 70, 89, 97, 121, 128
Crampel, Paul, 191–2
Crimean War, 45–6
Cromer, Lord, 97–8, 118, 129, 146, 150, 195, 209, 224
  see also Baring, Evelyn
Cyprus, 120
Cyrenaica, 2, 10, 18–19, 36, 104, 141

Dahomey, 5
ad-Damar, 41, 212
Damascus, 30
Damietta, 124–5

Danakil Desert, 69, 83, 168
Dara, 133, 135, 137
Dar al-Kuti, 190
Dareios I, Persian king, 63
Dar es-Salaam, 192
Darfur, 1, 10, 19, 24, 36–8, 50, 52, 54, 56, 58–9, 67, 71, 73, 82, 86, 92–3, 95, 99, 103, 126–7, 132–3, 135, 140, 144, 146, 159, 170, 189, 194, 245–6
Dariyya, 60
Dar Runga, 190
Dawra, 15
Deir Zubayr, 200
Delanghe, Commandant F., 182–3
Dhanis, Baron, 212–14, 217
Dilke, Sir Charles, 118
Dilling, 131
Dinguiraye, 21, 105
Dinka, tribe, 141, 154
Djibouti, 64, 148, 151, 185, 191, 213–14, 241
Dogali, Battle of, 169–70, 187
Dongola, 32, 35–9, 49, 103, 144, 174, 195, 206, 208–12, 217, 232
Dufferin, Lord, 128
Dufile, 156–7, 175, 197

East Africa Company, British, 178–81, 183, 185
East India Company, British, 31, 62, 70, 75
Edward, Lake, 34, 88
Efrata, 81
Egypt, Egyptians, xii, xiv, 1–2, 4, 6, 14, 25–32, 39, 180
  and Britain, 62, 127–30, 244, 249–50
  and British invasion, 121–6
  and Central Africa, 57, 82, 88–9
  and Ethiopia, 66–7, 72–3, 83–5
  and Red Sea, 69–71, 157
  and Sudan, 107, 194, 220, 244
  army of, 37, 39, 43, 45, 53–4, 99–100, 103, 124, 135, 162, 176, 238
  army units of:
    3rd Battalion, 232
    11th Battalion, 228, 238
  development of, 29–30
  dual control, 100, 103, 112–13, 126, 128
  empire of, 247

and its disintegration, 157
European immigrants, 49–50, 94, 100
finances of, 94–9
Mahdist attacks, 161–2, 172, 181–2, 187, 194
nationalists, 102–103, 111–12
travellers in, 32, 141
Emin Pasha, 91, 94, 141, 155–8, 174, 177–80
English, George B., 27
Entebbe, 192
Entoto, 165
Equatoria, 52–3, 55–7, 59, 68, 73, 82, 87–9, 91, 93–4, 101, 103, 127, 154, 155–7, 177–8, 181–2
Eritrea, xiii, 1, 95, 158, 168, 172–3, 187, 198, 205, 207, 218, 243–4
Ethiopia, xii, xiv, 1, 4, 34, 40, 51–5, 61, 70, 73, 75–6, 89, 127, 146, 149, 153, 159, 167, 180, 192, 218, 244
British invasion, 64–6, 69, 72, 75
Egyptian invasion, 66–7, 72–3, 83–5, 93–5
expansion to the Nile, 215–16
and Harar, 157
and Italy, 71–2, 184–6, 195, 220, 241
Mahdist invasion, 72, 144, 162–8, 175–6, 189

Fadl al-Mawra Muhammad, 156–7, 177–8, 181–3, 190, 193, 197
Fashoda, xiii, 1, 24, 87, 110, 181, 184, 196–7, 206, 213–16, 218–19, 221, 230, 249
French party at, 236, 238–40
Fatma, wife of Umar, 20
Fazoghlu, 35–6, 46, 49–50, 52, 73
Firket (Ferkeh), 32, 209, 231
Fisher, Captain Jackie, 120
France, French, xiv, 1
and central Africa, 184, 192, 199
and Dreyfus affair, 240
and Egypt, 25–7, 29, 45, 54, 69, 79, 151, 157, 178
and Ethiopia, 215–16, 239
and Marchand, 240–2
and Obok, 151
revolution, 121, 127

and Suez Canal and Fresh Water Canal, 62–3
in West Africa, 22, 196, 198–9, 247–8
Fulani, 1, 11–14, 21, 105
Futa Jalon, 9, 18, 20, 23–4, 52, 124–5
Futa Toro 9, 18–21

Galam, 22
Galla, 78, 79, 166
Gambetta, Leon, French Premier, 112–13
Gano, 5
Garibaldi, Giuseppe, 69
Gatacre, Major General William, 224, 226, 229
Germany, Germans, xiv, 71, 88, 96–7, 126, 240, 249
in East Africa, 178–80, 184, 240
Gessi, Romolo, 59, 66, 91, 101, 113, 154, 189–91
Gezira, 230
see also Jazira
Ghana, 4
Gibraltar, 229, 240
Giegler, Carl, 113–14, 129
Girouard, Lieutenant Percy, 209, 211–12
Giza, 36
Gladstone, Prime Minister William, 172
Gobir, 11, 13–16, 105
Gojjam, 83–4, 170–1
Gondar, 50, 77, 80, 83, 84, 170, 175, 189
Gondokoro, 51, 52, 59, 89, 182, 197
Gordon, Charles, xii, 51, 59, 68, 77–8, 89–91, 94, 100–101, 137, 140–3, 145–6, 151–2, 166–7, 189, 251
Graham, General Sir Gerald, 140, 148
Granville, Lord, Foreign Secretary, 112
Great Bitter Lake, 63
Great Lakes, 57, 59, 71, 82, 86–8, 95, 143, 146, 149, 157–8, 178–81, 189–90, 196, 219
Greece, 12, 86
War of Independence, 31, 36, 38, 42, 53
Grenfell, General Sir Francis, 161–2, 234
Grey, Sir Edward, 200
Guardafui, Cape, 61, 67, 70, 82, 147, 188
Gudu, 13, 105
Gundet, battle, 83
Gwandu, caliphal capital, 16–17
tribe, 55, 61, 141

Hadendowa, tribe, 55, 61, 141
al-Hafir, 210–11
Haile Malakot, king of Showa, 79
Haile Mariam, 172
Haile Mikhail, king of Shoa, 79–80
hajj, 10, 19–20, 22, 24, 50, 60–1
Halfiyeh, 231
Hamasien, 78, 153, 165
Hamdan Abu Anja, 160–4, 170
Hammuda Idris, 209
Harar, 68, 71, 79, 83, 121, 149, 151, 154, 164, 166, 226
Hausa, Hausaland, 1, 10–13, 15–17, 19, 25, 44, 105
Hayatu al-Said, 190
Hejaz, 30, 54, 60–1
Heligoland, 179
Hewett, Admiral Sir William, 122, 153, 164
Hicks, Colonel William, 135–7, 139, 141, 148, 242
Hoskins, Admiral Sir Anthony, 122
Hosn bin Naya, 227
al-Hudi, 226
Hunter, Major, 149–50, 151
Hunter, General Archibald, 212, 221–3, 226, 228
Hunzinger, J.A.W., 83–4

Ibn Khaldun, 3, 17, 138
Ibrahim, son of Muhammad Ali, 31, 36, 38–40, 43, 47, 50, 55, 57
Ibrahim, Sultan of Darfur, 58
Ilorin, 16
India, 3, 5, 12, 25, 27, 30, 61, 65, 70, 76, 122, 127, 140
army of, 66, 125, 165, 195, 209
Indian Ocean, 61–2, 68, 93, 157, 178, 192, 241
Indonesia, 3
International Commission, 93, 98
al-Iqayqa (al-Engeige), 231–2
Iraq, 137
Ismail, son of Muhammad Ali, 36–7, 40–1, 47, 50, 52, 142
Ismail, Khedive of Egypt, 55–7, 65–7, 70, 78, 83–5, 90–2, 94–7, 111, 127
deposed, 100

Ismail Aiyub, 58–9
Ismail Haqqi, 61
Ismailia, 63, 122–5
Istanbul, 69
Italy, Italians, xiv, 1, 52, 60, 69–71, 152, 157–8, 240
advance into Eritrea, 177, 179, 195, 205, 207, 218
and Ethiopia, 82
and Kassala, 187–8
and Massawa, 166–8, 171
treaty cheating, 173–4

Ja'aliyin tribe, 40–2, 231
Jabal Qadir ('Mecca'), 109–12, 114, 132–4, 137, 242, 248
al-Jabarti, 32–3
Jayli wad Adam, Mekk, 246
Jazira, 47
see also Gezira
Jebel Marra, 58
Jebel Royan, 230
Jebel Surgham, 231–4
Jeddah, 19, 38, 50, 62
Jenne, 5
Jephson, 156
Jerusalem, 137
Jibril ibn Umar, al-Hajj, 11
Jihad, Jihadists, 1, 3–4, 6–7, 9–10, 13, 17–18, 22, 25, 159, 247
al-Jira, battle, 83, 154, 167
Juba River, 68, 70

Kaarta, 18–20, 22
Kaba, 133
Kabalega, king of Bunyoro, 89, 94
Kafr el-Dawa, 119–20, 122, 124
Kanfu Hailu, 53
Kano, 15
Karamallah Kurqusawi 139, 141, 154–5, 163, 168
Karari, 103
Kassa Hailu, 54–5, 65, 75
Kassa Mercha, 76–8, 81
see also Yohannes, emperor
Kassala, 54, 61, 73, 92, 114, 144, 152, 167, 187, 189, 195, 198, 200, 205, 208, 217, 222, 223, 242

Kassassin, 125
Katsina, 15
Kawwa, 109, 111
Kebbi, 15–16
Kenfu, 75
Kenya, xi, xiii, xvi, 1, 157, 178–9, 185, 192, 219, 241, 244, 250
Keppel, Commander Colin, 229–31, 235
Keren, 83, 173
Kerreri Hills, 232–4
Khalid Pasha Khusraw, 55, 60
Khartoum, 33, 37, 43–4, 47, 49, 51, 54, 58, 61, 86–8, 92, 101, 106–108, 111, 113–14, 134, 137–9, 147, 163, 178, 182, 190, 212, 216, 220–1
  siege of, 139–43
Khasso, 9, 22
Khurshid Ali, 51–2, 54
Kilimanjaro, Mount, xi, 178, 179
Kinana, tribe, 110–11
Kirkham, John, 77–8
Kismayu, 68–70, 71, 82, 84, 93, 147, 179–80, 188
Kisumu, 192, 219
Kitchener, Major General Herbert, xii, 1, 145, 162, 195, 207–12, 216, 220, 222–4, 226–9, 235–6
  and Fashoda, 238, 242
  promoted, 239
Kitchener, Colonel Walter, 243
Kordofan, 35, 37–41, 43, 49–52, 55, 92, 105–107, 109, 126, 132, 135–6, 146, 158–9, 170, 222, 225, 242–3, 245
Korti, 37, 141, 143
Koshi, 212
Kufit, 167
Kwari, 53–4, 74
  see also Qwari
Kyogo, Lake, 74, 882

Lado, 155–6, 182–4, 197–8, 212, 217, 219, 230, 241
Lagarde, Léonce, 213–14, 218, 239
Lahej, Emir of, 62
Lamu, 180
Lasta, 75, 77, 81
Leopold II, King of the Belgians, 89, 181, 184, 197–8, 213, 241

de Lesseps, Ferdinand, 62–3, 121–3
Lewis, Colonel David, 226, 234, 242
Libya, xv, 6, 111, 191, 194, 249
Liotard, Victor, 199–200, 214, 220
Lokota, 247
London, xi–xii, 96, 112, 118, 120, 122, 138–9, 145, 179, 186, 195, 207, 209, 211, 240
Loring, William, 66, 82–3
Lupton Bey, Frank, 154
Lyttelton, General Neville, 229

MacDonald, General Hector, 226, 234–5
Madibbu Ali, 132–3
Magdala, 66, 76, 78–81, 84
al-Mager, 153
Maghreb, 1, 3, 29
Mahdi, *see* Muhammad Ahmed
Mahdists, 67, 102, 146–58, 205–207, 221, 224, 247
  defence of Sudan, 210–13, 220
  enemies, 194–206
  invasions, 154–76, 178, 186–7, 189–90
  and Italy, 186–7, 200
  wider effects, 194–6
Mahmadu Lamine, 23–4
Mahmud Ahmed, 223–6, 228
Mahmud Sami al-Barudi, 102, 113
Makonnen, Ras, 173–4, 201–202, 204
Malet, Sir Edward, 124, 128
Malta, 224, 229
Mamelukes, 25–8, 30, 32, 34, 36–7, 40
Mangasha, Ras, 171–2, 175, 188, 200–202
Manz, 84
Marabiete, 80
Marchand, Captain J.B., 1, 87, 184, 198–9, 206, 211, 213–14, 218–19, 229, 240
  at Fashoda, 236, 238–40
Mareb River, 83, 165
Mariatu, wife of Umar, 20
Masai, tribe, 219
Masina, 18, 20, 22, 24
Massawa, 31, 54, 60–2, 65–8, 70, 73–4, 79, 82–3, 85, 93, 150–2, 154, 165
  Italian occupation, 166–8, 176, 230, 233
Mauritania, 3–4
Maxwell, General John, 226, 235
McKillop, R.F., Pasha, 69, 93

Mecca, 19–20, 30, 49, 60, 104–105, 137, 139, 148, 247
Medina, 20, 30, 49, 60, 105, 110, 137, 139
Menelik, Ethiopian emperor, 76, 78–85, 150, 165–6, 169–71, 211, 213
   becomes emperor, 172
   campaign of Adowa, 201, 205
   and France, 214–16, 239
   and Italy, 173–4, 184, 188, 200
Merowe, 211–12, 216
Metemma, 142
   battle, 172, 174, 175, 223
Mexico, 12, 45–6
Michel, Charles, 215
Milz, Jules, 181–2
Mocha, 31
Monteil, Captain, 184, 199, 214
Morocco, xv, 1, 3–4, 6, 8, 105
Mozambique, 179
Muhammad, the Prophet, 1, 21, 104, 137, 140
Muhammad, emir of Harar, 166
Muhammad Ahmad, al-Mahdi, xii–xv, 1, 24, 44, 52, 103, 126, 131–45, 147, 159–60, 189–91, 242–3, 247
   death of, 143, 145, 175
Muhammad Ali, khedive of Egypt, 27–32, 34–6, 38, 42–3, 45–7, 53, 60–1, 67, 73, 94, 103–11, 146, 177
Muhammad-Ali-Polis, 46–7
Muhammad al-Amin al-Kanemi, 14, 18, 21, 191, 247
Muhammad al-Barudi, 115
Muhammad Belo, 16, 20, 24, 247
Muhammad Bey Khusraw, 36
Muhammad Bey Sulayman, 113
Muhammad Bishara, 211
Muhammad al-Hilali, 57
Muhammad IV Husain, sultan of Darfur, 51
Muhammad Khalid, 133, 135, 140
Muhammad el-Kheir, 140–2
Muhammad Rauf Pasha, 68, 70, 100–103, 106–10, 113, 132
Muhammad Retib Pasha, 66
Muhammad Said, 133–4
Muhammad al-Sanusi, 111
Muhammad al-Shallali, 114, 132

Muhammad Sharif Pasha, 102–103, 106
   khalifa, 111, 243
Muhammad Abu al-Suud, 107–109
Muhammad Uthman Abu Qarja, 140, 182
Muhammad ibn Ali al-Sanusi, 10, 191
Mundu, 183
Mwanza, 192

Nafata, king of Gobir, 13
Nairobi, 219, 241
Nakheila, 226
   battle, 227–32
Napata, 33, 47
Napier, General Robert, 76–7, 165
Naples, kingdom, 69
Napoleon Bonaparte, 26, 29, 31, 42
Napoleon III, 62
Nasir, pretender to Taqali, 55
Navarino, Battle of, 31
Niger River, 4–5, 10, 18, 22, 192, 247, 249
Nigeria, xv, 1, 196, 246–7
Nile River, 10, 19, 27, 30, 32, 34, 49–51, 86, 88, 92, 109, 175
   Blue Nile, 34, 37, 41, 43, 46, 50–1, 86, 88, 113, 139, 180, 216
   White Nile, 33–4, 37, 40, 47, 49–52, 56–7, 74, 86–9, 104, 113–14, 136, 139, 157, 175, 180, 184–6, 197, 216, 219, 227, 231, 242, 244
Nimr, chief of the Ja'aliyin, 41
North Sea, 179, 183
Nuba Hills, 38, 44, 52, 55–6, 73, 106–107, 133, 136–7, 139, 144, 146, 154, 163, 170, 174, 246
Nubar Pasha, 89, 96, 138
Nubia, 32, 211
al-Nujumi, Abd al-Rahman, 160–3, 167–8, 175, 209
Nupe, 16–17

Obok, 64, 67–8, 82–3, 85, 148–51, 214
Ohrwalder, Father Josef, 134
Omdurman, 37, 44, 47, 103, 157, 221–2, 224, 226, 229–31
   battle, 231–6, 240, 242, 251
Ottoman Empire, 25, 27–8, 30, 38, 54, 60–1, 70, 84, 97, 105, 113, 137, 146, 151, 246
Oyo, 5

Pagans, paganism, 7–8
Palestine, 26
Paris, xii, 27, 96, 112, 122, 184, 240
Parsons, Colonel, 223, 242
Peninsular War, 29
Perim Island, 64
Piedmont-Sardinia, 29, 69
Piracy, 30
Port Said, 60, 95, 119–20, 125
Portal, Gerald, 169, 180–1, 183, 186
Portugal, Portuguese, 5, 72
Ptolemy II, king, 63

al-Qadarif, 154, 187, 222–3, 242
al-Qallabat, 153, 157, 167, 170–1, 187, 222
Qapudan, Salim, 51–3, 56, 87
Qinis, 144, 160
el-Qubba, 142
Qwari, 53, 74–5
  see also Kwari

Rabeh al-Zubayr, 91–92, 159, 186, 189–90, 192–4, 199, 245–6, 248–9
al-Radad, 137
Radman Pasha, 149
Railways, 184–5, 192, 211–12, 219, 222, 225, 230, 241
al-Rajjaf, 182, 197, 206, 214–16
Ramleh, 124
Ras el-Tin, palace, 117, 119
Rashid Bey Ayman, 110, 112
Red Sea, xi–xii, xv, 19, 25, 27, 31, 38, 49–50, 54–6, 60–4, 68, 70, 73–4, 82–3, 86, 92, 99, 144, 147, 205, 209, 212, 222, 249
Renkh, 221, 238
Renzi, Azande chief, 183
Rhodes, Cecil, 212, 230
Riaz Pasha, 102
Ricci, Alessandro, doctor, 39, 48–9
Rizeyqat, tribe, 133
Rodd, Rennell, 184
Rome, 173
Rosebery, Lord, Prime Minister, 180–1, 184, 186, 200
Roseires, 242
Royal Navy, 26, 62, 64, 119, 153
  Mediterranean Fleet, 97, 185, 187, 207

Rubattino, Raffaele, 68–9, 70
Rudolf, Lake, 216
Rufa'a tribe, 41, 54
Russia, 97, 240
Russo-Turkish War, 84, 97
Rwanda, 89, 180

al-Sabaluqa, 230
Sa'd Rif'at, 153–4, 167
Sahara Desert, 2, 4–6, 9–10, 104, 143
Sahati, 168
Sahel, 1, 3–6, 8, 10, 17–19, 50, 131, 194
Sahle Sellassie, King of Shoa, 78–9
Said, khedive of Egypt, 55–6, 60
Saladin, 30
Salim Bey, 178
Salisbury, Lord, Prime Minister, 179, 185–6, 195, 200, 207–208, 211, 224, 239–40
Salt, Henry, 32
Samori, 18, 23–4, 131, 199, 246–9
Sanusi, 10, 19, 104, 159, 191
Saras, 39
Segu, 18, 22, 105
Senafe see Coatit
Senegal, 104
Senegambia, 3, 8–10, 104
Senhit, 153
Sennar, sultanate, 35, 37–41, 47, 51, 67, 111, 113–14
Seymour, Admiral Sir Beauchamp, 115–16, 118–22, 126
Shaiqiyah, tribe, 35, 37, 39–41, 55, 142
Shakka, 133, 135
Shaykan, 137–8, 142
Shendi, 40–1, 49–50, 142, 227
Shilluk, tribe, 51, 110, 230
Ships
  La Galissonnière (Fr), 116
  Inflexible, HMS, 120
  Invincible, HMS, 116
  Safieh (Mahdist), 238
  Tewfikieh (Mahdist), 236
  Zafir, gunboat (Egypt), 212
Shoa, 75–6, 78–81, 165
Sicily, 69
Sinai, 39, 123
Siwah, 39

Slatin Pasha, Rudolph, 133, 135, 137
Slaves, slavery, 5, 25, 31, 35, 38–9, 43–5, 48, 56, 59, 90, 189
  antislavery, 90
Sobat River, 34, 197, 215–16, 239, 241
Sokoto, caliphal capital, 16–17, 20, 23, 247
Sokoto Caliphate, xv, 19, 21, 23–4, 36, 50, 55, 104, 143, 149, 190–2, 246–9
Somalia, xiii, 1, 67–8, 70–1, 79, 82, 85–6, 93–4, 144, 146, 150–1, 179, 188, 194, 216, 218, 244
Songhai Empire, 8
South Africa, xiv, 164
  Boer War, 219
South Sudan, Republic of, xii–xiii, xv, 86, 244
Spain, 2, 4, 6, 29, 105, 140
Speke, J.H., 56, 87
Stanley, Henry Morton, 156, 174, 177–8, 180
Stewart, General Sir Herbert, 142
Suakin, 19, 31, 38, 49, 50, 54, 60–2, 70, 73, 92–3, 140, 147–9, 151, 160, 163, 174, 209, 222–3, 241
Sudan, xii, xiv–xv, 1, 22–3, 179–80, 244
  and Egypt, 19, 35, 39, 54, 102–103, 146
  railways in, 49
Sudd, 34–5, 40, 51–2, 87–8, 127, 154–5, 163, 182, 186, 197, 215–16, 220, 244
Suez, 50, 61–2, 122, 125, 153
Suez Canal, 50, 56, 62–5, 68, 82, 95–6, 118, 121–5, 147–8, 151
Suez Canal Company, 60, 70, 82, 95, 126, 147
Sulayman Pasha Niyazi, 135–6, 148
Sulayman (al-Zubayr), 189–90
Syria, xiv, 25, 31, 42, 46, 53, 56

Ta'aisha tribe, 143
Tadjoura, 83, 150–1, 157, 214
Taitu, Ethiopian Empress, 165–6, 202–203
Taka, 54–5, 61, 74, 92, 153
Tamai, 141
Tampura, 200
Tana, Lake, 50, 83–4, 86
Tanganyika, xi, 157, 179, 194, 241
  Lake, 184, 192, 242
Taqali, kingdom, 44, 55, 106–107, 109, 137, 154, 159, 163–4, 174–5, 245–6

Taufiq, Khedive of Egypt, 97–8, 100, 111, 113, 115, 117–18, 121, 156
el-Teb, 141–2
Telegraph, 61, 92–3, 95, 103, 114, 138, 151, 195, 207
Tel el-Kebir, 122, 125, 132, 141
Tessama, Dejazmatch, 215–16
Tewodros, Ethiopian emperor, 64–5, 75–81, 164–5, 175
Tigray, 75–7, 79, 81, 83, 165–6, 172, 188, 200, 205
Timbuktu, 5, 18, 22–3, 199, 247
Toro, 89, 157, 178
Toynbee, Arnold, 87
Trajan, Roman emperor, 63
Trinkitat, 139–40
Tuareg, 5
Tumat River, 46
Turin, 32
Tushki, 161–2, 173–4
Tussun, son of Muhammad Ali, 60

al-Ubaiyid (el-Obeid), 37–8, 43, 49, 54, 113–14, 133–7
Ubangui River, 190
Ubangui-Chari, 191–2, 199
Uele River, 183, 214
Uganda, xi, xiii, xvi, 1, 178–80, 183, 185–6, 192, 196, 213, 216–19, 241, 244, 249–50
Umar, son of Makk Adam, 134
Umar, al-Hajj, 18–24, 52, 55, 104–105, 131, 246–8
Umar Salih, 156
Umberto, king of Italy, 174
Umm Diwaykarat, 243
United States, 6, 82
Upper Nile region, 159, 163, 177, 180, 185–6, 196, 199, 207, 213, 220, 241, 244–5
Urabi, Ahmad, 102, 111, 113, 115–19, 121–4, 126–7, 135, 144, 156
Urabi Daft'allah, 182, 206, 214
al-Urdi, 211
Usuman dan Fodio, 10–22, 24, 36, 44–5, 104–105, 131, 192, 194, 246–8, 251
Uthman Digna, 139–41, 148, 153, 163, 167, 209, 222–6, 228
Uthman Isa al-Azraq, 209
Uthman Jarkas al-Birinji, 47

Uthman Rifqi, 101–103
Uthman Shaykh el-Din, 243

Vandeleur, Lieutenant Seymour, 248
Victoria, Lake, 34–5, 56–7, 86, 88–9, 178–80, 218, 241
Victoria, Queen, 65–6, 145, 192, 240
Vincent, Sir Edgar, 128

Wadai, 1, 10, 18–20, 50, 91, 144, 146, 149, 190–1, 246, 249
Wadelai, 178, 181–2, 197
Wad Hamed, 230
Wadi Halfa, 32, 35–8, 92–3, 141, 143–4, 161, 174, 195, 207–208, 211, 218, 221
Wad Madani, 38, 41, 47
Wagshum Gobeze (Emperor Tekle Giyorgis II), 16, 77–8, 81
Wahhabi, 20–1, 30, 60, 146
Wallo Galla, 80–1, 84
Warquit, Queen of Wallo Galla, 81
Wauchope, General Andrew, 229, 234
West Africa Conference, 148–9, 168, 181, 184–5, 195
West Indies, 6

Wichali (Ucciali), Treaty of, 173–4, 184
Wilson, General Sir Charles, 95, 142–3
Wingate, General Sir F.R., 134–5, 211, 236, 243
Witu, 180
Wolkait, 41
Wolseley, Lieutenant General Sir Garnet, 122–4, 126, 140–1, 145, 208

Yambio (Gbudwe), 245
Yemen, 30–1, 150
Yunfa, king of Gobir, 13–14, 105
Yusuf Asher al-Shallali, 113
Yusuf bin Muhammad al-Sharif, Sultan of Wadai, 190

Zalait, rocks, 51
Zanzibar, xv, 56, 68–70, 87, 93, 147, 155–6, 179–80, 185, 249
Zaria (Zazzau), 15
Zauditu, daughter of Menelik, 165
Zeila, 68, 70–1, 79, 85, 101, 149–52, 166, 201–202
al-Zubayr Rahma Mansur, 57–9, 67, 91, 93, 189, 245

Dear Reader,

We hope you have enjoyed this book, but why not share your views on social media? You can also follow our pages to see more about our other products: facebook.com/penandswordbooks or follow us on X @penswordbooks

You can also view our products at www.pen-and-sword.co.uk (UK and ROW) or www.penandswordbooks.com (North America).

To keep up to date with our latest releases and online catalogues, please sign up to our newsletter at: www.pen-and-sword.co.uk/newsletter

If you would like a printed catalogue with our latest books, then please email: enquiries@pen-and-sword.co.uk or telephone: 01226 734555 (UK and ROW) or email: uspen-and-sword@casematepublishers.com or telephone: (610) 853-9131 (North America).

We respect your privacy and we will only use personal information to send you information about our products.

Thank you!